Popular Controversies
in World History

Contents

VOLUME THREE
The High Middle Ages to the Modern World

VOLUME FOUR
The Twentieth Century to the Present

Introduction

In the countless history courses I've taught over the years, the one question that invariably appears at some point (usually from a nonmajor who has to take the course for some general education requirement) is: "Why should we study history?" This is not an idle question, but an esoteric one that goes to the heart of what history is and what it can tell us. Usually, the student asking that question has the notion that history consists of a static set of "facts," unchanging (or, at least, it should not change) and ultimately meaningless for modern life. Students often buy into Henry Ford's famous take on the subject, "history is more or less bunk," rather than George Santayana's maxim, "those who cannot remember the past are condemned to repeat it." In the end, neither of these perspectives is especially true or helpful. This is because both writing history and understanding history are complex activities. They are our attempts to make sense of the past, usually drawing from incomplete or biased accounts of what actually happened. Even when the accounts are complete, the interpretations of history can vary radically depending on the perspective of the person writing. Perhaps the best explanation of the problem comes from the novelist Aldous Huxley, who, in his novel *The Devils of Loudun*, said "The charm of history and its enigmatic lesson consist in the fact that, from age to age, nothing changes and yet everything is completely different."

This work proceeds on the assumption that history is not a subject, but rather an activity. The activity of history engages the capability of students to use reason. On a purely anecdotal basis, I've asked many of my colleagues which skills they believed were the most important for their students to possess a high proficiency in when they begin college. Almost invariably, the two top answers were writing and critical thinking. In *Taxonomy of Learning*, developed in 1956 by Benjamin Bloom as an effort to show the evolution of mental skills in pyramidal form, critical thinking skills are integral to the third and fourth levels: application and analysis. The students who ask why it is important to study history are proceeding on the assumption that history is only an activity that engages the first two levels: knowledge and comprehension. If that were all there is to history, then Ford may have been right. However, application and analysis are also key to understanding, without which one cannot reach the final two levels of Bloom's *Taxonomy*—synthesis and evaluation—which are essential to the creation of history. So, to summarize, critical thinking skills are key to moving from the first two levels—knowledge and comprehension—to the highest levels—synthesis and evaluation. In order to understand and, eventually, to write history, critical thinking is the transitional, indispensable skill.

Judging once again from my unscientific survey of my colleagues, it is one of the skills with which many students who are entering college struggle. This realization was the genesis of this project. *Popular Controversies in World History* takes as its subjects the topics over which there has been considerable historical debate. Some of these topics will not be familiar to students, but many of them will. Did the Great Flood, described in both the biblical book of Genesis and the Epic of Gilgamesh, actually happen? Is the lost continent of Atlantis just a myth, or was really such a place? Is the Shroud of Turin the actual burial cloth of Jesus Christ? Was William Shakespeare the sole author of all of the plays attributed to him? Who was the "man in the iron mask"? Did Franklin D. Roosevelt allow the Japanese attack on Pearl Harbor to happen as a pretext for the U.S. entrance into World War II? Did Lee Harvey Oswald act alone in assassinating John F. Kennedy in Dallas? These questions and more reveal that history is not a static set of facts, but rather a living, expanding set of ideas and interpretations. To understand those interpretations and formulate those ideas, critical thinking skills are paramount in importance.

The purpose of this work is to present the varying perspectives on events like these. These topics, as well as the ability to think critically about them, are vitally important parts of the social science curriculum at both the secondary and postsecondary levels. Each chapter takes a particular topic that has generated controversy either within the historical profession or in society as a whole and offers pro and con points of view, allowing readers to draw their own conclusions. The work covers all eras of human history, both before and after the advent of the written record. Each chapter in *Popular Controversies in World History* is formatted in the style of a historical debate, with a "pro" and a "con" section that presents contrasting perspectives. In most cases, both of these perspectives are or have been widely held within academia and supported by scholarship. The readers are then given the opportunity to exercise their critical thinking skills to evaluate the evidence presented by each side, to assess the validity of the arguments made by the authors, and eventually to determine which conclusions they accept or reject.

Of course, I could never have presented these arguments, ranging across so many eras and subdisciplines of history, by myself. This work represents the efforts of 62 other scholars with whom I have had the privilege to work. In addition, much of the early work on this project, especially determining the format to be used to accomplish our goals and formulation of the various questions to be debated, was done in conjunction with Geoff Golson, to whom I give due credit. I'd also like to thank the editorial and production staff at ABC-CLIO, including David Tipton, editorial manager; Barbara Patterson, who administered the considerable paperwork involved; Kim Kennedy-White, who helped me refine the manuscript submissions; and Donald Schmidt and his team, who oversaw the production work to turn the manuscript into a book. Without the efforts of such a fantastic team, this work would not have been possible.

References

Bloom, Benjamin S., et al., eds. *Taxonomy of Educational Objectives: The Classification of Educational Goals.* New York: Longmans, Green, 1956.

Huxley, Aldous. *The Devils of Loudun.* New York: Harper, 1952, p. 259.

Santayana, George. *Life of Reason, Reason in Common Sense.* New York: Scribner's, 1905, p. 284.

Contributor List

Claire Brennan
James Cook University, Townsville, Australia

Heather Buchanan
University of Michigan, Dearborn, Michigan

Joseph P. Byrne
Belmont University, Nashville, Tennessee

Cenap Çakmak
Muğla University, Muğla, Turkey

Justin Corfield
Geelong Grammar School, Geelong, Australia

Mark Dickens
University of Cambridge, Cambridge, United Kingdom

Todd W. Ewing
Williams Baptist College, Walnut Ridge, Arkansas

Michael Greaney
Center for Economic and Social Justice, Washington, D.C.

Harald Haarmann
Institute of Archaeomythology, Luumäki, Finland

Chris Howell
Red Rocks Community College, Denver, Colorado

Peter N. Jones
Bauu Institute, Boulder, Colorado

László Kocsis
South East European University, Tetovo, Macedonia

John Lee
Utah Valley State University, Orem, Utah

Annette Morrow
Minnesota State University, Moorhead, Minnesota

Thaddeus Nelson
Columbia University, New York, New York

K. T. S. Sarao
University of Delhi, Delhi, India

Anita Sharma
University of Delhi, Delhi, India

Talaat Shehata
Columbia University, New York, New York

Caleb Simmons
Florida State University, Tallahassee, Florida

Juliette Wood
Cardiff University, Cardiff, United Kingdom

I

The Ark of the Covenant is in Axum, Ethiopia.
(This idea has led to many investigations, publications, and media reports.)

PRO Talaat Shehata
CON Thaddeus Nelson

PRO

To better understand this argument—that the Ark of the Covenant is not lost, but that it is actually safe and in the town of Axum in Ethiopia—one needs to comprehend both the biblical and nonbiblical history of the ark. The reader will also need to gain more insight as to how throughout history different groups in many different nations have attempted to seize and, often for their own self-interest, coopted and then manipulated the concept of being God's *chosen* people. It's within that multifaceted paradigm that by the end of this section, the reader will decide for her- or himself as to the validity of the concept and the *actual* reality of a chosen people and which group, if any, should be accorded that title. But, as shall be explained, the reader will discover that the Ark of the Covenant is at the *core* of any such designation, and its possession has led some in the Ethiopian Coptic church to make such a claim.

In Exodus 25:1–2, the Old Testament states that "The LORD said to Moses, 'Speak to the people of Israel that they take for me an offering; from every man whose heart makes him willing you shall receive the offering for me.'" Then, it continues in Exodus 25:8, that the people of Israel should "make me a sanctuary, that I may *dwell* in their midst." It further stipulated in Exodus 25:9, that "According to all that I show you concerning the pattern of the tabernacle, and of all its furniture, so you shall make it." In Exodus 25:10–22, God elaborates on the primary constructs of the ark. It would be made from "acacia wood; two cubits and a half shall be its length, a cubit and a half its breadth, and a cubit and a half its height." Then, God tells Moses:

"And thou shalt overlay it with pure gold, within and without shalt thou overlay it, and shalt make upon it a crown of gold round about. And thou shalt cast four rings of gold for it, and put [them] in the four corners thereof; and two rings [shall be] in the one side of it, and two rings in the other side of it. And thou shalt make staves [of] shittim wood, and overlay them with gold.

And thou shalt put the staves into the rings by the sides of the ark, that the ark may be borne with them. The staves shall be in the rings of the ark: they shall not be taken from it. And thou shalt put into the ark the testimony which I shall give thee. And thou shalt make a mercy seat [of] pure gold: two cubits and a half [shall be] the length thereof, and a cubit and a half the breadth thereof. And thou shalt make two cherubims [of] gold, [of] beaten work shalt thou make them, in the two ends of the mercy seat. And make one cherub on the one end, and the other cherub on the other end: [even] of the mercy seat shall ye make the cherubims on the two ends thereof. And the cherubims shall stretch forth [their] wings on high, covering the mercy seat with their wings, and their faces [shall look] one to another; toward the mercy seat shall the faces of the cherubims be. And thou shalt put the mercy seat above upon the ark; and in the ark thou shalt put the testimony that I shall give thee. And there I will meet with thee, and I will commune with thee from above the mercy seat, from between the two cherubims which [are] upon the ark of the testimony, of all [things] which I will give thee in commandment unto the children of Israel." (Exodus 25:11-22, King James Version)

Finally, in Exodus 29:42–45 (King James Version), the Lord states:

"[This shall be] a continual burnt offering throughout your generations [at] the door of the tabernacle of the congregation before the LORD: where I will meet you, to speak there unto thee. And there I will meet with the children of Israel, and [the tabernacle] shall be *sanctified* by my glory. And I will sanctify the tabernacle of the congregation, and the altar: I will sanctify also both Aaron and his sons, to minister to me in the priest's office. And I will *dwell* among the children of Israel, and will be their God. And they shall know that I [am] the LORD their God, that brought them forth out of the land of Egypt, that I may *dwell* among them: I [am] the LORD their God." (emphasis added)

With that very clear knowledge in mind, the Israelites would consistently be in one in a state of endless *Shekhinah*. *Shekhinah* in Hebrew, as in Arabic with the word *S'akina*, is found in the Quran in numerous verses; the word means a state of total peace and tranquillity. In this case, this absolute reassurance and calming feeling was bestowed upon the people of Israel as a direct consequence of their individual and collective *knowing* that God was *always* with them.

Then, in Exodus 26:31–33, a precise description is given as to how a veil would separate the ark from the priests and congregation. Even Aaron and his lineage, who were designated by God as the future priestly class, were not allowed to enter the resting place of the ark too often. They were and are expected to undertake preestablished rituals *prior* to entering the area within which the ark rested. The ark was viewed by all to be resting in an area that would become known as the Holy of Holies. That area was held in *total* piety and reverence.

With that said and done, it's quite clear that not much more was left to the imagination, let alone to be debated, within the ranks of the faithful. To all Jews, God is established, beyond any shade of doubt, to not only be the Almighty Creator of life and the universe but also to be a dynamic and active deity *within* past history and *within* its unfolding present and future. God has constantly projected and established his concern for the people who *first* chose him by declaring to them that they are his chosen ones. He would judge them, as he would other non-Jews. God would also save those he deems worth saving, as he would other non-Jews. Throughout history, God would reveal himself in multifaceted ways, either through his prophets, the historical events, the laws, or the priests. Practicing and believing Jews were of the strong conviction that God's *divine* actions have, and will continue to the end of time, to penetrate and permeate the unfolding contours of history at his own choosing. All Jews needed, and will forever need are a strong belief in God's potential and a readiness to *act* and *interact* with God's people, when he sees fit that events dictate that he would do so.

According to numerous sources, the ark contained the original Ten Commandments, Aaron's rod, and a small pot filled with manna. Manna in Exodus 16:14, is described as available in the early morning, after the dew had evaporated. It was a staple mode of daily consumption by the Israelites, which especially sustained them while they were wandering for those 40 years with Moses on their journey to the Promised Land. Similar to coriander seed in texture, it was white in color. It resembled the early morning frost on green lawns. Often, besides having it ground, it was baked by the Israelites into little cake-like or small flat doughnut (without the holes) shaped pieces. They had the taste of cake baked in oil. It was also claimed in the Old Testament that manna, especially in its raw form, tasted like a honey wafer. Gathering the manna each day, as they had been instructed by Moses, the Israelites were expected to consume only that amount for their daily sustenance. The primary reason for that directive was that it was usually extremely hard to store any of it overnight. The manna would usually decompose and begin to excrete a putrid smell. It was only on the sabbath that they were permitted to collect double the amount that they usually had grown accustomed to gathering during the week. The Israelites decided that if they doubled-up on their usual daily intake of the manna immediately prior to the sabbath, then there wouldn't be enough hours in a day for it to go completely to waste. According to this thinking, it was better to lose half the manna than all of it, so that their collective daily needs on the next day, immediately following the sabbath, could be met. It seemed to work for them. That overwhelming gratitude by the people of Israel for manna's life-sustaining qualities during their days of hardship, earned it a very special *honored* presence, next to the Decalogue stones (Ten Commandments) and Aaron's rod. It could also be perceived as the Lord's way of getting the Israelites to honor and demonstrate extreme appreciation for nature's life-sustaining *gifts*.

Historicity and the Bible

Academic interpretations of the Hebrew scriptures vary and consider the evidence in light of hypotheses about biblical sources and the relationship between biblical and outside data, a relationship that is considered on a case-by-case basis. In the case of the Ark of the Covenant, the biblical text is so specific in its descriptions that it seems almost a certainty that it was written about an actual object still known to the Hebrew people—the specificity would seem out of place and unnecessary otherwise. But the Exodus during which the Ark was meant to have been created is another matter. There is no evidence of the 600,000 people described in the Bible as having left Egypt for Canaan. Even one-tenth that number would be expected to leave considerable archaeological evidence—litter, in essence. It is entirely possible that the exodus occurred with a much smaller group, and that this group built the ark. There is also a theory that Canaan's conversion to the Hebrew religion took place not because of invasion from an outside force but because of an internal revolution, which makes it much less clear when and where the ark would have been built.

Many sections of the Ten Commandments were already existent in the laws of numerous ancient civilizations. In ancient Egypt's religious texts, the laws and prohibitions against murder, theft, and crude injustice were very well evident in the consciousness and practices of Egyptians as they entered a temple or shrine that was dedicated to their god Osiris. According to the Egyptians, he was the god that would stand judgment on them upon their death. But, most biblical and Quranic scholars are of the strong conviction that the Ten Commandments went far beyond all moral codes established by either the Egyptians or any of the other ancient civilizations. The Jewish faith represented a clean break with any of them and was explicit in its monotheism. The unsurpassed majesty and innate *goodness* of God was present for all to witness. The hidden and most intimate thoughts and desires of the human mind and heart were, for the first time, being held accountable to the highest moral laws. It was a most sacred and awesome responsibility for all who wished to believe in an incontestable Supreme Being. The Israelites clearly had their work cut out for them.

With the strong feeling of there being a *choosing*, and therefore having become a *chosen* people of God, the Israelites *knew*, as it was stipulated in Deuteronomy 7:6–11, that "the Lord [their God was] God, the steadfast God, with those who love Him and keep His commandments He keeps covenant and faith for a thousand generations. . . . Therefore, [they needed to] observe conscientiously the Instruction—the laws and the rules—with which [he charged them]." In that context, the sanctuary, which had become known as the Ark of the Covenant, also became a moving one. In the exodus out of Egypt, the ark and its bearers, who were priests, preceded the Israelites out into the Sinai Desert and across the Jordan River. The Bible claims that with the parting of the Red Sea by Moses, with the intervention of God, the priests and the Israelites were able to cross over on dry land, until their feet touched the banks and the sea folded back onto itself. The same dry conditions, as stated in Joshua 3:15–17 to 4:10–11, 18, occurred when the priests carrying the ark, followed by the Israelites, crossed the Jordan River. The ark was present at the capture of Jericho. Prior to the fall of Jericho, and in a daily ritual, seven priests carried it, also carrying seven rams' horns as trumpets. Joshua was known to have isolated himself with the ark, to "consult it." The ark occupied a prominent location in the center of activity of the Israelites, when Joshua read to them the law. The ark was also "consulted" after the defeat in the battle against Benjamin at Gibeah.

It's within this context that one begins to get a clearer idea of how the ark, hundreds of years later, might have found its way to Axum in Ethiopia. But, first, it would have to be stolen, lost, and subjected to the possible threat of destruction or annihilation before any ruler of Israel would even entertain the thought that he and his people could temporarily part with it. In the Bible, it is stipulated that during Samuel's rule, the ark was lost to the Philistines, after Israel had withstood two separate defeats. The first defeat was at Ebenezer. Samuel and the Israelites thought very long and hard as to how they could restore their status, honor, and receding fortunes. They decided to have the ark hauled from the temple in Shiloh, where the Ark was resting, and place it before the troops, when they fought the Philistines a second time. They lost again. Only this time, the Philistines, to spite the Israelites for their demonstrated audacity and willingness to face them again in battle so soon following the first defeat, captured the ark and returned with it to their homeland. The Bible continues relating the events by stipulating that each town to which the ark was taken within the Philistine homeland was afflicted by plagues of mice and hemor-rhoids. Totally paralyzed by their populations' conditions, the Philistines, like the pharaoh before them in Egypt prior to the exodus, consulted their priests and diviners and concluded, after seven torturous months, that it would be best to return the ark to the Israelites. After that was done, and with much rejoicing by the Israelites shortly thereafter, the ark was neglected. After residing for 20 years in Kirjath-jearim, it was taken by Israel's new king, Saul, to lead his army, once again, against the Philistines. Despite the fanfare prior to the battle surrounding the ark, Saul never bothered to do what most earlier rulers of Israel did prior to going into battle against an enemy, and that was to "consult" it. By both the ruler and the people, the ark remained neglected for Saul's entire reign.

King David removed it from Jerusalem when he fled the city as a conse-quence of a conspiracy by Absalom. Then, he changed his mind and had his priest Zadok return it back to Jerusalem. But, it was King David who had earlier resolved to construct in Zion a large tabernacle, within which the ark would be placed. In the interim, he agreed to have the Levites oversee the ark's safety.

Festivals to which numerous animal sacrifices were ritually performed, along with the regular feeding and blessing by the priests of the large gathering masses of poor at the slowly reconstructed tabernacle entrance, became a consistent practice during King David's rule. It was with the arrival of King Solomon, the son of King David, that the newly constructed temple was completed. In its interior, a Holy of Holies area was provided for the ark. The ark would contain only the two stone tablets that had the Ten Commandments engraved on them. The Israelites saw Solomon worshiping at the ark more often than he had earlier done, after God had promised him in a dream that he would bestow wisdom upon Solomon. With the destruction of the temple, after Solomon's death, the ark disappeared. Rumors circulated wildly among the Israelites as to its ultimate resting place. One view stated that it had been taken to Babylonia. Another view claimed that it had never been taken out of Jerusalem; instead, it was hidden beneath the temple, in a dark area where wood for the temple was stored: all theories that appeared to be driven by idle priests, prone to gossip and conjectures. Whether it was a ruse consciously created by some of those priests to distract the public's knowledge as to its actual destination, in time, possibly will be determined by continued and determined archaeological and historical research and further acquisition of material and written evidence.

The important matter is that it's at this precise juncture in history that Ethiopian Christian Copts strongly held, and continue to hold, to the view that King Solomon and the queen of Sheba's son Prince Menelik I was coopted by one of Solomon's high priests. He was informed that the ark was to be removed from Jerusalem and needed a safe sanctuary far away—the "ideal" location, Ethiopia. Another rendition of Menelik I's role in the disappearance of the ark was that he knew nothing of its acquisition by one of Solomon's old priests and was only informed about it a few weeks after his departure from Jerusalem, on his way back home to Ethiopia. In either case, he acquired the ark, and his duty as Solomon's son was to find a safe sanctuary for it, immediately upon his arrival. Another version as to the whereabouts of the ark has been claimed by a few Muslim historians; the prophet Mohammed's cousin 'Ibn Abbas, the earliest founder of Quranic thought and clarification, has been attributed with the view that the ark with Moses' Rod (instead of it being referred to as belonging to Aaron) lies in the Lake of Tiberius, and that it will be restored on the last day of creation. How the ark initially found its way into the lake, historically, seems quite vague. But it seems that numerous theories abound, in Judaism, Christianity, and Islam. Where the final resting place of the ark actually is, from the archaeological and historical evidence currently available, will require much more excavation and precise documentation. But, in the interim, it appears that the pitched battle that had existed between the Beta Israel lost Jewish tribe in the northwestern highlands of Ethiopia and the majority population of Ethiopian Christian Copts colored and played a significant role in the insistence by

Worshipers gather for Lent at the Church of Our Lady Mary of Zion in Axum, Ethiopia, where some say the Ark of the Covenant is housed. (Franco Taddio/Stockphotopro)

Ethiopia's Christians that the ark actually found its way over the past 2.5 millennia to Axum.

With the legendary folklore that circulated *within* the majority Ethiopian Christian Coptic population from the 14th to the early 17th centuries regarding the courage and ferocious fighting that members of Beta Israel were able to withstand from all Ethiopian Christian advances on them, the church elites began to fear the overall ideological impact of Beta Israel on their extensive Christian following. Numerous ways by which they felt they could attempt to neutralize their growing influence within the ranks of their Christian followers was to tone down a few notches the aggressive rhetoric against Beta Israel, which had evolved unabated over the past two millennia. They allowed Beta Israel to acquire more work as artisans and tenant farmers. Beta Israel became identified, in the minds of the majority Ethiopian Christian population, as being very skillful carpenters and masons, who played an extremely important role in the construction of local and regional churches and palaces. Most of these changes occurred during the thriving Gondar dynasty. This, in time, allowed many members of Beta Israel between 1632 to 1755 CE to settle the urban areas. Beta Israel grew much more influential during that period, in the large Ethiopian Amarinia and Tigre-speaking communities. Increasing land grants were awarded to Beta Israel. A parallel track, which was also pursued by the elites within the church, was to not only attempt to neutralize Beta Israel's growing influence in the minds and hearts of the church's Ethiopian Christian faithful, but, most significantly, to appropriate the most holy of holy symbols—the ark. The logic being that, with the acquisition of the Ark of the Covenant as the ultimate prize that any Jewish or Christian group could dream of "owning," then, according to the elites within the church's thinking, it would not only stop the "bleeding" of many of their Christian faithful to the alien intrusive presence of the Beta Israel but, most importantly, it would *legitimize* their church *forever* in relation to Beta Israel, or for that matter, any other non-Christian or up-and-coming "renegade" religious group within the church. So, therefore, in their minds, that would justify any false and inaccurate claims that would be made as to the *genuine* ownership of the Ark of the Covenant, or for that matter, toward what they saw as their potential real rivals for such a claim, the Beta Israel. To permanently silence the Beta Israel, by 1755 to the late 19th century, Ethiopia's Christian Copts in the Gondar province scapegoated the Jewish tribe as their collective economic and social fortunes declined. That scape-goating technique was the usual boiler-plate sort, which has often been used with precision and sadistically against vulnerable minorities by dominant majorities throughout world history—single them out and criticize them (question their loyalty, patriotism, and so forth), demonize them, and then kill them. The Ethiopian Christian Copts in the northwestern highlands were only too happy to unload the Beta Israel in the late 1970s, 1980s, and 1990s onto modern Israel, in the airlifts that carried most of them to their new homeland. That way, no group within Ethiopia could ever again contest Ethiopia's Christian Copts' actual direct connection to ancient Israel and, according to them, their justifiable claim to the *sole* ownership of the original Ark of the Covenant.

With that in mind, therefore, the ark placed in Axum, within the treasury building, could be any representation of the original ark, as could be found in most synagogues during their ritual religious services throughout the world. It would be taken out in a few religious processions so that it would be exhibited to the faithful, and it would indirectly convey to the Jewish and non-Jewish world that God made certain that Ethiopia's Christian Copts were the *actual* descendants of his chosen people through Menelik I, the son of King Solomon and the queen of Sheba. It would then be safely hidden behind the veil in the church and an actual "smoke screen" would be created by a few of the priests, which created a sense of awe among the uninformed or possibly an illiterate segment of the parishioners. They would regard that smoke spewing forth from behind that veil as the actual presence of the Lord within their house of worship—as had been mentioned in the Old Testament. Some earlier researchers who had a quick glimpse of the purported ark behind the veil in Axum concluded that, as a result of their expertise with ancient and medieval artifacts and treasures, the ark in the Church of Our Lady Mary of Zion did not appear to date back any farther than the early to mid-14th century. They felt that the priests and the Ethiopian Christian Copts directly connected with the church were being rather disingenuous, which would bring the neutral observer to question why there was the need for the caginess and deception. Is it an attempt by this Ethiopian Christian group in its rural northwestern highlands setting to coopt the Jewish faith as a whole (or for that matter, any other faith), and possibly, in their own way, have all Jews and non-Christians convert to their Christian faith—after all, as they would have others believe, who does God "live" with through the ark? Or might there be some other reason(s) behind the need to have others believe that they actually have always had sole ownership of the ark for over the past 2.5 millennia? Clearly, the religious and historical plot continues to thicken.

So, therefore, in the continuing academic and historical searches, debates, and attempts to prove beyond a shadow of doubt the *genuineness* of the ark in the treasury building in Axum, Ethiopia's Christian Coptic church officials should be much more transparent and willing to allow professional scientists and archaeologists in to view the ark and, if possible, be allowed to perform scientific tests that would not in any way disturb the sanctity of the ark but would put to rest permanently any doubts concerning the actual final resting place of the original ark. It would clearly and very strongly not only benefit the scholarly and scientific community but the Ethiopian Christian Coptic church as well. It would forever establish the truthfulness of their claim. The well and vigorously researched scientific data need to be shared with the public, so that the historical narrative regarding the Ark of the Covenant can be verified.

References and Further Reading

Budge, Wallis. *The Queen of Sheba and Her Only Son Menyelek*. London: Martin Hopkinson, 1922.

Burstein, Stanley M. *Ancient African Civilizations: Kush and Axum*. Princeton, NJ: Markus Wiener Publisher, 1997.

Carew, Mairead. *Tara and the Ark of the Covenant: A Search for the Ark of the Covenant by British Israelites on the Hill of Tara, 1899–1900*. London: Royal Irish Academy, 2003.

Curtin, Philip D. *African History*. New York: Longman, 1995.

Curtin, Philip D. *Image of Africa*, Vols. 1 and 2. Madison: University of Wisconsin Press, 2004.

Curtin, Philip D. *On the Fringes of History*. Columbus: Ohio State University Press, 2005.

Hancock, Graham. *The Sign and the Seal: The Quest for the Lost Ark of the Covenant*. Clearwater, FL.: Touchstone Books, 1993.

Huggins, Willis Nathanial, & John G. Jackson. *An Introduction to African Civilizations: With Main Currents in Ethiopian History*. Westport, CT: Greenwood, 1969.

Littman, Sheba Enno. *The Legend of the Queen of Sheba in the Tradition of Axum*. Charleston, SC: BiblioLife, 2009.

Pankhurst, Richard. *The Ethiopian Borderlands: Essays in Regional History from Ancient Times to the End of the 18th Century*. Trenton, NJ: Red Sea Press, 1997.

Robert, Dana L. *Brief History of Missions*. Oxford: Wiley, 2009.

Shillington, Kevin. *History of Africa*. New York: Palgrave Macmillan, 2005.

Tibebu, Teshale. *The Making of Modern Ethiopia, 1896–1974*. Trenton, NJ: Red Sea Press, 1995.

Wilson, Marvin R. *Our Father Abraham: Jewish Roots of the Christian Faith*. Grand Rapids, MI: Eerdman's, 1990.

CON

Between the exodus from Egypt and Solomon's construction of the first temple in Jerusalem, the Ark of the Covenant played an important role in the narrative presented in the Hebrew Old Testament. However, following the construction of the temple in the mid-10th century BCE, the ark's role lessened, and it nearly disappeared from the Old Testament. In modern times, the absence of the Ark of the Covenant has been questioned by some, and an interest has been taken in locating it. Some who have attempted to do so claim that the ark may have disappeared from the Bible's historical narratives because it was removed from the temple and from Judah. The theories on why this is so vary between sources, but two widely supported proposals identify the Cathedral of Maryam Tseyon, or Mary of Zion, in Aksum, Ethiopia, as the final resting place of the ark; however, there is much evidence against this theory.

Story of Theft by Queen of Sheba's Son

The earlier story of the Ark of the Covenant's exodus to Aksum is found in the Ethiopian epic Kebra Nagast, translated as "The Glory of Kings." This narrative concerns the queen of Sheba, found in I Kings 10 and II Chronicles 9, and her visit to King Solomon, ruler over Israel and Judah. According to the Kebra Nagast, before returning to her country, the queen of Sheba conceived a son with King Solomon, after he tricked her into submitting to his will. Although born in Ethiopia, the queen's son, Menelik, visited his father years later and won his favor. Menelik refused his father's offer to stay in Judah and be king, saying he had promised his mother he would return to Aksum. King Solomon, grieved to see his now-favorite son leave, required his advisers to send their first-born sons to Aksum with Menelik to become his aides and advisers. These children of Judah could not bear to leave their country and their religious

An Ethiopian miniature depicting the meeting of Solomon and the Queen of Sheba. (Giraudon/Art Resource, NY)

heritage, so they plotted with Menelik to steal the Ark of the Covenant and bring it to Ethiopia. Their plan succeeded, and along with the ark, they are said to have brought Yahweh (God) and his favor to Ethiopia, thus supplanting Israel and Judah as his home. This narrative shows Menelik as the beginning of an Ethiopian royal dynasty that continues David's family, and through this, the covenant between Yahweh and David.

The legend of the Kebra Nagast has resonated through Ethiopian history for many centuries. Until the end of the reign of Emperor Haile Selassie in 1974, the Ethiopian constitution officially recognized the ruling dynasty as descending from King Solomon and the queen of Sheba through Menelik. Similar beliefs were often noted for other governing figures, said to have been of the lines of those who accompanied Menelik from Judah. Perhaps the most recognized modern effect of the Kebra Nagast is the theory that the Ark of the Covenant remains in the Cathedral of Maryam Tseyon, protected and used annually in the Timkat festival each January. This stance can be found in a tour book written by Girma Elias in 1997, *Aksum: A Guide to Historical Sites in and around Aksum*. The Davidic lineage of Ethiopian royalty and the presence of the Ark of the Covenant have both been supported by the Ethiopian Orthodox Church. Through this, the Kebra Nagast has served as a legitimizing national epic behind both the Ethiopian political power and church authority.

Story of Journey to Ethiopia by Way of Egypt

A contrary history of the ark to that contained in the Kebra Nagast was proposed by Graham Hancock (1992) in his book, *The Sign and the Seal: The Quest for the Lost Ark of the Covenant*. Hancock's investigation is framed by his communications with an Ethiopian cleric who claimed to protect the ark in the Cathedral of Maryam Tseyon in Aksum. Various issues of historicity prevented Hancock from embracing the traditional narrative of the Kebra Nagast and led him to develop an alternative route for the movement of the ark between Judah and Aksum. Hancock's theory begins with King Manasseh of Judah removing the ark from the temple. The officiating priests could not bear to destroy the ark or allow it to be lost, so Hancock believes they then brought it to a Judean settlement at Elephantine in Egypt. From there, he proposes, it would have been brought to a group of Jews in Ethiopia, around 470 BCE. The ark remained there until 330 CE, when Ethiopian Christians brought it to Aksum. According to Hancock, this history was remembered but became altered over time and developed into the legend of the Kebra Nagast.

Reasons to Doubt Ark Is in Ethiopian Cathedral

Both of these stories present claims that the trail of the Ark of the Covenant leads to Aksum, Ethiopia. Both narratives present reasons to doubt that the ark now resides in the Cathedral of Maryam Tseyon. Manifold archaeological finds lead to questions concerning the legend of the Kebra Nagast and the presumption that the story told in I Kings 10 and II Chronicles 9 refers to a ruler from ancient Ethiopia. Both the Kebra Nagast and Hancock's theory also contradict the biblical narrative and the modern scholarly interpretation of it.

History of Kebra Nagast Doubted

The most obvious points of contention concern the questions of the historicity of the Kebra Nagast. The primary issue among these is the identification of Ethiopia with the biblical Sheba. Most scholars propose that the biblical Sheba was the historical Saba. The center of this kingdom is recognized as having been in southwest Arabia, in modern-day Yemen. However, some discussion concerning the possibility that Saba, or Sheba, may still have been used in reference to Ethiopia exists. Some authors cite the historian Josephus, who called the queen of Sheba the queen of Egypt and Ethiopia. However, in Josephus's time, the term *Ethiopia* would have been attributed to the kingdom of Meroe in modern Sudan, not the modern nation of Ethiopia. Clearly Josephus's writing cannot be seen as supporting the narrative of the Kebra Nagast.

A further possibility of support comes from a royal inscription that refers to Saba. The inscription appears to be an attempt to lay claim to the rule of the Sabaean people in Ethiopia by a ruler named D'amat. Linguistic evidence and material remains indicate that the Ethiopian Sabaeans represented in the inscription were closely linked to the larger kingdom in Yemen and may have represented a group of immigrants from the south Arabian kingdom. While these inscriptions and cultural remains show evidence of Sabaeans in Ethiopia, none can be dated earlier than the eighth century BCE. Biblical scholars date the reign of Solomon to the middle of the 10th century BCE. This indicates that the Sabaean people of Ethiopia were likely in Ethiopia too late for the narrative in the Kebra Nagast to be factual. In fact, the earliest writing known today placing Sheba in modern Ethiopia is Michael of Tinnis's *History of the Patriarchs of Alexandria*, written between 1047 and 1077 CE. Thus Ethiopia was likely not known as Sheba during the time of Solomon and probably was not home to a Sabaean culture at the time either. This calls into question the narrative of the Kebra Nagast; if the queen of Sheba was not Ethiopian, the story of Menelik's bringing the ark to Ethiopia does appear to be based on anachronisms rather than historically accurate terms.

One of the key points of importance of the story in the Kebra Nagast is that it shows Ethiopia as a direct recipient of Yahweh's grace and of the religion of Solomon. Tradition states that the ark as well as the Davidic line resided in Ethiopia from the time of Menelik to the present. Thus Ethiopia was supposed to have been a Jewish, then a Christian, nation, under David's descendants since the time of Solomon. However, the Jews of Ethiopia likely did not arrive until the middle of the first millennium BCE. This may have occurred as a result of the neo-Babylonian conquest of Judah, which would have led some living in Judah to flee. This would mean that the earliest Jewish presence would have been in the fifth and sixth centuries BCE. This was a number of centuries after the life of King Solomon in Judah. Clearly this calls into question the legend that the queen of Sheba led her people in converting to Solomon's religion and that her son began a Davidic monarchy in Ethiopia in the 10th century BCE.

Multiple Aksum Gods

Of further concern is the evidence that the rulers of Aksum followed gods other than Yahweh, which contradicts the national legends of Ethiopia. The supreme deity appears to have been Mahrem, recognized in conjunction with Ares. Mahrem was seen as a divine supporter of the Aksumite king and was named as the ruler's invincible father. This would have created a divine monarchy, legitimizing the king with a heavenly patron. Additionally the Aksumites worshiped the local gods Astar and Bahar as well as Ilmuqah, Nuru, Habas, Dhat Himyam, and Dhat Ba'ada from south Arabia. The Yahwist faith that one might expect from the Kebra Nagast was not present in the ruling class of Aksum before the fourth century CE. Clearly the queen of Sheba's or the Ark of the Covenant's presence did not lead to a Judeo-Christian government in Ethiopia in the 10th century BCE.

In about 324 CE, the Ethiopian king, Ezana, began to convert his nation to the Christian faith. Under King Ezana the Ethiopian coins that were minted originally showed a divine symbol composed of a disk and a crescent, just as his predecessors' coins had. This symbol likely represented Mahrem or some other form of religious iconography. During his reign this coinage symbol was replaced with a cross, indicating a conversion to Christianity. Ethiopian Christians also began to travel to Jerusalem on pilgrimages in the fourth century CE. The Ethiopian conversion appears to have been from a faith native to Ethiopia or south Arabia, and not Judaism. It is difficult to support the ark's presence in Ethiopia from the 10th century BCE to the present, as the Kebra Nagast suggests, without an accompanying Judeo-Christian faith arriving through a Solomonic influence.

Portrayal of Queen of Sheba

A further issue concerning the Kebra Nagast is its portrayal of the queen of Sheba. She is depicted as an opulent ruler, able to travel with hundreds of camels, asses, and donkeys, each loaded with gifts for King Solomon. This suggests her power over a kingdom with rich and plentiful resources. Menelik is also presented as a grand ruler. He is accompanied by an assemblage of aides and advisers, who assist in the ruling of Ethiopia. These images of the queen of Sheba and Menelik are intertwined with the Ethiopian legend of the Ark of the Covenant's arrival in Aksum and its continued presence there throughout the centuries. Because of this, it is necessary to ask what the royalty and polities would have been like in ancient Ethiopia, because they may support or call into question the Kebra Nagast's narrative and its ties to the Old Testament.

The earliest evidence for a monarchy in the region comes from a series of inscriptions that names D'amat as ruler over Tigray and Eritrea. One such inscription is the previously mentioned one that also contains the name Saba. The dating of the inscription to the eighth century BCE serves to limit the earliest period of a powerful ruler in Ethiopia. This period saw the emergence of early state-level sites under D'amat, as evident in the growth of settlement sites, which before this were only the size of hamlets and towns. Since this transformation can only be traced to the eighth century BCE, the state-sized sites attributable to the D'amat monarchy could not have been contemporaneous with Solomon's reign and the narrative of the queen of Sheba. Instead, had the queen of Sheba, who lived at the same time as King Solomon, been from Ethiopia, she would have been from a region full of small towns and hamlets. The rich and powerful queen of the Old Testament and the Kebra Nagast very likely could not have been from such small settlements and have offered the gifts these sources attribute to her.

The state-level phase of Ethiopian settlement represented by the D'amat inscriptions came to a close ca. 400 BCE. The following period was marked by the absence of the powerful ruling elite, present during the reign of D'amat. It

Haile Selassie and the Rastafari Movement

The Rastafari movement, named for Selassie's precoronation name Ras Tafari Makonnen, holds that Selassie was god incarnate and the 225th monarch in the Solomonic dynasty. He is held as the *messiah* and the reincarnation of Jesus Christ. The movement is a syncretic religion owing much to Judaism and Christianity, but deviating sharply from them as well (though many Rastafari do consider themselves Jews or Christians). Rastafari who identify themselves with the Ethiopian Orthodox Church tend to hold the Kebra Negast in high esteem, and the movement in general particularly reveres the New Testament book of Revelation and the messianic prophecies of the Old Testament.

Selassie had nothing to do with the origins of the movement, and he neither accepted its claims of his divinity nor condemned the Rastafari. He shared spiritual and political ideologies with the movement, though, and the Rastafari position is that it is not necessary for Selassie to claim to be god, he simply is. Likewise, they do not accept his death, and credit it to a conspiracy or hoax.

saw the return to sites the size of hamlets and towns, following what appears to have been a collapse of the D'amat culture in Ethiopia. This style of culture continued until about 150 BCE, which marked the beginning of the Aksumite period. The Aksumite period saw the emergence of a new ruling class and the buildup of sites. The rulers appearing in the Aksumite period, including Ezana, would be those who later kings and emperors of Ethiopia would use as a link to the past and to Menelik and the queen of Sheba. However, there is no archaeological evidence of a connection between the pre-Aksumite cultures and those of the Aksumite period. While the majority of sites show no evidence of a continuation of culture, excavations at Matara have shown a clear break between these two periods. This absence of a connection does more than throw doubt on the official narrative of a chain of rulers. If the Ark of the Covenant had been in Ethiopia during the pre-Aksumite period, the lack of connection between D'amat-period sites and Aksumite-period sites offers no means for the ark to have been protected and passed on from generation to generation across the period of collapse.

The Kebra Nagast does present attempts to connect the reign of Menelik, which would have been in the 10th century BCE, to the Aksumite period and post-Aksumite period, which began ca. 1000 CE. While Ethiopian tradition held that the nation's ruler was a descendant of Menelik and that his power came in an uninterrupted line from Menelik's first dynasty, it also presented the titles of judges, generals, scribes, priests, and other officials as being those found in the Kebra Nagast for Menelik's entourage of advisers from Judah. However, there is no evidence of these titles being used before the post-Aksumite period. What appears to have happened is that titles used for governmental and cultic officials during the period in which the Kebra Nagast was written were anachronistically attributed to their equivalent in the Kebra Nagast. This tantalizing evidence of a connection between the period of Solomon's reign and post-Aksumite Ethiopia appears to offer no actual evidence of such ties.

Hancock Theory also Problematic

Hancock's narrative of the Ark of the Covenant's coming to Aksum around 330 CE, after having been held in a Jewish temple at Elephantine, Egypt, until the mid-fifth century BCE, may sidestep various historical issues concerning the story in the Kebra Nagast, but his overall support of the ark's presence in Aksum is based on issues that are logically problematic. The major historical theory Hancock presents to explain the travels of the ark is that he sees little role for the ark in the biblical narrative after the time of Solomon and the construction of the temple. However, there is little reason to believe that the end of the mention of a role for the Ark of the Covenant in the Old Testament story marks its physical disappearance from Judah and Israel.

The initial and probably most important argument against the assumption that the ark vanishes from biblical history and then appears in Ethiopia is that the ark does not disappear from the story at all. II Chronicles 35:4 mentions the ark and its return to the temple. Part of Josiah's reform apparently was to bring the ark back to the temple after it had been removed. Additionally it states that the Levites had been carrying it and protecting it during its absence from the temple. This shows a clear logical flaw in Hancock's argument, because the ark's absence from the Bible cannot be sustained as evidence of its disappearance from Judah. The verse in II Chronicles also fails to support the travel of the ark to Egypt; it presents the ark as having been in the care of the Levites, without any mention of it having left Judah. There is no clear record of the disappearance of the ark from the temple in the biblical narrative, not even by the time of Manasseh, when Hancock posits it was lost. Instead, the Old Testament appears to very easily answer Hancock's concern of what happened to the ark; it was returned to the temple.

It is not possible to wholly argue away Graham Hancock's theory of the ark's lessening importance in biblical history by looking to II Chronicles 35, because he argues that this may represent a conspiracy to hide its loss. However, the Old Testament's theology and history do offer an explanation as to why the ark would have been less important following the construction of the temple or why it subsequently was mentioned fewer times. The ark's original purpose among the new followers of Yahweh was to serve as a representative of their God with them, a throne on which he sat. Before the completion of the temple, the ark was easily brought from one town to another, allowing for the worship of Yahweh to take place over a wide area, without requiring a centralized place of cultic focus. The construction of the temple centralized the worship at Jerusalem.

Thus, after King Solomon's completion of the temple, worship was focused at the temple. The Ark of the Covenant then theoretically played a lesser role, because there was no need for it to travel from one town to another. The temple itself became Yahweh's throne on Earth, from which he protected Jerusalem. As in other ancient Near Eastern cultures, this would also have aided the consolidation of the monarchy, because the control of the temple and the official cult would have become tied with the royal family through the palace.

Issue of Centrality of the Temple

The biblical narrative clearly shows a focus on the Temple and away from other cultic sites, which would lead to a lesser importance for the Ark of the Covenant, but archaeologists have uncovered evidence that these other cultic sites were not neglected and that the temple was only one of many place where Yahweh was worshiped. This may appear to give pause to the explanation that the ark almost disappears from the narrative because of a focus on the temple. While there were many sacred sites at the time of Solomon's construction of the temple and throughout the following centuries, this was not the context in which the narrative was written. The book of I Kings was not written during Solomon's reign, but during the reign of King Josiah, during the sixth century BCE. Josiah attempted to reform the worship of Yahweh in Judah, removing holy sites outside of Jerusalem and focusing all cultic practices in Solomon's temple. When I Kings was written, it was only natural to mirror this new religious system instead of a historically more accurate one. The Ark of the Covenant is missing from the biblical narrative not because it had disappeared, but because the authors sought to reinterpret history in a way that did not require the ark's presence and where the ark may actually have detracted from the theology of the central importance of the temple in Jerusalem.

Hancock's Conspiracy Theory

Graham Hancock's argument for the possibility that the Ark of the Covenant was taken from Jerusalem is based on the presence of gaps in the biblical narrative. He posits that the absence of the ark from history is caused by a cover-up conspiracy to assuage the guilt over the loss of such an important relic. This argument is similar to one used by some who support the Kebra Nagast as an accurate history and who look to the same gap as a reason to believe the ark was stolen. This argument is not only specious, but it also goes against modern understanding of the composition of the Old Testament and the developing theology of the temple. There appears to be no reason to believe that the Bible's narrative does away with the ark, because it is mentioned following Solomon's lifetime and after the reign of Manasseh, the two points where its physical disappearance had been posited.

Argument of Ark's Role in Aksum

Modern supporters of the theory that the Ark of the Covenant is currently in the Cathedral of Maryam Tseyon in Aksum often point to its use in an annual festival and the presence of a clergyman to guard the ark and care for it. Graham Hancock uses conversations with this mysterious guardian as a frame for his novel and as a final proof of its presence. However, there are a number of relatively recent events that throw these modern claims of the ark's guardian into question.

The initial modern point of contention concerning the Ark of the Covenant's survival in Aksum occurs between 1526 and 1542 CE. In this period, Ahmad Gran Muslim Amir of Harar invaded Ethiopia and succeeded in destroying the Cathedral of Maryam Tseyon. Although modern Ethiopians hold that the ark was successfully removed beforehand and hidden, there have been contradictory reports. Between 1769 and 1772, James Bruce, an Irish traveler, visited Ethiopia. He reported in his book that while he was there, the king told him that Ahmad Gran was able to destroy the ark within the cathedral. Bruce later wrote that the king falsely claimed the contrary as well. Because of the contradictory nature of Bruce's account, it is difficult to take either position as the truth, but it is certain that the Cathedral of Maryam Tseyon was destroyed once around the period of Ahmad Gran.

Following Ahmad Gran's destruction of the cathedral in the early 16th century, King Sartsa Dengel led the construction of a small replacement cathedral on top of the ruins following his coronation in 1579. Tradition holds that the ark was returned to Aksum, either for the coronation of King Dengel or soon after his reign. In 1611 the Cathedral of Maryam Tseyon was again destroyed during the Galla War, and again the ark would have been threatened. The modern building was constructed during the reign of Emperor Fasiladas, between 1632 and 1667. Had the ark made its way to Ethiopia at any point before this, it would have had to survive two destructions of the church that tradition marks as its home, as well as other insurgencies and uprisings. This would be quite a feat for a 3,000-year-old wooden box. Taking into account Ethiopia's natural environment, it seems unlikely that it would have been in any condition to survive at all, because the warm moist air of Ethiopia does not preserve wood well.

More Recent Ethiopian Legend

A more recent Ethiopian legend has presented an idea as to how the Ark of the Covenant may have survived these tribulations in spite of the 3,000 years of wear. The theory states that what is recognized as the ark in the Cathedral of Maryam Tseyon is not the Ark of the Covenant, but the inscribed tablet on which Moses presented the Ten Commandments. This stone would be much more likely to have survived the millennia between the reign of Solomon and the present day. However, this myth appears to be a more recent creation, and it contradicts the Kebra Nagast, which states that Menelik stole the Ark of the Covenant. While this new twist on the older legend may attempt to explain the survival of an item from the 10th century BCE, it suffers the same failings as the theory that the ark was brought to Ethiopia that early. Additionally, if the stories that a stone is now in the cathedral were shown to be true, it would certainly not support the idea that ark had been moved to Ethiopia.

Practice of Ark Replication

A final note belongs to the Ethiopian practice of replicating the Ark of the Covenant. Throughout Ethiopia, many churches are noted as having their own *tabot*, or ark. This term, as noted above, is used in reference to their altar tables, which take on a symbolic meaning similar to the Ark of the Covenant in the Cathedral of Maryam Tseyon. When Graham Hancock watched a ceremony where the ark was taken out of the cathedral by priests and paraded through the streets of Aksum, he said that he knew it was a copy. The guardian of the ark had remained in the Cathedral of Maryam Tseyon, while the *tabot* was carried forth. This was likely a symbolic copy of the ark, similar to those used throughout Ethiopia. There is no reason to make the same assumption as Hancock did that the real ark remained in the cathedral during the procession. It is far more likely that any ark kept there would be a copy. The guardian refuses to show the Ark of the Covenant to anyone, and past guardians have stated that they had only seen it a few times in their lives. Without concrete proof of the ark's existence, such as a viewing and analysis of the materials, it is impossible to present any ark in the Cathedral of Maryam Tseyon as more than a symbol of what the true ark is imagined to be. This position is only strengthened by the historical issues concerning the stories of the ark, the likelihood that the ark would have been destroyed, or at the very least deteriorated by this point, and the changing legend as to the actual nature of the ark. An object is certainly being held today in the Cathedral of Maryam Tseyon in Aksum that Ethiopian tradition has labeled the Ark of the Covenant, but all evidence points to it being a relatively recent creation. And until positive evidence to the contrary is produced, this is the most reasonable conclusion.

References and Further Reading

Elias, Girma. *Aksum: A Guide to Historical Sites in and around Aksum*. Addis Ababa, Ethiopia: Mega Printing Enterprise, 1997.

Grierson, Roderick, and Stuart Munro-Hay. *The Ark of the Covenant*. London: Weidenfeld and Nicolson, 1999.

Hancock, Graham. *The Sign and the Seal: The Quest for the Lost Ark of the Covenant*. New York: Simon and Schuster, 1992.

Hoberman, Barry. "The Ethiopian Legend of the Ark." *Biblical Archaeologist* 46, 2 (1983): 112–14.

Lambdin, Thomas O. *Introduction to Classical Ethiopic (Ge'ez)*, Vol. 24. Harvard Semitic Studies. Winona Lake, IN: Eisenbrauns, 2006.

Mendenhall, George E. *Ancient Israel's Faith and History*, ed. by Gary A. Herion. Louisville, KY: Westminster John Knox Press, 2001.

The Modern Translation of the Kebra Nagast (the Glory of Kings). Trans. by Miguel F. Brooks. Lawrenceville, NJ: Red Sea Press, 1996.

Munro-Hay, S. C. *Aksum: An African Civilisation of Late Antiquity*. Edinburgh: Edinburgh University Press, 1991.

Munro-Hay, Stuart. *The Quest for the Ark of the Covenant: The True History of the Tablets of Moses*. New York: I. B. Tauris, 2005.

Pritchard, James B., et al. *Solomon and Sheba*, ed. by James B. Pritchard. London: Phaidon Press, 1974.

2

The Greek city-states were "democratic" by our modern American definition.

PRO   Cenap Çakmak
CON   John Lee

PRO

Whether the polis, city–state regime of ancient Greece may be viewed as a clear precedent and example of democratic evolution and development is a question that attracts a great deal of attention from analysts and political scientists. Opponents argue that the polis order cannot be taken as a precedent for the current understanding of democracy and its practices because of some of its visible defects and antidemocratic characters. They make particular references to the institution of slavery, which was widely practiced and keenly preserved in the city–states, the polis, implying that it is not proper to speak of a presence of democratic order in a place that relies on such an immorality.

There are other serious objections to accepting the polis regime as the initial form of democratic governance in the modern world. A commonly held objection stresses that this regime may not be seen as democratic simply because it denied equal status to all inhabitants in the cities, recalling that only a small group of people were entitled to cast their votes in the election process. Exclusion of women—and other disadvantaged groups—from the right to vote as well as recognition of wealthy people as true citizens with full entitlements stand out as other major objections. Skeptics, therefore, argue that the methods of legislative action and mode of governance employed in the ancient Greece were not truly democratic.

However, while these objections are valid and address part of the actual picture, a more thorough review and evaluation will reveal that the polis may be in fact seen as a major precursor for the current democratic practice and institutions. To this end, the above objections only refer to some deficiencies of the polis regime and do not constitute sufficient evidence for ruling out its ability to serve as the initial form and first example of democratic rule.

Above all, it should be noted that the opponents fail to consider the definition of the term democracy when staging their objections; they are instead focused on the defective elements of the polis order. But we have to keep in mind that a regime will always be flawed regardless of its achievements and the progress made over time. Who could point to a current democratic regime as the perfect rule today? Take the U.S. system; despite novel arrangements and visible accomplishments, only one of the two major parties is likely to win the presidential elections. Or consider a number of political systems that introduce election thresholds to attain stability in government and legislation. How is it possible to reconcile the basic premises of democracy in light of the obstacles faced by small parties that are unable to win seats in the parliament because they receive less popular support? Yet we still call the regimes fulfilling the basic requirements a democracy and democratic despite grave flaws and serious defects. Therefore, we must investigate whether the polis fulfills the basic requirements of a democratic rule instead of focusing on its defects.

There are at least three major reasons for regarding the political regime and design as implemented in ancient Greek cities, where direct participation was allowed in the rule of their respective nations, as the forerunner of the modern understanding of democracy. Above all, in order to appraise whether the political regime implemented in the polis of ancient Greece was democratic and the initial form of current democratic regime, we have to rely on an objective and authoritative definition of the term democracy. In addition, we must also identify some basic requirements for such a definition. And if the regime in the polis fits in the framework defined by these requirements and definition, then there should be no objection as to whether that regime was truly democratic.

In this case, the set of requirements identified to determine whether a regime is democratic or not should be employed objectively; in other words, the defects and immoral aspects of the polis democracy should not mislead us to conclude that it is not as democratic, despite meeting the criteria and preconditions for being a democracy. If, in its simplest sense, democracy is government by the people and ruled by the majority, we must look at the political regime in the polis to determine whether these two basic criteria are met.

Second, unfair elements and immoral practices in city–state democracies should not discourage us from seeing this regime as the initial example of modern democracy. Criticizing a regime or mode of governance because of its defects and flaws is different from defining the same regime as undemocratic. Whether a regime is democracy is determined via the basic criteria employed for defining the term, and once it is concluded that a given regime is a democracy, its flaws should not lead us to conclude otherwise.

In fact, modern democracies have suffered from serious flaws with respect to fair representation, greater participation, and equality before the law. But they have remained as democracies despite these flaws and shortcomings. It should also be noted that current democracies—even the most advanced ones—have to deal with similar problems to a certain degree. Despite novel arrangements and progress over time, women's participation in government and legislative bodies is still meager in many countries. To deal with this problem, some advanced democracies rely on policies of affirmative action. Low voter turnout rate—for instance in the United States—is a big problem that needs to be addressed for fairer representation and a more legitimate rule. These are all real and serious problems; however, we still define these regimes as democratic simply because they meet the basic criteria for being a democracy.

The same should also be true for the city–states of ancient Greece. It is true that not all citizens were entitled to cast a vote in a polis; it is also true that slaves were leading a miserable life, and we acknowledge that views of ordinary people who have a right to vote were easily won over by eloquent speakers. But we still observe the same problems in different forms and degrees. Yet we regard the current regimes as democracy despite these problems. Why should we not do the same with the poleis of ancient Greece?

Third, whether the democratic experience in the ancient Greek cities has influenced emergence of democratic regimes in the following centuries is a matter of controversy that needs extensive scholarly inquiry. Regardless of whether it has served as a source of inspiration, this experience represents the forerunner of the modern understanding of democratic practice. In other words, we still have to rely on the basic requirements employed to define the term democracy when attempting to determine whether the experience in the polis is actually democratic, even if we conclude that subsequent regimes and modes of governance did not follow the path and precedent set by that experience.

History needs to be progressive and linear; and for this reason, developments following the experience in the polis of the ancient Greeks are not necessarily affected by that experience. After all, people might not have liked it and may have wanted to replace it with another form of rule, perhaps an alternative means of rule could have replaced democracy as experienced by the ancient Greeks. Therefore, even if a historical survey concludes that the practices in poleis did not set a precedent for the subsequent generations, this will not necessarily mean they were not governed by some form of democracy.

Defining the Term Democracy

In his famous Gettysburg Address, President Abraham Lincoln defined democracy as "government of the People, by the People and for the People." Since then, this definition has gained wide acceptance by thinkers, pundits, and scholars. Lincoln's seminal definition refers to three key elements of democracy: that democracy derives its legitimacy from the people's commitment to it; that the people extensively participate in governmental affairs and processes; and that democracy actually seeks to realize the common welfare and safeguard the rights and freedoms of individuals.

Obviously the key in this definition is the "people." It is known that the term democracy literally means people's government and that it was created by combination of *demos*, meaning "people" and *kratia*, meaning "government."

The Acropolis of Athens as viewed from the Hill of Philopappus (also known as the Hill of the Muses). The Acropolis contained both the civic and religious buildings of the Athenian city-state. Its position on a high limestone outcrop provided defense from neighboring city-states. (iStockphoto)

It is also evident that the current usage of the notion of democracy has evolved from its Greek original *demokratia*. This implies that the current usage of the notion of democracy may be etymologically linked to the democratic regime as practiced in ancient Greece's city-states.

This practice represents the most direct form of democracy; in this system, all citizens met periodically to elect their rulers and other state officials, enact legislation, and discuss governmental issues. Of course it was far from being perfect; slaves, women, and foreigners were not entitled to cast a vote and express their views in assembly meetings.

Despite the flaws, this direct democracy fulfilled the fundamental criteria referred to above. Especially Athens displayed the great achievements in creating a more fair and just regime that ensured greater popular participation in government and legislation. The Athenian democracy, backed by additional reforms in 460 BCE, heavily depended on the popular assembly as the primary sovereign authority. All governmental decisions were made by this institution or required its approval.

More important, there were no restrictions imposed upon those who wanted to participate in the process of government or legislation; basically, anybody was entitled to debate or propose in assembly meetings. Of course there were downsides associated with this practice. The assembly was convening frequently; therefore, ordinary citizens were rarely able to attend every meeting; as a result of this, a few leading eloquent speakers who were able to articulate their cause dominated the entire process of legislation and rule-making. Yet, popular participation was so extensive and visible that every citizen entitled to participation in the process attended such meetings and held legislative or administrative positions at least once in their lifetime.

The citizens were also allowed to serve in the military and the judicial system. Every judicial decision could be appealed to a citizens' board. Some officers who held key positions were elected by popular vote, and they—generals and treasurers, for example—could be removed from the office by the assembly. Office terms of the elected actors were brief so that others would have the opportunity to serve in governmental posts. Only a few positions in the military were subject to appointment rather than election.

The idea of direct democracy was perfect in theory; but there were serious flaws in practice. Women were excluded from political rights despite being considered full citizens by law. Men slaves and foreigners were also disallowed to participate in the political process. Most important, despite the novel arrangements, aristocrats were still influential in the government and legislation bodies.

However, it is fair to argue that democracy was at work at least in principle because all of the basic requirements were being met. Political leaders and thinkers, in addition, clearly articulated the general rules for application of democracy. The Athenian democracy paid utmost attention to public devotion and the ability and competence of those who were recognized as citizens.

To this end, it will be useful to recall a definition provided by Pericles, a famous ruler in Athens who consolidated democracy in this polis, for the notion of democracy:

> The administration is in the hands of the many and not of the few. But while the law secures equal justice to all alike in their private disputes, the claim of excellence is also recognized; and when a citizen is any way distinguished he is preferred to the public service, not as a matter of privilege but as the reward of merit. Neither is poverty a bar, but a man may benefit his country whenever be the obscurity of the condition. (Fisher, 1901: 99)

Of course, this does not necessarily mean that the actual practice of democracy in poleis has met these criteria and expectations in full. Nonetheless, popular participation in political processes was extensive and fulfilling; popular choice and the decision by the majority were so crucial in decision making that as famous political scientist Stephen D. Tansey recalls, in ancient Greek city–states, "because the majority of citizens had to be convinced if the community were to act, it seems a very high standard of information and debate was often obtained alongside great commitment and loyalty to the state" (Tansey, 2004: 171).

Direct democracy as exercised in poleis was not ideal or perfect; but it was operational and involved all necessary components for greater popular participation in legislation and decision making. *Ecclesia*, the legislative body that also checks the executive body, was open to males over 18 years old. It was subsequently authorized with a practice of *ostrakismos*, under which citizens may convene once a year to determine who has the tendency to become a tyrant. If at least 6,000 citizens declare someone to be implementing this practice, he would be expelled from the community. This was a mechanism envisaged to protect the democratic character of the polis; undoubtedly, it has been abused, and innocent people were unjustly driven away from their domiciles. But malpractice or abuse does not necessarily mean that the idea or the system as a whole was wrong and undemocratic. We all know that judicial errors are still commonplace despite advanced technology and interrogation techniques.

In addition to *Ecclesia*, Athens also had a larger popular assembly, which solely dealt with law making. It consisted of 500 members; 50 being from each *deme*, smaller geographic districts in the city created for better representation. This arrangement was conceived to ensure fair and equal representation of 10 *demes* in the assembly. The *demes* were actually designed as electoral districts; special attention was paid to make sure that aristocrats would constitute a minority in every *deme* so that democracy would be consolidated further.

Representatives from each *deme* were entitled to chair the assembly for one-tenth of the entire year—or 36 days. Chairing the assembly was made possible via a board formed by these representatives. An Athenian citizen was elected randomly to chair this board every day; therefore, it was quite possible for *any* Athenian citizen to become chairman of the board and the entire assembly.

The Athenian people also elected the chief commander of the city–state, the *polemarkhos*. Ten additional commanders, *strategos*, each being one *deme*, were appointed to serve as assistants to him. All these arrangements were introduced for a better and fairer representation in the political institutions of the city–state. Whether these measures have worked is a different story; what really matters is to determine if these measures and arrangements are strong enough for us to conclude that these create a democratic regime. The answer must be yes.

Pericles introduced further safeguards for extensive and greater popular participation; under *graphe para nomon*, every citizen was vested with the authority to protect the fundamental laws and file a lawsuit in request of annulment of a law on the grounds of unconstitutionality. In consideration of reluctance of poor citizens to seek governmental posts and jobs because of lack of financial resources, Pericles also introduced legislation under which those who attend sessions of legislative bodies were entitled to a certain amount of remuneration and allowance. Every member in the *Ecclesia* had the right to speak and make statements, propose a draft bill, and ask for a secret session. The plenary sessions were inaugurated with a call asking who would like to take the stage for a word.

Pericles' Funeral Oration

If there is one individual who is best remembered for reforming the government of Athens, it is Pericles. He transformed the city–state from an aristocracy to an empire in the brief span of his 40 years in office. First as a soldier and then as a statesman, Pericles built Athens into a place of prominence on the Greek peninsula, turning the city's former allies into subject cities, which paid tribute to Athens for protection from the Persian Empire. Although technically still a democracy, debate has raged through the ages as to how much Pericles was led by the citizenry and how much he led them.

Near the end of his time in office, he led Athens into the Peloponnesian War, which would result in the destruction of the city some 25 years after his death. It was after the first year of the war that Pericles delivered his famous funeral oration, attributed to him by Thucydides, which comments on how the Athenian form of government sets them apart from their rivals.

> Our constitution does not copy the laws of neighboring states; we are rather a pattern to others than imitators ourselves. Its administration favors the many instead of the few; this is why it is called a democracy. If we look to the laws, they afford equal justice to all in their private differences; if to social standing, advancement in public life falls to reputation for capacity, class considerations not being allowed to interfere with merit; nor again does poverty bar the way, if a man is able to serve the state, he is not hindered by the obscurity of his condition. The freedom which we enjoy in our government extends also to our ordinary life. There, far from exercising a jealous surveillance over each other, we do not feel called upon to be angry with our neighbor for doing what he likes, or even to indulge in those injurious looks which cannot fail to be offensive, although they inflict no positive penalty. But all this ease in our private relations does not make us lawless as citizens. Against this fear is our chief safeguard, teaching us to obey the magistrate and the laws, particularly such as regard the protection of the injured, whether they are actually on the statute book, or belong to that code which, although unwritten, yet cannot be broken without acknowledged disgrace. (Thucydides 1914: 121–22)

Source: Thucydides. *History of the Peloponnesian War, Done into English by Richard Crawley.* New York: Dutton, 1914.

In addition to such mechanisms, Pericles also wanted to equip the direct democracy with noble arrangements, including *isonomia* and *isegoria*. *Isonomia* referred to equal treatment of all before the law; according to Pericles, laws provide the same equality for all in personal affairs. In addition, the laws give equal rights for all citizens regardless of their status or rank to participation in political processes. Only merit shall be considered in appointment to governmental posts or other political positions.

Pericles' *isegoria* seeks to ensure freedom of expression for all citizens. Pericles holds that citizens act based on a unique thinking and reasoning; for this reason, he further believes that the citizens should not only participate in state affairs but also do so in accordance with their views. According to him, democracy is based on pluralism and decisions are taken after lengthy deliberations and discussions over diverse views and approaches.

Do the Flaws of Polis Make It Undemocratic?

Polis democracy is mostly criticized for its flaws; critics make particular references to its failure to attract participation of large groups, including women, slaves, and foreigners, in political processes, with there being domination of a small and privileged group in administration, despite novel arrangements and its impracticality.

Problem of Restricted Political Participation in Poleis

It is argued that polis democracy fails to maintain a democratic rule because it excludes women, slaves, and foreigners from inclusion in political processes. This is a very accurate and legitimate criticism; however, polis democracy may not be declared as undemocratic just because it is a defected system and fails to ensure greater popular participation. It should be recalled that not only polis democracy but also most modern democracies suffer from this problem.

Only males were entitled to participation in political decision making in Athenian democracy; Pericles went even further requiring males be born to citizen parents for such entitlement. The elite members were more prone to marriages with foreigners, while the poor mostly married locals; because of the rule, therefore, a substantial number of elites lost citizenship, thus being excluded from political process. Likewise, women had a lower status in Athens; as a consequence of this status, they were denied participation in political processes.

That said, it should be recalled that a number of modern democracies have experienced similar problems. Thomas Jefferson, one of the leading founders of American democracy, owned some 400 slaves. Blacks were not entitled to cast a vote or participate in political processes in a number of modern democratic countries even as late as 20th century. Likewise, extension of suffrage to women is a fairly recent phenomenon; there were still some European countries where women were not allowed to run in the elections in 1970s.

Despite measures taken to address such problems, a number of significant flaws still remain visible in several modern advanced democracies. Above all, women are not fairly represented in many countries. Interest by women in governmental posts is fairly weak; and even if they develop a keen interest, male domination in administrations and legislations is still prevalent and influential.

With the exception of a few countries that have introduced legislations under which a certain percentage of the legislative posts must be filled by women, most modern democracies fail to ensure fair representation of women in government and parliament.

Another problem with respect to poor popular participation in political processes of modern democracies is the visibly low turnout rate. This is a common problem especially in less politicized societies and some advanced democratic states. For instance, turnout rate is around 40 percent in the United States and 60 percent in many European countries. So this suggests that poor political participation is still a problem in modern democracies, despite measures taken to address this problem. This problem notwithstanding, we never consider calling these regimes undemocratic; the same should be the case with the polis.

It is also true that despite measures taken to ensure participation of citizens from all backgrounds and classes in political decision-making processes, eventually only a small number of people gain access to governmental posts and executive positions. Eloquent speakers as well as wealthy citizens eventually established control over the poor and ordinary citizens. For this reason, direct democracy as practiced in poleis was referred to as some sort of aristocracy.

Because the votes of the citizens were crucial in decision making, convincing holders of the right to vote was also important. Citizens uninformed about the matter under review and discussion had to make up their minds based on what had been said on the stage by the speakers who often relied on a strong rhetoric to get what they wanted. This was often the case because most of the citizens holding the right to vote did not get sufficient information because of time constraints and infrequent attendance in the meetings. This made them rely on the arguments by eloquent speakers. It is upheld that citizens were mostly deceived or misinformed by a small number of eloquent speakers who were specialized in convincing ambivalent crowds. Critics, therefore, argue that a regime where the influence of a small number of people is visible and extensive cannot be regarded as a democracy, suggesting that the polis democracy was not a real democracy.

These criticisms are certainly relevant; but the same flaws are frequently observed in many advanced democracies as well. With a few exceptions, politics is something that only wealthy people would participate in within developed or developing countries considered to be democratic. Even though every citizen is entitled to make political decisions and express interest in governmental posts in democratic countries, this is not always possible because of de facto obstructions and barriers.

The case in the United States is especially illustrative; election campaigns often require large sums of money in this country; for this reason, presidential candidates are focused on attracting more funds to finance their campaign. It is also commonplace to observe that presidential candidates are often well-educated and often rich individuals; this implies that although common and ordinary citizens may run for presidency, theoretically the presidential post is actually reserved for some privileged political actors. It should be recalled that despite its long democratic experience, the United States first elected a black president as late as 2008.

Or consider the impact of media in the elections held in modern democracies; media effect is strongly criticized because of its determinative influence over the election results. People are misinformed or misled by propaganda or media publications; voters may cast their votes based on false or inaccurate information in modern democracies. This implies that modern democracies are actually no different from the polis democracy, in that governmental and administrative positions are sometimes occupied by advantaged groups, including the wealthy, the well educated, or elites.

It is certainly true that there were inherent problems with the direct democracy in the polis that lead in some degree to impracticality. For one thing, the polis democracy was missing a strong and working institutional setting. The composition of the existing institutions was often volatile, making the decision-making process unstable and fragile. A substantial number of citizens virtually did not have time to attend every session; and even when they did, they were uninformed about what was being discussed and reviewed.

Efficiency of the deliberations held in large areas, *agora*, was also controversial. It was pretty likely for the attendants to get distracted because of the large audience and untidy setting. In such an environment, rhetorical approaches and eloquent speeches were pretty influential in shaping the opinions and views of the delegates present at the meetings.

However, it should be recalled that this sort of direct democracy is still being practiced in the modern world. Even though there is no widespread application of it, some small towns in the United States and districts in Switzerland are ruled by such a system where *all* residents who are entitled to participate in the decision-making process convene to discuss their problems and take the proper measures accordingly. Besides, to make a decision on whether direct democracy is really democratic is not relevant to whether it is practical. In other words, a system does not need to be practical in order to be defined as democratic. Thus, we have to admit that polis democracy is actually the initial form of modern democracy if it meets the basic requirements to be considered so, even if it involves some impractical arrangements.

Did Direct Democracy in Greek Poleis Inspire and Influence Other Communities in Coming Ages?

Whether the regime in ancient Greek cities has influenced other societies and nations in the coming ages matters for the sake of locating a deterministic linkage between the democratic character of this order and the modern understanding of democracy. In other words, if modern democracy is an outcome and culmination of progress made throughout a process initially started by the Greek democracy, then this would mean that Greek democracy is a true inspirer of modern ages.

We are not so sure as to whether the mode of governance in Greek poleis did actually have such an impact over the nations in subsequent ages. However, the practice of direct democracy—just as it was exercised in Greek city–states—in at least some parts of the modern world must be somewhat of an inspiration. This should suggest that people actually like this form of participation because of its directness and ability to ensure fairer representation.

But the crucial question is of course whether representative democracy, the modern practice prevalent all around the world, is an evolved and tailored version of direct democracy in Greek city–states. This is a challenging question that requires a great deal of scholarly effort and extensive research.

However, even if we assume that there is no link whatsoever between the modern development of democratic order and the primitive form of government in Greek city–states that lacked a strong institutional setting, this would not necessarily mean Greek poleis were not truly democratic.

Above all, it should be recalled that democracy was only limitedly practiced in ancient Greece. Not all city–states relied on direct democracy as a form of government; Athens appeared to be a leading example of direct democracy. It is generally held that some of its rulers—Solon and Pericles—played the greatest role in the consolidation of direct democracy in this city–state. Their reforms helped a democratic form of governance to emerge; however, they met with serious opposition and reaction from circles with aristocratic tendencies and ambitions.

It is also worth recalling that democracy was only briefly experienced and practiced in ancient Greece. There are some obvious reasons for the collapse of the democratic order in the poleis. The primary reason appears to be the opposition by some philosophers and thinkers because they upheld that it was simply too dangerous and illogical to leave the task of government to the hands of ordinary people.

What is more, defeats in the wars led to a conclusion that suggests democracy was to blame and that if the city had been ruled under an aristocratic regime, they would not have had to deal with the dire consequences of these defeats. All these factors eliminated democratic regimes in ancient Greece, leaving no model for near future generations.

References and Further Reading

Fisher, George Park. *Outlines of Universal History*. New York: American Book Company, 1904.

Hansen, M. H. *The Athenian Democracy in the Age of Demosthenes*. New York: Oxford University Press, 1987.

Hignett, Charles. *A History of the Athenian Constitution*. New York: Oxford University Press, 1962.

Ober, Josiah. *The Athenian Revolution: Essays on Ancient Greek Democracy and Political Theory*. Princeton, NJ: Princeton University Press, 1998.

Ober, Josiah. *Mass and Elite in Democratic Athens: Rhetoric, Ideology and the Power of the People*. Princeton, NJ: Princeton University Press, 1989.

Ober, Josiah, and C. Hendrick, eds. *Demokratia: A Conversation on Democracies, Ancient and Modern*. Princeton, NJ: Princeton University Press, 1989.

Robinson, Eric W., ed. *Ancient Greek Democracy: Readings and Sources*. Hoboken, NJ: Wiley-Blackwell, 2004.

Sinclair, R. K. *Democracy and Participation in Athens*. New York: Cambridge University Press, 1988.

Tansey, Stephen D. *Politics: The Basics*, 3rd edition. New York: Routledge, 2004.

CON

The history of the Greeks was one of ascendancy to heights of intellectual and scientific achievement that was rivaled by no other ancient world civilization. During the Golden Age of Athens, the Greeks were well known for their philosophical, scientific, and cultural achievements. The source of this achievement may never be known completely. Some historians believe that the source of Greek achievement was due to their subjugation of slaves as workers for their glorious civilizations, the enslavement of women, and the promotion of Greek militarism as well as Greek elitism as the forces for their glorious cultural achievements. The purpose of this section is to show that the Greek achievement was founded on the use of slaves, the enslavement of women, or the promotion of militarism and elitism in the Greek society.

Slavery's Role in the Greek Society

As a factor in the rise of Greek culture, slavery has been presented as crucial to the development of leisure and comfortable living that allowed Greek men to cultivate the intellectual life of the Golden Age of Greece. The slaves worked hard to mine the silver in the earth to produce the wealth that allowed for the comfortable conditions for intellectual pursuits of the scholars of the Greek revolution. The historical origin of slavery cannot be ascertained readily, because of the lack of written materials. Furthermore, the existent materials such as written plays and Greek literature only describe them in commonly accepted stereotypes and do not give detailed description of the true state of slaves in Greek society. Historians believe that there is a mention of slavery in Homeric writings in 1200 BCE. At this time, there is a description of slavery as a form of private property ownership. So, a chieftain could own about 50 slaves per household in a typical Greek family. In the same Homeric writings, there are stories of slave-raiding parties, with their war enemies taken as treasure or reward of their war exertions. But the Homeric writings make no mention of a slave trade or slave dealers. It seems that we may have concluded that slave trafficking was not even existent at the time. In the Homeric time, slavery seems to be a limited institution and not very

Greek capital with slaves, Corinth, Greece. (Scala/Art Resource, NY)

widespread. We also observe that masters were kind and treated slaves well and slaves were trustworthy and loyal to the master (Lloyd 1988).

Later, slavery became an institution in Greece as well as a way of life. Slaves usually originated from various sources, such as one being in debt to someone and working the debt off for a period of time to the master; as those the various Greek societies captured during their war campaigns against one another's cities; or those who were born into this status as children of slaves. Furthermore, some slaves were orphaned or left to die as babies, but then were rescued and later turned into slaves for the people who had raised them. In addition, when a family needed money, they would sell their daughters into slavery in order to survive off the price for their children; sometimes children were kidnapped and placed into slavery for the support of Greek living.

The Greek slaves played an important role in Greek society and their status was dependent on how much labor they contributed to the society. For example, Greek slaves could work in the house being managed by the women of the house. They could participate in the family rituals and sacrifices, but they were limited in their political participations in the government. These household slaves were considered higher-class slaves. However, they could not enter the gymnasiums (schools) or the public assembly where the political discussions took place. Moreover, they were not considered citizens of the city because they were the property of the master. These Greek slaves were also part of the treasury and Athenian police force. The lower classes of slaves were consigned to menial labor, such as a mineworker in the silver mines, where the life expectancy was very short.

It was after the Dark Ages that the trading of slavery begins as a monetary transaction where a slave could be sold for 10 minae ($180 US), if he was healthy and strong. A weaker or older slave could be sold for 1/2 minae ($9 US). The price of slavery was subject to market pressures in the economy. If there were a war or battle, the price would usually go down, because the supply was plentiful, and the price would go up if the supply were low. Thus, the slaves were treated as an economic property subjected to the flow of the marketplace.

Among the general slave population, female slaves were usually the lowest status slaves, because of the bias against females in general. They would usually take care of the house: shopping, child care, wool working, and cooking. They also served as wet nurses for the newborn children or as cooks. They also served unofficially as confidants of their mistresses or their masters. At times, the limits could be taken advantage off by the masters. Sexual abuse and rape were not uncommon. The masters usually destroyed the babies of these unions. The female slaves were not treated very well in some families.

In the period from 800 to 600 BCE, the role of slavery expanded because of the expansion of the Greek city–states in their exploration of the Mediterranean world. The Greek city–states began to urbanize their cities, utilized coinage, and started to focus on handicrafts as a manufacturing process. In ca. 600 BCE, there was a strong impetus to use slaves in these handicraft industries and take them away from agricultural use.

The city–states started to employ them legally in jobs as checking for counterfeit coinage and as temple slaves. They were public slaves, who had more independence than privately-owned slaves. Thus, the slaves were used to help in manufacturing handicrafts and industrial production in the Greek cities, which helped the Greek economy to prosper and supported the city–states.

Some historians believe that slavery was not that important to the overall survival of the Greek society. There were some societies such as the Spartans that allowed a modicum of freedom from slavery as well as rights for the slaves. Some historians have claimed that the Greeks had so much free time because they enslaved many people. These historians stated that slaves were important for family life, business life, and political life of the city–state. Slavery allowed the Greeks to become urbanized and free to pursue other occupations not attached to the land. They allowed the urbanization of the city–state and freed the Greeks to pursue more intellectual pursuits. These historians have claimed that the ancient Greeks might have been unable to pursue their individual interests and achievements without these slaves. As a result, the city–states depended on the enslavement of many people to support their manufacture and handicraft industries and allowed them to survive in the ancient world. In addition, those who had slaves had more free time to participate in direct democracy, because they could take days off from work to take part in the election process. Furthermore, they could participate in the 40 or so assembly elections during the year. Thus, the slaves indirectly allowed the Greeks to participate in their government and produce democracy as well as to govern the city–state.

The Subjugation of Women Supported the City–State

Greek society was male centric both in status and perception of the role men, but the dependency on the subjugation of women was relative. In some Greek city–states, the women were considered lower class citizens. Men had the right to vote, to take legal action, and to own property in Athens. Women were considered vehicles for the procreation of the species and were needed for intercourse for men. The females were raised and nurtured until they could be used for marriage to another male. Women were then required to manage the household and the children that came through their pregnancies. They were assisted by their women slaves in the raising of families and their husbands in the working world. Women usually received their education in their homes, consisting of domestic duties and chores as well as managing their husbands' slaves or economics.

In the Athenian democracy (475 BCE), men had written several stereotypes of Greek women into their acceptable literature. The men were responsible to control and maintain their women's sexual appetite, because in the Greek psychology and philosophy, women were lustful and could not restrain their appetites. Greek men were by nature controlled by reason and were more able to master themselves with this natural ability. Aristophanes noted in *Lysistrata* that men should satisfy and control their women's sexual desire in order to preserve their reputation and also to procreate an heir for the man's property. Aristotle also noted that young women needed to avoid masturbating, because they could not control their temptations as well as young boys could. Such were the prevailing stereotypes of women as inferior and uncontrollable animals during Athenian times.

Even in their living spaces, women were confined and limited in order to prevent illegitimate intercourse between the two sexes, because the males had to make sure their property went to rich and intelligent sons or grandsons. The living quarters of women were separated from the male quarters in the houses. The women were often escorted to places, because women were deemed necessary for men's survival. Many men believed that women could not protect themselves from other men. Furthermore, women were separated from men into separate quarters during their social engagements. The social spaces were very much limited for the women of Athens.

The ideal Athenian women was as such an obedient servant of the husband or father whose major responsibility was to procreate and train children, manage the house, spin wool, weave cloth, and prepare the food. They were as such domestic servants of the husband and showed a continual social role that was on the surface subjugating and demeaning in the modern context. Their role was to allow men the freedom to pursue their democratic and civic responsibility.

The Athenian women had many different positions in the society. Some women were prostitutes, who plied their trade through the streets of Athens. They lived in places that would be the equivalent of today's brothels, and the law limited the amount that they could charge the client. They were supposed to weave and cook for the brothel owners. Other women were courtesans or party girls that entertained the men with instruments or intelligent conversations. They went to parties or symposiums where they entertained the male guest at these parties. Some of them owned their own homes where they would entertain men. Concubines became mistresses to men and sometimes would be the outlet for men in a social or relationship manner.

Despite the relative dependence on the low status of women, there were some communities, such as those of the Spartans, that allowed their women higher status, as well as some women who attempted to compete with men in the male-dominated society. The Spartans allowed their women to compete and train with the men in their military exercises. They allowed them to wrestle naked as well as compete in the sports competition and the physical exercises. Some of the Spartan women could own property with the men as well as help to manage the finances during their marriage to Spartan men. Women were encouraged to develop their intellect, own more than a third of the land, and they could marry at a later age than their sisters in Athens. Husbands were usually away at military exercises, but this allowed their wives greater authority in the homes.

Other areas of dominance of women were as priestesses in religious ceremonies and cults. In John Breton Connelly's (2007) *Portrait of a Priestess: Women and Ritual in Ancient Greece*, the author gathered several epic, lyric poems, speeches, and epigrams to support the function of the priestess in the religious life of the Greeks. Priestesses were either nominated, purchased the position, or were elected to the position of priestess. They were bedecked with white linen cloth and performed animal sacrifices for the goddesses. Priestesses had legal and financial benefits as well as social respect. They could own property, had freedom from taxation, and were given priority to hear from the Delphic oracle. Their personal safety was ensured, and they could have front row seats at competitions. They could put their seal on documents and sanctuary law. They could charge a fee for their services from the initiate. The priestesses performed 145 religious ceremonies and ruled over 40 cults during the history of the Athens. In this book, women were as much of equal status as the men because of their religious importance and administration of the temple rituals.

In other religious areas, the women had outlets where they could express their lives and emotions freely in religious exercise. The women, who worshiped Dionysus, were known as *Bacchants* or *Maenads*. They would leave their husbands and families to dance with Dionysius and honor the wine god during their festivals. They would even suckle wild beasts, even if they had newborn children, if they were not hunting and ripping apart the beasts. Female slaves could participate in religious rituals such as the Eleusinian mysteries. These were limited outlets for the Greek women to express their freedom and individual energies outside the domestic sphere.

There is evidence that some women could read and write as well as discuss the current issues of the day. Vase paintings suggested that women could gather and discuss various issues. Women, however, did not socialize with the men if they were considered respectable women. Women could participate in various cults that allowed socialization and dominance of women such as the Maenads of the Bacchus cults of Greece. There was some advantage for women to manage their property and estates, but women could not sell or dispense of the property without permission of their husbands (or fathers). They were also allowed to receive gifts from others and to inherit property if there was no male heir, but this was discouraged. Finally, women could receive a dowry from their fathers, which guaranteed the marriage if the husband did not want to lose the dowry.

In conclusion, some women were relatively independent and well regarded by men in the society. They also held equal status in the religious rituals of the 40 major religious cults in Greece and could influence the men in their ideas toward life and philosophy. Despite the few examples of women's independence, the subjugation of women allowed men the freedom to participate in political life, and left the other outlets (religious and philosophical) on which the women could spend their energies. The men were able to have freedom to pursue their intellectual quests as well as make civic contributions in the government.

The Intellectual Environment Created by Militarism

Militarism is the doctrinal view of politicians and the military that society should be dominated by ideas embodied in a military culture and heritage centered on the ideals of war. Militarists believe that discipline is the highest social policy and that the social order should support the military. National policy is focused on preparing for military strategy and maintaining war operations. Usually, social oppression follows the enforcement of military order on civilian society. Militarism justifies the use of force in diplomatic and international relations and believes that the civilian people are dependent on the goals of the military, which militarists believe is more important than social welfare. Therefore, militarism is undemocratic and antidemocratic in its outlook and respect of civilian welfare. The entire society's economy and culture are utilized to support the goals and objectives of the military in the society. The national budgets and economy are centered on the realization of military goals and attacking other opponents. Politically, the military will hold two offices: military officers and civilian leaders. Usually, in the democratic government, there would be limitations on the holding of two offices at the same time. Militarism is founded on the premise that freedom of speech and association will be limited, because the society will support military services goals, concepts, policies, and war.

The Athenian army and the Spartan helots pursued a militarily dominant policy of society and political diplomacy. The Spartans were known for their physical

---

The Plague and the Peloponnesian War

The Peloponnesian war between Athens and Sparta lasted nearly 30 years, and during the first year, Athenian spirits were running high. According to the Athenian historian, Thucydides, the following summer the city was struck by a plague that had been spreading throughout the eastern Mediterranean. The Athenians, crowded together inside the city, were easy prey for the plague, which spread rapidly. As a result, somewhere between a quarter and a third of the Athenian population perished, including the city–state's inspirational leader Pericles. Thucydides also caught the plague, but he recovered, and his account is the main historical description of what happened. According to his *History of the Peloponnesian War*, the plague caused a general despair that led Athenians to turn their backs on the gods, which might be argued to be a contributing factor to the city's destruction by the conclusion of the war.

---

training of their male and female youth in sports and military contests. The entire society was focused on training the soldier and the use of armies as part of the militarism of the Spartan society. The Greek society was focused on maintaining the war department of the city–state. They had to defend themselves from the onslaught of foreign enemies as well as take over. As a result, the society was focused on preparing, maintaining, and supplying the defense of the city–state.

Militarism became the central policy of the state, because it had to defend itself through maintaining high amounts of the army and navy. The Greek society invented catapults, fortifications, phalanxes, and the trireme battleship to aid their conquest of land and territory. The Athenians focused on developing their navy by building trireme ships and training sailors to transport their soldiers to war. They built and maintained one of the strongest navies in the Greek world. This navy was used in several wars, such as the Peloponnesian war with the Hellenes. The Spartans utilized their civilian army as their choice of military tactics in producing the phalanxes. The Spartans used helots or militarily trained slaves to man their armies. These helots were Messinian soldiers who had been captured and made military slaves. They would take the children of the helots and raised them in communal camps where the boys and women were trained in tactics of war and hand-to-hand combat. They would eat together, train together, and be educated together so that they would become a united armed force. These helots became hardened under Spartan-like conditions of challenge and combat. They were like the special forces of the army who were specifically trained for battle and combat. Some historians say that the training was so tough that it made the marines look like weaklings. These Spartans were well known for their fierceness and toughness in battle, and they had a reputation of being a militarily oriented society.

These two military societies came into conflict during the Peloponnesian war (431–404 BCE) where they attacked each other during several years of battles and military struggle. It was fought between Athens and Sparta and their respective allies from the Greek world from Sicily to Istanbul to Crete. The war originated because the Spartans were afraid of Athenian power over the Peloponnesian coast. It continued until Lysander, the Spartan general, defeated the Athenian fleet in the battle at Aeogospotomi in 405 BCE, where it was starved to death by cutting off its supplies. The power of the Athenians collapsed. The war was a struggle between sea power and land power, with Athens dominating the Aegean coast and Sparta dominating the land of the Peloponnesian in the Greek peninsula. It was a struggle because Sparta could not dominate Attica or the territory around Athens, and because Athenians would withdraw into their forts in Athens while being supplied by sea power. On the other hand, the Athenians could not establish bases on the Peloponnesian coast because of the strength of Spartan land power until the war ended at Dellium in 424 BCE. Between the years of 423 and 421 BCE, the Athenian alliance weakened and rallied behind Sparta, because of the defeat at Mantinea in 428 BCE. Finally, in 405 BCE Lysander was able to defeat Athens in a battle at Aeogospotami and surround Athens so it could not get supplies.

Athens continued to flourish during the age of Pericles because of the military might of Athens. Military magistrates who managed the struggle between the two powers ruled the society. However, they were limited in their power by the civilian assembly, which both checked and balanced their power. In fact, it was probably the civilian assembly that sued for peace after the Spartan defeat of 403 BCE. They wanted to rest from the continual warfare and depletion of their prosperity. The building projects of the Athenians were contributed from the rich property owners or aristocrats. However, the poor also had a say in the decision over which building to construct and who to hire for their construction. However, the peace maintained by the militarism of Athenian battles created the peace necessary for the survival of the city–states.

Greek Elitism and Pursuit of Excellence of Greek Culture

The idea of Greek elitism is based on the belief or philosophy that the views of those members of an elite or select group—with outstanding personal abilities, intellect, wealth, specialized training, or distinctive traits—must dominate society even if their policies may not support the society as a whole. Elitism also means that the power is concentrated in the hands of the elite or a special class of people. Elitism has the special characteristics of long-term training or study in a particular discipline or practice; a long track record of skill in a particular art or profession; a history or background in a discipline such as military or martial arts; and having great wisdom in a particular field or discipline.

The Greek elitism can be found in the emphasis toward excellence and virtue in their philosophy and worldview. This elitism is founded on the striving after excellence and training in the arts, military, and political culture of the Greeks. They call this concept *arête* or civil excellence as a person or society. Plato's *Republic* and Aristotle's *Ethics* discuss that the ideal attitude toward life is to strive for outstanding qualities in its leaders and civilian population. An oligarchy ruled some of the city–states, where the power rested in a small segment of elite and educated families. Many argued that wealthy Greeks ruled behind the Greek government, controlling policy with their wealth and influence. They were an exclusively powerful segment of society that ruled the rest of the society with their power over the economy of the state.

Even in Spartan government, this view of elitism was supported by the enactment of a constitution that gave representation to an upper class of Spartans, but also eliminated a life of luxury for the society. Lycurgus, the Spartan founder, created a system of government that had two kings, five *ephors* or executives, a council of 30 elders, and a general assembly comprising all male citizens. Full citizenship was given to an elite known as Spartiates who fought wars for the society. The Spartans also limited luxurious imports from foreigners and discouraged the ownership of private property as well as democratic ideas, but this created equality among Spartans because all had life and status in common to support the state. As a result, an elite could not develop to rule Spartan society, because the citizens supported the state completely, and not any elitist social class.

According to some historians, the Athenians lived modestly and did not have many luxuries. The economy was dependent on maritime trade and agriculture, but most of the food was imported from outside. The cultural achievements were supported from money from the Delian league, which was maintained by diplomacy and Athenian naval power.

Athens gave equal status for the poor through their first government created by Solon in 594 BCE. Solon created a new constitution that attempted to mediate social conflict between the poor and rich in the sixth century BCE. The reforms he enacted were intended to relieve financial burdens by cancelling the debts of the poor and destroying the law of mortgages for the rich. He also allowed access to political participation for the poor, which had depended on the amount of property and the birth status of the candidate for office. The lowest class was called *thetes* (laborers), who could take part in the general assembly, but not run for office. Solon also banned the export of agricultural products except for olive oil. He also offered to abolish their system of weights and measures for a universal system adopted by the other countries in Mediterranean. Solon constructed a supreme court manned by archons or magistrates elected from the people in the assembly. These laws allowed the foundation for democracy of the lower class to develop during Pericles's times.

During Periclean times, the government was structured with 10 generals who were elected by the citizens. In Athens, the government was run by 10 *strategoi* or generals who were elected by 10 clans to conduct military exploits, receive diplomats, and direct political affairs. The magistrates comprised the next level of power; they were elected every year to do administration tasks for the government functions, such as police. The Great Assembly was an assembly of citizens who were elected to cast votes on various laws. There were about 6,000 elected citizens who were able to vote on various issues. They were able to pass a law with legal immunity. Finally, there was a Council of the Boule, which was managed by 500 representatives and ruled on legal procedures and processes. They also ruled over decisions made in the General Assembly and administrative details of the government. This form of government seems like it was conducive to a ruling by oligarchy or the military in the society.

Greek Elites and Pericles's Government

Despite this structure, when Pericles was made *Strategos* in 445 BCE, he initiated several reforms that would make the votes and the rights of the poor citizens heard in the assembly. One of the rules was the allowance of *thetes*, or Athenians without wealth, to occupy public office. He also had a special salary or *misthophoria* that was paid to citizens who attended the assembly so they did not need to be employed elsewhere and could just focus on the political life. With these two reforms, he enabled the assembly to function effectively, gave his people public service rights, and created the first polis or city–state in Greece. However, it was the emphasis on civic virtue and civic participation that allowed the elite of Greece to participate in these democratic assemblies.

The government established the principle of equality in its policy of supporting the poor and giving them equal say in Athenian government, but it was balanced with wise leaders and an elitist class in the government. This could have been exploited because the poor were extremely poor or they had no knowledge of the laws. So the Athenian democracy enacted three policies: (1) give an income to public civil servants; (2) seek and supply work to the poor; (3) give land to property-less villagers; public assistance for invalids, orphans, and indigents; and other social assistance. It was the first ancient welfare systems for the poor that also allowed them to participate in civilian life. Thus, even the poor Athenian civilians could participate in Greek public life regardless of income or wealth, but they were led by wise political leaders in the *strategoi* or military leaders in their participation in government.

In conclusion, the Greek city–states depended for their survival upon their domination of slaves, subjugation of women, the expansive role of the military, and the guidance of an elite leadership. The Greek city–states depended on the labor of slaves to increase the leisure and free time necessary for the pursuit of democratic activities of the Greeks. In addition, the Greek city–states' subjugation of women allowed men the freedom and space to guide and govern the city–states. It also disenfranchised a majority of the population in order to allow the men to guide the city-states. Furthermore, the Greek city–states needed the military to protect and expand natural resources to support the economy of the city–states. Finally, the Greek city–states were guided by an elite class of educated and wise leaders, despite the spread of the vote to the poorer classes.

References and Further Reading

Canterella, Eva. *Pandora's Daughter*. Baltimore: Johns Hopkins University Press, 1986.

Connelly, John Breton. *Portrait of a Priestess: Women and Ritual in Ancient Greece*. Princeton, NJ: Princeton University Press, 2007.

Finley, M. I. *Slavery in Classical Antiquity: Views and Controversies*. Cambridge: W. Heffer and Sons, 1960.

Lloyd, Janet. *Slavery in Ancient Greece*. Ithaca, NY: Cornell University Press, 1988.

Murnagham, S. *Women and Slaves in Greco-Roman Culture: Differential Equations*. New York: Routledge, 2002.

Rich, John. *War and Society in Greek World*. New York: Routledge, 2007.

Westerman, W. L. *The Slave Systems of Greek and Roman Antiquity*. Philadelphia: American Philosophical Society, 1955.

Wiederman, Thomas. *Greek and Roman Slavery*. New York: Routledge, 2001.

3

The Ogham Celtic script is derived from the Norse Rune script.

PRO　Justin Corfield

CON　Harald Haarmann

PRO

A number of inscriptions survive from early medieval Ireland, and these have a script on them, which have become known as the Ogham Celtic script. The exact reason why they have been ascribed this name ("Ogham") is unknown, but it is thought to have been derived from the Irish word for the mark made by a sharp weapon—possibly as the inscription would have had to have been made with a sharp weapon. However, another possibility exists, that this early script was derived from the Norse Rune script, as there was much interaction between Scandinavia and Britain throughout their histories.

There are a number of spurious theories about the origins of the Ogham script that need to be dispensed with before the positive assertion of Ogham as derived from the Norse script can be made. Unlike traditional inscriptions of the period (and indeed of later periods), the inscription itself is sometimes on the "flat" of the stone, but can also be found around the edges, with a number of "notches" that would have had to have been made with a strong (and sharp) metal instrument. Altogether there are several hundred inscriptions in the Ogham script that have survived—counts by scholars vary from around 400 to 507— most have been completely deciphered. When first faced with the problem, there was some doubt over the decipherment—indeed there were some who queried the nature of the script, but with the help of "bilingual" stones from England, linguists have worked hard on the Ogham script and have been able to identify a number of vowels and consonants and work out the number of differences between them. The result of their work has been a tabulation of an alphabet that consists of 25 characters. It has also been worked out that the writing, on the edges of the stone, has to be initially read upward on the left-hand side of the stone, and then downward on the right-hand side.

The reason for the adoption of the script is in doubt. Originally there was a theory that the Ogham alphabet was designed by the Irish, and it was specifically created by a number of Druids, presumably a small select group, for the sole reason of having letters that would be incomprehensible to people who spoke Latin.

At the time of the earlier inscriptions, in the early fifth century, there were many issues over the cultural expansion from Britain—where Latin was widely spoken after 400 years of Roman rule, albeit coming to an end. It was during the same period that Saint Patrick was conducting his missionary work among the Irish—traditionally arriving in Ireland in 432 CE after the mission of Palladius in 431 CE. Even if the dates are not that accurate, it is clear that the Ogham script was being used at the same time as the initial spread of Christianity.

Thus, according to the theory that the Ogham script was a Druidic one, the Irish devised this script with some form of nationalistic intent and came up with what was essentially a cryptic alphabet that would serve as some form of code. This idea was widely voiced by the writers James Carney and Eoin MacNeill, who drew on the early work of Robert Alexander Stewart Macalister (1870–1950), who held a chair at University College, Dublin, from 1909 until 1943, and had been involved in extensive research and publications on ancient Ireland and archaeology in Ireland. Macalister had studied in Germany and would have been familiar with the Runes there. However, he was adamant about the nationalistic origins of the Ogham script, and his famous work on the Ogham script was *Corpus Inscriptionium Insularum Celticarum*, although Robert Welch's *The Oxford Companion to Irish Literature* did note that some of his work was "marred by idiosyncratic theories—most notably the view of ogam [Ogham scripts]" (1996: 323). Carney and MacNeill believed that the script might have links to secret five-fingered hand signals, which were used in Cisalpine Gaul (modern-day northern Italy) from the early sixth century. If this were so, there would be some clear and systematic pattern to the adoption of a script for largely nationalistic (and political) reasons.

Much of the basis for this Druidic invention of the script also comes from the medieval texts *Auraicept na nÉces, In Lebor Ogaim* ("The Book of Ogham") and several others. These clearly state that 25 scholars devised the script, each of whom gave his name to one letter of the script's alphabet. While this is clearly an interesting story and tradition, like many other medieval stories, many feel it has no historical basis. The idea of the 25 "wise men" is similar to many other bardic traditions whereby stories from ancient history have been retold for generations, and although they do become an important part of the local folklore, they are not accurate accounts of historical events. Indeed most linguists see a close association of the Ogham script with trees. This can be seen with the *b* signified by a single stroke, also known as *beithe* (birch), and the *s* with four strokes for *sail* (willow). The link with trees has seen another theory that the script came from marks on tally sticks. Raised by the Swiss-born Rudolf Thurneysen (1857–1940), who made a detailed study of the early Irish language, this has gained a number of adherents.

Although it is possible that the script might be in some form of purposely designed code, especially given the shortage of writing equipment during the period, many scholars have criticized this theory. They feel that the script is essentially a transliteration system in which the Irish have managed to put their words into a script, and that the sounds made in the Irish language were so unlike those in Latin that a new script was more appropriate. This has led scholars to compare the Ogham script with the Younger Futhark, or Scandinavian runes, with which there are some clear similarities.

Charles Graves (1812–1899) raised the first ideas about the link between the Ogham script and some Germanic and Nordic runes. A mathematician and also the bishop of Limerick, he was born in Dublin, the son of a lawyer who became the chief police magistrate of Dublin. After a brilliant academic career, Graves became a professor of math-

Stone bearing an inscription in Ogham, County Waterford, Ireland. (Michael Carter; Cordaiy Photo Library Ltd./Corbis)

ematics at Trinity College, Dublin, in 1843. An Anglican, he was made dean of Castle Chapel, Dublin, in 1860, and four years later was appointed as dean of Clonfert. Two years later he was appointed as bishop of Limerick, Ardfert, and Aghadoe, becoming one of the last bishops appointed before the disestablishment of the church of Ireland. However, he held the position for 33 years, until his death. Working on many mathematical problems, Graves became interested in Irish history and the Brehon laws, which form much of the basis of the Sister Fidelma murder mystery stories published in the 1990s and the 2000s. This led him to conduct a study of the Ogham script, and Graves traveled around making notes of inscriptions and checking on others. It was through his work that much of the decipherment was carried out, and Graves himself was able to compare the inscriptions with Nordic runes, noticing a large number of similarities in their style and the method in which they were written. As an eminent scholar on a range of topics, he lectured frequently about them.

To draw any conclusions about the Ogham script, one of the most important areas to investigate is just where the surviving inscriptions are located, what they contain, and what their purpose is believed to be. Certainly it is highly likely that there were many more inscriptions that have not survived, and it is also easily possible that archaeologists might uncover new inscriptions in the future.

Within Ireland, most of the inscriptions come from Kerry or Cork. Many were out in the open until recently with the antiquary John George Augustus Prim (1821–1875) managing to save those in Dunbell by taking them to the

National Museum of Ireland. Many have subsequently been saved in local museums.

Although most identified with Ireland, there are Ogham inscriptions that have been found in Wales (especially Brecknockshire) and also a number that have been located in some parts of England, the Isle of Man, Scotland, and the Shetland Islands. Damian McManus identifies 382 inscriptions, and there are some for which scholars query whether or not they contain the Ogham script. The University College of Cork lists about 400 inscriptions, many of which were copied by the antiquarian Abraham Abell (1783–1851). From a Quaker family from Cork, Abell was very interested in archaeology and helped found the Cuvierian Society, which was a forerunner of the Cork Historical and Archaeological Society. A linguist of note, he became fascinated by the Ogham inscriptions. R. A. S. Macalister in 1945 recorded 507 inscriptions, and three more had been found by 1949.

The Ogham inscriptions in Wales often include some Latin names, and of the eight that have been found in England, five were in Cornwall and two close to the Cornish border, in Devon. There is also an isolated one that was recovered in Silchester, in Hampshire, and it is presumed to have been written by an Irish settler or perhaps was moved at some later stage. There were three Ogham inscriptions in Scotland—subject of a learned paper by the Scottish antiquarian James Carnegie, 6th Earl of Southesk (1827–1905)—and five from the Isle of Man. Except for the inscription at Silchester, all the other inscriptions were found from around the Irish Sea. All the Ogham inscriptions are on stone, and it seems obvious that they might have been used on paper that has not survived; very few written records survive from this period, earning it the name the Dark Ages. Two appear in later manuscripts—one in the *Annals of Inisfallen* (1193) and the other, a fictional inscription in the *Book of Leinster*, a Middle Irish saga in which reference is made to some texts. It therefore seems likely that the script originated in Cork or Kerry and was later adopted by small groups elsewhere—certainly from around the Irish Sea. This spread is compatible with either the theory that the script comes from the Nordic runes or that it was invented by a small clique of Druids anxious to keep out British influences.

In order for this large number of inscriptions, over a long period of time, to have been in a script that had been invented by the Druids to prevent the Romans and the Romano-British from interpreting them would mean that the society of the period for the region around the Irish Sea—where the inscriptions are found—would have had to have been dominated and controlled by a small elite who were able to dictate the language in use. This might have come about from visiting Druids—certainly the tales of early Christian saints and martyrs of the same period had people traveling extraordinary distances to spread their teachings. It is possible, but the question is whether this is likely. If all the Ogham inscriptions were dated from roughly the same period, again, this would be possible. But some of the inscriptions date from long after the fifth

Casting the Runes

As the Christian era unfolded in Ireland, the church banned other written alphabets from use; among these were both Norse runes and Ogham. Associated with witchcraft and paganism, both forms of communication were used in similar ways in Irish popular folklore. One way in which common people sought divine knowledge for life events was by casting the runes, much like the throwing of dice, but with specific rules of determining what the meaning of the different characters might be for the person's future. Just as Nordic runes were used for casting (and still are by modern Wiccans), stones with Ogham script inscribed were also used to invoke protection, good health, and financial success.

century—the ones from the Isle of Man date from the 11th and 12th centuries. That a small Druid circle could keep so much control to use a script devised as a code and keep it in use for 600 years seems far less likely.

The similarities between some of the letters of the Runic alphabet and the Ogham inscriptions lend to the belief that the two scripts are related. So did they use a sharp implement to carve them on stone? The idea of the Runic alphabet would have met with some problems in Ireland where the literate might have had trouble capturing the sounds of the Irish dialect or language. Thus the script developed from a spoken language and was devised—as with most other written languages—from a need to convey the spoken language in a permanent form. Indeed many of the Ogham inscriptions mark the boundaries or ownership of land. A much more modern example of this was the Manchu language, which was exclusively spoken until the early 17th century when the Manchus started taking control of parts and later the whole of China. As they moved from a nomadic people to ones involved in the complex work of administration, the Manchu language needed to be written down, and the Manchu writing, from what was originally a Tungusic language, started to be written in a script not that dissimilar from Mongolian. This is only natural, and it seems likely that the Ogham inscriptions had to be introduced as a way of helping with the administration of parts of Ireland and also places farther afield. Indeed the inscriptions largely date from a period when the Indo-European inflectional endings started to be dropped and are, instead, being replaced with a more distinctive series of initial mutations and a considerable variation in consonant quality.

Although many people are mentioned on the stones, there is only one who is known from other sources. This is one from Wales, which refers to Vortiporius, who ruled in Dyfed and is mentioned in Geoffrey of Monmouth's famous *Historia Regnum Britanniae* ("History of the Kings of Britain"), and the stone, which was found at Castell Dwyran, in Carmathenshire, in South Wales, is believed to be his gravestone.

The greatest quandary for many historians was the discovery of the "Ogham Stone" at Silchester in 1893. This has provided scholars with much debate over its origins and why it was found in Silchester, although it is possible that it was moved there at a later date. There were even suggestions that it was a fake, but that theory has been dismissed in favor of the idea that somebody familiar with the Ogham script, possibly from Ireland or Cornwall or Wales might have moved to Silchester and was buried there with the stone marking his grave.

As to the inscriptions themselves, most of them consist of names of people, with the vast majority describing relationships such as "A son of B" (A *maqi* B) or "A from the tribe C" (A *maqi mucoi* C). Most of the surviving inscriptions list people, with some tribal affiliations, and only rarely other information. This means that much of the interpretation over the origins of names comes from the names used. Many of these seem to be personal descriptions of people, with names like "Alive like fire," "Born of the Raven," "Yew of Battle," or "Chief in Battle." These are clearly pagan names, which can be clearly differentiated from the Romano-British names in use at the time. However, a few of the later Ogham inscriptions, which have been found on the Isle of Man or the Shetland Islands, contain what are clearly Viking names. Indeed the 11th-century Ogham inscription found in the churchyard of Kirk Michael has some Viking runes within it, showing a possible relationship between the two.

Although the geographic spread of the inscriptions and what is contained on them do suggest a development of a script similar to Nordic runes, the major argument in favor of this comes from the reason why these inscriptions were made in the first place. The nature of the wording on them suggests that they were either used to plot land ownership or possibly as tombstones. Either way, they were meant to be read and understood by other people. There would be no point in having a field or land demarcated by an inscription that was only legible to a small Druidic elite. The whole purpose of modern signs such as "Private Property" or "Trespassers Will Be Prosecuted" is to stop or dissuade unauthorized people from entering land. This means that they must be clear and intelligible to anybody. And this would be the same with the stones that have carvings in the Ogham script.

Scholars have debated the reason why a number of the Ogham inscriptions are on stones on which, or from which, crosses have been carved. In a number of cases it is clear that the carving of the cross predates the inscription, clearly showing a Christian influence. As mentioned before, the emergence of the Ogham script coincides with the missionary career of Saint Patrick, but the crosses on the stones used for the script show that the use of the Ogham script is clearly not incompatible with Christianity and in fact seems to be able to happily coexist with it.

Furthermore, some of the stones have inscriptions on them, not only in the Ogham script but also in Latin. This is clear on the vast majority of the surviving inscriptions from Britain (but not those from Scotland). As with the Rosetta Stone (which had three scripts), these "bilingual" stones were used to decipher the Ogham script in the first place. The inscriptions in Latin would be particularly useful for the Romano-British as well as for the learned people in Ireland, so why have them also in the Ogham script? The only reason for this is that there must have been people who could read the Ogham script but who could not read Latin. Thus the marker or tombstone—whatever the purpose of the original stone—would be legible to people, whichever script they could read. It would, therefore, not be hard for some educated people in those days to understand both by simple comparison of the inscriptions, and therefore the idea that the Ogham script was a secret code cannot really be sustained.

So, the absence of evidence supporting other theories about the origins of the Ogham script, the similarities between the Ogham script and the script found on Norse rune stones, and the obviously pagan features on many of the extant Ogham examples prove that the script could not have been Irish or Celtic in origin, but rather Norse.

References and Further Reading

Brash, Richard Rolt. *The Ogam Inscribed Monuments of the Gaedhil in the British Islands: With a Dissertation on the Ogam Character*. London: George Bell and Sons, 1879.

Carney, James. "The Invention of the Ogom Cipher," *Ériu* 26 (1975): 53–65.

Clarke, Amanda, Michael Fulford, Michael Rains, and Ruth Shaffrey. "The Victorian Excavations of 1893." Silchester Roman Town—The Insula IX Town Life Project. Reading, UK: University of Reading, 2001. Available at www.silchester.rdg.ac.uk/victorians/vic_ogham.php (accessed May 30, 2010).

Fulford, Michael, Mark Handley, and Amanda Clarke. "An Early Date for Ogham: The Silchester Ogham Stone Rehabilitated." *Medieval Archaeology* 44 (2000): 1–23.

Graham-Campbell, James, and Colleen E. Batey. *Vikings in Scotland: An Archaeological Survey*. Edinburgh: Edinburgh University Press, 1998.

Macalister, Robert Alexander Stewart. *Corpus Inscriptionum Insularum Celticarum*. Dublin: Stationary Office, 1949.

MacNeill, Eoin. "Archaisms in the Ogham Inscriptions," *Proceedings of the Royal Irish Academy* 39 (1929): 33–53.

McManus, Damian. *A Guide to Ogam*. Maynooth, Ireland: An Sagart, 1991.

Montfort, Paul Rhys. *Nordic Runes: Understanding, Casting and Interpreting the Ancient Viking Oracle*. Rochester, NY: Destiny Books, 2003.

Welch, Robert, ed. *The Oxford Companion to Irish Literature*. New York: Oxford University Press, 1996.

CON

As a topic of cultural memory, the originality of the Ogham (Ogam) Celtic script has always been an agenda of national identity among the Irish. The debate is heated on whether or not Ogham is a Celtic innovation in writing technology or merely an adaptation of Norse runes. As will be seen from the evidence provided, this section contends that the Ogham script is, indeed, a Celtic innovation.

Origin and Distinctiveness of Ogham

Ogham is the oldest of the scripts in which the national language of Ireland, Irish, has been written. Irish is a representative of the Gaelic (Goidelic) branch of the Celtic languages, like Manx (formerly spoken on the Isle of Man in the Irish Sea) and Scottish-Gaelic. As an instrument of writing technology, Ogham carries much more symbolic meaning than the Latin alphabet, which is used to write many languages around the world.

This self-contained connection of Ogham and Irish as an identifier of Celtic culture may be compared to how the Armenian alphabet is exclusively associated with Armenian, the Georgian script with Georgian, or the Hangul script with Korean. Like Ogham, these scripts were devised to serve as a means of written communication in locally specific cultural environments and for speech communities whose languages are clearly distinct from other languages that surround them.

Left: runestone recovered from the from Viking site of Hedeby in present-day Denmark. Right: illustration of Ogham inscriptions on a standing stone from Ireland. (Library of Congress/Green, John Richard: *History of the English People*, 1902)

The popular debate about whether the Ogham script is an original Celtic innovation or a derivation from the runic script gains momentum when considering the symbolic value of Ogham as an identifier of Irish culture. The discussion in this section unfolds beyond the partisanship of revived druidism and beyond the sentimental agenda of Celtic cultural activism. However heated the popular debate may be, there is one instance that can provide a conclusive and substantiated answer and thus clarify the origins of Ogham. This is the scientific study of the history of writing. The arguments presented here speak in favor of the originality of the Ogham script as a Celtic innovation in writing technology.

The proper handling of categorizations, conceptualizations, and terminology poses a special challenge to any assessment of the origins of writing systems. In the reflections about writing systems and their origins—whether scientific or popular—much confusion has been caused by misconceptions about the principles of writing technology and about relationships between individual scripts. To avoid the pitfalls of generalizing categorizations and imprecise terminology, some pertinent issues of writing research will be highlighted in the following, particularly focusing on the principle of alphabetic writing relating to Ogham.

What Kind of an Alphabet Is Ogham?

Ogham is a script that operates with signs that render single sounds. This makes it an alphabet that is a special type of writing system. Alphabets follow the principle of a one-to-one correspondence of sign and sound. Each single letter stands for one individual sound. Historical orthography may blur the perspective. In the spelling of American English, the writing of the word "thru" is closer to the basic alphabetic principle than the rendering of the same word as "through" in British English, where keeping with the spelling an older (medieval) stage in the phonetic development of the English language is still reflected. In most languages using varieties of alphabetic scripts, though, the one-to-one correspondence of sign and sound is much more clearly recognizable than in writing English (e.g., in Spanish, Hindi, Russian, or Finnish).

Alphabets distinguish themselves from scripts such as Babylonian cuneiform or Japanese Hiragana, where a sign corresponds to a syllable (composed of several sounds), and also from logographic writing such as the Chinese characters or the Naxi script in southern China. In logographic scripts, ideas or concepts are rendered with the help of stylized pictures of the things denoted or the ideas described. The simplified Chinese characters of today are highly stylized and no longer disclose their origins as picture symbols. The signs can be visually identified as miniature images in the script used by the Naxi in their ritual books.

The Ogham script belongs to a certain subcategory of alphabetic writing. The Ogham signs render both consonants (such as *p, d,* or *m*) and vowels (such as *a, e,* or *u*) in writing. This sort of writing all the sounds of a language is typical of those alphabets that were or are in use in Europe, for example, the Greek, Cyrillic, Etruscan, Latin, runic, Ogham, and other scripts. These alphabets are different from the varieties of the alphabet that were or are in use in the Near East, the Orient (Saudi Arabia, Iran, Pakistan), and northern Africa, for example, the Phoenician, Hebrew, Arabic, and other scripts. The signs of the latter alphabets only render the consonants—not the vowels—of the languages that are written with such letters.

In the evolutionary history of writing, the alphabet is the youngest type of script that originated in the first half of the second millennium BCE. Before then, only syllabic or logographic scripts had been in use. The "complete" alphabetic writing, with signs for consonants as well as vowels, is the youngest version that was elaborated in the first millennium BCE. The Greeks elaborated the first complete alphabet in the eighth century BCE—as a derivation from the Phoenician script—for writing the Greek language.

There is no prototype alphabet from which all others would have derived. At a certain time in cultural history, writing systems made their appearance in the Near East. These writing systems were organized according to the "one-sign for one-sound" principle. This is true for the Proto-Sinaitic, the Phoenician, Ugaritan, and other variants of local scripts. All these early alphabets are original scripts in the sense that they were crafted—independently—on the basis of the alphabetic principle. Thus, the Phoenicians were inspired by the same writing technique as the people from Ugarit, the ancient harbor on the Syrian coast, without borrowing letter forms from each other.

This process of crafting local scripts by applying the alphabetic principle as a writing technology repeats itself throughout history and has produced a number of unique innovations like Ogham and other scripts (see above). In this context, the notion of "originality" applies to various local scripts, although they represent a common type of writing, and that is sign use according to the alphabetic principle. For instance, the Armenian script that originated in the fifth century CE was inspired by a Syrian version of the alphabet. The Armenian alphabet is categorized as an "original" script, because it introduces a new property, namely a set of indigenous signs that are not derived from any other sign repertory. The same is true for Ogham. This script has been inspired by the alphabetic principle to write Latin. And yet, the Ogham signs are all original and not derived from the forms of Latin letters (unlike runes, which are derived from Latin letters).

Also in the case of some derived alphabets, it is legitimate to speak of an original script, provided it introduces a new property in its system (e.g., the Greek alphabet, which deviates from its source, the Phoenician script, by using both consonant and vowel letters). Conversely, the Latin alphabet is not an original script, because it operates on the same basis (that is, writing consonants and vowels) as its source, the Etruscan alphabet, which, in turn, is an adaptation from the Greek alphabet.

Is Ogham Associated with the Runic Script in Celtic Folklore or Historical Sources?

Even before scholars in the field of writing research clarified the multifaceted trajectories in the history of the alphabet in the past century, there had been valuable knowledge available about old historical relationships between scripts.

This knowledge was preserved in historical literary sources, and it was also reflected in popular tales.

Especially with alphabetic scripts, a certain respect for the origins radiates from the web of local cultural memory. The ancient Greeks knew that the source of their literary tradition was the Phoenician script, and they proudly hailed this cultural heritage. Roman literary sources show that the masters of the Mediterranean were conscious that they had been taught writing by their Etruscan neighbors, a historical truth that has been corroborated by the findings of writing research. The Slavs, who write their languages with the Cyrillic alphabet (i.e., Russians, Belorussians, Ukrainians, Bulgarians, Macedonians, Bosniaks, Serbians), have always known that their script was derived from the Greek alphabet. A similar consciousness about historical cultural relationships has also been typical of cultural memory in India. There is a widespread awareness among educated people from that country that the origins of their alphabetic tradition lie in western Asia.

If Ogham were somehow related to runic, some whatever spurious allusions to that relationship would be expected to be found in the rich Irish literary tradition that goes back as far as the early Middle Ages. In medieval Irish literature, there is no reference to any foreign script from which Ogham might have been derived. Interesting information about the use of Ogham to write on stones and on wooden sticks comes from the early Irish epic "Táin Bó Cúailnge" ("The Cattle Raid of Cooley"). This epic was composed in the seventh century CE; the oldest extant manuscript from which its text is known dates to ca. 1100. In none of the sources do we find any connection between Ogham and runic.

And yet, neither the nonscientific literature nor any popular account about Ogham can be regarded as authentic in regard to the identification of the origins of this script. For this purpose, the findings from writing research have to be inspected with more scrutiny, paying special attention to comparative methods.

Typological Comparisons between Ogham and Runes

There are undeniable similarities in the Ogham and Runic scripts that evoke curiosity as to their relative nature. A historical relationship can be conceived between the two, with the older Runic script providing the source for the younger Ogham. However, scrutiny of the emergence of the two writing systems, their social functions, the composition of their sign inventories, and their techniques reveals that any historical interconnection between the two can be reasonably ruled out. The major similarities are listed below; analysis of these speaks in favor of regional and independent developments.

Separate origins for Ogham and Runic outside Roman state territory

The Runic script and Ogham originated on the periphery of Roman colonial territory in northern Europe. The findings of modern writing research point to the islands of Denmark (Jutland, in particular) and northern Germany (Schleswig-Holstein) as the area where runic writing was elaborated around 100 CE. Ogham originated on the northwestern fringe of the area of Ireland occupied by the Romans. This island always remained outside direct Roman political control, albeit in contact with the Roman world. The earliest inscriptions in Ogham date to the fourth (possibly to the third) century.

The fact that the two scripts in question were elaborated outside the borders of the Roman state is no coincidence. The prestige pressure that was exerted by Latin—as a language of the state, as a means of intercommunication among all the ethnic groups in the Roman Empire, as a medium of higher education and civilized lifestyles—on local speech communities within Roman-held territory was so strong that any attempt to create an independent script for writing a local language would have been doomed to failure.

This dual aspect of dependence and independence from Latin has been high-lighted for Celtic cultural heritage in Ogham: "The richness of Early Irish litera-ture is a paradox: it owes its existence to the example and challenge of Latin, but also to the independence of Ireland from the Roman Empire. If Ireland had been part of the empire, Irish would have had a status similar to that of British [the Celtic spoken in Britain], one local language among many, overshadowed by the immense cultural prestige of Latin" (Charles-Edwards 1995: 736).

The Germanic population that lived within Roman territory became ac-quainted with the runes but did not use them frequently. While specimens of ru-nic inscriptions are rare in the Roman area, they are more numerous in southern Scandinavia. The Celts of Britain did not use Ogham, and it was also unknown to the Celts who lived in Gaul (modern France). The Gaulish Celts used the Latin alphabet to write their language, although not on a regular basis.

If the runes were the source of Ogham, an exchange of writing technology would be expected through cultural intercommunication between the Germanic and Celtic populations within Roman territory as would the mutual occurrence of runic and Ogham inscriptions in the areas of contact. However, there is no evidence of this. The runes cannot have influenced the emergence of Ogham through later contacts either. When the Scandinavian Vikings reached Ireland (late eighth century CE), Ogham, which had been used there during previous cen-turies, was in decline.

Separate cultural contacts of Celts and Germanic tribes with the Romans

The knowledge of writing technology, and of the Latin alphabet in particular, in northern Europe was promoted by trade relations the Romans entertained with Germanic peoples and the Celts. Of special interest to the Romans were the trade contacts between Germanic people and Roman merchants in the northeast. There was a prosperous trade of amber from the coast of the Baltic Sea (in the regions of former Prussia and today's Lithuania), which was in the hands of Germanic middlemen. Trade with the Gaelic Celts from Ireland unfolded across the Irish Sea. These trade relations in the northwest (with the Gaels) and those in the northeast (with the Germans) functioned separately, without any Germanic-Celtic joint ventures that would have made the diffusion of writing know-how from one culture to the other plausible.

As for the contacts between Ireland and Britain, in addition to trade, cultural exchange was vital for "continuing kinship links between the aristocracy either side of the northern part of the Irish Sea during the first half of the first millennium C.E." (Mytum 1992: 29) and must be considered. Social relations between elite families living on both sides of the Irish Sea, which is on both sides of the territorial border of the Roman Empire, certainly furthered idea diffusion either way. The knowledge of alphabet-based Latin literacy was one of the cultural goods Celtic aristocrats on the British side had to offer their kinfolks in Ireland.

Apparently, the local traditions of writing, Runic in the northeast and Ogham in the northwest, were both inspired by literacy in the Roman world, although they evolved under locally specific conditions of cultural contact and independently in the two distinct cultural areas.

The Latin alphabet as a source of inspiration for Ogham derivation for Runes

The inspirational source to base the local scripts among the Celts and the Germanic peoples on the alphabetic principle of writing definitely has to be sought in the Roman world (that is, with Latin), although the ways in which the Latin script inspired the composition of the Runic and Ogham systems differ locally.

The influence of two contemporaneous traditions of writing known in the western part of the Roman world can be distinguished in the runic letter forms: the Latin alphabet and varieties of the so-called Alpine alphabets that had been inspired by Etruscan writing and were used for writing local languages in the Alps (e.g., Raetic, Camunic). Those who elaborated the runic script and composed its sign inventory drew on the graphic material that they found in the Latin letters and in the sign forms of the Alpine scripts.

The composition of the Ogham inventory of signs differs markedly from that for runes in that the graphic shapes of Ogham letters are, in their appearance, completely disconnected from any of the letter forms of the Latin or runic alphabets. In stark contrast to the shapes of the runic letters, Ogham signs are devised as highly abstract motifs and testify to Celtic inventiveness.

So, although writing technology among the Gaels of Ireland was obviously inspired "by the Latin alphabet, the framers of Ogham showed remarkable independence of mind in their choice of script, their alphabetic sequence, and the sounds they chose to represent" (McManus 1996: 342).

The *Book of Ballymote*

Written around 1391, the *Book of Ballymote* is the only source purporting to describe the invention of the Ogham script for the writing of Primitive Irish language, crediting the Celtic god Ogma with the invention of the script. The book was a compendium of different sources on ancient Greek, Roman, Celtic, and Christian knowledge, but one section, the Auraicept na n-Éces, details the invention of Ogham. Up until the Christian era, the script was kept by Druids as a sacred method of communication. Rather than writing the characters on paper, Druidic priests used finger Ogham, or even shin or nose Ogham, to communicate with other scholars. During the Roman period, Julius Caesar, unaware of Ogham's existence, noted that the Druids resisted the art of writing, and instead seemed to memorize large amounts of poetry. It was not until the onset of Christianization that the druidical colleges began to decline and Ogham began to appear in public. The mysteries of the script were gone, however, as it appeared on monuments, usually next to a Latin translation of the text.

The grouping of letters in Ogham (unknown in runic)

The 20 signs of the Ogham script are distributed in four groups with five letters each. The distribution in the stone inscriptions is the following: (1) *N, S, V, L, B*; (2) *Q, C, T, D, H*; (3) *R, Z, NG, G, M*; (4) *I, E, U, O, A*. A fifth group (called *forfeda*, "additional letters"), comprising signs for rendering the diphthongs *EA, OI, UI, IA*, and *AE*, was added later when Ogham was used for writing manuscript texts. The signs to write consonants consist of scores that are incised to the left and right of an imagined stem line or diagonally across it. The stem line is equal to the arris of the stone that is inscribed. Vowels are written by carving notches on the arris).

The organization of Ogham as a system of intentionally designed score-and-notch motifs makes it a true "cipher," that is a secret code. Ogham might have been intended to be a cipher by its very creators, and, as a secret code, it was handed down from one generation of guardians of druid knowledge to the next in secluded circles.

A unique terminology in Irish exists to describe the infrastructure of the sign system and the composition of its graphic constituents:

- *aicme*, "group of letters" (literally "family")
- *feda*, "letters" (plural of the word for "wood").

The Ogham letters have a tally-like shape, suggesting that they might have been transferred to form an inventory of script signs from an older system of reckoning with tally sticks.

- *druim*, "stem line" (literally "ridge")
- *flesc*, "stroke (score, respectively)" (literally "twig").

The convention to group letters, typical of Ogham and untypical of runic, is not unique for the Ogham alphabet but was inspired by Roman grammatical tradition. "It is now generally accepted that the grouping of the letters can be derived from the classification found in Latin grammarians of the first through the fourth centuries C.E." (Russell 1995: 210).

The distinct order of Ogham letters (unknown in runic)

The order of letters in Ogham also differs markedly from that of the runic. In runic, the first to sixth letters form the sequence *f, u, th, a, r, k*. Futhark is the name for the runic alphabet in several local varieties, while the Ogham script is styled the Beithe-luis-nin (after the names of the first, second, and fifth signs).

Separate conventions of naming letters for Ogham signs and runes

Knowledge of the alphabetic principle (via the Latin alphabet as its manifestation) associates the diffusion of another idea, that of the acrophonic principle, which is reflected in both the Ogham and runic scripts. According to the acrophonic principle, the letters are given names using words whose initial sound is the one rendered by the corresponding sign in writing. The acrophonic principle for name giving was known through the works of Roman grammarians, who documented the literary norms for Latin, among them Terentius Varro ("De lingua Latina") and an anonymous treatise "Rhetorica ad C. Herennium"—both dating to the first century BCE—Fabius Quintilianus ("Institutio oratoria") of the first century CE, Aelius Donatus ("Ars maior") of the fourth century.

The names for individual letters in Ogham are associated with such concepts as trees (e.g., alder, birch, oak) or with natural phenomena (e.g., earth, field, rod of metal). Contrasting with this tradition, runic letters are associated with animals (e.g., aurochs, horse), divinities (e.g., Tyr, Ing), and so forth.

The preference for plants for naming script signs (Ogham) in the Celtic tradition is in accord with the famous ornamental style in Celtic art, which is oriented at plants and their parts. Also in the Germanic tradition of ornamental design, there is a certain preference that is distinct from the Celtic. The visual arts among the Germanic tribes are known for their exquisite animal motifs. The animal style in art finds its parallel in giving names of animals to some of the Runic letters.

Different periods of writing on stone for Ogham and runes

Stone was used extensively as a surface for inscriptions for both Ogham and runes. There are significant differences between the Celtic and Germanic tradition, though.

These differences concern the techniques for engraving letters on the stony surface and placing inscriptions and also the time span when stone was used as a writing surface.

Writing on stone with Ogham is a tradition that is separated by cultural chronology from the heritage of rune stones. Stones were inscribed with Ogham centuries before runes were used on such a surface. From the beginnings of Ogham literacy, stone was the preferred surface. The early runic literacy differs markedly, because inscriptions are placed on portable objects. When runes began to be used to write on stone (fifth century CE), the custom of Ogham stone inscriptions had already been flourishing for almost two centuries. Later, when the number of rune stones (inscribed and ornamentated memorial stones) increased in the Germanic cultural domain (i.e., since the seventh century CE), the use of Ogham on stone was already declining. "It has been suggested that the apparent seventh-century demise of orthodox ogam may have been the result of Christian disapproval, rather than replacement by a more effective system [i.e., the Latin alphabet]" (Redknap 1995: 758).

Those who are inclined to look for a historical relationship between Ogham and runes should consider a possible drift of idea diffusion from the Celtic to the Germanic cultural area (and not vice versa) as regards the tradition of inscribing stones. In this context, cultural chronology speaks in favor of the higher age of this medium among the Celts.

Ogham traditional runic texts differ markedly in inscription engraving technique. Ogham signs are written in a way that the edge (or arris) of a stone serves as the stem line on which notches (for vowels) are carved and from which scores (for consonants) are engraved in both directions. In contrast, runic inscriptions appear in straight rows or bands on the surface of the stone, with no regard for the edge.

The Area of Influence and Cultural Chronology of Ogham

Hundreds of inscriptions in Ogham have been preserved on the most durable material, on stone. The texts are found on stones with memorial function, mostly gravestones. The finds concentrate in the southern and central part of Ireland (some 330 inscribed stones) and also in Britain, namely in the southwest and northwest of Wales (some 150 stones). There are only a few dozen stones with Ogham inscriptions from Cornwall, the Isle of Man, and Scotland.

The oldest known engraved stones with Ogham inscriptions are from Ireland, dating to the pre-Christian era, that is to the fourth and possibly to the third century CE. The stones in Britain are younger and date to the early Christian period (fifth century).

All Ogham inscriptions on stone stem from regions with Celtic population, that is, separated from the areas with early settlements of Angles and Saxons.

The chronology of writing technology in the British Isles shows the following stages:

- Latin alphabet (dominating between the first and fourth centuries);
- Ogham (in Ireland in the fourth century);
- Ogham (in Britain in the fifth century), coexisting with the Latin alphabet;
- Ogham (in Ireland from the fifth to seventh centuries), coexisting with the Latin alphabet;
- Anglo-Saxon Runic script (in Britain from ca. 650 to ca. 900), coexisting with the Latin alphabet;
- Latin alphabet (dominating since the Middle Ages, with scholastic Oghams continuing in Irish manuscripts of the post-seventh-century era).

The language of the Oghams on stone is archaic Irish. The texts are monolingual in Ireland, while in Wales, the inscriptions are usually bilingual (Irish and Latin) and digraphic (Ogham and Latin letters). The language of the Ogham texts in manuscripts is Old Irish.

Social Functions of Ogham Contrasted with Those of Early Runes

The original function of using Ogham for commemorative purposes started in the pre-Christian era and continued into the Christian period. The Christianization of the Celts of Ireland dates to the fifth century and is associated with the missionary work of Saint Patrick. Soon after the new religion had spread among the islanders, Irish monks went to Wales and Scotland to do missionary work themselves. They carried Ogham and the Gaelic language in their cultural "baggage." These two markers of Irish identity disappeared from Wales later, and Ogham declined in Scotland as well, but Gaelic continued to be spoken there (i.e., Scottish-Gaelic).

In addition to names, the Ogham inscriptions on gravestones do not contain much information of historical value. The names refer to an individual person and to a family group and are arranged according to a formulaic order: so-and-so, son of so-and-so. These stereotype formulas in monolingual Irish inscriptions find their counterpart in the bilingual texts (including Latin) in Britain.

The case with texts with memorial contents is different:

> The use of Ogham on memorials seems to have given them special power. Some mention deities as tribal ancestors such as Dovinia of the Corcu Duibne. It seems that Ogham stones were important markers indicating property ownership . . . and perhaps these rights were all the stronger through their statement in a magical script. (Mytum 1992: 55f.)

In the old days, many Celts believed in the magical properties of the Ogham signs. These beliefs are echoed in the popular Irish tales. Against this background, it becomes understandable why Ogham was also used for writing spells, namely to make the magical cipher infuse the meanings of words and the contents of phrases with supernatural power.

The original functions of the runes differ markedly from those of Ogham. While texts in Ogham appear in a religious context on immobile objects (i.e., stones), runic inscriptions are found on portable objects (e.g., a woman's fibula, a bone comb, spearheads, shafts of various kinds). Most of the early runic inscriptions are very short, containing only one or two words. Of these, one is usually a name, perhaps of the owner of the inscribed object. In the early phase of the use of runes (i.e., until about 400 CE), the range of subjects treated in the inscriptions is quite narrow. Runic literacy of the early centuries is characterized by "the complete absence of any inscriptions dealing with cult, administration, literature, law, and so on" (Williams 2004: 270).

During the Middle Ages (ca. 950–ca. 1150), when literacy in runic flourished among the Anglo-Saxons in Britain and the Scandinavians, Ogham, in its religious function, was no longer in use and lived on only as scholastic Ogham, this being a bookish medium. As such, Ogham was used in manuscripts since the eighth century and in Ireland only. The subjects in the manuscripts are related to the script itself and to its role in Irish literary history. Ogham was taught in schools until the 17th century, and it was never forgotten as a symbol of Irish culture. For written Irish, the only language that was once rendered in the Ogham script, the Latin alphabet has been in use since the Middle Ages.

As this section has shown, there are multiple reasons for arguing that the Ogham script did not derive from Norse runes. Culturally, the influence of the Romans was much more pronounced than that of the Scandinavians. Linguistically, there are more dissimilarities than similarities in characters and organization between the Ogham script and Norse runes. Finally, the script's function within Christian society aligns it more closely with Celtic origins. Bringing all of this evidence to bear proves the point that Ogham was of Celtic derivation rather than Norse.

References and Further Reading

Charles-Edwards, Thomas. "Language and Society among the Insular Celts AD 400–1000." In Miranda J. Green, ed., *The Celtic World* (pp. 703–36). New York: Routledge, 1995.

Elliott, Ralph W. V. "The Runic Script." In Peter T. Daniels and William Bright, eds., *The World's Writing Systems* (pp. 333–39). New York: Oxford University Press, 1996.

Haarmann, Harald. *Foundations of Culture. Knowledge-Construction, Belief Systems, and Worldview in Their Dynamic Interplay.* New York: Peter Lang, 2007.

Haarmann, Harald. *Historia universal de la escritura.* Madrid: Gredos, 2001.

McManus, Damian. *A Guide to Ogam* (Maynooth Monographs 4). Maynooth, Ireland: An Sagart, 1991.

McManus, Damian. "Ogham." In Peter T. Daniels and William Bright, eds., *The World's Writing Systems* (pp. 340–45). New York: Oxford University Press, 1996.

Mytum, Harold. *The Origins of Early Christian Ireland.* New York: Routledge, 1992.

Redknap, Mark. "Early Christianity and Its Monuments." In Miranda J. Green, ed., *The Celtic World* (pp. 737–78). New York: Routledge, 1995.

Russell, Paul. *An Introduction to the Celtic Languages.* New York: Longman, 1995.

Sawyer, Birgit. *The Viking-Age Rune Stones and Commemoration in Early Medieval Scandinavia.* New York: Oxford University Press, 2000.

Williams, Henrik. "Reasons for Runes." In Stephen D. Houston, ed., *The First Writing: Script Invention as History and Process* (pp. 262–73). New York: Cambridge University Press, 2004.

4

The "Trial of Socrates," described by Plato, was an actual event that occurred in 399 BCE, rather than merely a philosophical device used by Sophists in teaching Apologia.

PRO   Todd W. Ewing

CON   John Lee

PRO

In 399 BCE, the people of Athens tried Socrates on charges of impiety and corruption of the city's youth. During the customary daylong trial, both sides presented their case, and in the aftermath the jurors found the philosopher guilty and sentenced him to death. Since the timing of the execution conflicted with a religious festival, in which a ship traveled to the island of Delos to commemorate the return of Theseus, no executions could occur until its return. During the interval, despite attempts to persuade Socrates to escape into exile, he awaited his sentence, which involved drinking hemlock. The ship returned and, amid his friends, he calmly allowed the sentence to be carried out. These elements, on the surface, appear to present a straightforward account of the demise of a prominent citizen of Athens around the close of the fourth century BCE. Yet, in the aftermath of his execution, controversy about his life and teachings prompted accounts from both friends and detractors. From the sources, a complex—and contradictory—image of Socrates emerged, which has prompted scholars to revisit the account of the trial and call into question its historicity. Perhaps, in one sense, Socrates has been placed on trial again.

The critics point to the fact that Plato, one of Socrates's followers, immortalized his teacher in his many philosophical works. Yet, in what has been called the "Socratic problem," in many cases, the line between what Plato advocated and what came out of the mouth of Socrates is blurred. Thus, one is left to puzzle over what, if anything, originated with the master. Further, since Socrates never wrote anything himself, there appears to be no independent source to evaluate Plato's work. The only other surviving contemporary writings are those of Xenophon, whose portrait of Socrates differed from that of Plato; and Aristophanes offered not only another image of the philosopher, but a disparaging one. Aristotle, a student of Plato, commented in a few places on the differences between his teacher and Socrates, but did not provide enough material on the subject to provide evidence for clear-cut answers. Thus, one is left to consider the possibility that Plato fictionalized the account of Socrates's demise in order to create a platform to present various philosophical ideas, such as the nature of justice, piety, and the immortality of the soul. Plato's contemporaries then supposedly seized on this same means to propose and propagate their own ideas, and in the course of time, the myth of Socrates became historical "fact."

The debate about the various elements of his life and thought has multiplied, and the conclusions are varied. Yet, given the impact Socrates has had on subsequent thought and history, one is compelled to wade through the morass and seek some firm answers. Four issues move to the forefront in the discussion: (1) the reality of the trial, (2) the "Socratic problem" and the validity of the sources, (3) an understanding of the actual charge, and (4) the nature of Socrates's execution. No irrefutable answers are available, yet some evidence exists allowing the trial of Socrates to be securely anchored in historicity.

Before addressing the heart of the controversy, one must discuss the reality of an actual trial. Leaving off the discussion about sources and the nature of the charge for now, an examination of the external elements is in order. Meletus, Anytus, and Lycon, men about whom very little is known, prosecuted Socrates for impiety. Plato has his teacher indicate the charge that he is one who "corrupts the youth and does not believe in the gods the state believes in, but in other new spiritual beings" (Plato, *Apology* 24B–C). Xenophon similarly cited the charge as, "Socrates is guilty of rejecting the gods acknowledged by the state and bringing in strange deities: he is also guilty of corrupting the youth" (Xenophon, *Memorabilia* I.i.1). Of note, Diogenes Laertis, a historian of philosophy writing in the third century CE, reported the charge in the same terms (Laertius, *Lives* I.V.40). He asserted that the accusation continued to be posted in the Metroon, a temple that also housed the city's archives. Granted, he received this information secondhand, but given the correspondence with earlier sources, one finds difficulty in believing that he fabricated this claim. Indeed, his citation of Favorinus indicates that he did not simply lift the material from Xenophon or Plato. Furthermore, even opponents of Socrates confirmed the reality of the trial. In 393 BCE, apparently in response to Plato's *Apology*, Polycrates wrote an attack on Socrates, utilizing a fictional speech of one of the plaintiffs, Anytus, to give the "true" reasons for Socrates's guilt. Unfortunately, this work is lost, but many writers in antiquity make reference to the "speech." In his *Apology*, Xenophon, along with other whose works are now lost, countered Polycrates with their own version. Most scholars consider Xenophon's address to the "Accuser" a reference to Polycrates and not the actual plaintiff (Marchant 2002: ix–x). Anton-Hermann Chroust attempted to reconstruct this lost work in 1957, and noted that the responses to Polycrates took issue with his version of the charges and not the actual event (Chroust 1973: 6). Among the other lost works include those by Lysias and Theodectos (Stryker and Slings 2005: 74).

Also, a trial for the cause of impiety was not necessarily a unique event. The friends of Pericles faced charges of impiety at the beginning of the Peloponnesian war. Plutarch records three such impiety trials. Pheidias the sculptor faced charges that he had stolen gold that covered the statue of Athena, but worse, he had included the likenesses of himself as one of the figures on the goddess's shield. Aspasia, Pericles's mistress, also faced the charge because she allegedly supplied freeborn women to him. Anaxagoras faced charges of impiety. Although the sources disagree, the indication is that the philosopher questioned the nature of the sun and moon (Bauman 1990: 37–38). Diagoras the poet faced indictment for impiety in 415 BCE for mocking the Eleusinian mysteries, and Diopeithes the seer is purported to have promoted a law punishing those who did not properly acknowledge the gods or who inquired into the nature of the heavens. Despite some question about these sources, one could agree with Robert Parker's assessment about Diepeithes's proposed law, that "there is no very strong reason to be suspicious" (Parker 2000: 47).

In the end, the writers of antiquity did not question the reality of a trial, nor is the concept of an impiety trial an alien concept. Yet, one could still argue that many of the sources and examples rest on tenuous supports. The sources appear to contradict one another, and one is still left with the "Socratic problem." If the sources cannot be trusted, how can the historicity of the trial be maintained with any certainty?

Among the surviving sources, four are contemporary, or near contemporary, with the life of Socrates. Aristophanes, the comic writer, wrote *Clouds* in 423 BCE, and a later revised version. Among the works of Plato, four works relate to the trial and death of Socrates: *Euthyphro, Apology, Crito*, and *Phaedo*. Xenophon also contributed to the corpus with his own *Apology* and *Memorabilia*. Aristotle was born 15 years after Socrates's death, and although he never knew the philosopher, he spent 20 years at Plato's academy. The *Ethics* provides comments, not about the trial and execution, but about Socrates's teaching, so as a direct source, it can be set aside for now. Later writers and philosophers wrote about Socrates, but when reconstructing the historical man, as mentioned above, these works tend to be placed in the background as suspect. Once again, the problem surrounding the primary sources is that they all seem to present a different picture of Socrates.

Aristophanes presented a character named Socrates, who, unsurprisingly, runs a "think shop." There he rests in a basket suspended above the ground, contemplating the heavens and expounding his views. His students wander about below involved in a variety of studies. The farmer, Strepsiades, in an effort to escape his growing list of creditors, enrolls in an effort to learn the art of making the weak argument strong. He fails in his endeavor and sends his son Pheidippides, who masters the art and helps his father. Yet, in the end, the son turns on him, and he realizes that he has created a monster and thus wreaks vengeance on the school by burning it down. The play associates Socrates with

In this 18th-century engraving, ancient Greek philosopher Socrates holds a cup of hemlock. After being convicted by a court of corrupting the youth of Athens, Socrates chose to be true to his principles by drinking the poison rather than trying to secure a release through bribery or an escape attempt. (Library of Congress)

the natural philosophers and Sophists of the day, who were renowned for their art of rhetoric and charging people large fees for instruction. Aristophanes obviously caricatured his subject, so its use as a means of discovering the historical Socarates can be dismissed; but he presented a portrait of the man that became reality in the minds of Athenians, much like modern sketch comedy parodies politicians, placing distorted images in the public's mind. Plato indicated this truth by having Socrates mention "Aristophanes' comedy" as a distortion of his teaching (*Apology* 19C).

Plato's *Apology*, on the other hand, presents a polished speaker, well versed in the art of speaking. Indeed, despite the traditional claim that he did not prepare a speech beforehand, Socrates presents a formal, "forensic" court speech (Burnyeat 2004). Indeed, the presentation follows all of the proper rhetorical rules. He begins with an exordium to his audience, moves to a prothesis, which states his case, and counters with a refutation. The speech concludes with a typical digression and a final peroration (Allen 1984: 63). This polished urbane Socrates does not match the portrait given by Xenophon, who paints him as a harmless sage dispensing practical bits of wisdom on careers and household management (Wilson 2007: 94). Indeed, even the exchange with Meletus in Plato's version seems to be constructed like a Socratic dialogue (Burnyeat 2002:

Plato's Account of the Death of Socrates

Plato's *Phaedo* contains the death scene of Socrates and presents the scene through the eyes of Phaedo, a close friend of Socrates:

> Crito made a sign to the servant, who was standing by; and he went out, and having been absent for some time, returned with the jailer carrying the cup of poison. Socrates said: "You, my good friend, who are experienced in these matters, shall give me directions how I am to proceed." The man answered: "You have only to walk about until your legs are heavy, and then to lie down, and the poison will act." At the same time he handed the cup to Socrates, who in the easiest and gentlest manner, without the least fear or change of color or feature, looking at the man with all his eyes, Echecrates, as his manner was, took the cup and said: "What do you say about making a libation out of this cup to any god? May I, or not?" The man answered: "We only prepare, Socrates, just so much as we deem enough. I understand," he said: "but I may and must ask the gods to prosper my journey from this to the other world—even so—and so be it according to my prayer." Then raising the cup to his lips, quite readily and cheerfully he drank off the poison. And hitherto most of us had been able to control our sorrow; but now when we saw him drinking, and saw too that he had finished the draught, we could no longer forbear, and in spite of myself my own tears were flowing fast; so that I covered my face and wept, not for him, but at the thought of my own calamity in having to part from such a friend.

Source: Plato, *Phaedo*, Project Gutenberg, www.gutenberg.org/files/1658/1658-h/1658-h.htm. (accessed May 31, 2010)

---

144). Trust in Plato's account is further diminished with the "Socratic problem." Plato, in other works, has obviously placed his own ideas in the mouth of Socrates, showing developed philosophical concepts, such as that of ideal forms. The assumption is, then, that if Plato is guilty in one place of using Socrates as a mouthpiece, he is guilty elsewhere too, and determining the line between the historical and the fictional man is impossible. One must admit that most likely Plato has not presented a verbatim account of the content of the trial speech. To suggest as much shows a complete misunderstanding of classical literary technique. The possibility certainly exists that he has inserted his own ideas into his master's mouth to promote a particular concept. Yet, one is left to wonder about which particular Platonic teachings are set forth in the *Apology*. The purpose of the work does not seem designed to promote a particular philosophical idea, but instead, focuses on vindicating the memory of Socrates. Plato could not have accomplished some sort of didactic goal through a complete fiction in the face of Athenians who actually remembered the trial (Vlastos 1995: 6; Fowler 2005: 65.)

Xenophon's portrait, as mentioned before, is different. Whereas Plato claimed to be an eyewitness, Xenophon admits to having received his information secondhand through the auspices of Hermogenes, traditionally shown as one of the friends of Socrates. The contents of this *Apology* and the *Memorabilia* differ from Plato's accounts. These are presented in more of a narrative form, and he pursues a different agenda. Xenophon sought to create a picture of Socrates as one who faithfully respected the gods of Athens and participated regularly in the city's rituals. One looks in vain for some kind of Socratic harmony, in which the texts could be placed side by side. The *Memorabilia* has been demonstrated to be a response to Polycrates's work and thus, Xenophon has shaped his work accordingly. Some of his assertions about being present with Socrates are suspect and obviously a literary device, but one cannot rule out his claim to have actually heard the teacher on occasion (Marchant 2002: xiii, xiv). Once again, though, one is left with an unsettling uncertainty about the validity of the contents of his work.

Leaving aside the "Socratic problem" for now, what can be known from the sources at hand? Aristophanes, as said, can be dismissed as a concocted image that is not "historical." Plato and Xenophon have obviously fabricated elements and style for their own purposes. Yet these two authors can be mined for a historical "core." Xenophon wrote long after Plato, and he may have known of the latter's efforts to give an account, but one does not find him simply "plagiarizing" (Marchant 2002: x). Various components can be found that correspond in their respective works, showing that each of them was at least acquainted with actual elements that served as part of the backdrop for their own agenda. More significant is that these elements are not essential to their basic argument, and thus there would have been no reason to fabricate them. For example, the charge itself is not something that either would have fabricated. Indeed, both report the charge of impiety and corruption of the city's youth (Plato, *Apology* 24B; Xenophon, *Apology* 11, 12; *Memorabilia* I.i.1).

Other elements correspond. Both make reference to Chaerephon's inquiry of the Delphic Oracle, in which Socrates received his mantle as wisest among men (Plato, *Apology* 21A; Xenophon, *Apology* 14). Both refer to an exchange with Meletus even though Xenophon merely gives an excerpt as opposed to Plato's actual dialogue (Plato, *Apology* 24A–27D; Xenophon, *Apology* 20). Both have him defending against each of the charges, albeit with different emphases. Plato has Socrates refer to the "god" and the "gods" in more vague terms, associating his individual "spirit" with the divine; whereas Xenophon talks about the defendant's association with various city cults. Although the latter likely exaggerates, they both indicate that he addressed this charge (Plato, *Apology* 27D; Xenophon, *Apology* 12–13). The inference that some kind of alternative fine could be paid is reflected in both of these works, even though it is garbled in the tradition, since Xenophon states that he refused to allow his followers to pay (Plato, *Apology*

38C; Xenophon, *Apology* 23). Regardless of the amount or the attitude behind the counteroffer, all accounts recall Socrates making some statement about a fine.

One other element may not only illustrate an association with an actual event in the trial, but serves as an example of how Xenophon extrapolated. In *Apology* 39C–D, Plato "prophesizes" about the "grievous" fate of those who unjustly condemned him. Xenophon related that he prophesized about how Anytus's son, despite advice, would "fall into some disgraceful propensity and will surely go far in the career of vice." This fulfillment is most likely an extrapolation to provide a vindication of Socrates, but reflects an original factor in the trial (*Apology* 29–30). Further, both reference his confidence in facing death. One has difficulty seeing how, or why, both would create an element that does not seem to promote their literary agenda (Plato, *Apology* 41D; Xenophon, *Apology* 27, 32–33). Finally, in connection with his imprisonment, both authors refer to an attempt by his friends to engineer his escape, which he rejected (Plato, *Crito*; Xenophon, *Apology* 23). Once again, they do so without any obvious borrowing from each other, but unconsciously incorporate real life events into their works.

For modern readers, Plato's and Xenophon's literary liberties erode confidence. Yet one must remember that authors in antiquity utilized a different methodology in presenting events and especially speeches. As Thucydides explained in his well-known axiom on the speeches in his work, he simply attempted to capture the essence of what his subjects said, not to provide a verbatim report (Thucydides 2003: i.xxii.1). In the case of the *Apology* of Plato, Charles Kahn noted the distinction between it and the other dialogues in that it is the content of a public speech more in the line of Pericles's funeral orations, thus "quasi-historical" (1996: 88). Doubtless, Plato and Xenophon both placed words in Socrates's mouth. The contrast between the polished Plato and the mercenary Xenophon is obvious, but both seem to have captured the essence of Socrates even as they attempted to exonerate a man pilloried by his own community. They both drew upon their own experience of the man, coupled with recollections of statements he made and attitudes he held. Furthermore, Plato was not being deceitful in his efforts. He certainly based his ideas on some formative teachings of Socrates, to which he felt free to add his own thoughts in order to arrive at what he assumed to be a logical conclusion (Guthrie 1969: 33–34). Yet, once again, this appears to beg the question: If Socrates is a construct of Plato and Xenophon, then, is there any historicity?

One is forced to deal with the "Socratic problem" and whether the historical man can be separated from the literary creation. In the end, no definitive statements can be asserted, but some conclusions can still bring one into the arena of historicity. The usual approach in the search for the historical Socrates is to divide Plato's works into a chronological schema of early, middle, and late. The assumption is that the earlier dialogues would reflect more of Socrates's actual teachings and ideas. Yet, as Plato progressed and matured in his philosophical thinking, he began to incorporate his own ideas into his Socratic vehicle. Most efforts to separate Plato from Socrates search for stylistic and philosophical developments, which although problematic still offer insights, despite objections (Allen 1984: 8–9; but see Wilson 2007: 101).

Robin Waterfield provides an excellent summary of the four main points used to demonstrate a contrast between Socratic ideas and later Platonic influences. First, there is a contrast between the ideas that one will always choose what is best versus being controlled by one's appetites. Second, Socrates rejects the typical Greek attitude that one could justify harming one's enemies, but in works chronologically identified as later, such as the *Republic*, the idea is actually championed. Third, Socrates limits his inquiries to discovering moral issues, as opposed to a focus on metaphysical explorations of the ideal (which Aristotle seems to associate with his "friends" [i.e., Plato] in *Ethics* I.vi.1). Finally, Socrates seems to proclaim that he himself knew nothing definite as opposed to a later confidence of certainty (Waterfield 1990: 12–13). One must admit that these do not offer definitive proofs about what is distinctly Socratic, but they create a defensible position that a progression of ideas exists in the Platonic corpus. Further, those works that show a mature development of ideas are stylistically linked to works associated with *Theaetetus*, which does offer an external historical anchor. A reference in its introduction is made to the siege of Corinth, which is dated at 369 BCE. Therefore, since the *Apology, Crito,* and *Phaedo* associated with the works are stylistically distinct, the implication is that they are earlier works. One can, with logical consistency, maintain a certain amount of confidence of the existence of a "Socrates" closer to the man himself. With some justification, W. K. C. Guthrie calls the *Apology* the most "Socratic" of Plato's works (1969: 157–58). Although skeptics complain about the inevitable reality that one can never completely separate the Platonic Socrates from the actual man, there is truth in the statement that the *Apology* does not contain any utterance that the actual Socrates could not have reasonably stated publicly (Stryker and Slings 2005: 78).

Plato provided glimpses of the real Socrates, which calls into question the validity of Xenophon's portrait. Along with the *Apology* and the *Memorabilia*, Socrates is the main character in the *Oeconomicus*, a work on managing the estate, and the *Symposium*, which deals with conversations at a dinner party. Socrates appears to be less witty and not as profound in Xenophon (Guthrie 1969: 15). The contrast appears to suggest that one is correct and that the other should be jettisoned in the search for Socrates; and most scholars favor Plato as more authentic. Yet, as Waterfield points out in defense of Xenophon's image of Socrates, a philosopher does not always dwell upon the lofty, but most likely provided occasional advice on practical matters (1990: 19–20). Plus, he did not demonstrate the capability of gleaning the more profound insights of his teacher as Plato could and so dwells upon matters that specifically interested him. Also, where Xenophon does take license, one is reminded once again of the literary habits of the classical world. Xenophon is utilizing firsthand encounters, anecdotes from his friends, as well as his own limited extrapolations to portray Socrates as a harmless wise man (Wilson 2007: 96).

Guthrie summed up the best approach to the apparent discrepancies in the sources when he indicated that Socrates had to have been a "complex character," with many aspects to his personality. Thus, when each of these writers approached their subject, they did so with their own interests and agenda (Guthrie 1969: 8–9). They did not erase the foundational essence of Socrates and the pivotal events in his life, nor is their literary exaggeration a deceitful fabrication. When one considers other historical persons in antiquity, the same tendencies apply. Jesus of Nazareth, a peasant from Galilee, carried on a teaching ministry until he ran afoul of the Jewish and Roman authorities, who executed him. His followers quickly interpreted his life and work, and not all of them agreed on the details, but the essential historical facts remain. Alexander the Great rose to prominence and conquered the Persian Empire. Those who wrote afterward presented him either as a brute or a visionary. Regardless of how one viewed him, the ancient Near East had become Greek. Harmodius and Aristogeiton assassinated Hipparchus because of a family slight, but later Athenians elevated them as the "tyrant slayers." The motives had been changed, but the essential historicity of the event remains. Likewise, in the case of Socrates, Xenophon and Plato may have colored events with their own style and program, but they did not lose the basic historicity of their master defending himself before the court of Athens, under a charge of impiety.

Another controversy that circulates around the trial of Socrates concerns the motives of the prosecutors. On the surface, Meletus and his associates accused the philosopher of impiety, but this charge seems difficult to define for modern scholars. Also, the suggestion has been put forth that this action served only as a mask for political motivations (Stone 1989: 138–39). Before addressing this view, one must understand the nature of the charge of impiety. Socrates is being accused of not believing in the gods of Athens and of introducing new divinities. The former is not simply a charge of atheism, although this must have been a concern for some of the jurors, but that he did not actually participate in the civic cults, which, being the social creature he seemed to be, is implausible (McPherran 1998: 163–64). Yet, philosophical skepticism is not the only crime of which he was accused. He had not been the first to question the nature of the gods, but the latter part of the charge is more significant. Even in *Euthyphro* Socrates quoted the charge that he is "a maker of gods" (3B) before a reference to the city's gods. He and Meletus were most likely referring to the claim that he had his own divine spirit that gave him advice on occasion (*Apology* 31C–D). Xenophon apparently did not understand the underlying issue and focused on demonstrating where Socrates did participate in the civic cults. Plato, however, seemed to understand the true nature of the charge. Socrates not only questioned the nature of the gods as worshiped in Athens, but also suggested the existence of a personal spirituality that superseded the state cults. What made him particularly dangerous was that he had a popular following among the children of prominent citizens in Athens.

The modern approach to the trial is to assign political motives to his adversaries. This belief usually stems from Socrates's so-called antidemocratic statements and his relationships with Critias and Alcibiades. Both of these men were associated with oligarchic forces, and Critias stood among the Thirty Tyrants who butchered many in Athens in 404 BCE (just five years before Socrates's own trial). Yet, because of the amnesty in the aftermath of the democratic restoration, charges could not be brought for earlier political crimes. So those seeking to accuse Socrates of political subversion in connection with these off-limit events had to change the charge to a religious one in order to accomplish his destruction. Thomas Brickhouse and Nicholas Smith offer the best refutation of political motivations. In truth, Socrates did make criticisms of democratic practices (see *Apology* 25C for example), but his connection to those who disrupted the city is more to the point. Both Alcibiades and Critias were his known associates, and the assumption persisted that Socrates encouraged them in their destructive activities. Xenophon attempted to address this issue (*Memorbilia* I.ii.12), but once again, he is actually answering Polycrates. Plato's *Socrates*, however, does not mention these associates and the so-called corruption of them; so, if political issues did hang in the background, one wonders why he would not have addressed them a full defense (Brickhouse and Smith 1989: 71, 73–74).

In actuality, one must remember that political motives could have been in the background, but not those suggested above (Parker 2002: 151). Unlike modern Western democracies, Athens did not attempt to separate religion and state. A threat to the state cults equated with a threat to the state. The charge did stem from Socrates's personal divinity, which could undermine the civic cults, and, in the minds of the Athenians, this made Socrates a danger (Wilson 2007: 32–33). In turn, he could continue to teach others to follow his example of undermining the social values of the city (Parker 2002: 153–54). One must remember that the trial took place during a time of social and civic turmoil. Athens had recently lost the Peloponnesian war and witnessed the dismantling of their entire empire. The more recent horrors of the Thirty Tyrants and the upheaval of democratic forces left the people sensitive to any activities that could further disrupt their already crumbling social and political order. Perceived attacks on religion in times of stress tend to bring out those conservative champions of traditional beliefs who feel compelled to protect their society. One need only look back to the spate of impiety trials during the turmoil of the Peloponnesian war. The reason Meletus and his cohorts targeted Socrates most likely stemmed from his public prominence—and even because of personal animosity. For example, Anytus had personally clashed with Socrates over the career choice of his son (Xenophon,

Apology 29–30). Furthermore, in the antisophist environment of the time, this may have encouraged Meletus and Lyco. Given the animosity that Socrates could provoke and the popular perception of his arrogance, he may have said or done something that antagonized the wrong person at the wrong time.

The last assault on the historicity of Socrates's trial and execution concerns the actual sentence itself. In Plato's *Phaedo*, one is confronted with a Socrates who calmly appropriates the poison. While chastising his friends for their grief, he quips with his executioner and continues to philosophize about the soul. He drank the hemlock, which slowly deadened his legs. He then lay down to wait for the poison to slowly turn his extremities "cold and rigid" (*Phaedo* 118A). Once it reached his heart, he uttered his last words and quietly expired. This scene has been traditionally rejected on the grounds that it does not portray an accurate description of death by poison. Thus, Plato is obviously fictionalizing in order to create a picture of a man with impressive and heroic character, who died in stoic control of his mind and actions (Brickhouse and Smith 2004: 263).

The assaults on Plato's version are commonly found in two recent articles. Christopher Gill commented on the contrast between Plato's depiction of death by poison and that given by other classical writers, such as Nicander. The latter's description is much more violent with convulsions and choking (Gill 1973: 25–28). More recently, Bonita Graves provided more clinical evaluations of hemlock poisoning symptoms in connection with Socrates's death (1991: 156–68). These represent what appeared to be definitive medical proof that Plato had sacrificed historical events for his own philosophical agenda.

Yet, Enid Bloch has impressively dismantled the arguments of Plato's critics (2001: 255–78). She reexamines not only the ancient sources, but also draws exhaustively on historical evidence from medical explorations of the use of hemlock. She effectively dismantles the argument against Plato's veracity. First, she specifies that Plato never actually used the word hemlock, but only "the drug." Later writers identified it with hemlock, which in reality refers not just to one plant, but to a wide variety of plants in the same family, some of which can cause convulsive seizures, but one, which does not (Bloch 2002: 259–60, 262). Second, she provides two accounts that present ways in which the specific hemlock plant is utilized, providing symptoms that coincide with those described by Plato. The 19th-century toxicologist John Harley experimented on himself on two different occasions by taking doses of hemlock (Harley, 1869). In both cases, he described the heaviness of the legs and the onset of paralysis, but commented on his ability to maintain clarity of mind. The second account is the tragic incident of a tailor whose children presented him with what they thought was a wild parsley sandwich. Instead, they accidentally poisoned him. The physician at the hospital interviewed all involved and cataloged the symptoms, which involved a heaviness of the legs, paralysis, and asphyxia with no convulsions

(Bloch 2001: 263–64). In the final analysis, one cannot definitively reject the plausibility of Plato's account of the end of his master's life.

The challenge to the historicity of the events surrounding the death of Socrates will never cease. Indeed, as Guthrie comments, if all scholars agreed on the various issues, then the conclusions about Socrates would be suspect (1969: 8–9). As long as the "Socratic problem" exists, one will always have a seed of doubt about the "historical" Socrates. Yet, certain facts can be maintained plausibly in the face of critics. In 399 BCE, Athens put a man named Socrates on trial for impiety. Nobody in antiquity disputed that fact. The charges are consistent with precedent and seem to be based on actual beliefs about the gods promoted by Socrates (beliefs that neither Plato nor Xenophon needed to fabricate to further their own agendas). That his followers did take liberties with the actual words of Socrates is not in dispute, but once again, the practice is consistent with ancient practice. The actual man himself can still be glimpsed behind the literature of the classical world, and his trial continues to stand as a milestone event in the history of both Greece and humanity.

References and Further Reading

Allen, R. E. *The Dialogues of Plato*, Vol. 1. New Haven, CT: Yale University Press, 1984.

Aristophones. *Clouds*, trans. Jeffrey Henderson in *Aristophanes: Clouds, Wasps, Peace*. Loeb Classical Library, Vol. 488. Cambridge, MA: Harvard University Press, 1998.

Aristotle. *Nicomachean Ethics*, trans. H. Rackham. Loeb Classical Library, Vol. 73. Cambridge, MA: Harvard University Press, 2003.

Bauman, Richard. *Political Trials in Ancient Greece*. New York: Routledge, 1990.

Bloch, Enid. "Hemlock Poisoning and the Death of Socrates: Did Plato Tell the Truth?" in *The Trial and Execution of Socrates: Sources and Controversies*, ed. Thomas C. Brickhouse and Nicholas D. Smith. New York: Oxford University Press, 2001.

Brickhouse, Thomas C., and Nicholas D. Smith., eds. *Routledge Philosophy Guidebook to Plato and the Trial of Socrates*. New York: Routledge, 2004.

Brickhouse, Thomas C., and Nicholas D. Smith., eds. *Socrates on Trial*. New York: Oxford University Press, 1989.

Burnyeat, Myles F. "The Impiety of Socrates," in *Plato's Euthyphro, Apology, and Crito: Critical Essays*, ed. Rachana Kamtekar. Lanham, MD: Rowman and Littlefield, 2004.

Chroust, Anton-Hermann. *Aristotle: New Light on his Life and on Some of his Lost Works*. Notre Dame, IN: University of Notre Dame Press, 1973.

Diogenes Laertius. *On the Lives and Opinions of Eminent Persons in Philosophy*. Translated by R. D. Hicks. Loeb Classical Library, Vol. 184. Cambridge, MA: Harvard University Press, 1925.

Fowler, Harold North. *Plato: Euthyphro, Apology, Crito, Phaedo, Phaedrus*. Loeb Classical Library, Vol. 36. Cambridge, MA: Harvard University Press, 2005.

Gill, Christopher. "The Death of Socrates." *Classical Quarterly* 23 (1973): 25–28.

Graves, Bonita M., et al. "Hemlock Poisoning: Twentieth Century Scientific Light Shed on the Death of Socrates." In *The Philosophy of Socrates*, edited by K. J. Boudouris. Athens, Greece: Kardamista Publishing, 1991.

Guthrie, W. K. C. *Socrates*. New York: Cambridge University Press, 1969.

Harley, John. *The Old Vegetable Narcautics: Hemlock, Opium, Belladonna, and Henbane*. London: Macmillan and Co., 1869.

Kahn, Charles. *Plato and the Socratic Dialogues*. New York: Cambridge University Press, 1996.

Marchant, E. C. *Xenophon: Memorabilia, Oeconomicus, Symposium, Apology*. Loeb Classical Library, Vol. 168. Cambridge, MA: Harvard University Press, 2002.

McPherran, Mark L. *The Religion of Socrates*. University Park: Pennsylvania State University Press, 1998.

Parker, Robert. "The Trial of Socrates: And A Religious Crisis?," In *Religion in Socratic Philosophy*, edited by Nicholas D. Smith and Paul B. Woodruff. New York: Oxford University Press, 2000, 40–54.

Stone, I. F. *The Trial of Socrates*. New York: Anchor Books, 1989.

Stryker, E., and S. R. Slings, "On the Historical Reliability of Plato's Apology." In *Plato's Euthyphro, Apology and Crito: Critical Essays*, edited by Rachana Kametkar. Lanham, Md.: Rowman and Littlefield, 2002.

Thucydides. *History of the Peloponnesian War*. trans. C. F. Smith. Loeb Classical Library, Vol. 108. Cambridge, Mass.: Harvard University Press, 2003.

Vlastos, Gregory. "The Paradox of Socrates." In *Studies in Greek Philosophy: Socrates, Plato, and their Tradition*, Vol. 2, edited by David Graham. Princeton, NJ: Princeton University Press, 1995.

Waterfield, Robin. *Xenophon: Conversations of Socrates*. New York: Penguin, 1990.

Wilson, Emily. *The Death of Socrates*. Cambridge, MA: Harvard University Press, 2007.

CON

The ancient world speculated about the origins of the universe and the natural forces like wind, lightning, and heat in the world. Some of the ancients wrote about these speculations in myths and epics that used events as rhetorical devices rather than actual chronicles of historic events. These myths and epics were testimony that ancient people were always questioning their world as expressed through stories. In this vein, the achievement of the ancient Greeks was that they were willing to deal with these questions in a factual and thoughtful way rather than using stories. They were already asking how the world was made, and they believed that basic elements were the original elements of the world. These ancient people were called the pre-Socratics, and they saw individual facts and created theories to explain the universe through natural laws. Consequently, these pre-Socratics began the elementary roots of science. However, the Greek approach began to change with the rise of a group of itinerant philosophers known as the Sophists. Some philosophers claim that the historic character of Socrates came less from the actual person than from the Sophists stance on the world. The purpose of this section is to trace the origin of Socrates's philosophy and compare it, in terms of style and content, to that of the Sophists' in order to show that the story of the trial of Socrates, as described by Plato, was more likely a sophistic device rather than an actual chronicle of an event.

Pre-Socratics

In discussing Socrates, we need to understand the foundations of philosophy especially with the Greeks. The Greek philosophers asked basic questions about the nature of reality. What is it? What is it made of? What are the elements of world? By what law is nature made? The pre-Socratics, who flourished during the early age of Greek prosperity, thought about these questions. These pre-Socratics, such as Thales and Anaximander, worked on speculating whether water and the boundless or infinite were the foundation of the universe. Heraclitus declared that the fundamental element was fire and that the world had neither beginning nor end. For example, Democritus speculated that atoms were the fundamental units of the universe. These pre-Socratics' thoughts became the fundamentals for the philosophies of the Sophists and Socrates.

The Sophists

The Sophists were a group of teachers who journeyed around Greece to teach young men for money. They questioned the nature of reality and the nature of human conduct. What can we know about nature? Does nature exists outside of human perception? What is the good life? They were instructors of rhetoric, reasoning, and skepticism to the rich people of Athens. Many of the Athenian

---

Socrates on Sophism: Plato's *Protagoras*

Plato reveals much about either his own or Socrates's attitude toward Sophism in his *Protagoras*. The dialogue is between Socrates and Protagoras, the supposed first Sophist:

> You are going to commit your soul to the care of a man whom you call a Sophist. And yet I hardly think that you know what a Sophist is; and if not, then you do not even know to whom you are committing your soul and whether the thing to which you commit yourself be good or evil.
> I certainly think that I do know, he replied.
>
> Then tell me, what do you imagine that he is?
>
> I take him to be one who knows wise things, he replied, as his name implies.
>
> And might you not, I said, affirm this of the painter and of the carpenter also: Do not they, too, know wise things? But suppose a person were to ask us: In what are the painters wise? We should answer: In what relates to the making of likenesses, and similarly of other things. And if he were further to ask: What is the wisdom of the Sophist, and what is the manufacture over which he presides?—how should we answer him?
>
> How should we answer him, Socrates? What other answer could there be but that he presides over the art which makes men eloquent?
>
> Yes, I replied, that is very likely true, but not enough; for in the answer a further question is involved: Of what does the Sophist make a man talk eloquently? The player on the lyre may be supposed to make a man talk eloquently about that which he makes him understand, that is about playing the lyre. Is not that true?
>
> Yes.
>
> Then about what does the Sophist make him eloquent? Must not he make him eloquent in that which he understands?
>
> Yes, that may be assumed.
>
> And what is that which the Sophist knows and makes his disciple know?
> Indeed, he said, I cannot tell.

Source: Plato, *Protagoras*, Project Gutenberg, www.gutenberg.org/files/1591/1591-h/1591-h.htm. (accessed May 31, 2010)

---

politicians sent their sons to be trained by the Sophists, because the Sophists taught their sons how to reason and argue, which were the basic skills of a politician. Rhetoric was the tool that the Sophists used when attempting to persuade others to their views. They used irony, repetition, and logic to teach their students how to argue with other people. Logic allowed the Sophists to teach the students how to analyze critically the opponent's argument for flaws as well as to organize their speeches to persuade other people with good reasons. They were similar to

Greek red-figure vessel of a Sophist instructing a student in rhetoric, from Cerveteri, an ancient city northwest of Rome, 480 BCE. (Jupiterimages)

the modern-day lawyers of the day, who use the same methods to argue in court for their defendants and questioning witnesses.

In the Sophist questioning, they decided that knowledge was based on individual opinion and perceptions. They decided that a person's experience was relative to him and there were no absolute truths of life. This means that if a person said an object is orange and another person said it was red, they were both right according to their senses. As a result, the Sophists doubted that we can know anything for sure, and all knowledge is relative to the person.

Despite their doubt of knowledge, they believed that the study of human beings and examining their behavior was the proper subject for philosophy. In their education of others, they attempted to understand the best life to lead. They believed that excellence could be taught to their students. This meant that as philosophers they wanted to understand politics, psychology, and government, because these subjects focused on human beings in their teachings. They questioned the customs and traditions of human society because they wanted to know how best to train their students.

The Sophists, due to their questioning of beliefs and through fostering a climate of tolerance for new beliefs, are credited with creating democracy in Athens. Through their training of the leaders of the Athens, they allowed the leaders to learn the process of argumentation and to understand new ideas. These processes allowed the attitude of freedom to be maintained by these leaders. This freedom of the mind was carried into the Athenian government, where through the force of persuasion, they were able to create an open place for the discussion of new ideas. This discussion of opposing arguments allows unpopular views to be voiced in the assembly. As a result, the roots of democracy began with the Sophists teaching these leaders how to reason and to think democratically. However, as Athens grew more powerful, many people wanted a status quo and to keep power in the government. These Sophists would question their leaders' motives and reasons, and through this they created antagonism among the leaders of the day.

Protagoras (490–420 BCE) is generally regarded as the first Sophist. He believed, like Socrates, that virtue could be taught, because men had the ability to learn virtue. Protagoras was the first teacher of virtue, and he studied the use of language as a way to teach virtue. Protagoras also said that he viewed all truth as dependent on the individual. His famous quote is: "Man was the measure of all things." This statement indicates his belief in relativism. Furthermore, Protagoras believed that we cannot know whether there are gods, because life is too brief and because of the mystery of the subject. However, he viewed that man was the measure of all things or that all truth depended on him. He also said that if you have two arguments, usually the one that you avoid the most is the more truthful of the arguments. This belief shows a type of argument (Guthrie 1971: 262–63).

Others include Gorgias, Prodicus, Hippias, Lycophron, Callicles, and Cratylus. Gorgias (487–376 BCE) originated from Sicily. He made use of paradox and exaggeration as methods of persuasion in rhetoric, which Socrates used in the *Apology* (Kennedy 1972: 31). Prodicus (465–415 BCE) believed in the importance of the exact use of words and style in rhetoric, which Socrates also believed about philosophy. Hippias of Elis (was born about the middle of the fifth century BCE), contributed the meaning of words, rhythm, and literary style to the rhetorical art. Lycophron was a Sophist who believed that law was a convention made by man. Callicles argued that laws were made by men for their own interests and not by gods. Cratylus, another Sophist, believed that words changed so much that communication was impossible. All these Sophists echoed themes that Socrates would emulate or challenge in Plato's dialogues.

Socrates: Background

There was one philosopher thought to be a Sophist, because some of his beliefs were similar. This philosopher was Socrates (470–399 BCE), who was born in the artisan class. He was very educated, and he fought in a war. People thought he was very disciplined, because he could stand for a long time and endure cold weather. He married a woman named Xanthippe, who was his wife for a long time. Socrates used to go into the *agora*, the marketplace, to discuss philosophy with young people. He conducted dialogues discussing ethical and human issues.

Many contemporaries thought he was a Sophist because of the way he conducted arguments. He attempted to conduct a rhetorical discussion like the Sophists would. He would ask questions by giving a definition and answer with another question until the essence of the definition was found. Through constant questioning and doubt, he would find the essence of the words or topic of discussion. He attempted to open the listener to other possibilities than their own beliefs. This was called the Socratic method.

Diogenes Laertius, a Greek historian, wrote the *Lives and Opinions of Eminent Philosophers* in 300 CE. In this book, he claims that Protagoras was the creator of the Socratic method because he created a method of arguing that was similar to the Socratic method. They both argued claims by putting forth a counterclaim and then choosing the one that was least acceptable to argue. By doing this, they could find the truth by examining the strengths and weaknesses of the counterclaims.

Like the Sophists, Socrates believed that philosophy was the most important study of man. He also believed that excellence could be taught to the student, but that teaching helped the student remember his own thoughts about virtue. Thus, Socrates felt that virtue was an important part of life, and living virtuously was the best way to live like the Sophists.

Socrates had mixed opinions about the Sophists. He did praise them as being better educators than he himself was, and he also sent a student to study under the Sophists. His contemporaries also believed him to be a Sophist, because he taught like them. For example, Aristophanes, a comic playwright, also associates Socrates with being a Sophist.

But Socrates challenged the skepticism and relativism of the Sophists. As a result, Socrates differed with the Sophists on philosophical issues, but he used Sophist tools to seek the truth.

The *Apology*: A Sophists defense

In the *Apology*, Socrates uses many of the Sophists' tools to teach his beliefs about philosophy, virtue, and the moral conduct of life. The charges against him were the same charges that the Athenian leaders leveled against the Sophists. They were questioning the traditions, religions, and philosophical basis of the Athenian society. Socrates was also questioning the basis and the tolerance that the Sophists had developed, because many Athenians were too conservative to allow for tolerance.

Socrates challenged many of the aristocrats as well as taught the children of these aristocrats. Because of these challenges to their thinking, many of the aristocrats and leaders thought he was corrupting the youth of the city and challenging religion. He made these young people think! The leaders felt threatened because this type of thinking could mean the end of their power. Socrates was very similar to the Sophists in that he made people think about the assumptions on which they based their ethics and knowledge. Socrates claimed he had been told by an oracle to embark on this mission of questioning in order to find wisdom. He knew he did not have all the answers, but the leaders thought that they did. Socrates challenged this and took away their pretence to wisdom. As a result of being exposed, they felt threatened because they felt their influence over the people would be reduced. As a result of Socrates's seeking for wisdom, he disturbed the guardians of the society, who brought him up on charges of corrupting the youth. The *Apology* strongly supports the belief that Socrates acted like a Sophist in his life, even up to his death, to the point of using Sophistries to defend himself in the court. Furthermore, Socrates even had people questioning their own immortality and their religion, because he too had to face death because of his Sophist-like attacks against the conservative leaders.

In his use of Sophist tools in the *Apology*, Socrates uses a logical argument of generalization and exceptions in his defense against corruption of youth. Socrates was defending himself against the charges of being a corrupter of youth by comparing himself as only one corrupter of the youth among many supporters of the youth. Socrates raises the question that if there is only one corrupter, how can he influence so many people? Is he the only exception? He is using a Sophistry to logically point out a fallacy or untruthfulness of the charge to his side. This Sophism was displayed when he was questioning Miletus and posing questions like a Sophist would in court.

Socrates was accused in the Athenian court of having taught evil men such as Critias, Alciabiades, and Charmides, who had rebelled and attacked the Athenian state in the past. His defense, another sophistry, was to say that he did not teach them anything or that his teachings had nothing to do with their evil lives. This is a Sophism that attempted to exclude him by explaining that there might be other choices than what they accused him of. He is pointing out that they chose their evil lives and that his teachings had nothing to do with their evil actions.

He adds to this defense that if he had corrupted the youth, he did this involuntarily and so must be absolved of the charges. If a man involuntary commits evil, it may be true in a transcendental way to absolve responsibility. However, in a practical sense, it absolves all criminals of responsibility, because they all would say that they committed it because of other forces. Thus he says that it is relative to the person. He also defends himself by saying the relatives did not charge him with the crime, so why should he be held responsible. These relatives should have witnessed against him for corrupting the youth.

In terms of his defense about not believing in gods, he uses another Sophism by saying that he believes in the sons of gods or lesser divinities. He was also practicing the minimal religious rituals of the times. In saying that he believes in these lesser divinities, he does not commit himself to believing in the state gods or to those of the Greek mythology. He is just saying he does not know about them. This is similar to Protagoras's belief about the gods. In addition, he supports his belief in this demon or guiding spirit that led him to this philosophical journey. Socrates also is saying that this is unimportant to the paramount duty of doing right and self-examination, which is the core of religion.

In the last part of his speech, he tries to distance himself from the Sophists, but maybe he is trying to claim that he is a better Sophist. He believes that he was on a divine mission to seek wisdom and to support the youth, which was accidental and nebulous, but he still went ahead with his questions. He also states that he will subject himself to divine will, because he doesn't know anything about the afterlife, other than as a long sleep, which again cast doubts on issues in which people believe. Socrates also sees that his judges appear a little haughty, but he continues teaching as well as philosophizing until the end in order to get the judges to question their assumptions. In a sense, he was teaching as his student Plato would teach to a Sophist whom he disliked. However, Socrates attempted to portray human excellence throughout the trial.

Many historians have claimed that Plato hated the Sophists and the Athenians because of their condemnation of Socrates. Because of this hatred, he denied democracy, liberalism, and relativism as threats to true philosophy, which involves finding the ideals of life and the virtues of excellent living. Plato saw that Socrates used many of the Sophists' tools, but he went further in using them to seek the absolute truth and values in life. As a result, Socrates portrayed himself as a transitional philosopher using the Sophists' methods to find the absolute values of the classical philosopher.

References and Further Reading

De Romilly, Jaqueline. *The Great Sophists in Periclean Athens*. Trans. Janet Lloyd. Oxford: Clarendon, 1992.

Denyer, Nicholas, ed. *Protagoras and Plato*. New York: Cambridge University Press, 2008.

Diogenes Laertius. *Lives of Eminent Philosophers*. Trans. R. D. Hicks. 2 vols. Cambridge, MA: Harvard University Press, 1959.

Guthrie, W. K. C. *The Sophists*. New York: Cambridge University Press, 1971.

Kennedy, George. *The Art of Persuasion in Greece*. Princeton, NJ: Princeton University Press, 1963.

Kerferd, G. B. *The Sophistic Movement*. New York: Cambridge University Press, 1981.

Rankin, H. D. *Sophists, Socratics and Cynics*. London: Croom Helm, 1983.

Schiappa, Edward. *Protagoras and Logos*. Columbia: University of South Carolina Press, 1991.

Sprague, Rosamund Kent, ed. *The Older Sophists: A Complete Translation by Several Hands*. Columbia: University of South Carolina Press, 1972.

5

Pushyamitra Sunga, a Hindu ruler in the second century BCE, was a great persecutor of the Buddhists.

PRO   Caleb Simmons
CON   K. T. S. Sarao

PRO

Throughout much of its history, Hinduism has been promoted as a religion of tolerance. Even with the modern movement of Hindu revivalism, where fundamentalism predominates, these same practitioners argue that Hinduism at its core is tolerant of other religious traditions because of the multiplicity of goals and paths covered by the umbrella term *Hinduism*. However, the historical narrative of an individual identified as Emperor Pushyamitra Sunga has surfaced to combat the claims of religious tolerance. Emperor Sunga is said to have persecuted Buddhist monastics. This is a hotly contested issue by Hindus and non-Hindus alike, primarily in India, given the surge for a Hindu nation by the *Hindutva*. Literally "Hindu-ness," the *Hindutva* is a movement that incorporates several political parties that push for the secular democracy of India to be converted to a Hindu state.

To better understand the situation, the character of Pushyamitra Sunga and the text from which we have learned about him must be examined, and the biases the author may have had must be evaluated. Then, the historical setting in which he rose to power must be examined. This setting includes religious, cultural, and political elements. This will show that many of the religious parameters constructed into neatly organized categories simply did not exist in that time. Also, it will become evident that the Buddhists made strong political alliances with several of the enemies of the Sunga Dynasty. Upon the assessment of these elements, it can be concluded that Pushyamitra Sunga did engage in an active campaign against Buddhist monastics, but that the assault was motivated by politics rather than religion.

The Historical Pushyamitra Sunga

Pushyamitra Sunga was born in 215 BCE during the reign of the Mauryan Empire in India. The background of his family is not clearly given in any historical texts. However, in *Brhadaranyaka Upanishad* and the *Ashvalayana Shrauta*

Stotra, the Sunga family is referred to as an accomplished group of teachers from the Vishishta-advaita gotra, the school of qualified nondualism started by Ramanuja Achraya. This link would place Pushyamitra within a lineage recognized as one of the six orthodox *darshanas* (philosophical schools) by the *Manavadharmashsta* (The Laws of Manu), a text composed slightly earlier that promoted a social order based on the Vedic society and Brahmanic authority derived from Brahmans, the priestly caste (*varna*) within this system and the center for religious practice and piety.

B. N. Puri has argued that the Pushyamitra is of Persian descent based on the suffix of *mitra* on his name, but this is not likely because the term *mitra* is a common Sanskrit word meaning *friend* or *companion*. Because of the linguistic commonality between Persian and Sanskrit, both being early Indo-European languages, similar terms are not unusual. Therefore, Pushyamitra literally means "the one who is a supreme companion," which, as we will see, is a deceptive title with regard to his relationship with the emperor.

Pushyamitra is found in many historical texts and there is little debate that he was a historical figure. The most important of these texts is the *Mahabhashya*, written by Patañjali. It is unclear if this author is the same as the famous grammarian Patañjali, or if this name was used to legitimize the texts as is sometimes done in ancient cultures. Whatever the case, the *Mahabhashya* contains a detailed history of the rule of the Sunga clan as well as their predecessors, the Mauryas. Despite this account and others like it confirming the existence of a historical character named Pushyamitra Sunga, according to Baij Nath Puri (1957) in *India in the Time of Patañjali*, the *Bhagavata Purana*, a text about the Sunga ruler Bhagavata around 170 CE, makes no mention of Pushyamitra in its listing of the lineage of Sunga rulers. Again the reason for the omission is unclear, but it could be the result of internal struggles for power or an oversight by the sage composing the text, because, as we will see, Pushyamitra had strong ties to the Mauryan Empire and might have been mistaken as the last Mauryan ruler.

Pushyamitra established himself as a great warrior under the Mauryan emperor Brihadratha. Eventually he was promoted to *senapati* (literally, "lord of the army"), the head general over the Mauryan army. According to B. G. Gokhale in *Buddhism and Asoka*, in 188 BCE, while Brihadratha was examining his forces, Pushyamitra Sunga assassinated the emperor and established himself as king. Others have dated his ascension three years later, marking the date of Brihadratha's assassination in 185 BCE. Upon ascending to the throne, Pushyamitra moved the capital of the empire to Pataliputra. He also began to patronize Brahmanic temples and shrines as evidenced in temple inscriptions at Ayodhya, Barganga, and other locations. His militaristic prowess was always upheld, because he continued to refer to himself as *senapati* even after becoming *maharaja* (emperor). These inscriptions also serve as historical markers, because they were often established after some great feat by the patron. Because of this, however, the accounts are often exaggerated to exalt the patron even more.

Horse Sacrifice Legend

The Ayodhya inscription discusses one very important aspect of the reign of Pushyamitra, the *ashvamedha* horse sacrifice. This story is corroborated in Patanjali's *Mahabhashya* and in popular culture by the second- to third-century CE poet/playwright Kalidasa in his epic drama *Malavakagnimitra*. The *Malavakagnimitra* is centered on Pushyamitra's son and successor, Agnimitra, but goes into detail concerning Pushyamitra's two horse sacrifices. Thus, the tale of Pushyamitra's sacrifices must have been somewhat common knowledge. The horse sacrifice is a very important Vedic ritual in establishing the religious life of Pushyamitra and eventually perceiving his relationship with Buddhism. It was a means by which the social and cosmic orders were upheld and was a form of propitiating the Vedic pantheon. This ritual was only to be performed by "righteous" kings as mandated by *The Laws of Manu*.

The sacrifice also has strong ties to the epic tradition of Brahmanic Hinduism. The Pandavas in the *Mahabharata* and Dasharatha in the *Ramayana*, two of the most important epics of the tradition, perform this sacrifice as the righteous and rightful kings. The sacrifice was used as a threefold confirmation of legitimacy, wealth, and power. The king was legitimated as the rightful king because he was the one who preserved the social order by placating the deities. He displayed his wealth not only through sacrificing his best horse, but also through staging a lavish festival surrounding the ritual. His power was shown by allowing his best horse to wander the kingdom unrestricted for one year. This would demonstrate that as far as the horse could roam in a year was under the protection of the king. This is crucial for the Sunga Dynasty, because both rituals were performed after victorious military campaigns against a Greek coalition, which was formed between the Greeks (*yavanas*)

A horseman, detail from a the gate of a Buddhist stupa, from Bharhut, Madhya Pradesh, Late Mauryan Period, Sunga dynasty, 180–72 BCE. (Indian Museum, Calcutta, India/Giraudon/ The Bridgeman Art Library)

and Indians, particularly Buddhists. This will be discussed in much greater detail below.

There may have also been internal reasons for the first of Pushyamitra's *ashvamedhas*. His son, Agnimitra, the central character in Kalidasa's drama, had been sent away to serve as viceroy of Vidisa. Vidisa is also possibly an independent kingdom that Pushyamitra had ruled over while he was *senapati* in the Mauryan kingdom. Given Agnimitra's eventual overthrow of the kingdom, Vidisa might have been where disgruntled generals were sent. There seems to have been a certain tension between the father and son either resulting from this posting or an event that resulted in Agnimitra being sent to Vidisa. The filial ties would soon be mended, because Agnimitra's son, Vasumitra, was chosen to escort the horse during its year of roaming. This was a high honor usually bestowed on the kingdom's greatest warrior. This act would solidify the relationship and secure the stability of the Sunga Dynasty and its succession.

Persecution of Buddhist Monastic Community

Thus far there has been no mention of persecution of the Buddhist monastic community, although it is evident that Pushyamitra has strong ties to Brahmanic Hinduism. The ancient sources that accuse Pushyamitra of slaughtering Buddhists are the *Divyavadana*, a Buddhist text that contains a history of Indian rulers and their relationship to the *sangha* (the Buddhist community) and the *Ashokavadana*, the narrative of the life of Ashoka Maurya. In a very brief account, the *Divyavadana* states that Pushyamitra Sunga was one of the greatest persecutors of the Buddhist community in Indian history. According to this account, Pushyamitra sought council from various ministers as to how to become as famous as the great Ashoka, a Mauryan ruler who converted to Buddhism, which will be discussed in greater extent below.

Several ministers explained that Ashoka had become so popular by establishing 84,000 Buddhist reliquaries (*stupas*) around the empire and suggested that he do the same. However, a Brahman minister suggested that he would become more famous than Ashoka if he were to eliminate Buddhism and the *stupas*, and thus the memory of Ashoka. Pushyamitra heeded the Brahman's advice and began attacking Buddhist monasteries. Pushyamitra not only attacked the monks and nuns, he is also reported to have offered a reward for anyone who killed a monk upon the presentation of the dead body. The account given in the *Ashokavadana* is quite similar but goes into greater detail on Pushyamitra's use of the four-element army consisting of elephants, cavalry, chariots, and infantry in his attack on Buddhist monasteries. This presentation of Pushyamitra Sunga is quite different from most of the previous examples given. Therefore, the context of Pushyamitra's ascension and the shift in religious patronage must be examined to reconcile the various accounts.

Jain Dharma

Focusing on self-discipline, nonviolence, and education, Jainism or Jain Dharma originated in India in the sixth century BCE. It shares with Buddhism and Hinduism the notion of karma and the quest for enlightenment; like some sects of both of those faiths, the reverence for life leads to the practice of vegetarianism, veganism, and even the sweeping of the ground before one's footsteps so as to avoid killing insects underfoot. The Jain cosmology is similar to that of Hinduism, and the Ramayana and Mahabharata are important texts, though Jains interpret them somewhat differently. There is also a similarity to many Christian and Jewish sects in antiquity: fasting and a denial of material wealth and worldly goods are important aspects of many Jain practices. Jain monks of the Digambar sect do not even wear clothes, considering them an unnecessary material possession.

Rulers Prior to Sungan Rule

Prior to the Sungan rule, the majority of the Indian subcontinent had been ruled by the Mauryan Empire. Since its inception, the dynasty had been very diverse in its religious patronage. The founder of the empire, Chandragupta Maurya (ruled 322–298 BCE) was a patron of the Jain tradition established by Mahavira. This tradition was considered a heretical *shramana* movement by followers of the Brahmanic tradition. The *shramanas*, which also include Buddhism, were traditions that denied the authority of the Vedas and the caste system. These teachings placed the *shramana* traditions at odds with Brahmanic tradition because both the Vedas and caste were their central tenets of belief. Chandragupta, however, also patronized various temples that would now be classified as Hindu. This tradition of patronage to several varying religious tradition was not unusual for the time.

The neatly divided categories of "Hindu," "Buddhist," or "Jain" did not exist yet. Therefore, the ability to follow a multiplicity of paths was not uncommon. The dominant religious tradition was what has been described above as Brahmanic Hinduism, but to view this as a unified movement would be anachronistic. The beliefs and ritual would vary widely based on region and cultural differences. The common thread was the Vedic sacrifice and caste, with the priest class as the sacrificial officiates, but different shrines that followed a different philosophical path (*darshana*) or were devoted to a different deity would jockey for position even within what today we would call Hinduism. Thus it would be a fallacy to view the positioning for patronage as a battle simply between Hindus and Buddhists. It was a much more complex arena. However, with the conversion of Emperor Ashoka, the tension between the loosely connected Brahmanic traditions and the Buddhists grew and perhaps united the groups with another thread, that of anti-*shramana*.

Chandragupta is also important to our discussion because of his relationship with the Greek Seleucids. According to Appian of Alexandra in his *History of Rome: The Syrian Wars*, when Seleucus I entered India to conquer the Mauryan territory, he was met with greater resistance than he had planned. Thus he entered into a marriage alliance with Chandragupta. In accordance with the treaty, Seleucus was also given 500 war elephants and Chandragupta received several Persian provinces. Several Greek historians also remained in the Mauryan court to chronicle the new Greco-Indian ally.

Ashoka Maurya

Ashoka Maurya (ruled 273–32 BCE) was the third ruler of the Mauryan Empire. Early in his reign, he conducted many great military campaigns and eventually united all of south Asia under his banner. However, after his last victory in Kalinga, he realized the suffering caused by his brutal search for power and converted to Buddhism. He then began promoting the Buddhist doctrine of non-violence (*ahimsa*). This religious experience was also an interesting political move that would discourage violent coups d'état of his government, but would also alienate many followers of the Brahmanic traditions.

Ashoka began to promote Buddhism in many ways that made it the dominant religious tradition of the time. In addition to the 84,000 *stupas* he was said to have constructed, he sent missionaries throughout the empire and beyond. He even sent his son Mahindra and his daughter Sanghamitra, both Buddhist monastics, to the island of Ceylon (Sri Lanka) to spread the Buddhist Dharma. He himself is said to have developed a lifestyle very close to that of an ascetic. Much of the history of Ashoka's promotion of Buddhism is preserved in rock edicts he constructed throughout India.

Many of these edicts suggested religious tolerance; however, his patronage was causing Buddhist monasteries to grow while many of the Brahmanic temples and shrines suffered from the lack of support. The patronage of the Buddhist monasteries was so great, according to Hirakawa Akira's (1990) *A History of Indian Buddhism*, that it began to stifle the economy. Patronage was not the only problem that arose from Ashoka's promotion of Buddhism. In accordance with the doctrine of *ahimsa*, Ashoka made animal sacrifice, the center of Vedic ritual, illegal. Therefore, he essentially outlawed the practice of the Brahmanic tradition. As a result, a Brahmanic countermovement was established, with the *Dharmashastras* (Law Codes) as the collections of central rules by which life should be conducted, centered on sacrifice and purity and pollution of caste. Pushyamitra later became the epitome of this countermovement.

Ashoka also remained allied with the Greeks. He continued to exchange ambassadors with them and even mentioned the Greek rulers in many of his rock edicts. After Ashoka, the Mauryan Empire continued this relationship with

Buddhists and the Greeks, but gradually the rulers became weaker and weaker until Pushyamitra successfully overthrew the empire by assassinating Brihadratha in front of the army. After the assassination, the Mauryan Empire became divided. The northwestern portion was subsumed into the Greek Bactrian Empire, the central region became the Sunga Empire, and the eastern region was reclaimed by the Kalingas, led by the Jain king Kharavela. Thus the majority of the subcontinent abandoned patronage and practice of the Buddhist tradition. Because of the loss of much patronage by the Sunga Empire, tension arose between the Buddhists and the rulers. With the Greeks nearby and former generals, such as Yajnasena, forming hostile relationships with the Sungas and establishing their own independent states, the stage was set for the Buddhist monasteries to become political adversaries of the Sunga Empire.

The Pushyamitra Sunga Era

Pushyamitra Sunga began to distance himself from the practices of the Mauryan rulers and to establish a lineage that would place himself as the rightful king. This practice can be seen throughout south Asia when new rulers rose to power. The change was not regarded as new and innovative, but as potentially detrimental; therefore, the emperor must have been positioned within the broader history of the region. The horse sacrifice also served as a form of legitimization. The first of the two horse sacrifices was performed in Pataliputra, the very site of the edict where Ashoka had forbidden animal sacrifice. It also served as the substitute for the festivals called *samayas* that the Mauryan Empire had established. Thus Pushyamitra was seeking not only authentication, but also the approval of the people. His need for authentication by both people and the scribes that formed lineages through ancestry charts seems to validate the conversation that was the setting for the mention of Pushyamitra in the *Divyavadana*.

While Pushyamitra seems to have been accepted by many of the people, there was a movement against his rule. Puri suggests that a rival Buddhist viceroy from the then-defunct Mauryan Empire, Damstranivasin, who had established an independent kingdom, offered the Greek king Demetrius his daughter if he attacked the Sungas. P. C. Bagci (1946), in an *Indian Historical Quarterly* article, suggests that the Krmisa mentioned in *Manjusrimulakalpa* is Demetrius. The narrative seems to fit, but his conclusion is not accepted by all scholars. Damstranivasin beseeches Demetrius for the alliance on the basis that Pushyamitra is anti-Buddhist. Since the Sunga Empire had usurped the power of a Greek ally, Demetrius agreed, and the first of two Greek invasions during the reign of Pushyamitra had begun. Demetrius is also linked to the Buddhists in the Hathigumpha Inscription, where he is referred to by the name Dharmamitra, the friend of the Dharma. These invasions are widely documented in both Indian and Greek chronicles as well as archaeological evidences. The motivation, whether political or religious, seems to have been steeped in the conflict of Buddhism and Brahmanism.

First Greek Invasion of Northern India

During this time of turmoil concerning the power structure of the former Mauryan Empire, the Greeks under Demetrius, whether because of an alliance with Damstranivasin or simply to expand their kingdom, invaded northern India. The exact date of the invasion is unclear, but most scholars would agree that the *Yavana* invasion of Demetrius came within the first 10 years after Pushyamitra claimed the throne of Magdha by killing Brihadratha, ca. 187–77 BCE. Details of the invasion are given in several sources, including Kalidasa and Patañjali, as well as in the *Gargi Samhita* in the *Yuga Purana* and in an inscription at Hathi-gumpha. In *Buddhism and Asoka*, B. G. Gokhale notes that Greek coins featuring Demetrius wearing the scalp of an elephant, an obvious link to India, have been found well into the central region of Sunga territory.

The invasion was very successful in the beginning. The forces led by Demetrius conquered the lands of northern India, forcing Pushyamitra Sunga to retreat and move his capital to Rajagriha, where he would subsequently be attacked by the Kalinga king Kharavela, who obviously felt threatened by the approaching army. Amid the attacks mounting from both sides, Pushyamitra had a brush of good fortune. Demetrius and his forces learned of a civil war that was breaking out in his kingdom, and he was forced to withdraw from the campaign. Pushyamitra seized the opportunity to present himself as the *senapati* who had repelled the foreign invasion. It was at this moment in history that Pushyamitra offered the first of the horse sacrifices in Pataliputra as an example of his power and in no doubt to repay the fortunate turn of events that the gods had orchestrated. Thus Pushyamitra Sunga was able to solidify himself as the emperor of northern India.

Rule of Pushyamitra in Northern India

With Pushyamitra now the uncontested ruler, he began to punish those who had sided against him. Among the most outspoken of these groups were the Buddhist monasteries. The Buddhists in the western Punjab region had openly sided with the Greek invaders, so they were treated as political enemies of the state. Had Pushyamitra been lenient on the traitors, he would have been viewed as a weak ruler, which would have facilitated attempts to overthrow him. In this context, the claims of Buddhist texts alleging cruelty against the Buddhist monasteries and a bounty for the heads of dead monks during Pushyamitra's reign seem fully plausible. His attempt to extinguish the Buddhist *sangha* correlates with his attempts to extinguish political rivals. In the *History of the Sunga Dynasty*, B. C. Sinha (1977) holds that later in his reign, Pushyamitra lessened his persecution of the *sangha*, and the construction of several Buddhist *stupas* are attributed to his patronage, although this has been disputed by several scholars. However, this leniency was short lived because the second Greek invasion also was tied to the Buddhist community.

Second Greek Invasion

The second Greek invasion during the rule of Pushyamitra came near the end of his reign. The leader of this invasion was the Greek king Menander, Demetrius's successor, who is forever linked with Buddhism as the pious King Milinda of the *Milinda Panha*. His Bactrian kingdom extended from Kabul in modern-day Afghanistan to the Punjab in modern-day Pakistan, where his capital of Sagala was located. He is said to have converted to Buddhism after his discussion with the Buddhist sage Nagasena, as told in the *Milinda Panha*. From Menander's conversion onward, he was a great patron of Buddhism and its monasteries within the subcontinent's northwestern regions.

Much of the Buddhist art of the time reflected Greek influence. In iconography, the Buddha is portrayed with curled hair, a popular characteristic of Greek gods and busts. Even representations of Menander have elements of Buddhism within them. In a relief of the king found on the *stupa* in Bharhut, Menander is depicted holding an olive branch, which shows his relationship to Greek goddess Dionysus, and a sword with the symbol of the three jewels of Buddhism. His coins also illustrate the importance of Buddhism to his court through the depiction of the Buddhist eight-spoked wheel. Thus Buddhism is linked to one of the Sunga's neighboring kingdoms against which they vied for territory and power.

The details of the second Greek invasion are slightly more nuanced than the campaign of Demetrius. The motivation behind the campaign is not entirely obvious. What is clear, however, is that the conflict took place while the horse for the second sacrifice was roaming freely under the guard of Pushyamitra's grandson Vasumitra and his forces. It seems as though Menander took this ritual as an opportunity to attack the divided forces of Pushyamitra. Sinha argues that the horse might have wandered past the Indus River (*Sindu*) into the Greek territory. This would have been an affront to the Bactrian king for several reasons. First, if the horse were to roam into the terrain of Menander, the Sunga legion would follow it. The presence of a foreign army would certainly be enough to incite conflict. Also, the presence of the horse could be taken by Menander as a claim by Pushyamitra to the region, because the purpose of the ritual was to show the far reaches of his kingly influence. The theory of the horse breaking the boundary of the Indus seems less likely, because evidence shows that Menander's armies marched into the middle of the country (*madhyadesa*) before being pushed back and ultimately defeated in a decisive battle at the banks of the Indus by the legion under Vasumitra that was guarding the sacrifice horse.

The second invasion proved to be the flagship by which the Sunga Empire was solidified. The Greek armies were quickly expelled by the Sungan forces, and the war against Menander was exalted as a total annihilation of the enemy. However, the complete vanquishing of the Greek forces must be called into question, because Menander was able to expand his territory in the western portion of the Aryavarta, which, given its name (literally, "the Noble Sustenance"), must have been a region that produced great wealth for the ruler. Despite this small setback, Pushyamitra staged the more elaborate of the *ashvamedhas* and established himself and the Sunga Empire for several generations. With a stronghold on the region for many years to come, Pushyamitra's successors were able to loosen their policies concerning Buddhists and once again patronize multiple religious traditions.

Conclusion

In conclusion, Pushyamitra Sunga actively engaged in a war against Buddhism with many different motivations, most of which were directed back to the establishment of political stability for himself and his lineage. Coming as he did from an orthodox Brahmanic family, Pushyamitra was aware of the Mauryan preference for the anti-Brahmanic *shramana* movements. He may have even been directly affected by the lack of patronage given to Brahmanic pandits if his connection to the Vishishta lineage is accurate. Upon usurping the throne, he needed to create a niche for himself in light of the great Emperor Ashoka; therefore, he distanced himself in religious patronage and sought to erase many of the injunctions created by the former king as retold in the *Divyavadana* and the *Ashokavadana*. The conflict was then multiplied when Buddhist monasteries sided with the foreign Greek invaders led by Demetrius. As a result, Pushyamitra performed an animal sacrifice that directly transgressed Buddhist doctrine. Then he sought to eradicate the traitors by attacking them with his armies and offering rewards for their slaughter. After a period of brief relaxing of his sanctions, a conflict arose between the Greco-Buddhist king Menander and the Sungas. While the policies of Pushyamitra were harsh, they were clearly not misguided. He saw Buddhism as a threat to his ascension to the throne of the empire, and this proved to be true several times. It was only through the elimination of many Buddhists and their allies that the Sunga Dynasty was established and found stability in the region.

References and Further Reading

Akira, Hirakawa. *A History of Indian Buddhism: From Sakyamuni to Early Mahayana*. Honolulu: University of Hawaii Press, 1990.

Albright W. F., and P. E. Dumont. "A Parallel between Indic and Babylonian Sacrificial Ritual." *Journal of the American Oriental Society* 54, 2 (June 1934): 107–28.

Bagci, P. C. "Krmisa and Demetrius." *Indian Historical Quarterly* 22 (1946).

Bhandarkar, Ramkrishna Gopal. *A Peep into the Early History of India*. Bombay: D. B. Taraporevala, 1930.

Cowell, Edward B., and Robert A. Neil. *The Divyavadana: A Collection of Early Buddhist Legends*. Amsterdam: Oriental Press, 1970.

Gokhale, B. G. *Buddhism and Asoka*. Baroda, India: Padmaja Publications, N.D.

Nath, Jagan. "The Pusyamitras of the Bhitari Pillar Inscription." *Indian Historical Quarterly* 22 (1946).

Puri, Baij Nath. *India in the Time of Patanjali*. Bombay: Bhartiya Vidya Bhavan, 1957.

Sinha, Binod Chandra. *History of the Sunga Dynasty*. Varanasi, India: Bharatiya Publishing House, 1977.

Smith, R. Morton. "On the Ancient Chronology of India (II)." *Journal of the American Oriental Society* 77 (October–December 1957): 266–80.

Smith, R. Morton. "On the Ancient Chronology of India (III)." *Journal of the American Oriental Society* 78, 3 (July–September 1958): 174–92.

Strong, John S. *The Legend of King Asoka, A Study and Translation of the* Asokavadana. Princeton, NJ: Princeton Library of Asian Translations, 1983.

Upreti, Kalpana. *India as Reflected in the Diyavadana*. New Delhi: Munshriram Manoharlal Publishers, 1995.

CON

King Pushyamitra Sunga (ca. 184–48 BCE) is generally regarded as the symbol and leader of the Brahmanic revival that took place when the dynasty of the Mauryan kings, the alleged supporters of non-Brahmanic faiths, was brought to an end. The majority of the textual sources dealing with the Sungas link them to the Brahman caste. Thus, the end of the Mauryan Dynasty at the hands of Pushyamitra Sunga is seen as a victory of Brahmanic anti-Buddhist forces that had been silently at work. In other words, it is generally held that after the end of the Mauryan rule, Buddhism not only lost the royal favors it had enjoyed under kings such as Ashoka, but, as a result of the persecution by Pushyamitra Sunga, it also lost most of what it had gained earlier. Thus it has been suggested that other than destroying Buddhist monasteries and *stupas* and killing Buddhist monks, he caused greater damage to Buddhism by letting unfavorable forces loose against it. As we will see, nothing could be further from the truth.

Pushyamitra Sunga was the commander in chief of the last Mauryan king, Brihadratha. After assassinating his master, he captured power and laid the foundations of the Sunga Dynasty. His extensive empire, with its capital at

---

Ashoka (304–232 BCE)

One of the last Mauryan rulers, Ashoka governed the Indian empire when it was at its largest: his territory stretched from Afghanistan and Iran to Assam and Bangladesh and covered most of the Indian subcontinent. His military prowess helped to expand the previous bounds of the empire, and at some point in his 40-year reign he became a convert to Buddhism, which was then in its early centuries. Ashoka's conversion is traditionally credited to guilt over his treatment of his brothers (whom he executed) and the death toll of his victory in the Kalinga War. Whatever the case, his piety was noted by his people, and he left behind 33 inscriptions in stone—on pillars, boulders, and in caverns—popularly called the Edicts of Ashoka.

The edicts are mostly moralist and prescriptive, calling for kindness, generosity, fairness in the execution of justice, and the protection of many animals (including, pragmatically, all four-footed animals that are not useful or edible). It is a feature of the edicts that they generally call for behavior that is moral in intent but practical in execution, not focused too greatly on self-denial or self-burden.

Pataliputra (modern Patna), included the cities of Ayodhya, Vidisha, and Vidarbha (Berar) and extended in the south up to the Narmada River. The accounts in the *Ashokavadana*, the *Divyavadana*, and *Tāranātha's History of Buddhism* also show him as being in control of Jalandhar and Shakala in the Punjab.

Warfare seems to have been the mainstay of the reign of Pushyamitra and other kings of his dynasty. He and his descendants warred with the Andhras, Kalingas, Greco-Bactrians, and possibly the kingdoms of Panchala and Mathura (which may not have been under Pushyamitra's rule). Pushyamitra himself fought at least three major wars. One of these wars was fought against Yajnasena, the king of Vidarbha, who had remained loyal to the Mauryan Dynasty after the coup d'état. He fought the other two wars against the Greco-Bactrians, in all probability against King Menander (Milinda of the Buddhist text *Milindapanha*), whose kingdom lay to the northwest of his empire. The Greco-Bactrians had attacked northwestern India in circa 180 BCE. They eventually captured much of the Punjab, perhaps ruling from Mathura for a while, and may have even ventured as far as Pataliputra. However, in the end, Pushyamitra's forces in all likelihood recaptured Mathura toward the close of the second century BCE and may have driven the Greco-Bactrians out of the Punjab.

After establishing himself firmly on the throne, according to N. N. Ghosh (1945), Pushyamitra is alleged to have run the affairs of his kingdom with the help of his contemporary Brahman scholars, such as Manu (the author of the *Manusmriti*) and Patañjali (the author of the *Mahabhashya*) and reestablished the sacrificial ceremonies of Vedic Brahmanism. As animal sacrifices and old Vedic rituals were completely discouraged by the Mauryan rulers, who were followers of heterodox faiths such as Buddhism and Jainism, his performance of two *ashvamedha yajnas*, as K. P. Jayaswal (1918) writes, is viewed as an anti-Buddhist activity of a king who was a fundamentalist Brahman. Scholars such as Haraprasad Sastri (1910) feel that actions such as discouraging the animal sacrifices by Ashoka were a direct attack on Brahmans, because much of their power and prestige lay in the fact that they alone could perform sacrifices and thus act as intermediaries between the people and the gods. Such actions, these scholars tell us, deprived Brahmans of their long-enjoyed privilege of guiding the religion of the masses.

Sastri further maintains that the *dhamma-mahamattas* (ministers of piety) employed by Ashoka for the propagation of his policies destroyed the reputation of the Brahmans and that such an action was particularly resented by the Brahmans, because it came from a *shudra* king. Further, it is alleged, Ashoka had acted against Brahmanism by "showing up the false gods," who, until then, had been worshiped in Jambudvipa. Another well-known scholar, U. N. Ghoshal (1966), also feels that the propagation of Buddhism during the Mauryan period had disturbed the Brahmanic social and religious order.

There are also some scholars who feel that even if the atrocities committed by Pushyamitra as reflected in the *Divyavadana* are viewed as exaggerated, the acute hostility and tensions between Pushyamitra and the monks could not be denied. There thus are many scholars who view King Pushyamitra Sunga as a fanatical Brahman king who persecuted and tyrannized the Buddhists by killing them and destroying their holy places. Then there are some other scholars who take a somewhat lenient view and believe that Pushyamitra may not have been an enemy of Buddhism but that he certainly withdrew royal support and was responsible for creating an environment that the Buddhists found unfavorable for their own activities.

Accounts of Pushyamitra's So-Called Anti-Buddhist Activities

To critically examine the various textual references that mention the so-called anti-Buddhist activities of Pushyamitra Sunga would be worthwhile. The most important and perhaps earliest reference is from the *Divyavadana* (and its constituent part, the *Ashokavadana*). According to this Sarvastivadin text of the second century CE, when Pushyamitra asked his ministers how he could obtain everlasting fame, most of them told him that, as long as Buddhist law remained, he would have to construct 84,000 *stupas* as his predecessor King Ashoka had, but one of the priests told him that he could obtain everlasting fame by doing the opposite—destroying the Buddhist religion. According to this text, Pushyamitra chose the latter route and also put a bounty on the heads of Buddhist monks. Then he went to the Kukkutarama monastery at Pataliputra, intending to destroy the Buddhist region. According to these ancient accounts, he was turned away three times at the gate of the monastery by a lion's roar before he slaughtered the monks and destroyed the residence of the organization. Continuing in this way through the country, he arrived in Shakala, the modern-day Sialkot in the Pakistani Punjab, where he issued the edict of awarding a gold piece for each head of a Buddhist monk that was brought to him. According to the legend, this activity was only ended when the Yaksha Damshtranivasin, the guardian spirit of Bodhi living in this region, enabled Pushyamitra's army to be crushed, Pushyamitra to be killed, and the Maurya dynasty to come to an end.

The *Vibhasha*, a Sarvastivadin-Vaibhashika text dated in the second century CE, chronicled that Pushyamitra hated the Buddhist religion and burned holy books; destroyed *stupas*; demolished monasteries, including 500 monasteries on the borders of the kingdom of Kashmir; and slaughtered monks. According to this source, Pushyamitra was supported with *kumbhandas, yakshas*, and demons that enhanced his powers and made him invincible until he approached the Bodhi tree during his destruction of Buddhism and was vanquished by the deity of that tree, which had taken the form of an extremely beautiful woman in order to be able to approach the king.

This story is also repeated in the *Shariputraparipriccha*, a Mahasamghika text translated into Chinese between 317 and 420 CE. But the story in this text, besides being much more detailed, shifts the anti-Buddhist operations of Pushyamitra Sunga from the northwestern part of the Indian subcontinent to Bihar in the east,

The *Aryamanjusrimulakalpa*, which belongs to the early medieval times, mentions Pushyamitra Sunga in abusive terms such as *Gomimukhya* (cattle-faced) and *Gomishanda* (Gomin, the bull) in an allusion to the Vedic sacrifices that were revived under the Sungas. This text, while talking about the "evil actions" of Pushyamitra against Buddhism, tells the legend of Pushyamitra demolishing monasteries and venerable relics and killing monks after capturing the east as well as the entry into Kashmir and being defeated and dying after he turned north.

Also, Tāranātha, the celebrated Tibetan Buddhist historian, mentions that "the *brahmana* king Pushyamitra, along with other *tirthikasās*, started war and thus burnt down numerous Buddhist monasteries from the *madhyadesha* to Jalandhara. They also killed a number of vastly learned monks. As a result, within five years, the doctrine was extinct in the north" (Tāranātha 1970: 121).

Archaeological Evidence Supporting Persecution Hypothesis

Besides the textual evidence, archaeological evidence is also put forward in support of "anti-Buddhist" actions of Pushyamitra and other kings of the Sunga Dynasty. For instance, John Marshall (1955, 1975) writes that at Takshashila there is evidence of some damage done to the Buddhist establishments about the time of the Sunga. Marshall proposes that the Sanchi *stupa* was vandalized during the second century BCE before it was rebuilt later on a larger scale, suggesting the possibility that the original brick *stupa* built by Ashoka was

Buddhist stupa at Sanchi, India. (Mark Weiss)

destroyed by Pushyamitra and then restored by his successor, Agnimitra. Similarly, N. N. Ghosh (1945) writes that the gateway of Bharhut was built not during the reign of Pushyamitra but by his successors, who followed a more tolerant policy toward Buddhism as compared to Pushyamitra, a leader of Brahmanic reaction. The destruction and burning of the great monastery of Ghositarama at Kaushambi in the second century BCE is also attributed to the Sungas. For instance, J. S. Negi (1958) notes that G. R. Sharma, who was responsible for most of the excavation work at Kaushambi, was inclined to connect this phenomenon with the persecution of Buddhism by Pushyamitra. Similarly, according to P. K. Mishra:

> Although archaeological evidence is meager in this regard, it seems likely that the Deorkothar stupa, geographically located between Sanchi and Bharhut, was destroyed as a result of Pushyamitra Sunga's fanaticism. The exposed remains at Deorkothar bear evidence of deliberate destruction datable to his reign. The three-tiered railing is damaged; railing pillars lie broken to smithereens on stone flooring. Twenty pieces of pillar have been recovered, each fragment itself fractured. The site offers no indication of natural destruction. (2001)

Critique

Many Indologists, including K. P. Jayaswal (1923), H. C. Raychaudhary (1923), R. C. Mitra (1954), and D. Devahuti (1998), have expressed skepticism about the truthfulness of the Buddhist legends regarding the persecution of Buddhism by Pushyamitra Sunga. Raising serious doubts about the authenticity of the legend, Etienne Lamotte (1988), for instance, has pointed out that the only point on which the sources concur is the destruction of the Kukkutarama of Pataliputra "in the east." If there was an encounter between Pushyamitra and the Yaksha Damshtranivasin and Krimisha, it is impossible to pinpoint where exactly it took place: at Sthulakoshthaka in the Swat Valley, at the Dakshinavihara on the heights above Rajagriha or in Avanti, at the gates of Kashmir, or in Jalandhar. This is also the case with the death of Pushyamitra, which variously takes place under the Bodhi tree at Bodh-Gaya, on the shores of the southern ocean, or somewhere "in the north." Thus Lamotte points out, to judge from the documents, Pushyamitra "must be acquitted through lack of proof" (1988: 109). Agreeing with Lamotte, D. Devahuti (1998) also feels that the account of Pushyamitra's sudden destruction with all his army, after his promulgation at Shakala of a law promising *dinaras* for the heads of Buddhist monks slain by his subjects, "is manifestly false." Taking recourse to similar argument, R. C. Mitra, too, feels that "The tales of persecution by Pushyamitra as recorded in the *Divyavadana* and by Taranatha bear marks of evident absurdity" (Mitra 1954: 125).

H. C. Raychaudhury (1923) and Romila Thapar (1991) also do not believe in the persecution theory. Raychaudhury, for instance, points out that the ban on animal sacrifices did not necessarily entail antagonism toward the Brahmans for the simple reason that the Brahmanic literature itself lays stress on *ahimsa*. For instance, the *Chandogya Upanishad* mentions the importance of nonviolence and the futility of giving too much importance to sacrifices alone. Ashoka did not only ban the sacrifice of those animals that were sacrificed in *yajnas*, but even others.

Thapar opines that Ashoka's frequent exhortations in his edicts for showing due respect to Brahmanas and Shramanas hardly point to his being anti-Brahmanic in outlook. In fact, Raychaudhury notes that some of the *dhamma-maha-mattas* were concerned specifically with safeguarding the rights and welfare of the Brahmans. Haraprasad Sastri's (1910) contention is that Ashoka was powerful enough to keep the Brahmans under control, but after him a conflict began between his successors and the Brahmans that only ended when Pushyamitra assumed power, and that Pushyamitra's action was the manifestation of a great Brahmanic revolution is also indefensible.

As pointed out by Raychaudhury, some of the Mauryan kings were themselves followers of Brahmanism. For instance, according to the *Rajatarangini*, a text belonging to the early Medieval period that deals with the history of Kashmir, Jalauka was not only a zealous *Shaiva* and an open supporter of Brahmanism, but he was also quite unfriendly toward Buddhism. And Thapar writes that "since the Mauryan empire had shrunk considerably and the kings of the later period were hardly in a position to defend themselves, it did not need a

revolution to depose Brihadratha" (Thapar 1991: 201). The fact that Pushyamitra was assassinated while he was reviewing the army does not indicate there
was a great revolution. On the contrary, it points rather strongly to a palace
coup d'état taking place because by this time the organization of the state had
sunk so low that subordinate officials were happy to work under anyone who
could give them assurance of a more competent administration. Moreover, as
Thapar points out, had it been a great Brahmanic revolution, Pushyamitra would
have received the assistance of other neighboring kings such as the descendants
of Subhagasena from the northwest.

The testimony of the Buddhist legends also appears doubtful on various other
counts. The earliest texts that mention these legends are chronologically far
removed from the Sungas. The traditional narrative in the *Divyavadana*, for
instance, can, at the earliest, be dated to two centuries after Pushyamitra's death.
It is more likely that the *Divyavadana* legend is a Buddhist version of Pushyamitra's attack on the Mauryas and reflects the fact that, with the declining influence
of Buddhism at the imperial court, Buddhist monuments and institutions would
naturally receive less royal attention. Moreover, the source itself, in this instance
being Buddhist, would naturally exaggerate the wickedness of anti-Buddhists.

Further, at the time of the Sungas, *dinara* coins (Roman *denarious* gold coins)
were not prevalent. The earliest period during which they came into circulation in
India was the first century CE. Most interestingly, this legend of persecution in
which a *dinara* is offered as an award for the head of a monk is first related in the
Ashokavadana in connection with the persecution of the Jainas and the Ajivikas by
Ashoka and clearly appears to be a fabrication. To say that Ashoka, whose devotion to all religious sects is undeniable through his edicts, persecuted the Nirgran-
thas or the Ajivikas is simply absurd, and so is the story of Pushyamitra Sunga.
Thus, as pointed out by Koenraad Elst, "the carbon-copy allegation against Pushyamitra may very reasonably be dismissed as sectarian propaganda" (Elst, 2005).

Probity of the *Divyavadana* is also grievously marred by the fact that Pushyamitra Sunga is mentioned as a descendant of Ashoka, whereas he did not
belong to the Mauryan Dynasty, a dynasty of non-Brahman background. In fact,
this very fact flies in the face of the hypothesis that Pushyamitra persecuted the
Buddhists because he was a Brahman. Similarly the argument that the Brahman
backlash became intense because the Mauryas were *shudras* does not seem to
hold. Besides the fact that the Mauryas are mentioned as *kshatriyas* in the
Divyavadana, Raychaudhury has pointed out that the *Purana* statement that all
kings succeeding Mahapadma Nanda will be of *shudra* origin implies that
Nanda kings after Mahapadma were *shudras* and not the Mauryas, because if it
referred to succeeding dynasties, then even the Sungas and Kanvas would have
had to have been listed as *shudras*.

There is really no concrete evidence to show that any of the Maurya kings
discriminated against Brahmanism. Ashoka, the most popular Maurya king, did

not appear to have any vulgar ambition of exalting his own religion "by showing up the false gods" of Brahmanism. Thus the theory of a Brahmanic persecution under Pushyamitra loses much of its raison d'être. The policy of Pushyamitra Sunga appears to have been tolerant enough for the simple reason that if he were against the Buddhists, he would have dismissed his Buddhist ministers. Furthermore, the court of Pushyamitra's son was graced by Bhagavati Kaushiki, a Buddhist nun. Moreover, there is overwhelming evidence to show that Buddhism actually prospered during the reign of the Sunga kings.

As Thapar notes, many scholars have actually argued that archaeological evidence casts doubt on the claims of Buddhist texts of persecution by the Sungas. An archaeological study, recorded in *Ancient India,* of the celebrated *stupa* at Sanchi proves that it was enlarged and encased in its present covering during the Sunga period. The Ashokan pillar near it appears to have been willfully destroyed, but Marshall (1955) suggests that this event may have occurred at a much later date. According to D. C. Sircar (1965), the Bharhut Buddhist Pillar Inscription of the time of the Sungas actually records some additions to the Buddhist monuments "during the supremacy of the Sungas." The Sri Lankan chronicle, *Mahavamsa,* admits the existence of numerous monasteries in Bihar, Avadha, Malwa, and the surrounding areas during the reign of King Dutthagamani (ca. 101–77 BCE), which is synchronous with the later Sunga period.

Conclusion

It may not be possible to deny that Pushyamitra Sunga showed no favor to the Buddhists, but it cannot be said with certainty that he persecuted them. Though the Sunga kings, particularly Pushyamitra, may have been staunch adherents of orthodox Brahmanism, they do not appear to have been as intolerant as some Buddhist texts have shown them to be. The only thing that can be said with certainty on the basis of the stories told in Buddhist texts about Pushyamitra is that he might have withdrawn royal patronage from the Buddhist institutions. This change of circumstances under his reign might have led to discontent among the Buddhists.

It seems that as a consequence of this shifting of patronage from Buddhism to Brahmanism, the Buddhists became politically active against Pushyamitra and sided with his enemies, the Indo-Greeks. As H. Bhattacharyya and colleagues (1953) suggest, this might have incited him to put the Buddhists down with a heavy hand. Thus if in some parts of Pushyamitra Sunga's kingdom a few monasteries were at all pillaged, it must be seen as a political move rather than a religious one. Moreover, in such cases the complicity of the local governors also cannot be ruled out.

Jayaswal (1923) has referred to another interesting aspect of the declaration made by Pushyamitra Sunga at Shakala, the capital and base of Menander. According to him, the fact that such a fervid declaration was made not only at a place that was far removed from the center of the Sunga regime but also in the capital city of his arch enemies, points to reasons motivated by political considerations.

After Ashoka's lavish sponsorship of Buddhism, it is quite possible that Buddhist institutions fell on somewhat harder times under the Sungas, but persecution is quite another matter. Thus it would be fair to say that where the Buddhists did not or could not ally themselves with the invading Indo-Greeks, Pushyamitra did not beleaguer them. In any case, after the end of the Sunga Dynasty, Buddhism found congenial environment under the Kushanas and the Shakas, and it may be reasonable to assume that Buddhism did not suffer any real setback during the Sunga reign even if one could see some neglect or selective persecution of Buddhists. As Lamotte writes: "Far more than the so-called persecution by Pushyamitra, the successes of the Vishnuite propaganda during the last two centuries of the ancient era led the Buddhists into danger, and this was all the more serious in that it was a long time before its threat was assessed" (1988: 392–393).

References and Further Reading

Aryamanjusrimulakalpa, The. K. P. Jayaswal, ed. and trans. *An Imperial History of India*. Lahore: Motilal Banarsidass, 1934.

Bhattacharyya, H., et al., eds. *Cultural Heritage of India*. 2nd rev. ed. Vol. II. Calcutta: Ramakrishna Mission Institute of Culture, 1953.

Chakravartty, Gargi. "BJP-RSS and Distortion of History." In *Selected Writings on Communalism*, edited by P. Lahiri, 166–67. New Delhi: People's Publishing House, 1994.

Devahuti, D. *Harsha: A Political Study*. 3rd rev. ed. Delhi: Oxford University Press, 1998.

Divyavadana, The. P. L. Vaidya, ed. Darbhanga: Mithila Institute of Post-Graduate Studies and Research in Sanskrit Learning, 1959.

Elst, Koenraad. "Why Pushyamitra Was More 'Secular' than Ashoka." 2005. http://koenraadelst.bharatvani.org/articles/ayodhya/pushyamitra.html (accessed June 1, 2010).

Ghosh, N. N. "Did Pusyamitra Sunga Persecute the Buddhists?" In *B.C. Law*, Vol. I, edited by D. R. Bhandar. Poona, India: Bhandarkar Research Institute, 1945.

Ghoshal, U. N. *A History of Indian Public Life*. Bombay: Oxford University Press, 1966.

Jayaswal, K. P. "An Inscription of the Sunga Dynasty." *Journal of the Bihar and Orissa Research Society, Patna* 10 (1923): 203.

Jayaswal, K. P. "Revised Notes on the Brahmin Empire." *Journal of the Bihar and Orissa Research Society, Patna* (September 1918): 257–65.

Lamotte, E. *History of Indian Buddhism: From the Origins to the Śaka Era*, trans. by Sara Webb-Boin. Louvain-la-Neuve, Belgium: Insitut Orientaliste: 1988.

Marshall, J. H. *A Guide to Sanchi*. 3rd ed. Delhi: Manager of Publications, 1955.

Marshall, J. H. *A Guide to Sanchi. Taxila*, Vol. I. Delhi: Bharatiya Publishing House, 1975.

Mishra, P. K. "Does Newly Excavated Buddhist Temple Provide a Missing Link?" *Archaeology, A Publication of the Archaeological Institute of America* (April 2001). Available at http://www.archaeology.org/online/news/deorkothar/index.html (accessed June 1, 2010).

Mitra, R. C. *The Decline of Buddhism in India, Santiniketan*. Birbhum, India: Visva-Bharati, 1954.

Mukhopadhyaya, S., ed. *The Aśokāvadāna*. New Delshi: Sahitya Akademi, 1963. Translated by John S. Strong as *The Legend of King Ashoka: A Study and Translation of the Aśokāvadāna*. Princeton, NJ: Princeton University Press, 1983.

Negi, J. S. *Groundwork of Ancient Indian History*. Allahabad, India: Allahabad University Press, 1958.

Raychaudhury, H. C. *Political History of Ancient India: From the Accession of Parikshit to the Extinction of the Gupta Dynasty*. Calcutta: University of Calcutta, 1923.

Sastri, Haraprasad. *Journal of the Asiatic Society of Bengal, Calcutta*, (1910): 259–62.

Sircar, D.C., ed. *Select Inscriptions Bearing on Indian History and Civilization*, Vol. I, 2nd rev. ed. Calcutta: University of Calcutta, 1965.

Tāranātha's History of Buddhism in India. Lama Chimpa and A. Chattopadhyaya, trans. Simla: Indian Institute of Advanced Study, 1970.

Thapar, R. *Ashoka and the Decline of the Mauryas*. New York: Oxford University Press, 1991.

6

The Shroud of Turin is actually the wrapping shroud of Jesus.

PRO   Justin Corfield
CON   Thaddeus Nelson

PRO

The Shroud of Turin, held at the Turin Cathedral in northern Italy, has long been thought to be the burial cloth of Jesus Christ. It was used to wrap around Jesus's body after the Crucifixion and was left in his tomb when he "rose from the dead." There are several plausible theories over how it has survived, and indeed its history dates back to the late Middle Ages and is known with a fair degree of certainty. There is also much scientific evidence for the probability that it was genuine, with the main evidence against it being the carbon dating conducted in 1988 of some pieces.

The Jewish tradition of burial was to wrap the body in a cloth and bury the person on the same day of death. In the case of Jesus it was after his body had been taken down from the cross and his body was placed in the tomb prepared for him. In the New Testament of the Bible, all four Gospels (Matt. 27:59; Mark 15:46; Luke 23:53; John 19:40) refer to the body of Jesus, after it was taken down from the cross, as being wrapped in a "linen cloth"—Matthew mentions in addition that the cloth was "clean," and John mentions "cloths" (plural). Following the Resurrection, Mark refers to the sight of a man dressed in a white robe (16:5), with Luke referring to two men in "dazzling cloths" (24:4). John adds an extra piece of information that when Simon Peter and another disciple entered the empty tomb, they saw "the linen wrappings lying there. And the napkin that was about his head, not lying with the linen clothes, but wrapped together in a place by itself" (20:6–7). There are no other references in the Bible to the burial shroud. However, given the nature of the death of Jesus and his "rising from the dead," it seems likely that one of his followers would have kept the cloth. There have been numerous other surviving relics connected with Jesus, but the Shroud of Turin has been the most studied of these.

In about 1355, Geoffrey (or Geoffroi) de Charny, Lord of Lirey, in France, seems to have first publicly showed a cloth that he claimed was the Shroud of Jesus. He was a French landowner and soldier and was involved in much of the fighting at the start of the Hundred Years' War. He defended Tournai against the English in 1340, and two years later fought at the Battle of Morlaix, again fighting the English. Five years later, he took part in a Crusade, going to Smyrna (modern-day Izmir, Turkey), and in 1349 was involved in a French attack on Calais. Captured by the English, he was taken to England as a prisoner, but seems to have been ransomed soon afterward, returning to France and writing a book on chivalry, which gained attention in scholarly circles. Geoffrey de Charny was killed by the English at the Battle of Poitiers in September 1356, and it is known that his wife publicly displayed the shroud soon afterward.

Although many sources cite his wife as being the person who first displayed the shroud, the earliest medieval written mention of the shroud dated from 1389, in a memorandum of the Bishop d'Arcis of Troyes. This refers to the shroud having been exhibited some "thirty-four years or thereabouts" beforehand, putting it within the lifetime of Geoffrey. The relatively specific mention of "thirty-four years" certainly ties in with the last years of Geoffrey's life—the battle of Poitiers being one of the major events in French history at that time. Seeming to confirm the connection between Geoffrey de Charny and the shroud, in 1855 a small pilgrim's medallion from the period was found and taken to the Muse'ee de Cluny in Paris. It shows the arms of Geoffrey de Charny and his wife Jeanne de Vergy and has a small depiction of what could be the shroud. It seems to indicate that some people might well have gone to the shroud as pilgrims in order to pray there for inspiration and would then get a medallion as a souvenir. Although Geoffrey may have been the first to exhibit the shroud, it is easily possible that it might have belonged to his wife.

Geoffrey and his wife's son, also called Geoffrey de Charny, inherited the shroud, which he exhibited at Lirey in 1389—the event that led to the bishop's memorandum. His daughter Margaret de Charny gave the shroud to Louis I of Savoy in 1453, and it was owned by the House of Savoy (later Kings of Italy) until the 20th century. The great-grandson of Louis, Emmanuel Philibert, moved the shroud to Turin in 1578, and his son Charles Emmanuel I, started plans for a special chapel for the shroud, which was installed in the Guarino Guarini Chapel in 1694. It was then exhibited at the marriages of various members of the House of Savoy—in 1737, 1750, and 1775—and in 1821 it was displayed to mark the accession of Charles Felix as King of Savoy, and in 1842 to mark the marriage of Victor Emmanuel II, who in 1861 became the first king of Italy. After negotiations which started in 1973, in 1983 it was finally bequeathed by the great-grandson of Victor Emmanuel II, King Umberto II of Italy (in exile since 1946) to Pope John Paul II, and although it has remained in Turin Cathedral, it is the property of the papacy.

If the history of the shroud is known for certain back to 1355, the historical mystery surrounds what happened to it during the 13 centuries after the Crucifixion, if it is genuine. John's Gospel clearly describes the shroud, so there is the probability that it might have been taken by one of the followers of Jesus. If so, it is likely that it would have been treasured by the early Christians, but this is

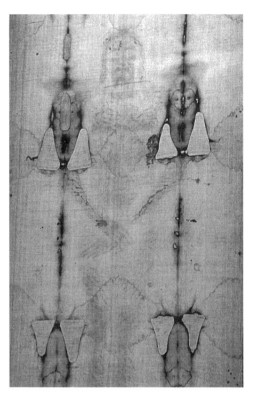

The Holy Shroud, a fourteen foot-long linen revered by some as the burial cloth of Jesus, on display at the Cathedral of Turin, Italy. (AP Photo/Antonio Calanni)

all supposition. Most historians now identify the shroud with the Byzantine relic known as the Mandylion or "Image of Edessa," held in Constantinople until the city was sacked in 1204. It was a cloth that purported to have on it the face of Jesus Christ, and there is some evidence—written and visual—that the face on the Mandylion and the shroud were similar.

The Mandylion had been taken to the city of Constantinople in September 944 by pilgrims from the city of Edessa (modern-day Urfa), in southern Turkey, where it was claimed to have been held since the sixth century. The city has some links with the Bible, with some historians identifying it as the biblical city of Ur, although this is disputed by the vast majority of historians. Located along a major caravan route, in common with many other places in the region, Edessa had a small Christian community. A Roman headquarters, it had been used by the Emperor Valerian in 260, and in the fourth century, Saint Ephram had lived there, founding a school of theology. The people in Edessa followed the Nestorian beliefs, which were found to be at variance, theologically, from those of the Byzantine rulers, and the school was closed in 439. The city was captured by the Sassanids in 605, retaken by Heraclius, and then captured by the Arabs in 639 who brought Islam to the city. What happened to the shroud during this period is a matter of pure conjecture, but its transfer to Constantinople in 944 is mentioned in contemporary Byzantine documents.

The contemporary description of the Mandylion was that it was a picture of Christ "which was not made by human hands." There is also a reference made by the rusader Robert de Clari who described a "figure" on a cloth or shroud, which was held at the Church of Saint Mary at Blachernae in Constantinople and was shown to the public each Friday. The original account by Robert de Clari still survives in the Copenhagen Royal Museum. However, with the destruction of Constantinople during the Fourth Crusade in 1204, the relic—like many others—was lost.

To link the shroud with the Mandylion rests not just on the few necessarily vague written accounts. The face on the shroud is well known, and it shows the image of a man with a fairly distinctive face and beard, with several easily noticeable facial features. There are some images of the Mandylion surviving, and all these show a similar face—indeed they only show the face. This has been easily explained by the shroud having been folded in half, and then in half again, with the face in the center of the exposed piece of cloth. It would then have been mounted on a board and a lattice covering put on top to draw attention to the face, as seems to be the case in the images of the Mandylion. The folding of it seems likely, as the shroud shows the naked image of a man, and the Byzantines would probably have hidden this, especially with their belief that it was of Jesus. The earliest surviving image of the Mandylion dates to about 1100 CE and is in a fresco above an arch in the Sakli "Hidden" Church in Goreme, in Cappadocia, in central Turkey. There are also two images of the Mandylion from the 12th century. One is in a Serbian church at Gradac in modern-day Croatia, and the other is at Spas Neriditsa near Novgorod in the Russian Federation, with a later one surviving at a monastery at Studenica, Serbia, dating to the 13th century. A Byzantine coin from 945 shows an image of Christ similar to that on the shroud, and there is also a 12th-century mosaic portrait of Jesus in the cathedral at Cefalu, in central Sicily. However, it should also be pointed out that a coin from the reign of Justinian II (reigned 685–695 and again 705–711) has a similar portrait of Jesus, as does another Byzantine coin of 692. This seems to imply that the image of Jesus resembling the face on the shroud was well known long before the Mandylion came to Constantinople.

If the Mandylion and the shroud are the same, there are a number of possible connections that tie Geoffrey de Charny's family to the sacking of Constantinople in 1204. One tradition ties it to Hugh de Lille de Charpigny, who was present at the sacking, and it later ended up with lands at Aegion in Greece, somehow passing into the de Charny family, probably through his friend and companion-in-arms Guillaume de Champlitte, who was also at the sacking of Constantinople and whose wife, Elizabeth de Mont St. Jean, was the sister of Pons de Mont St. Jean, the great-grandfather of Geoffrey de Charny. Another possibility was that it might have come into Geoffrey de Charny's family through his wife Jeanne de Vergy. One of her great-great-great grandfathers was Otho de la Roche, who also took part in the sacking of Constantinople in 1204. A third link exists, and this involves the Knights Templar.

The Order of the Poor Fellow-Soldiers of Christ and the Temple of Solomon, better known as the Knights Templar, was a secretive Crusader military order established in 1119, with strong ties to central France, from where many of its leaders came. The order was known to possess many secrets and had been established in Jerusalem with a particular interest in holy sites, having carried out its own excavations at the site of the temple in Jerusalem. There has long been much controversy about a "head" known as "Baphomet," which was used in some of their meetings and revered by the knights. When the order was destroyed in 1307, interrogations of the knights were unable to reveal exactly what "Baphomet" was—certainly no trace of it has been found, and historians and pseudo-historians have debated whether or not it could refer to the shroud, or even the head of Jesus or John the Baptist. There have been many theories, and one curious one worth noting is that by authors Lynne Picknett and Clive Prince (1994). In their book *Turin Shroud—In Whose Image?*, Picknett and Prince have gone as far as to suggest that it was the image of the head of Jesus used by Leonardo da Vinci in the making of the Shroud of Turin—using early photography—meaning that the shroud is a late medieval creation, but it does actually show the head of Jesus.

There is one crucial piece of evidence for case of the Templars having the shroud, or at least having access to it. This comes from a Templar preceptory in Templecombe, Somerset, England, where Molly Drew, during World War II, discovered an old panel painting that was revealed after the plaster had fallen. It showed the image of a Christ figure, with a face similar to that on the shroud. Given that the order was suppressed in 1307, and with carbon dating placing Drew's panel back to about 1280, the link between the shroud and the Templars seems possible. Holger Kersten and Elmar Gruber (1994), in their book on the shroud, suggest that the wooden piece could have been part of the box in which the shroud might have been kept.

The Templars were involved in the sack of Constantinople, and the connection between Geoffrey de Charny and the Knights Templar is close, although he himself was not a member of the order. When the last grandmaster of the Templars, Jacques de Molay, was burned at the stake outside Notre Dame Cathedral, Paris, on March 18, 1314, his close aide who was burned with him was Geoffrey de Charnay (*sic*), the preceptor of Normandy for the Knights Templar. Historian Noel Currer-Briggs has traced that the man burned with Jacques de Molay was the uncle of Geoffrey de Charny, who put the shroud on public display in about 1355.

Whether the shroud was held by the de Charny family since the sacking of Constantinople, or whether it was held by his wife since that time, or even whether it was owned by the Knights Templar, it is clearly possible that Mandylion and the shroud could be the same item; and given their similarities, it seems probable that they were the same. This, therefore, manages to push back the existence of the Shroud of Turin to as far back as the sixth century, when it was celebrated as being in Edessa. The written records cannot provide any more information, but there is plenty of evidence on the shroud itself that provides far more positive evidence that it was the burial cloth of Jesus Christ.

The image on the shroud has been minutely examined and found to clearly not be made by paint. There are several theories over how it could have been formed. The microanalyst Walter McCrone (1990), from Chicago, has maintained that the image on the shroud could have been made from iron oxide pigments using gelatin as a binding medium. The major problem with this is that the image on the shroud represents an extremely tall man, and some of the features show an odd perspective. The most prevalent theory about these questions is that the image on the shroud is capable of being formed naturally when a body is covered in various substances—as would have happened to the body of Jesus when it was placed in the tomb (John 19:40). Historian and author Holger Kersten, in his work with Elmar Gruber, ground aloe and myrrh, and the resulting experiment showed that it is possible to imprint the image of somebody onto a shroud-like garment. Kersten carried out several experiments, and this tended to back up his theory and also show how the image shown in the shroud was slightly misshaped, possibly resulting from the cloth closely following the contours of the body—the body being lain on the cloth, which was then used to cover it up. The cloth would then be stitched to help people carry the body of the deceased. The fact that the cloth follows the shape of the body explains the reason why the figure on the shroud was so tall, the image not being a two-dimensional image. Given that the exact method of treatment of the body of Jesus, and indeed others in Jerusalem during the same period, is not known for certain, it is clearly possible for the image to come from the person buried in the shroud without any supernatural significance being given to the existence of this image.

As the nature of the image can be easily explained, what it depicts needs close examination. There are many parts of the image that tally with the Gospel descriptions of the Crucifixion of Jesus, but there are discrepancies with medieval beliefs that are important, as some feel the shroud was created in the late Middle Ages. The most obvious is that the nails used in the crucifixion of the man whose image is left on the shroud were nailed through his wrists. Although church paintings of the period, and indeed for many centuries afterward, show the nails going through the palms of his hands, this would have been impossible in an actual crucifixion, as the palms were not capable of taking the weight of someone's body. Parts of the bones of a crucifixion victim were found in June 1968 to the north of Jerusalem in a burial ground, which can be dated to the time of Jesus. On these it is quite easy to see that the nails passed through the wrists. The next controversial point about the hands was that the thumbs of both hands couldn't be seen. This is because when the nail passed through the wrist, it led to a contraction of the thumb, evidence of which has been noted when experiments were done on amputated limbs. If the figure on the shroud had been faked, it seems unlikely that the forger would have both been able to transpose the nailing from the palms to the wrists and be aware of the effects of this on the thumbs. This therefore suggests that the image is of someone who was either crucified by the Romans or in a manner similar to that used by the Romans. However, there is a problem of rigor mortis. If rigor mortis had set in, it would, obviously, have been impossible to rest the hands of the figure in the shroud over his groin. This again tallies with the biblical account that the body of Jesus was taken down very soon after he had died. It has also led to theories that Jesus was thought to be dead when he was brought down from the cross—either having fainted or having been drugged.

A number of writers have been able to observe many other pieces of evidence of the image. There is clear evidence of flagellation, with the image on the shroud clearly having been naked at the time. It has also been possible to spot evidence of other parts of the biblical account of the death of Jesus—the Crown of Thorns and the spear in the side. These all tally with the Gospel accounts.

Historians and scholars have also studied the weave of the cloth. The method of weaving in a herringbone pattern was common in Syria at the time of Jesus, but unknown outside that region. Although this does suggest that the cloth came from Syria, it still does not prove that it was that of Jesus, although once again it points away from being made in medieval France. However, the pattern of the weave as well as the method of lying the body of Christ on the cloth is shown in a fresco in a church in Nerezi, near Skopje, the capital of Macedonia (the former Yugoslav Republic of Macedonia), dating from 1164, and also from the Codex Pray, a prayer book compiled in Budapest in 1192; as well as in an *epitaphion* from Thessaloniki in Greece, dating from the 14th century, all pointing to the fact that details of a cloth similar to the Shroud of Turin were well known for centuries. This once again suggests the link between the Mandylion and the shroud.

Historian Ian Wilson has been keen to prove the validity of the shroud or whether it was made after the time of Jesus. His book, *The Turin Shroud*, first published in 1978 and then enlarged as *The Blood and the Shroud: New Evidence That the World's Most Sacred Relic is Real* (1998), provides much of the detail on the shroud and the possible reasons for it being genuine. For most skeptics, the main reason for doubting its genuineness rests on a series of carbon dating tests carried out in 1988. These have been seen by many as proof that the shroud dates to the late Middle Ages. This would therefore mean that the cloth held by Geoffrey de Charny, first shown by either himself or his widow, is not the same one as currently in Turin Cathedral, suggesting that at some stage the medieval "original" (which may, or may not have been that of Jesus) was replaced by a late medieval "copy."

There is a strong belief in the infallibility of science, and many commentators have seen the carbon dating as proof that the shroud could not be that of Jesus. However, many serious doubts have arisen as to the accuracy of the carbon dating. The first reason for querying the carbon dating concerns the part of the shroud that was removed to be tested. As the Turin authorities were loath to let any significant part of the shroud be burned for carbon testing, the small piece that was tested—and destroyed during the testing—was from the edge of the cloth. This immediately raises the query whether it might have been a part of a

---

The Shroud of Turin Research Project

In early 1970s, a group of scientists, mostly from the United States, formed the Shroud of Turin Research Project (STURP). In 1978, 24 scientists from STURP spent five days gathering evidence from the shroud, resulting in a 1981 report that put to rest many of the theories of spurious origins:

No pigments, paints, dyes or stains have been found on the fibrils. X-ray, fluorescence and microchemistry on the fibrils preclude the possibility of paint being used as a method for creating the image. Ultra Violet and infrared evaluation confirm these studies. . . .

Microchemical evaluation has indicated no evidence of any spices, oils, or any biochemicals known to be produced by the body in life or in death. . . .

We can conclude for now that the Shroud image is that of a real human form of a scourged, crucified man. It is not the product of an artist.

Source: Shroud of Turin Web site. "A Summary of STURP's Conclusions." Available at www.shroud.com/78conclu.htm. (accessed June 1, 2010)

Renaissance repair—the shroud having been repaired on a number of occasions. However, the real problem over the carbon dating was the lack of a "control" test whereby material of a known date was burned and the results compared with those from the shroud.

The first pieces of the shroud removed for examination on November 24, 1973 were studied in detail by the Belgian textile expert Gilbert Raes, director of the Laboratory for Textile Technology in Ghent. At that time the amount of the shroud that would have to be removed for carbon dating was too big for it to be considered. However, 15 years later, technology had advanced such that one small piece was removed on April 21, 1988. This piece was cut away by Giovanni Riggi, a specialist in microscopy, but the method of testing it had changed. Initially, parts were going to be sent to seven laboratories. Subsequently, it was changed and a new protocol was reached with the British Museum, London, acting in a coordinating role. The tests involved pieces from the shroud being tested against two control specimens from cloth of a known age. As a result, as soon as the piece was detached from the shroud, in the full blaze of publicity and in front of witnesses, it was then taken into an adjoining sacristy where it was cut into three pieces, and the control cloth was placed in nine small tubes to be sent to three radiocarbon laboratories. The first three—an actual piece, along with two "control" pieces—were tested at Tucson, Arizona, with the next three tested in Zurich, and then the last three pieces were tested at the radiocarbon laboratory in Oxford, England. The various bodies agreed to communicate the results to the Vatican ahead of publicizing the details, and on October 13, 1988, at a press conference held in London, Edward Hall from Oxford, his chief technician Robert Hedges, also from Oxford, and Michael Tite from the British Museum in London announced the results. All they had with them was a blackboard upon which the dates "1260–1390" were written. Tite explained to the press that the radiocarbon dating had come up with that period of years to a 95 percent degree of probability, with the shroud's raw flax being made into linen possibly in or around 1325. Although many people feel that the carbon dating has proved that the shroud, in spite of all the circumstantial evidence tying it to the Mandylion, was made in the late medieval period, the scientific account of the carbon dating was not published until February 16, 1989, in the scientific journal *Nature* (Damon 1989).

There were, however, several problems involving the carbon dating. The first was raised by the right-wing Brother Bruno Bonnet-Eymard of the Catholic Counter-Reformation in the Twentieth Century. He pointed out that while the piece of the shroud was removed in front of cameras, the putting of sections of the piece into canisters for testing was done in secret by Tite and an elderly cardinal, and he accused Tite of having "switched" the samples. Kersten and Gruber suggest that this was because the image on the shroud was not "supernatural." They felt that the blood on the shroud proved that Jesus did not die on the cross but in the grave—or at any rate on the shroud. Others have suggested that the washing of the body of Jesus, necessary for the image to form on the shroud, might have been the cause of the blood.

However, Kersten and Grueber had a few other reservations over the whole carbon-dating process. As well as the possible switching of the pieces of the shroud and the two "control" cloths, they had queries over exactly which cloth was used as the control. The dates given by the three radiocarbon laboratories varied considerably, not just with the cloth from the shroud—presuming it had not been swapped—but with the tests on the cloth from the "controls." One of the pieces used in the control was stated, in *Nature* magazine, as coming from the cope of Saint Louis d'Anjou, great nephew of King (later Saint) Louis IX. However, despite efforts by Kersten and Grueber to track down the cloak, which had last been restored in 1965, they were not able to discover where it was now located. Kersten and Grueber went further and suggested that rather than testing the shroud against medieval cloth, it would have been important to test it against ancient cloth and cloth of a known date. They themselves had found plenty of ancient cloth from the Middle East at the Victoria and Albert Museum in London that could have been used.

Ian Wilson's (1998) criticism of the carbon dating is different. He pointed out that the carbon dating left many questions unanswered. The weave of the cloth of the shroud was different from the controls, and as each cloth was photographed by the various laboratories—many without scales so it is impossible to determine, to any degree of accuracy, the size of the pieces being tested—it would have been possible for even lay observers to guess which parts belonged to the shroud and which did not.

This leads to the study of pollen found on the Shroud of Turin. Trying to locate pollen was the idea of Max Frei, who was head of the Zurich police laboratory. He had written on the flora of Sicily and used clean strips of adhesive tape to remove pollen from parts of the shroud. By March 1976 he had been able to differentiate between pollen from 49 different plants on the shroud—one being from the cedar trees of Lebanon, and others from halophytes, plants that need a very high salt content that would have flourished around places such as the Dead Sea. He was able to prove that the shroud does have pollen of plants that are found only in the Middle East, and many found largely in the Holy Land. This proved that the cloth had been, for part of its history, in the Holy Land—presumably prior to it being taken to Edessa. The accuracy of his work was proven by the location of a rice pollen. This was easily explained because the Shroud of Turin was displayed from the balcony of the castle of Vercelli in northern Italy in 1494 and 1560, which at that time was in the center of the main rice-growing region in Europe.

Undoubtedly, questions remain about the shroud, and there are anomalies and gaps in the story of how it moved from Jerusalem to Edessa, how it survived the sacking of Byzantium, and how it ended up in France. However, all the theories of it being fake—as a painting or an early photographic image—can either be totally disproven or leave far more questions unanswered. For most people, including the hundreds of thousands of pilgrims who have flocked to Turin each time the shroud has been placed on public view, the shroud remains the burial cloth of Jesus.

References and Further Reading

Craik, Jamie E. "The Templars, the Shroud, the Veil and the Mandylion." *Templar History Magazine* 1, 1 (Fall 2001): 17–20.

Currer-Briggs, Noel. *The Shroud and the Grail*. London: Weidenfeld and Nicolson, 1987.

Goldblatt, Jerome S. "The Amazing Facts of the Turin Shroud." *Bulletin* (April 5, 1983).

Gove, Harry E. *Relic, Icon or Hoax? Carbon Dating the Turin Shroud*. Bristol, UK: Institute of Physics Publishing: Bristol, 1996.

Kersten, Holger, and Elmar R. Gruber. *The Jesus Conspiracy: The Turin Shroud and the Truth about the Resurrection*. Shaftesbury, UK: Element, 1994.

Laidler, Keith. *The Divine Deception: The Church, the Shroud and the Creation of a Holy Fraud*. London: Headline, 2000.

McCrone, Walter C. "The Shroud of Turin: Blood or Artist's Pigment?" *Accounts of Chemical Research*, 23:3 (1990) 77–83.

Picknett, Lynn, and Clive Prince. *Turin Shroud—In Whose Image?* London: Bloomsbury Books, 1994.

Damon, P. E., et al. "Radiocarbon Dating of the Shroud of Turin," *Nature* 337:6208 (February 16, 1989), 611–615.

Walsh, John. *The Shroud.* London: W. H. Allen, 1964.

Wilson, Ian. *The Blood and the Shroud.* London: Weidenfeld and Nicolson, 1998.

Wilson, Ian. *The Turin Shroud.* Harmondsworth: Penguin, 1979.

Wilson, Ian, and Barrie Schwortz. *The Turin Shroud: The Illustrated Evidence.* London: Michael O'Mara Books, 2000.

CON

The Shroud of Turin has become a highly recognizable symbolic object, tied to Jesus Christ, his death, and Resurrection as told in the Christian Gospels. The shroud is a piece of intricately woven linen cloth, roughly 4.3 by 1.1 meters in size. When unfolded, it appears to contain an image of a crucified body. Supposedly, the shroud was used to wrap Jesus after his Crucifixion and remained behind after his Resurrection. This story holds a place in the hearts of many believers, offering them a direct tie to important events lost nearly 2,000 years ago. While many are willing to accept this on faith, others have exposed the shroud to scientific inquest, meant to understand the actuality of such claims. In almost every case, the shroud has been shown to be either a forgery or an artistic piece passed off as real. In response to these results, many who believe that it is the burial cloth of Jesus have presented arguments to attempt to disprove the scientific studies. These arguments are often not valid, and no arguments have actually been presented as positive evidence that the shroud was tied to Jesus.

Evidence against Authenticity

Perhaps the first and most important piece of evidence against the authenticity of claims that the Shroud of Turin was used to wrap Jesus Christ in death is the history of the object. Clear points of concern surface from the early history of the shroud that illustrate it was recognized as a fraud from its first showing. The record of the shroud begins in the town of Livey, France, in 1355 CE, where it was owned by Geoffrey de Charny. He offered no explanation for the origin of the shroud but simply claimed that it was the burial cloth of Jesus. Near the end of 1389, Bishop Pierre d'Arcis wrote to Pope Clement VII, telling him of an investigation launched by his predecessor, Bishop Henri de Poitiers, and the final results of his study of the shroud. Bishop de Poitiers had told Bishop d'Arcis that an artist had confessed to him that he had created the work and that it was not the actual shroud in which Jesus was buried. Pope Clement VII, after weighing the evidence, declared that the shroud was a fake and that it could be displayed as a representation, but not as an authentic relic.

It would seem that after such a confession, the tale of the shroud should have ended in the late 14th century. However, Charny's granddaughter Margaret, resumed showing the shroud as authentic during the early and middle 15th century. During this period, there were additional questions of the shroud's authenticity, showing that it was not held as a reputable item during Margaret's ownership either. In fact, her husband recorded the shroud in his papers only as an image, not as the actual burial cloth of Jesus. In 1453 Margaret willingly sold the shroud to the Royal House of Savoy. While in their care, it was threatened by a fire in 1532, an event that will be important in further analysis of the shroud's authenticity. When the Royal House moved its capital to Turin in 1578, the shroud went with it. From this location, where it remains today, it gained its familiar name. In 1983 the Savoy family gave the shroud to the pope and the Catholic Church, which has not stated that it is authentic and instead leaves such matters to the faith of individuals.

This brief history of the Shroud of Turin offers a number of important points concerning the issue of authenticity. When Pope Clement VII considered the shroud, one point that his decision was influenced by was the fact that Geoffrey de Charny could not provide an explanation for its origins. This was a very forward-thinking methodology. To a modern archaeologist, a record of an artifact's origin and successive owners is its provenance. Modern scholars rely heavily on provenance, as did Pope Clement VII. Without such records, it is impossible for scholars to tie objects to their origins. What this means for the shroud is that not only is it impossible to state with a high degree of accuracy that it is authentic, but also there is no way to state that it even existed before 1355. Within the light of a confessed forger, this problem alone should cast doubt on the proposed linking of the shroud to Jesus around 30 CE.

Factors for Proving Authenticity

There remain many who still claim the shroud is in fact the burial cloth of Jesus. To best address these continued claims, we can easily look at what evidence would support such a position and see if it exists. Unfortunately, DNA from Jesus can't simply be found and compared to the portions of the shroud that appear to show blood. Since there is no such method of directly linking the shroud and Jesus, its epistemology must be approached. This means looking at how the shroud fits into the already established body of scientific knowledge about the past, based on the evidence that can be gathered.

One way the shroud would have to fit within the existing knowledge of Jesus is that it should date in creation to the early first century CE. This is so that its creation might predate the Crucifixion. Until 1989 this was an issue of great contention because it was very difficult to determine exactly when it was made. By the 1980s, the possibility of carrying out carbon-14 dating on the shroud became a reality, with more efficient methods that would not require the destruction of a large portion of the cloth. Carbon-14, or radiocarbon, dating measures the predictable decay of a specific type of radioactive carbon atom found in all organic material, carbon-14, over time to find an accurate date for the death of living things. The results, published in 1989, showed that the plants used in creating the fibers composing the shroud were most likely harvested between 1260 and 1390 CE. Such a date is strong evidence against the shroud being used to wrap Jesus's body.

Believers of the shroud's authenticity have not let the results of carbon-14 dating keep them from supporting a much older age. There have been numerous arguments as to the validity of these findings based on potential inaccuracies in the radiometric dating. The best-known claim of problematic carbon-14 dating focuses on the fire the shroud survived in 1532. According to proponents of the shroud's authenticity, the heat and chemical exposure in the fire would have contaminated the shroud, providing a more recent date through carbon-14 testing. Such a hypothesis is problematic for two reasons. First, carbon-14 dating of burnt or charred materials is a common practice in archaeology and can produce accurate results. Next, H. E. Gove (1996) makes the point that even if the fire were to somehow introduce additional carbon-14 to the shroud, in order for carbon introduced in 1532 to skew tests in the 1980s by 1,100 to 1,200 years, 86 percent of the carbon in the shroud would have had to originate in the 1532 fire. Such an inclusion of carbon is not only incongruous with scientific understanding of fires, but it also would leave an obvious addition of material that has never been found on the shroud. There is thus no reason to believe that the shroud changed its carbon makeup in 1532 in a way that would meaningfully alter the carbon-dating results of the 1980s.

While the 1532 fire could not have altered the shroud's dating, there are other hypotheses put forward in defense of a first-century dating, other possible influences on the outcome of the tests. One popular explanation is that the samples of the shroud taken for dating included threads from a modern repair and were thus skewed toward later dates by the inclusion of younger materials. This theory does not fit well with the actual events involved in sample selection. The process involved the oversight of two textile experts and inspection of the sample under magnification. Even the most modern stitching at the time of the tests would have been visible under a microscope and would certainly have been noticed by the experts. There is no actual evidence to support the existence of such thread in the area tested either, simply the guess of those who favor an earlier date for the shroud's manufacture. Without such evidence, researchers must rely on the opinion of the textile experts and not the guesswork of shroud enthusiasts.

An additional source of contamination, and a subsequent misleading carbon-14 analysis, that has been proposed is microscopic organic compounds, such as bacteria, on the surface of the shroud. Such a defense is erroneous based on both the methods used in analysis and in the ability of such materials to significantly alter the dating of the shroud. The carbon-14 testing was carried out at three separate universities, in Arizona, England, and Switzerland. Each facility used methods of cleaning the cloth to remove foreign contamination. Between all three sites, any significant source of contamination would have been removed by one method of cleaning or another. As with the 1532 fire, a large proportion of the sample, 64 percent, would have to be composed of modern contamination to turn a first-century date into a date in the 13th or 14th century. This would leave only 36 percent of the sample as the actual shroud fabric. The cleaning would not have left anywhere near this level of contamination. Even if they had, it would not have been capable of removing all of it, and certainly such a large amount of contamination would have easily been detected.

Claims that the radiocarbon dating of the shroud was inaccurate are a problematic example of ad hoc hypotheses, meant to explain away evidence contrary to one's desired outcome. There is no evidence to support any inaccuracies, and the methodology involved supports the position of the universities concerning the shroud's date. Methodologically, the analysis is robust. Three universities, using different preparation methods, arrived at similar dates, close enough to be beyond the likelihood of chance. To further assess the accuracy of the tests, each university tested three additional samples of cloth that were of known age. The results were similar to the shroud in the closeness among the universities' findings, but it is also possible from these data to say that the dates provided were accurate based on known information. This illustrates that the methods used were accurate and that the preparation and analysis of the shroud should be trusted as similarly accurate.

Basis of Arguments for Authenticity

With the work of Max Frei, supporters of the shroud's authenticity found some support for their position in pollen fossils. Supposedly these miniscule particles were lifted from the shroud's surface with tape and, when analyzed, they showed an origin in the Middle East. This would seemingly match the epistemological model of Jesus's life and place the shroud within the area of his burial. However, such agreement is not positive proof of a link between the two. It would offer no evidence of time frame or the owners of the cloth. This piece of the puzzle was also problematic in that it was not able to be repeated. In 1978 the Shroud of Turin Research Project (STURP) took another course of taped samples from the surface of the cloth. These lacked corroboration for the pollen fossils observed by Frei, calling into question his results as potentially missampled. It is important to stress that even if such pollen remains were on the shroud, this at best can be seen to place it at some point in the region that Jesus came from, but not provide ample direct evidence of use of the cloth in his burial.

While the 1978 STURP tape samples have been used in studying potential pollen samples, this was not the original purpose in collecting them. STURP lifted 36 samples from portions of the cloth both within the image and in areas with no apparent image in an attempt to find support for the idea that the shroud was not formed through artistic means. The findings were that the samples did not provide evidence of man-made pigments or painting and that the image was created through some other means. This theory has been prevalent since at least 1898, when the shroud was first photographed. In these, it appeared that the shroud was a negative image, dark where it should have been light and light where it should have been dark. Proponents of the theory that the shroud was used to bury Jesus state that no artist would have been able to produce such an image. A final point to support the shroud's authenticity concerns details that appear in the shroud that artists in medieval Europe would not have known about. If any aspect of the shroud's formation is truly beyond the ability or knowledge of artists in the 13th and 14th centuries, this would raise the question of how exactly the shroud was made. The question that must be asked is if any of these claims is true.

Arguments that Medieval Artists Could Not Have Crafted the Shroud

Arguments that medieval artists could not have crafted the shroud generally fall into two categories: unknown historical points and anatomical accuracies. The most widely stated claim is that the points in the shroud where the crucified victim would have had nails placed are in his wrist, not the hand, as was prevalently illustrated in artistic representations. Modern scientific study has shown that placing the nail in the hand would not have worked, as they cannot bear the weight of an adult human. However, the image on the shroud only has one such nail, and it appears to actually be in the lower portion of the hand, not the wrist. Other supporters have claimed that the flagellations shown in the shroud would have been unknown in medieval Europe. This ignores contemporary artistic representations of just such marks. No aspect of the shroud's imagery appears to be outside of the knowledge of potential medieval artists, and while this does not prove that it is constructed by such individuals, it means that this cannot be precluded either.

A second line of reasoning used to counter claims that the shroud is only an artistic interpretation concerns the anatomical details preserved in the image of the figure. If anything though, the anatomy present indicates in various ways that the shroud is just such a human endeavor. Perhaps the most important point is that the proportions and layout of the body do not match those of real humans. The body is extremely disproportionate to actual anatomy, appearing

The Face on the Shroud: Jesus or Leonardo?

Recent scholars, looking at the face on the Shroud of Turin, have come to the conclusion that what created the image on the shroud had to have been a photographic process, as the shroud contains no pigments and the image is in the negative. However, this has led to a question about who would have had both the knowledge and the materials to create such an image, and, most importantly, just whose face was used. Lillian Schwartz of the School of Visual Arts in New York has scanned the face on the shroud and come to the conclusion that it has the same dimensions as the face of Leonardo da Vinci, one of the few people at the time of the shroud's supposed creation who would have had the knowledge of both human anatomy and the photographic process needed to create such a forgery, as well as the access to the materials to carry it off. Using an early photographic device, a *camera obscura*, and a sculpture of his face, da Vinci could have used silver sulphate to make the fabric sensitive to light, leaving a permanent, negative image of the face on the sculpture—possibly his own.

tall and lanky. This has lead to the proposition that Jesus, if it was his burial cloth, would have suffered from a genetic disorder called Marfan's syndrome (Nickell 1993).

A better explanation may be found in gothic art, which frequently depicted humans in such a drawn out manner. Additionally, it has been noted that the hair seems to hang down as if the figure were standing, not laying recumbent, as would have been the practice in first-century Jewish tombs. This observation does not require that the shroud would have been created artistically, but it does not speak well of the defense that the shroud is perfectly correct in physical details. Of similar concern is the position of the legs, one of which is shown straight and out of place with the associated footprint. If a real body had directly created the image, one would expect a flexed leg to match with the foot. A final point is the clarity of the image. It appears that the cloth was wrapped around a still body and then not moved. Besides the difficulty in placing the body without significant movement, after death the body would have settled and moved slightly as rigor

Enhanced photograph of what is believed by some to be the face of Jesus Christ as it was impressed in the Shroud of Turin. (Chiesa Cattolica Italiana)

mortis released. What the shroud actually shows is an idealized individual whose positioning and physical body fit better with an artistic interpretation than an actual human corpse.

If the details of the shroud do not preclude artistic work and the biology of the individual suggests it, STURP's findings that there were no pigments involved in the creation of the shroud should be questioned. This is exactly what Walter C. McCrone did in 1989, using better equipment and a lifetime of experience as a microanalyist (McCrone 1990: 77–83). Using STURP's sample tapes, McCrone was able to detect two common pigments, red ochre and vermillion, as well as other evidence of painting on the shroud. McCrone was able to show clear evidence of the use of pigments in both the body and bloody images. He was also able to determine that the variety of red ochre used was not available until after 800 CE, offering additional evidence for the earliest possible dating of the shroud's creation. The presence of pigments is not at all surprising, as the bloody parts of the image remain red to this day, something that would not be expected from actual blood, which turns brown over time. When assessed in light of the details present in the shroud, McCrone's analysis indicates an artistic origin.

Persistence of Pro-Authentic Argument

At this point, it is clear that the Shroud of Turin was likely created well after the time of Christ's burial and that it shows evidence of being a man-made image. Even in light of these facts, individuals still claim that the shroud must have been the burial cloth of Jesus. To bolster their position, they present the interpretation of the shroud as a negative image, popularized by photographs taken in 1898, and to the fact that the image does not penetrate through the fabric of the shroud as evidence that no one in the 14th century could create it. Part of the interpretation of this position lies in theories about how the shroud's image may have formed through contact with Jesus's body. Like all claims, these should be analyzed before they are blindly accepted.

Proponents of the body contact theory hold that direct contact with the herbs and oils or their vapors used in cleaning Jesus would have marked the fabric with an image of Jesus's body. This model is quite problematic, as vapors do not travel in a straight line, nor are they focused in the way that would be necessary to form the image of the shroud. Attempts to duplicate this method of formation have met with failure, creating blurry images completely unlike that of the shroud.

Supporters of the shroud's authenticity claim it could not have been created through painting. Scientists who have studied the shroud have presented evidence that shows this likely is not true. Beyond his findings of paint on the shroud's surface, McCrone was able to locate an instructional book from the 1800s explaining a 14th-century technique for creating images that may have been used to make the shroud. In fact, this method appears to have been meant specifically for creating almost invisible images on cloth. This fits well with the date of forgery presented to Pope Clement VII. Joe Nickell (1983) added support to the theory that the shroud was painted by performing a trial of his own. By placing cloth over a model of a human and dabbing it with dye, he was able to present an image that matched the shroud. Nickell found that the images of both his reproduction and the actual shroud were not the true negative that shroud enthusiast claimed would be the result. The beard and hair of the individual actually appeared as positive images.

There is an epistemological argument against the idea that the shroud could not be a painting. This deals with how it fits into existing knowledge of Christian artistic traditions. As noted before, the body of Christ on the shroud fits better with gothic artistic tradition than actual human anatomy. The artistic representation of Jesus fits well with a long chain of development that began in the middle of the second century, when the first images of Christ appeared. Before this point, the anionic nature of early tradition prevented the creation of any divine images. A further step toward the shroud appeared in the sixth century, with the development of a theology of unmade images. These were icons supposedly created not by people, but by a divine act, a theory that will be explored more in depth at a later point. The shroud itself can be seen as a part of these artistic and theological traditions, which are also composed of artistic representations. This is not absolute proof that the shroud was a human-created item, but in conjunction with the evidence of paint, the impossibility of the vapor method of creation, and the proven existence of artistic methods for creating similar images, it is safe to say that the shroud was an artistic endeavor.

Basing on Belief

There remains one final argument that shroud supporters frequently fall back on when the overwhelming scientific and historical evidence is presented. Shroud proponents state that it was a unique item created through a onetime miraculous action that has never occurred since. In general, claims of divine origin and power are not considered scientific or acceptable as evidence in science, history, or archaeology. This is because they cannot be tested and disproved, a cornerstone of the scientific method as it is used across these disciplines. Such arguments are within the realm of faith and certainly are valid for people to embrace and believe if they choose. It is precisely because of this that faith cannot be disproved or otherwise assessed scientifically.

Much of the religiously based argument for the shroud's authenticity is based on the uniqueness of the Resurrection as told in the Gospels. The first major issue concerning this is that scholars do not all agree that the Resurrection in the Gospels, as interpreted today, is accurate. The Gospels were written well after the time of Jesus's life by at least a number of decades, and the story of a physical Resurrection may have been a later interpretation. It is likely that for the Jews of Jesus's time, the idea of a resurrection meant something different, referring to an inclusion in the community as a whole at the final day of God. Debate on this issue remains, and many individuals would eschew this interpretation in deference to their own faith-based beliefs, making it a relatively ineffectual point of contention. Still, it is important to remember that the events in the biblical narrative may not be accurate records of real-life history. Perhaps the largest biblical challenged to the shroud's authenticity is that the text does not mention it at all. Instead, it mentions a pair of cloths and nothing of a miraculous image. Various theories have voiced concern whether the shroud was one of these cloths or an original temporary cloth, but they lack support from historical sources, functioning more as ad hoc arguments.

Argument Based on Radiation Theory

Those who support the idea that Jesus's Resurrection removed the body from the tomb and subsequently altered the shroud look to the realm of physics for their validation. They posit that the body of Jesus could have been transformed into energy in the form of radiation. Physics does allow for such a transformation, but not within the confines of the biblical stories. The energy released in such a transformation would be extremely vast, sufficient to destroy the shroud and much of the surrounding countryside. It is possible to fall back to a faith-based position, effectively that the transformation occurred but was somehow divinely limited. This position reenters the realm of nonscientific evidence, with all the problems inherent in such a stance. Looking past the problem of the limited radiation force, we again are forced to deal with the issue of image clarity. Radiation can be focused through various scientific means. The transition of a body into energy would possess no such ability to focus itself, resulting in a distorted, or likely, undistinguishable image. Looking at it as an effect similar to a camera, an analogy made by some shroud proponents, it would be more like exposing an entire role of film to the sun and then taking a picture through the camera lens. The shroud would be expected to show a blackened circle instead of a human image. As a scientific argument, the focused radiation image hypothesis is unsupported and contrary to observable evidence.

A further argument made, based on the theory that Jesus's Resurrection released a form of radiation, concerns the 1989 radiocarbon dating of the shroud. The hypothesis is that the radiation may have altered the chemical makeup of the carbon isotopes in the fabric of the shroud. This would potentially cause the material to date to a much younger period than it was actually from. Potentially, this could be true, but scholars and shroud proponents have no method to prove it. This theory does not follow the scientific assumption of uniformitarianism, meaning, that it is not based on observable events that have happened, been recorded, measured, and studied. In short, scientists have never witnessed a divine resurrection and studied what it does to the radiocarbon age of fibers. While there is no way that the hypothesis of resurrection-altered carbon-14 cannot be disproved, neither can its supporters point to an event where this has been known to occur.

Conclusion

No matter what how intensely the Shroud of Turin is studied and found to be a 14th-century forgery, there will doubtlessly be some who continue to approach the question of the cloth's origin and nature from a faith-based position. There is nothing wrong with this, and for them the shroud will always be tied to the biblical story of Jesus's Resurrection. Using this belief as evidence to scientists, historians, and archaeologists remains impossible. These scholars work through methodology that does not function in the realm of faith, instead being limited by testability and uniformitarianism. Divine radiation and similar arguments that fail these requirements must then be left to people who already base their decisions on religious beliefs as to the origin of the shroud.

There are other explanations that have been formulated for the creation of the shroud in its many years of popularity. However, the evidence for such positions is often less robust than the theory of a painted shroud and is home to various holes of missing facts. One such theory is that the shroud was an early attempt at photography by Leonardo da Vinci. This is quite a puzzling idea, as the shroud clearly shows marks of paint and was known to exist before Leonardo was born. Not surprisingly, the cloth has also attracted tales of the Knights Templar. However, there is no historic evidence that the shroud was ever brought back from the Crusades by the knights. These fanciful histories are attractive in that they offer an explanation for the shroud's origin, which some consider hidden in mystery, but in the end, they ignore the scientific analysis of the shroud just as much as any explanation of the shroud being Jesus's burial cloth.

The concluding word on the Shroud of Turin must be this: it was not wrapped around Jesus in his tomb after he was crucified. There is quite a bit of evidence as to what actually occurred or to how the shroud came to be. While none of the evidence is, on its own, a definite point of proof, in conjunction they present a robust theory that cannot be ignored. The cloth was not known of until the 14th century, when it first went on display. Soon after this, an artist actually confessed to forging it through completely natural means. Modern analysis has come to support this interpretation. Radiocarbon dating places the shroud's creation at the time the confessor said it was. Historical and experimental studies have shown that the shroud could have been made during that period, even though it might appear strange to modern viewers. Finally, the presence of coloring agents on the shroud corresponding to the body and blood makes it quite clear that this was the method by which the image came to be.

Shroud supporters have attempted to argue against these points, finding potential areas of dissonance or questionable tests. By and large, these accusations have proven unlikely. It is also important to remember that even if something as important as the carbon-14 dating were found to be in error, this would not support the position that the shroud was originally used in the burial of Jesus. It is necessary that any such claims actually present positive proof, not just negative analysis of other studies. In the absence of such data, we must work from the null hypothesis that the Shroud of Turin was not used to bury the biblical Jesus.

References and Further Reading

Damon, P. E., et al. "Radiocarbon Dating of the Shroud of Turin." *Nature* 33 (February 16, 1989): 611–15.

Fagan, Garrett G., et al. *Archaeological Fantasies*. New York: Routledge, 2006.

Frei, Max "Nine Years of Palynological Studies on the Shroud," *Shroud Spectrum International,* 3 (June 1982), 3–7.

Gove, H. E. "Dating the Turin Shroud—An Assessment." *Radiocarbon* 32, 1 (1990): 87–92.

McCrone, W. C. "The Shroud of Turin: Blood or Artist's Pigment?" *Accounts of Chemical Research* 23 (1990): 77–83.

Nickell, Joe. *Inquest on the Shroud of Turin*. Buffalo, NY: Prometheus, 1983.

Nickell, Joe. *Looking for a Miracle: Weeping Icons, Relics, Stigmata, Visions and Healing*. Buffalo, NY: Prometheus, 1993.

Shermer, Michael. *Why People Believe Weird Things: Pseudoscience, Superstition, and Other Confusions of Our Time*. New York: Freeman, 1997.

7

A Staffordshire inscription points to the location of the Holy Grail; it may be in Wales.

PRO John Lee
CON Juliette Wood

PRO

The Holy Grail, substance of legends and myth, has been the subject of entertainment for countless generations of people and countries, especially Welsh and Scottish cultures. In their myths, legends, and stories, the Holy Grail has attracted the attention of scholars of literature and history to discover the ancient origins of this story. This legend has also provoked amateurs and professional scholars to discover the location of the Holy Grail. Several scholars have discovered inscriptions from Staffordshire, England, that point to the grail being located in Wales. This section attempts to support the claim of Staffordshire through the inscriptions and presents a discussion of an historian's interpretation of this claim.

The Holy Grail comes from the Latin *gradale* in the 19th century meaning dish or cup (Barber 2004: 95). It has also been associated with *krater* or the two handles on a cup or Greek vase. The word has been used in Catalonia in the wills and accounts of the people as two *gradales* or cups. In addition, it has been associated as a broad large dish, which was an object of value for the rich and the famous (Barber 2004: 96). The first use of the term grail as referring to the Holy Grail was in the medieval romances, with the origins of the word grail from the French culture.

The Legend of the Holy Grail

The Holy Grail was a cup, plate, or dish that Jesus Christ drank or ate out of during the Last Supper before his Crucifixion. Legend has it that Joseph of Arimathea, a Jewish Sadducee priest and a merchant, had it in his hand to catch the blood of Jesus Christ at the cross and had transported it to Wales, in England. It has also been claimed that Mary Magdalene, Jesus's female friend, had the cup. Also, some Mormon scholars have speculated that Mary Magdalene (along with other women, possibly) was married to Jesus Christ and that she produced heirs for him. The lineage of Christ was known as the sangreal or royal lineage. This forms the basis of the story of the Holy Grail, but there is an additional

Joseph of Arimathea collecting Christ's blood at the Crucifixion. From the Quest of the Holy Grail and the Morte d' Arthur, about 1300–1350. (The British Library/StockphotoPro)

twist that the Knights Templar had taken it to England on their journeys. This story can be found in Wales in the legends and mythologies of the Welsh people. These legends have placed Joseph of Arimathea as the central figures of the legends with Percival being the knight who saved the grail. The stories of King Arthur have the Knights of the Round Table searching for the grail in various places in Britain. These stories trace heroic episodes that the knights had to face trials before actually seeing the Holy Grail. The Cathars, a religious group, the Templars, a monastic knight group, and the Gnostics have been added to the legend as either carriers of the grail or part of Mary Magdalene's connection to the Holy Grail.

The First Theory of the Grail: Sangreal or the Royal Blood Line of Christ

The Holy Grail has also been symbolized as the holder or container of the royal bloodline or sangreal (blood royal) of Jesus Christ and the attendant seed of Jesus Christ. Mormon author Vern Grosvenor Swanson argues that Jesus Christ shed atoning blood to save the world, but he also donated his blood to a royal bloodline (Swanson 2006: 10). He proposes that Jesus was of the Judaic lineage, while Mary Magdalene and Mary were of the tribe of Ephraim (45). According to Mormon beliefs, these two tribes were separated in the past but reunited in the royal marriage of both lines in Jesus and his wives. Jesus was the inheritor of the Israeli kingship through his bloodline from David and married Mary, who was an inheritor of the Israeli royalty through the tribe of Ephraim. Together they created a royal family. Because of this royal family, through children of Jesus, they created a lineage that ultimately ended in Joseph Smith, who became the inheritor of the kingdom of Jesus Christ (Swanson 2006: 344).

Through an elaborate tracing from before the beginning of time, Swanson traces how the lineage of Jesus Christ went to Great Britain where Jesus learned the secrets of the gospel through the Druids in Britain and brought back this knowledge to Jerusalem (Swanson 2006: 41). As part of this lineage, Jesus was destined to be king. Jesus goes there to learn Nicodemus's trade, who is his caretaker, learns about his genealogy and family, teaches his family about his truth, and establishes a church in Glastonbury and learns of the Druidic mysteries (Swanson 2006: 42–44). The Druids were religious intellectuals who studied the stars, math, architecture, and other universal secrets. Then through three cultural imperatives, Swanson claims that Jesus had to have been married. The first were the Gnostics, where in the Gospel of Thomas, Mary Magdalene is portrayed as the receiver of special knowledge and mysteries and who had a special relationship with the savior, which implies marriage (Swanson 2006: 55). Then he proves that marriage was sanctioned by Judaic law as an obligation of a rabbi and every Jewish man (Swanson 2006: 71). Then he proves that Jesus had to have been married, according to Mormon belief, in eternal marriage as was obligatory for Jesus as well as his followers (Swanson 2006: 78). He then traces Jesus's travels through the medieval legends by claiming that King Arthur might have been a descendant of Joseph of Arimathea (Swanson 2006: 215). He links the Cathars, who believed that Mary and Jesus had sexual intercourse, which the Catholics refute (Swanson 2006: 237). Then he weaves the Templars into the tale as the bearers of another secret lineage (a false lineage) that was protected by them, and then to attempting to find another secret in the temple (Swanson 2006: 241). He finally cites a third temple that was built by the Templars in the church at Roselyn and hypothesizes that the three kingdoms represent the two lineages united as one in the third column. Swanson returns to the British theory of their descent from Israel and the Hebrews and uses DNA tracing to show the descent from Jesus to Joseph Smith, who is the *messiah* who will restore the gospel. He claims that Joseph Smith knew that he was descendant from Jesus Christ and therefore a king of Israel.

The Second Theory of the Grail: Arthurian Romances

The Holy Grail has been discussed in British literature for many centuries with the first discussion by Chrétien de Troyes, an author of knight stories and the author of *The Story of the Grail* (Barber 2004: 15). This story is about the encounter of Percival, who sees the grail in a procession. He has had to accomplish many trials to obtain even this vision. Chrétien writes three continuations that elaborate on this story by involving Sir Gawain (Barber 2004: 13–15). Chrétien conceives of the grail as a mystery and something that ignites awe in the beholder. He describes how Percival was confused by candles while seeing the grail (Barber 2004: 92). In addition, the grail is a holy thing that carries the Eucharistic sacrament. It is precious and made of gold (Barber 2004: 93). The grail is also a source of food, which supplies blood and wine to the Knights of the Round Table (Barber 2004: 101). In addition, Chrétien connects the grail to the Christian faith as the dish of the Lord's Supper (Barber 2004: 93–94). In addition, the grail is described as being used to heal Lancelot and other knights from wounds (Barber 2004: 101). Thus in Chrétien, the Holy Grail is a mysterious sacred object that provides miracles of healing, food, and spiritual nourishment for the knights.

The Holy Grail is next described by Robert de Baron, who wrote *L'Histoire du Graal* in the 1200. This story traces the history of the grail from the Gospels and places Joseph of Arimathea as the hero of the story (Barber 2004: 41). Joseph's brother-in-law, Bron, becomes one of the knights of King Arthur's Round Table. Arthur's father, Uther Pendragon, is the founder of the Round Table, but this is a parallel to the table of the Last Supper, the grail knighthood, and finally the Round Table itself. In the Round Table, there is one seat left vacant, which is supposed to be the seat of the future king of the Roman Empire, namely King Arthur himself (Barber 2004: 44). Finally, Percival is made keeper of the grail after Bron dies (Barber 2004: 45). This book is trying to link the Holy Grail with the Gospels and history. Furthermore, the grail symbolically becomes the dish or chalice of the Catholic Mass. For Catholics it is a symbol of the cup that collected Christ's blood and is intimately connected to the Mass (Barber 2004: 98). It becomes the ultimate symbol of Jesus Christ celebrating the Mass (Barber 2004: 98).

The third book is called *Perlesvaus* written by Jean de Nesle of Flanders in 1239. This book describes the character Perlesvaus as the assistant of Sir Lancelot as they trace the path of the grail to Arthur's castle (Barber 2004: 39). Perlesvaus attempts to defend the castle from 12 knights and he kills himself, but the Holy Grail appears and heals him (Barber 2004: 39). This story discusses Sir Lancelot's part in the grail legend.

The fourth book is *Lancelot*, which tells the story of Lancelot, Guinevere, and the ill-fated Camelot (Barber 2004: 57). The grail becomes a healer and a provider of food to these knights. The last grail book is by Wolfram von Eschenbach, a German writer around the turn of the twelfth century, who discusses the grail in the company of the angels in his *Parzival* (Barber 2004: 83).

In addition to the French origins of the grail, historians have proposed that it has derived from the legends of Celtic myths. Theodore de la Villemarque, in the *Conte populares Bretons* (1840), describes the grail in the bardic basins of

Celtic stories and legends (Barber 2004: 240). Villemarque believes that the Breton fables inspired the French romances with their ideals of the grail. Ernst Renan wrote *La poesie des race Celtiques*, which explains that the grail is a quest for sovereignty and an initiation of knights as contained in the poems of Peredeur's initiation (Barber 2004: 241). Thus the grail becomes the barding cups or initiation stories of the Celtic myths.

Richard Barber, the author of *The Holy Grail*, believes that the Holy Grail comprises the secret traditions of mystical practices suppressed by the Catholic Church (2004: 321). These practices were contained in a medieval book called *The Sworn Book*, which contained secret names and rituals that would allow the follower to obtain vision of Christ in 28 days. The rituals consisted of fasting, practicing Mass twice, praying, and reciting the prayers of the book (Barber 2004: 389). After performing these, the practitioner would obtain a vision or trance of Jesus Christ.

This is similar to the story where a knight, through self-discipline and denial as well as trials obtains, a vision of the Holy Grail (Barber 2004: 389). So the Holy Grail is this secret tradition that is hidden in *The Sworn Book*, and the Catholic Church suppressed the secret tradition because it threatened the ritual and the control of the priests by allowing individuals to achieve a vision by their own efforts in 28 days (Barber 2004: 389). These romances are for the select few who understand the symbolism of the Holy Grail. The Catholic ritual forced individuals to undergo the ardor of priesthood and recitation of the Mass for a longer period of time. These stories and legends have inspired the imagination and hope of many generations of readers. The Holy Grail has come to symbolize the perfection or the hopes of a generation and has been a symbol of the quest of the human soul for the divine. In recent years, the legend has become a target for conspiracy theories as contained in the book and movie *The DaVinci Code*. It has also become an expression for perfection and ardor in the newspapers and magazines. As a result, the Holy Grail has been a mysterious concept throughout Western literature and religion to symbolize the search for human perfection and imagination, which could be another origin of the grail.

The Third Theory: Staffordshire Location

The grail is placed in Staffordshire because of a stone called the Shepherd's Monument where an inscription is carved on the face. This inscription describes the lineage of Jesus Christ, who was supposed to have been entrusted to carry the grail unto the present day. This Shepherd's Monument is located in Shugborough Hall. The grail was also believed to have been hidden away in White Castle, which some historians believe is Whitton Borough Castle near the Shropshire border. It is at the Shropshire border that a cup that bears the name *grail* was discovered near a gravesite.

Shugborough Hall

One of the prominent sites in England related to grail lore is Shugborough Hall, the ancestral home of the Earls of Lichfield, in Staffordshire. Maintained today by the Staffordshire County Council and the British National Trust as a stately home open to public tours, Shugborough Hall is home to the Shepherd's Monument, which some believe points to the home of the Holy Grail. The monument, which was commissioned in 1748 by Thomas Anson, the earl at the time, is a marble slab depicting a group of shepherds examining a tomb, in a mirror image of Nicolas Poussin's painting "The Shepherds of Arcadia." The interesting part to grail lore is the seemingly haphazard arrangement of 10 Roman letters that many believe is a code pointing to the grail's location. Many have speculated on the code's meaning, and in 2004 two code breakers of World War II fame from England's noted Bletchley Park attempted to crack the code, but to no avail. However, in 2006 Louis Buff Parry, a Canadian cryptologist, claimed to have deduced some of the code's meanings, stating that the symbols indicated that the grail was buried somewhere close, although it has yet to be found.

The stone is hidden in a shepherd's monument built by Thomas Anson in 1748. In the monument, there is a marble tablet that is about 20 feet wide and 2 feet thick. The tablet has a picture carved in it of a shepherd and shepherdess contemplating heaven. The tablet has inscriptions on the bottom in two lines with 10 letters separated by periods. The stone inscriptions say D.O.U.O.S.V.A.V.V.M. An unknown hand inscribed these codes, but the builder, Thomas Anson, has links to the Prier de Sino, a secret society of Templar. Poussin, the French artists, drew an inverse image of the shepherd's stone that has the inscription on it. He has connections to the Prier de Sion (BBC, March 17, 2006). Some believe that Poussin inverted the letters as codes to the Templar (BBC, March 17, 2006).

Louis Buff Parry, a cryptologist, has attempted to translate the cryptic message. He says that the *D* and *M* stand for 1,500, the Roman numeral, which signifies the 1,500th verse of Genesis. The *VVA* stands for bloom or the bloom of Joseph that is contained in the 1,494th verse of Genesis. It believes the stone builder's stone has been lost. Parry believes that the stone will be found in Staffordshire and the Holy Grail will be discovered there (BBC, March 17, 2006).

Another cryptologist was an American code breaker who used a code matrix and discovered that if the letters *SEJ* were inversed they would create the word Jes or Jesus Defy. Historians believe that this was a symbol of a Christian sect that believed Jesus was an earthly prophet instead of the Son of God (BBC, November 26, 2004). He used this as a keyword for the rest of the code and discovered 1,2,2,3 as numbers in a code matrix on the side of the monument, which he believes will point to the location of the grail.

The location at White Castle also has shepherd's songs that might be linked to the one in Staffordshire (BBC, November 26, 2006). These songs denote the Arcadian or pastoral themes of the Staffordshire monument, and some historians believe this to be collaborating proof of the Staffordshire claim.

In conclusion, the Staffordshire claim is more believable because there is actual physical evidence claiming the existence of the grail. In addition, the Staffordshire claim has connections to actual people, who were connected with the Templar. In addition, there are two physical evidences—namely, Staffordshire and the White Castle location—that cite the shepherd song as part of the grail story. The other sources of the grail legend are based on speculation on royal lineage and romance stories, which are not as convincing as physical proof.

References and Further Reading

Baigent, Michael, Richard Leigh, and Henry Lincoln. *Holy Blood, Holy Grail.* New York: Dell, 1983.

Barber, Richard W. *The Holy Grail: Imagination and Belief.* Cambridge, MA: Harvard University Press, 2004.

British Broadcasting Company (BBC). "Code Points Away from Holy Grail." November 26, 2006. Available at http://news.bbc.co.uk/2/hi/uk_news/england/beds/bucks/herts/4040127.stm (accessed June 1, 2010).

British Broadcasting Company (BBC). "Holy Grail Lies 'at Stately Home.'" March 17, 2006. Available at http://news.bbc.co.uk/2/hi/uk_news/england/staffordshire/4818084.stm (accessed June 10, 2010).

Donington, Robert. *Wagner's "Ring" and Its Symbols: The Music and the Myth.* London: Faber, 1963.

Franke, Sylvie. *The Tree of Life and the Holy Grail.* East Sussex, UK: Temple Lodge Publishing, 2007.

Gardner, Lawrence. *Bloodline of the Holy Grail: The Hidden Lineage of Jesus Revealed.* Beverly, MA: Fairwinds, 2002.

Gardner, Lawrence. *The Magdalene Legacy: The Jesus and Mary Bloodline Conspiracy: Revelations beyond the Advance Code.* San Francisco: Weiser Books, 2007.

Glatz, Carol. "At Mass in Valencia, Pope Uses What Tradition Says Is Holy Grail." *Catholic News* (July 10, 2006).

Goering, Joseph. *The Virgin and the Grail: Origins of a Legend.* New Haven, CT: Yale University Press, 2005.

Hansen, H. T. "Foreword." In *The Mystery of the Grail: Initiation and Magic in the Quest for the Spirit*, by Julius Evola, Rochester, VT: Inner Traditions, 1996.

Loomis, Roger Sherman. *The Grail: From Celtic Myth to Christian Symbol*. Princeton, NJ: Princeton University Press, 1991.

Swanson, Vern Grosvenor. *The Dynasty of the Holy Grail: Mormonism Sacred Bloodline*. Springville, UT: Cedar Fort, 2006.

Wagner, Wilhelm. *Romance and Epics of Our Northern Ancestors, Norse, Celt and Teuton*. New York: Norroena Society Publisher, 1906.

CON

Legends regarding the location of the Holy Grail, the cup of Christ, with which Joseph of Arimathea is said to have caught the blood of Jesus at the Crucifixion, are many. The grail has been thought to be in Israel, Syria, France, England, and the United States, among many other locations. One of the most persistent grail legends has to do with a certain inscription on a monument in Staffordshire, England, which supposedly indicates that the grail is close-by. However, despite the fact that the inscription was made over 250 years ago, and intensive searches have taken place ever since, the location of the grail has never been determined. Despite the efforts of a legion of amateurs and many professional code breakers (such as the famed British cipher experts from Bletchley Park), nobody has ever been able to conclusively state exactly what the monument is communicating and even if it is regarding the grail. By looking through the history of the monument and its builder, we will be able to see that it is most unlikely that the encoded letters on the monument have anything to do with the grail.

Shugborough Hall is situated in Staffordshire, England, not far from the city of Lichfield. In the 17th century, a local lawyer, William Anson, purchased a house and some land, which became the core of an important estate. A new house was constructed to reflect the family's growing status, but the most significant change to the house and gardens was the work of the two great grandsons of the first William Anson, Thomas and George. Thomas, born in 1695, was a sophisticated, educated man with an interest in the classical arts and architecture of ancient Greece and Rome. His brother George, born in 1697, was a famous naval officer who sailed around the world between 1740–1744. During this eventful voyage, his ship captured a Spanish treasure galleon. The prize money made him immensely wealthy, and some of this wealth was used to improve the estate and the house. In 1747 he was named Lord Anson, and the following year he married Lady Elizabeth Yorke, daughter of the first Earl of Hardwick. The Ansons were a prominent family who wanted to create a setting befitting their wealth and prestige. Between 1745 and 1748, just before the new Lord Anson and his bride came to live at Shugborough Hall, the architect Thomas Wright carried out a number of extensions and improvements. Lord and Lady Anson had no children, and Thomas inherited his brother's fortune, which enabled him to make more improvements to the house and grounds. Thomas Anson was a member of the British Parliament and active in the local community. He commissioned his friend, the architect James Stuart, to design a series of eight monuments for the garden and parklands. The landscaped garden at Shugborough Hall is typical of the period, containing monuments and decorative statuary as well as plants. These structures embody both the sophisticated aesthetics of the 18th century and the personal ideals of an influential and cultured family. Subsequently, the family suffered severe financial reverses, and a large proportion of the house contents were sold in 1842.

Today the house and the estate are open to the public. Information about the Anson family during the period when the Shepherd's Monument and other monuments in the garden were being constructed can be found in the family and estate papers. Many of these have been deposited in the Staffordshire Record Office and the William Salt Library in Stafford. The history of the monument on the Shugborough Hall Web site is based on these sources. One of the monuments in the garden, known as the Shepherd's Monument, has become associated with the mystery of the Holy Grail and a secret society of warrior knights. It has a carved bas-relief based on a painting by the French painter Nicolas Poussin. The painting depicts shepherds gazing at a tomb inscribed with the words "Et in Arcadia Ego." There is also a series of cryptic letters, $_D$.O.U.O.S.V.A.V.V.$_M$., with the first and last ones lower than the rest. This is surrounded by a rustic stone arch, which in turn is set inside an outer structure carved in the Doric Greek style. The letters and the fact that the carved relief is a mirror image of Poussin's original painting have attracted the attention of cryptologists and grail hunters for whom the letters present a code that reveals the true meaning of the Holy Grail.

Background

The story of the Holy Grail first appeared in medieval romances written in Europe in the 12th century. The grail was a mysterious object associated with abundance and danger. It was identified with the cup from which the founder of the Christian religion, Jesus Christ, drank at the Last Supper on the night before his death. On that occasion, he blessed bread and wine and shared it with his apostles. This event is still commemorated among Christians in Communion services and in the celebration of the Mass. Accounts from the New Testament in the Bible say that a man named Joseph of Arimathea offered to bury Christ in his own tomb. According to medieval romances, Joseph used the same cup to catch Christ's blood as he was being prepared for burial. This event is not mentioned in biblical accounts. The combination of biblical and legendary material forms the basis for the medieval story about the Holy Grail, which was used by Jesus Christ and brought by Joseph of Arimathea to Britain during the time of King Arthur. The knights of King Arthur's court undertook a quest to find the Holy Grail, and a few worthy knights succeeded. After the quest was achieved, the grail was taken away into a supernatural realm and never seen again. Medieval romances were more concerned with the adventures of the knights than with the theological significance of an object associated with the sacrament of Communion and the Mass. However, since the revival of interest in Arthurian tradition in the 19th century, the grail itself has fascinated many writers. Numerous theories about its meaning, history, and present location have been put forward. In the context of the search for the true meaning and actual location of the Holy Grail, medieval romances are viewed not as fictional stories, but as codes that will lead to the discovery of a great secret. The knights who searched for the Holy Grail are equated with a real group of warrior knights known as the Knights Templar, or the Templars.

The Order of the Knights Templar was founded to defend Jerusalem and the Holy Land during the Crusades. When Jerusalem was finally lost, the Templars returned to Europe. They were wealthy and powerful and eventually they clashed with the king of France. At the beginning of the 14th century, the French king had the Templars in France arrested on false charges, claiming that they worshiped pagan idols and indulged in obscene practices. Although not everyone believed these charges, the Order of the Knights Templar was disbanded. When the accounts of the Templar trials were reexamined several

centuries later, some writers suggested that the Templars were persecuted not because the French king wanted to destroy a rival institution, but because the Templars had learned some esoteric secret during the years they spent in the East and that this secret threatened the power of church and government alike. There is no clear evidence that the Templars were involved with esoteric matters, and very few historians have considered the possibility very seriously. However, the idea that the Templars have guarded a secret connected with the Holy Grail has been a mainstay of popular alternative history. For such popular historians history is one vast conspiracy to hide a secret. Certain events, like the suppression of the Templars, and objects, like

Shepherd's Monument at Shugborough Hall in Staffordshire, England. (Getty Images)

The Knights Templar, the Holy Grail, and Pre-Columbian America

The 14th century was not a good time to be a member of the Knights Templar, which had until then been the most wealthy and powerful of the military monastic orders created during the Crusades. At the behest of the King Phillip IV of France, Pope Clement V disbanded the order in 1312, and remnants of the order spent the rest of the century trying to elude capture and possible execution. Legend has it, however, that the Knights Templar possessed the Holy Grail, the cup that Joseph of Arimathea used to catch Jesus Christ's blood at the Crucifixion. Recently, some scholars have argued that the last of the Knights Templar left France in 1398 aboard their ships, sailed first to Scotland, then following the Viking voyages across the islands of the North Atlantic, finally settling in North America almost 100 years before Christopher Columbus sailed.

According to the legend, a Scottish prince named Henry Sinclair led a group of Knights Templar to Nova Scotia, where their presence is testified to in the mythology of the Micmac Indians of the region. Some archaeologists claim to have found geometric arrangements similar to those used by the Freemasons, who claim their heritage from the Knights Templar. But what might be even more interesting to some medieval enthusiasts is the possibility that they may have brought the Holy Grail with them and that it is today somewhere in North America.

Poussin's painting and the Shepherd's Monument, hold a key that will ultimately unravel this conspiracy, if researchers apply the correct methods. In relation to Shugborough and its supposed connection with the grail, the proposed key to the code resides in a secret history of the Templars (Baigent Leigh and Lincoln 1996), mysterious structure and lines in the landscape (Andrews and Schellenberger 2005), and psychic visions (Collins 2004).

Romantic ideas about warrior knights and hidden codes provide the context for the suggestion that the Anson family who lived at Shugborough Hall were somehow involved with a society of secret Templars who had survived the suppression of the order in the 14th century. The letters and the carving on the Shepherd's Monument have been interpreted as a code that will lead to the Templar's greatest secret, the location of the Holy Grail. References to the monument in contemporary documents, many of them in the personal documents and letters of the Anson family, reveal a great deal about the family and their attitudes toward art and life. They do not support the idea that the code has anything to do with secret societies or the Holy Grail. What these references do reveal is a newly wealthy family with sophisticated tastes who had access to the art, architecture, and literature of classical Europe. They drew inspiration for how they wished to live their own lives from the classical Greek and Roman world, and they expressed these aspirations in the architecture and garden design of their home at Shugborough.

History

Three designers were involved in the construction of the Shepherd's Monument at Shugborough Hall. Thomas Wright of Durham, an architect, garden designer, mathematician, and astronomer, was employed by the Anson family to extend and improve the house, and he also drew the original design for the monument at Shugborough. The Poussin relief was executed by the Antwerp-born sculptor Peter Scheemakers from a print of the French painting by Bernard Picart. The Doric-style surround was added later by another architect designer, James Stuart, who was a friend of the owner and an important figure in the revival of interest in classical architecture and culture during the 18th century.

The origins of this so-called grail mystery, however, are not rooted in the 18th-century world of the Anson family. The grail mystery is linked to the 20th-century world of a group of French grail enthusiasts who created an organization called the Priory of Sion. They claimed that the Priory formed the inner core of the Knights Templar and guarded their most precious secret in order to provide an imaginative, but completely synthetic, history for this secret society. These modern enthusiasts produced a number of mysterious documents. They interpreted details in Poussin's painting, such as the tomb with its inscription and the figures who appeared to point to features in the landscape, as references to an actual place in southern France, supposedly the secret last resting place of the Holy Grail. However, neither the tomb nor the landscape in Poussin's painting reflects real geographic features. Poussin used this imaginary tomb inscribed with the words "Et in Arcadia Ego" in several paintings as a symbol for mortality and the transience of life. Although a structure was built several centuries later in the French countryside, no tomb existed when Poussin painted the Arcadian Shepherds in the 17th century, and it is unlikely that he ever visited this part of France (Putman and Wood 2005: 115–32). However, the authors of the most popular alternative history about the Holy Grail inserted the Shugborough monument, with its seemingly mysterious series of letters, into their speculative history about the French painting and the Priory of Sion (Baigent, Leigh, and Lincoln 1996: 190–91). Since then, a location with no prior links to the Templars or the Holy Grail has been absorbed into a dynamic, but unsupported, modern legend, and it has attracted new motifs of its own.

Not far from Shugborough is Bletchley Park, another country house in the midst of an estate. Code breakers at Bletchley Park, who worked for British intelligence during World War II, broke the infamous German *Enigma* codes. More than half a century later, the name still conjures up visions of secret agents, wartime espionage, and the fight against repression. Several new solutions to the meaning of the Shugborough monument were presented to the world media through the efforts of two code breakers who worked at Bletchley Park during World War II. This revived the wartime nostalgia associated with the place and provided a seemingly authentic source for decoding the secret (Shugborough Estate Web site; *The Guardian* November 26, 2004, 3; *The Times* November 26, 2004; *The Daily Telegraph* November 26, 2004).

The most dramatic solution, however, did not come from Bletchley Park but from an unnamed code breaker working in a secret intelligence organization. This solution explained the letters as a reference to the Holy Grail and to the belief that the Templars allegedly preserved an alternative religious tradition in which Jesus Christ was human, not divine. The letters were submitted to a series of code grids to yield a "solution," *Jesus H Defy*. This makes little sense as it stands and in no way solves the puzzle. Further interpretation identified the *H* with the Greek letter chi (*X*), and translated the *X* as *messiah/Christ*. The phrase is thus explained as *Jesus (the Deity) Defy*. The reasons for these changes have never been fully explained. The Greek *H* consistently refers to the letter *e* in the name Jesus, as in the abbreviation IHS, the first three letters of the name in Greek. The words *messiah* and *Christ* mean "the anointed one" not "deity." So, the code breaker adds more speculative history claiming that the Templars practiced an alternative Christianity that denied the divinity of Jesus. Unfortunately this has no more inherent sense than the original "code" and owes more to romantic ideas about the Templars and the popularity of alternative history than to any serious attempt to solve a code. In fact this is a circular argument. It asserts that the Templars practiced an alternative Christianity, without any concrete proof that this was so, uses this to interpret the "code," and then presents the solution as proof of the original assertion. References to code-breaking grids, an influential, unnamed code breaker from an intelligence network, the Templars, and the Priory of Sion are elements that make the contemporary grail legend so compelling. It is also these very elements that locate this explanation in the world of modern legend rather than history (Wood 2003). Indeed a reference to the "denial of Jesus' divinity" occurs in the paragraph immediately after the description of the Shugborough Hall code in the alternative history book where is was featured originally, so no code breaker need look very far (Baigent et al. 1996: 192).

Other solutions have been suggested for these cryptic letters besides a grail code. The 10 letters are separated by full stops, which implies that they are abbreviations for words. Several solutions offer Latin or English phrases using these letters. Margaret, countess of Lichfield, a member of the family presently occupying Shugborough, remembered a story she had heard as a child and proposed the following solution: "Out of your own sweet vale Alicia vanish vanity twixt Deity and Man, thou Shepherdess the way" (Shugborough Academy Web site). Although no trace of the story has ever been found, the explanation hints at the notion of vanity, and by extension, to a philosophy known as stoicism. This philosophy first appeared during the Hellenistic period (ca. third century BCE) and was popular among the educated Greco-Roman elite. Stoicism stressed that life and its blessings were transitory; therefore, a virtuous life was the basis of true happiness. The stoics belonged to the classical world that educated 18th-century men and women admired. Such sentiments would have appealed to members of the Anson family. Another solution also echoes the notion of life's brevity. *"Orator Omnia Sunt Vanitas Ait Vanitas Vanitatum."* This Latin phrase paraphrases a biblical verse in Ecclesiastes, "Vanity of vanities, saith the preacher, all is vanity" (*Billings Gazette* June 6, 2006). Both of these solutions echo the sentiments of virtuous living and endurance, which those in the 18th century attributed to the classical world. Either solution could be seen as a comment on a scene depicting the perfect pastoral world of Arcadia whose beauty is disrupted by death.

It is also possible that the letters are a personal memorial to the memory of a departed loved one. The first and last letters, *D. M.*, were a standard abbreviation for *Diis Manibus* ("To the Souls of the Departed") and were carved on Roman funerary monuments. The remaining letters might stand for the Latin phrase *"Optimae Uxoris, Optimae Sororis, Viduus Amantissimus Vovit Virtutibus."* This could be translated as "Best wife, best sister, the most loving widower dedicates [this] to [your] virtue." This is the most personal of the solutions offered. Once again the sentiments fit the poetic ambiguities of Arcadian symbolism popular with the Anson family and their circle. Depending on the date on which the inscription was carved, this could be a memorial to the parents of the Anson brothers who carried out improvements to the estate and gardens, or to Elizabeth, Lady Anson, who died in 1760. The cryptic letters may commemorate the affection between Lady Elizabeth (the wife and sister) and her husband (widower) who survived her by only a few years, or perhaps it may refer to the Anson's mother and father. It is even possible that the memorial commemorates an early and brief marriage of Thomas. Local records note the marriage of a "Thomas Ansin" to Anne Ridell in 1728. Although the exact identities of the wife and widower are still unclear, it does provide a solution to the code that becomes clear once it is "cracked" (Shugborough Academy, cited April 30, 2007).

If the Templars and the Holy Grail lie behind the monument and its mysterious lettering, then there should be some indication in the family papers or other documents. Secret codes are all too easy to manufacture if details are strung together independent of their historical and cultural contexts. The earliest element of the monument was based on a design by Thomas Wright (1711–1786), a mathematician, architect, antiquarian, and astronomer. The original design of a rustic arch on which this monument is based appeared in one of his books on architecture, which included a number of sketches for architectural features intended to adorn the houses of wealthy aristocrats. He described this collection of rustic follies and hermitages in terms of the fashionable images for past wisdom as "suitable for a Brahmin or a druid" (Harris 1979: plate A). Thomas Wright's interests mirrored those of his 18th-century patrons. He was erudite, elitist, intellectually playful, confident about the harmony of knowledge and creation, and stoical about the vicissitudes of fate. At first glance the imaginative Thomas Wright seems an ideal purveyor of codes and secrets. His scientific fame rests on his explanation of Earth's position in the Milky Way galaxy, but his attempt to produce a cosmology integrating divine, moral, and scientific views was full of unusual notions. He also wrote utopian fiction. He was a Freemason and he used codes and ciphers in the decoration of his own home. When he was young, Wright's father, thinking his son was mad, burned all of the young man's books. He was an antiquarian with a particular interest in the beliefs of the Druids. He made drawings of ancient stone monuments in Ireland that he believed had been built by the Druids. Eighteenth-century ideas about what the Druids believed were an important source for his fantasies about the past and the inspiration for many of his designs. There is no mention of Templars in his mystical worldview. In any event, Wright was not involved in the creation of the bas-relief whose imagery and inscription have suggested secret meanings to some observers. In the finished monument at Shugborough, the mirror image adaptation of Poussin's painting of shepherds near a tomb in Arcadia set within Thomas Wright's rustic arch was executed by the sculptor Peter Sheemaker. Another architect, James Stuart, designed and built several other monuments in the garden. He also surrounded both the carving and Wright's rustic arch with a portico in the Greek Doric style.

It is the Ansons, the owners of the estate, and how they fit into the cultural interests of the 18th-century intelligentsia that can tell us the most about Shepherd's Monument. Admiral George Anson, famous for his circumnavigation of the globe and newly enriched from sea booty, came to live at Shugborough with his wife, Lady Elizabeth Yorke, whom he married in 1748. His brother, Thomas Anson, was the owner of Shugborough. He was a member of the Royal Society and a founding member of the Dilettanti Society, a dining club devoted to the revival of classical art. Both of these organizations were devoted to intellectual pursuits and were not secret societies. Thomas's friend, James Stuart (1713–1788), who did much to revive the Greek style as an architectural fashion, added the Doric surround to the Shepherd's Monument.

The significance of a tomb in Arcadia is important in order to understand the meaning of the monument. The question to be resolved is whether it conceals an esoteric secret or whether it had personal meaning for the Anson family. There are indications that the Anson family thought of the estate in Arcadian terms. Arcadia was a region in ancient Greece devoted to farming and agriculture. For this reason it came to symbolize the virtues of the pastoral life, one that was simple, untouched by ambition or corruption, and unchanging. Educated men and women of the 18th century saw themselves as the inheritors of Greek and Roman values and began to remake their environment in the image of the Greek and Roman world. Collecting classical antiquities became fashionable, and gardens were designed to imitate a romanticized vision of the pastoral simplicity of

Arcadia. Paintings of classical subjects also became popular. The Duke of Devonshire, an acquaintance of the Anson family, owned an earlier version of the Arcadian shepherds looking at a tomb painted by Nicholas Poussin. He lent this painting to Elizabeth, Lady Anson, who made a copy, and there is a picture of her holding the sketch still in the Lichfield family collection. Elizabeth Anson was a talented woman, well read in classical literature. She described Shugborough as "Arcady" in a letter to her brother-in law, Thomas, whom she also addressed as "shepherd" (Harris 2006: 1–2).

The Roman poet Virgil wrote a series of poems called *Eclogues* set in an idealized Arcadia and praised the virtues of a pastoral life. The phrase "Et in Arcadia Ego" echoes a passage in one of these poems, and it appears in paintings by later artists with interests in classical myth. The contrast in Poussin's *Les Bergers D'Arcadie* (*The Shepherds of Arcadia*) between the pastoral scene and the inscribed tomb suggests the clever ambiguity so beloved of sophisticated painters and their classically educated patrons (Blunt 1996). Their wealth enabled them to indulge in the study of classical literature and extensive travel, and many of them amassed collections of classical art and paintings from contemporary artists that incorporated mythic references. They also wanted to emulate the ideals of the Greek and Roman world in their own lives. The phrase "Et in Arcadia Ego" is deliberately ambiguous. It refers both to the transience of life, "even in Arcadia am I (i.e., Death)" and to the beauty of eternity, "I (the occupant of the tomb) am in Arcadia." There is another detail that may link the more general taste for Arcadian symbolism with personal meanings for the Anson family. The phrase was inscribed on a funeral urn commemorating the death of Henry Pelham, a close friend and political ally. An urn was carved above the tomb in the Shepherd's Monument at Shugborough, although no such object appears in the Poussin painting. This may be another personal reference in the monument to the death of a friend. Another similarity between the Pelham and Shugborough memorials is the phrase *optimae uxoris*. It appears on both monuments and, like *diis manibus*, it is also found on Roman grave memorials.

A poem written in 1758 about the monument at Shugborough titled "Hermit Poem on an Emblematical Basso Relievo after a famous picture of Nicolas Poussin" mentions Arcadia and the fact that "life's fleeting moments gently steal away." The subject of this poem is the carving of Poussin's work, but there is nothing mentioned about the cryptic letters. Another poem, written in 1767, calls them "mystic ciphers," but does not give any indication of what they might mean. During that period both Lady Elizabeth and her husband had died and Thomas Anson had engaged his friend, the architect James Stuart, to make further additions to the park and garden. The first volume of Stuart's important book on architecture, *The Antiquities of Athens*, appeared in 1762, the year before he started working at Shugborough. One of the drawings included in the volume echoes some of the elements in the Shugborough inscription. It depicts a funereal shield with the letters *D.M.* and a Latin inscription (Stuart 1762). These classical references would have appealed to, and to some extent flattered, the accomplishments of the family and their circle of friends. In 1782 another friend, Thomas Pennant, came to visit Shugborough. He was a famous traveler who wrote an account of his travels through the British Isles at a time when such journeys were an impressive undertaking. He described both the gardens and Thomas Anson's attitude to them:

> The scene is laid in Arcadia. Two lovers expressed in elegant pastoral figures appear attentive to an ancient shepherd who reads to them an inscription on a tomb "Et in Arcadia" the moral resulting from this seems to be that there are no situations of this life so delicious but which death must at length snatch us from. It was placed here by the owner as a memento of the certainty of that event perhaps as a secret memorial of some loss of a tender nature in his early years for he was wont often to gaze on it in affection and fine meditation. (Pennant 1782)

This reference also describes the carving rather than the cryptic letters, but the author knew Thomas Anson personally. Pennant's description emphasizes the personal nature of the imagery and its connection with a stoic endurance of loss.

Conclusion

The announcement that the code had been cracked produced a flurry of interest, and, although this died down somewhat, the Shugborough Web site still contains a "Holy Grail" section. However, none of the details drawn from contemporary documents links the Shugborough monument to the grail or the Templars. What information there is about the interests of the Anson family places the monument firmly within the popular theme of a romantic, elegiac Arcadia, something that was widely known and appreciated in the 18th century. It is now clear, indeed it has been clear for some time, that Poussin painted an imaginary tomb. It was a symbol for mortality and he used it in several paintings. A structure was built on a site in the French countryside much later, and the link between the two was only made in the 20th century. Since the inscribed tomb did not exist when Poussin painted his vision of shepherds in Arcadia, there can be no connection with Shugborough or the family who commissioned the monument incorporating a version of his painting in the 18th century. Similarly the reversal of the composition, the urn, and the changed angles cannot be attributed to that fact that "Staffordshire was a hotbed of Masonic activity" (Baigent et al. 1996: 191). Nor can the figures and the lettering be interpreted as symbols pointing to "the location of the treasure—the tomb of god the holy blood and the holy grail" (Andrews and Shellenberger 2005: 88). The engraving used by Sheemakers was printed in reverse, and the broad rectangular composition of Poussin's landscape had to be compressed into a narrower, "portrait" frame. Aristocratic families, like the Ansons, especially when they possessed something that appears to be mysterious, attract just this sort of legend.

The information that we have about the Ansons and their monument presents a very different picture from the rather wild speculations that Admiral Anson could have captured the bas-relief based on Poussin's painting at sea from a Templar ship. The connections between the Shepherd's Monument and the Holy Grail are tenuous at best, requiring a sizable stretch of the historical imagination. Thus, the mystery at Shugborough is not in any way related to medieval romance about the Holy Grail, nor does it really concern any grail relic. Attempts to create and then solve a mystery focus on the meaning of the mysterious cipher and its possible link to esoteric ideas. The Shepherd's Monument at Shugborough Hall seems to have had a personal significance for the family. The exact nature of that significance remains unclear, but a likely explanation is that it commemorates the loss of some family member using the imagery of Arcadia. By examining the existing sources, many of them contemporary, with the construction of the monument, we can, however, understand the cultural and social context in which the Shepherd's Monument was constructed, revealing a much more conventional meaning than grail seekers might like to see.

References and Further Reading

Andrews, Richard, and Paul Shellenberger. *The Tomb of God, the Body of Jesus and the Solution to a 2000 Year Old Mystery.* Rev. ed. London: Little Brown, 2005.

Baigent, Michael, Richard Leigh, and Henry Lincoln. *The Holy Blood and the Holy Grail.* London: Corgi, 1996.

Baker, Andrew, "The Shepherdess's Secret." Unpublished manuscript at the Staffordshire Record Office.

Billings Gazette. "City Lights: Parmly Plus Pluck Solve Old Puzzle." Available at http://www.billingsgazette.com/news/local/article_7b9cd7d5-568d-5260-b42a-68dbb27aad71.html (accessed August 3, 2010).

Blunt, Anthony. *The Paintings of Nicolas Poussin.* London: Phaidon, 1996.

British Broadcasting Company (BBC). "Code Points Away from Holy Grail." Available at http://news.bbc.co.uk/1/hi/england/beds/bucks/herts/4040127.stm (accessed June 1, 2010).

Collins, Andrew. *Twenty-First Century Grail: The Quest for a Legend.* London: Virgin Books, 2004.

Harris, Eileen. "Cracking the Poussin Code: The Key to the Shepherd's Monument at Shugborough." *Apollo* (May 2006). Available through title search at www.archives.staffordshire.gov.uk (accessed June 1, 2010).

Harris, Eileen, ed. *Thomas Wright's Arbours and Grottos: A Facsimile. With a catalogue of Wright's works in architecture and garden design.* London: Scolar, 1979.

Morris, Steven. "Has the Mystery of the Holy Grail been solved?" *The Guardian* (November 26, 2004) Available at http://www.guardian.co.uk/uk/2004/nov/26/artsandhumanities.highereducation (Accessed August 3, 2010)

Pennant, Thomas. *Journey from Chester to London*: Chester, 1782.

Putnam, Bill, and John Edwin Wood. *The Treasure of Rennes-Le-Chateau: A Mystery Solved.* Rev. ed. Stroud: Tempus, 2005.

Shugborough Estate. Home page. Available at www.shugborough.org.uk/AcademyHome-156 (accessed June 1, 2010). Shugborough Academy lists the history of the monument and selections from newspaper articles:

Smith, Lewis. "War Codebreaker Cracks an Enigma of Love." *The Times* (November 26, 2004) Available at http://www.timesonline.co.uk/tol/news/uk/article395668.ece, (Accessed August 3, 2010)

Stuart, James, and Nicholas Revett. *The Antiquities of Athens.* 1762. Vol. 1. London: Princeton Architectural Press, 2007.

Tweedie, Neil. "Letters Remain the Holy Grail to Code-Breakers." *The Daily Telegraph* (November 26, 2004)Available at http://www.telegraph.co.uk/news/uknews/1477527/Letters-remain-the-holy-grail-to-code-breakers.html (Accessed August 3, 2010)

Wood, Juliette. "The Templars, the Grail and Just About Everything Else: Contemporary Legends in the Media." *FLS News: The Newsletter of The Folklore Society* 45:2 (2003).

8

Nestorius did not intend to argue that Christ had a dual nature, but that view became labeled Nestorianism.

PRO Mark Dickens
CON Annette Morrow

PRO

History is rarely kind to heretics, even less so to heresiarchs, those who devise systems of belief that lead the faithful astray. Their stories are usually told not by themselves, but by their opponents. In the process, they are condemned for questioning the religious *status quo* or offering innovative solutions to theological problems. Their beliefs are minutely scrutinized to discredit their views, and they are often accused of immoral behavior, as further evidence of their heretical thinking. Since those who triumph over the heretics often destroy most or all of their works, one can only evaluate them through the lens of their opponents.

Most heresiarchs are universally regarded by scholars as clearly opposed to the basics of the Christian faith as outlined in the Bible and interpreted by the church leaders since apostolic times. However, about Nestorius there is much less consensus; for the past century, theologians have held widely divergent views on his teachings. Was he truly a heretic or rather a victim of church politics whose views have been subsequently misinterpreted, in part due to the exalted status of his opponent, Cyril of Alexandria? This section proposes the latter view; Nestorius does not deserve to be labeled a heretic because he did not teach what he is accused of.

Before going further, the idea of a dual nature needs to be clarified. The word is misleading, since Nestorius undeniably argued that Christ had a dual nature. This position, known as Dyophysitism (from Greek *dyophysitai*, "two natures," referring to the divine and human natures of Christ), is also the orthodox Christian position articulated at the Council of Chalcedon in 451 and considered a primary article of faith by the Catholic, Orthodox, and Protestant churches today. It stands in contrast to the Miaphysitism (from Greek *mia physis*, "one nature") of the Oriental orthodox churches (Coptic, Ethiopian, Syrian, and Armenian Orthodox), who affirm only one nature in Christ. By contrast, Nestorius is accused of teaching that there were two *persons*, not two *natures*, in Christ (a crucial terminological distinction). This section, therefore, disputes the accusation that Nestorius taught "two persons in Christ."

Historical and Theological Background

After three centuries of surviving as an illegal religious sect within the Roman Empire, Christianity experienced a dramatic turnaround when Constantine I (306–337) issued the Edict of Milan (313), signaling the end of official state opposition to the faith. The Christianization of the empire proceeded apace over the next several decades, resulting in the proclamation of Christianity as the official state religion in 380 by Theodosius I (378–395).

The reprieve from persecution and subsequent state sponsorship of Christianity meant church leaders could turn their attention to unresolved theological issues that had been brewing for decades. There were both religious and political reasons for doing so. Church and state were increasingly interconnected, and most emperors viewed the ecclesiastical unity of the empire as inextricably linked to its political unity; solving theological problems had serious implications for governing the empire. Hence, beginning with Constantine I at the Council of Nicaea (325), emperors periodically convened ecumenical councils at which the gathered bishops debated issues vital to the doctrinal unity of the church.

The chief concerns at the first several ecumenical councils centered on two Christological issues: the relationship between the Son (Jesus) and the Father (God) in the Trinity and the relationship between divinity and humanity in Christ. The first concern was at the heart of the Arian controversy, which was addressed at the Ecumenical Councils of Nicaea (325) and Constantinople (381). The second issue, which was the core of the Nestorian and Monophysite controversies, dealt with at the Ecumenical Councils of Ephesus (431) and Chalcedon (451).

The essential problem is that the New Testament affirms both the divinity of Christ and his humanity, but does not clearly explain how the two interact with or relate to each other. Various biblical statements on this relationship can be interpreted in several different ways, notably John 1:14: "The Word became flesh and made his dwelling among us. We have seen his glory, the glory of the One and Only, who came from the Father, full of grace and truth" and Philippians 2:5–7: "Christ Jesus, who, being in very nature God, did not consider equality with God something to be grasped, but made himself nothing, taking the very nature of a servant, being made in human likeness."

Two contrasting views on the divine–human interaction in Christ were developed in the theological schools of Antioch (Syria) and Alexandria (Egypt). The Antiochenes followed a literal and historical approach to biblical exegesis, while the Alexandrians favored an allegorical and philosophical approach. The emphasis that Antioch placed on the historical facts of Jesus's life resulted in a strong focus on his humanity, whereas the more metaphysical approach of Alexandria produced a greater emphasis on his divinity. Important representatives of the Antiochene tradition include Paul of Samosata, Diodore of Tarsus, Theodore of Mopsuestia, John Chrysostom, and Nestorius. The Alexandrian school produced Origen, Athanasius, Apollinarius of Laodicea, Cyril of Alexandria, and Eutyches (both lists contain saints and heretics).

A corollary of these different theological emphases was their approach to the role of the logos, the preexistent Word of God that became incarnate in Jesus Christ. Antiochenes generally spoke of the logos dwelling alongside the human in Jesus, resulting in two logical subjects in Christ (called *logos-anthropos* or "word-man" theology). In contrast, Alexandrians described the Word taking on flesh to such an extent that it became the sole logical subject of the person of Christ, with the practical result that his divinity often eclipsed his humanity in their thinking (called *logos-sarx* or "word-flesh" theology). The union was one of essence or substance in which the human will was eclipsed by the divine will. All Christological statements in the Bible, including those about Jesus's birth, suffering, and death, were ultimately ascribed to the divine logos become flesh (and therefore to God).

Taken to their logical extremes, both viewpoints could end up in heretical thinking. The Antiochene Paul of Samosata (d. 275) taught that Jesus was merely a man in whom the Holy Spirit dwelt; whereas the Alexandrian Apollinarius of Laodicea (d. ca. 390) argued that the human mind in Christ had been replaced by the divine mind of the logos. Apollinarius also coined the phrase "one incarnate nature of the God Logos," later used by Cyril, who thought it came from Athanasius, the great champion of Nicene Christianity. The teachings of both Paul and Apollinarius were subsequently condemned by church councils. On the same basis, many scholars would also include as examples of the heretical potential in the two competing theological systems the names of Nestorius and Eutyches (representing Antioch and Alexandria, respectively), both condemned by the Council of Chalcedon (451).

Another key factor was the increasing rivalry between the apostolic sees (or patriarchates) of Antioch: Alexandria and Constantinople. Initially, there had been near equality among Rome, Antioch, and Alexandria, with Rome being accorded the status of "first among equals." However, Canon 3 of the Council of Constantinople (381) moved the new capital Constantinople into second place after Rome (a position strengthened by Canon 28 of the later Council of Chalcedon). This move particularly irked the patriarchs of Alexandria, who looked back to the evangelist Mark as their apostolic founder and had called themselves "popes" since the patriarchate of Heraclas (232–248). By contrast, any claim by Constantinople to apostolic foundation had to be fabricated (and was, in the person of the apostle Andrew).

The Rise and Fall of Nestorius

When Sisinnius I, patriarch of Constantinople, died in December 427, Emperor Theodosius II (408–450) chose Nestorius, a Syrian monk and disciple of Theodore of Mopsuestia, to replace him. Nestorius was consecrated as bishop of Constantinople in April 428. The church historian Socrates Scholasticus describes him as "distinguished for his excellent voice and fluency of speech," but his subsequent actions revealed the "violent and vainglorious temperament," of one who "continually disturbed the public tranquility" (Stevenson and Frend 1989: 287–88).

Whether or not Nestorius was as arrogant as Socrates claims, his actions reveal why the people of the capital nicknamed him the "incendiary" bishop. In his inaugural sermon he asked the emperor's assistance in purging the realm of heretics. When he attempted to impose his authority over the Arians in Constantinople, a fire and riot ensued in the city. Demonstrating both religious zeal and political naivety, Nestorius proceeded to attack immorality in public entertainment, to bring the city's monks under his ecclesiastical jurisdiction, to restrict the involvement of aristocratic women in ecclesiastical affairs, and to challenge the role of the Augusta (empress) Pulcheria, the powerful sister of Theodosius II. In so doing, he alienated the general population, the monks, the aristocracy, and the empress. This would haunt him during the subsequent theological controversy; while his opponent Cyril of Alexandria (412–444) "had an immensely strong personal power-base in his own church. . . . Nestorius had set almost everyone against him on the home front" (McGuckin 1996: 20).

Nestorius, Persian prelate and Patriarch of Constantinople who was deposed for his heretical views about the nature of Jesus Christ. (Mary Evans Picture Library/The Image Works)

Although these actions played a role in Nestorius's eventual downfall, the main complaints about him concerned his Antiochene Christological views and particularly his rejection of the term *Theotokos*, "Bearer/Mother of God," to describe the Virgin Mary. When the presbyter Anastasius preached against the use of *Theotokos*, saying "It is impossible that God should be born of a human being," Nestorius backed him up and began to also preach against the term, urging instead the use of *Christotokos*, "Bearer/Mother of Christ," since it avoided the implication that divinity had its source in humanity. However, as Socrates notes, he "acquired the reputation among the masses of asserting that the Lord was a mere man." Although Socrates concluded this was not what Nestorius actually taught, he critiqued him for not paying adequate attention to earlier theologians' use of *Theotokos* (Stevenson and Frend 1989: 288–89). Nestorius's rejection of the term was seen by the general populace, who increasingly venerated Mary, as an assault on their religious devotional life, and Pulcheria (a consecrated virgin with a reputation for prayer and good works) probably interpreted Nestorius's opposition to *Theotokos* as a personal attack (Russell 2000: 32–33). Meanwhile, to Cyril of Alexandria, Nestorius's position amounted to questioning the divinity of Christ.

Cyril wrote three letters, in increasingly urgent terms, attempting to bring Nestorius into line with his thinking on Christ's nature, but Nestorius stood firm. The dispute between the two came to a head with the Ecumenical Council that was called by the Emperor Theodosius, to meet at Ephesus on Pentecost in 431. Although Nestorius welcomed this as an opportunity to confront Cyril, the council was to prove his undoing, given the way his teaching and actions as patriarch had alienated so many. In anticipation of the council, Cyril wrote 12 anathemas, or accusations, which he attached to his final letter to Nestorius (Stevenson and Frend 1989: 307–8). To avoid excommunication, Nestorius had to agree to all 12 accusations. In issuing the anathemas, Cyril had clearly overstepped the authority delegated to him by Celestine. They presented a strong Alexandrian position to which no Antiochene could agree. Moreover, the dispute between Cyril and Nestorius had become so personal that the latter was probably beyond agreeing to anything the former proposed, even where there were grounds for genuine theological agreement.

The Council of Ephesus

In early June 431, approximately 200 bishops gathered in Ephesus. Apart from 10 who accompanied Nestorius, most were Cyril's allies, since John of Antioch and his delegation of 43 bishops had been delayed. Despite receiving a letter from John announcing their imminent arrival, the council began without them, under Cyril's leadership. Ignoring protests from the emperor's representatives and gathering in the Great Church of St. Mary the *Theotokos* in Ephesus, the council proceeded to depose and excommunicate Nestorius on June 22. Although summoned to appear, Nestorius refused, rightly understanding that he would not get a fair trial. When John and the Antiochene bishops arrived on June 26, they convened an alternate council and immediately deposed Cyril and Memnon, bishop of Ephesus and Cyril's ally, as well as excommunicated their supporters who refused to "anathematize the heretical propositions of Cyril" (Stevenson and Frend 1989: 309). When the pope's legates reached Ephesus on July 10, they supported Cyril, giving papal assent to Nestorius's deposition.

Nestorius's Letter to Cyril of Alexandria

At the Council of Ephesus, evidence against Nestorius, in the form of his correspondence with Cyril of Alexandria, was read. Ironically, it remains one of the only extant pieces of Nestorius's writing, as most others were destroyed after he was declared a heretic. In this segment, Nestorius explains his views on Jesus's nature:

Holy scripture, wherever it recalls the Lord's economy, speaks of the birth and suffering not of the godhead but of the humanity of Christ, so that the holy virgin is more accurately termed mother of Christ than mother of God. Hear these words that the gospels proclaim: 'The book of the generation of Jesus Christ, son of David, son of Abraham.' It is clear that God the Word was not the son of David. Listen to another witness if you will: 'Jacob begat Joseph, the husband of Mary, of whom was born Jesus, who is called the Christ.' Consider a further piece of evidence: 'Now the birth of Jesus Christ took place in this way. When his mother Mary had been betrothed to Joseph, she was found to be with child of the holy Spirit.' But who would ever consider that the godhead of the only begotten was a creature of the Spirit? Why do we need to mention: 'the mother of Jesus was there"? And again what of: 'with Mary the mother of Jesus"; or 'that which is conceived in her is of the holy Spirit"; and 'Take the child and his mother and flee to Egypt"; and 'concerning his Son, who was born of the seed of David according to the flesh"? Again, scripture says when speaking of his passion: 'God sending his own Son in the likeness of sinful flesh and for sin, he condemned sin in the flesh"; and again 'Christ died for our sins" and 'Christ having suffered in the flesh"; and 'This is," not 'my godhead," but 'my body, broken for you."

Source: *Nicene and Post-Nicene Fathers*, 2nd series, Vol. 14, edited by Henry R. Percival. Peabody, MA: Hendrickson Publishers, 1885.

Meanwhile, the Antiochene party refused to have anything to do with the "Cyrillians," to which the main council under Cyril responded by excommunicating any bishop who "has joined himself to the assembly of revolt" (Stevenson and Frend 1989: 310).

Theodosius was still backing Nestorius at this point, but his support was wavering. On July 17, he ordered that Cyril and Memnon be deposed along with Nestorius. All three were arrested in August, after which both sides wrote letters to the emperor, appealing their cases. Finally, on September 11, 431, Theodosius dissolved the council, sending Nestorius back to his monastery in Antioch, while Cyril returned in victory to Alexandria, having overcome the imperial judgment against him by the distribution of extensive bribes to the court in Constantinople, a practice he repeated later on to maintain his position of favor with the imperial family and to ensure that the Antiochenes would agree to the *Formula of Reunion* in 433 (Bethune-Baker 1908: 10–1; Loofs 1914: 55–56; Driver and Hodgson 1925: 279– 82, 349–51).

Over the next two years, the emperor and representatives from the two sides in the conflict conducted negotiations aimed at reconciliation. Cyril was especially motivated to see this happen, for the Council of Ephesus could not be considered as binding unless there was unanimous agreement to its decision. Without the support of Antioch, the ecclesiastical legitimacy of Nestorius's deposition was questionable and Cyril's position was vulnerable. Finally, in April 433, in response to an Antiochene proposal, Cyril wrote a letter to John of Antioch "to make peace between the Churches" and agreed to the Formula of Reunion, probably drawn up by Theodoret of Cyrrhus.

The Formula was a compromise theological statement that favored the Antiochene "two-nature" position over the Alexandrian "one-nature" position and made no mention of Cyril's contentious anathemas, but confessed Mary as *Theotokos* (Stevenson and Frend 1989: 314–15). As Loofs points out, Cyril "could have come to an agreement with him [Nestorius] as easily as with the Antiochians afterwards in 433, if he had not had . . . an interest in discrediting him" (1914: 41). As it was, to secure the peace, the Antiochenes had to accept the decisions of Ephesus as binding, including the deposition of Nestorius. Thus, in exchange for a theological agreement that he would have whole-heartedly agreed with, Nestorius was sacrificed and thereafter considered a heretic.

That Cyril had not abandoned his essentially "one-nature" approach is evident from a letter he wrote to fellow Alexandrians to defend his acceptance of the Formula of Reunion, in which he stated unequivocally "after the union [the Incarnation] we do not divide the natures from each other . . . but say 'one Son' and, as the fathers have put it, 'one incarnate nature of the Word'." This final phrase was a quote from the heretical Apollinarius, which Cyril believed to be from Athanasius (Stevenson and Frend 1989: 318). Although the Antiochene bishops agreed to acknowledge Cyril as orthodox, many initially refused to accept the deposition of Nestorius. However, by 437, all had finally agreed to this, many albeit reluctantly. Nestorius had become expendable and denouncing him was the price of theological peace: "John of Antioch . . . and Pope Celestine of Rome ended up taking the side of Cyril against Nestorius, not for theological reasons, but for church-political reasons . . . there is no evidence that they held a different viewpoint from Nestorius. Actually, all the evidence indicates that they held precisely the same view" (Braaten 1963: 252).

Accusations against Nestorius and the *Bazaar of Heracleides*

The standard accusations against Nestorius can be summed up as follows:

1. By rejecting the term *Theotokos*, he ignored the importance of the *communicatio idiomatum* (the idea that all the attributes of divinity in Christ can be attributed to his humanity and vice versa) and challenged (or even denied) the divinity of Christ, presenting him rather as a "mere man."

2. By calling the union of divinity and humanity in Christ a "conjunction" of the two natures and promoting a "prosopic union" rather than Cyril's "hypostatic union," he devalued the idea that "the Word became flesh."

3. By differentiating between Christ's humanity and divinity, he promoted "two persons," "two Sons," and "two Christs," rather than a unified person.

Did Nestorius actually teach any of these things? In order to determine this, his extant writings need to be analyzed. Until the late 19th century, this task was particularly difficult, since only a few of his works remained, nearly all in carefully selected fragments preserved in the Acts of the Council of Ephesus or the writings of Cyril and others or disguised as sermons of John Chrysostom (Bethune-Baker 1908: 23–25; Nau 1910: 335–58; Driver and Hodgson 1925; 382–98). However, the discovery in 1889 of the *Bazaar of Heracleides,* a Syriac translation of Nestorius's defense of his life and doctrine, gave scholars new insights into the teachings of the condemned heretic. The work, originally composed in Greek under the pseudonym Heracleides (so as not to attract the attention of those intent on burning Nestorius's writings), was probably finished sometime between late 450 and late 451, around the time of the Council of Chalcedon (Driver and Hodgson 1925: x; Bevan 2007: 42). Although there are no references to Chalcedon in the book, it has been proposed that Nestorius was actually summoned to the council, but died en route (Bevan 2007: 42–51).

As Driver and Hodgson (the English translators of the work) note that Nestorius's aim was to show that "his own condemnation at Ephesus was unjust" and "the vindication of Flavian [after the 449 Council] . . . was the vindication of all that he [Nestorius] had stood for." Over and over again he makes the point that his doctrines are consistent with the Bible, the Nicene Creed, and the Church Fathers (Driver and Hodgson 1925: xxix–xxxi). Some have questioned how much the *Bazaar* accurately expresses his position 20 years earlier during the height of the controversy. However, as Anastos has noted, "it remains legitimate to allow him to be judged by his own latest and most mature efforts" (1962: 121).

All commentators on the *Bazaar* agree that there are significant problems in understanding the text. A major objection concerns the unity of the book, which can be divided into two parts: a *Dialogue* between Nestorius and Sophronius (Driver and Hodgson 1925: 7–86) and an *Apology* by Nestorius (Driver and Hodgson 1925: 87–380). Some have maintained that, whereas the *Apology* is unquestionably by Nestorius, the *Dialogue* is the work of a later author, pseudo-Nestorius (Turner 1975: 306–8), but this idea has been disputed by others (Chesnut 1978: 392–98). Most scholars note the serious stylistic challenges the work presents, challenges that in part explain why Nestorius's ideas were never broadly accepted: "It is not possible . . . to gather together a series of quotations from the Bazaar which, without explanation of linkage, will give a coherent and connected account of the Incarnation" (Vine 1948: 188). Even Anastos, who regards him as "indubitably orthodox" and the "most brilliant theologian of the fifth century," describes the repetition in the *Bazaar* as "frustrating, wearisome, and painful" and concludes that his major defects were "the obscurity and prolixity of his style" (1962: 123, 140).

Nonetheless, careful consideration of both the *Bazaar* and the other extant fragments of Nestorius's writings can greatly help in dispelling some of the misunderstandings about his teaching that persist to this day. Although scholars continue to disagree over exactly what he taught, the work clearly shows that he denied (1) an essential union of the divine and human natures in Christ (i.e., a union of the essence or substance of each nature); (2) any transformation from Godhead to manhood or vice versa in the Incarnation; (3) the idea that Christ was just another "inspired man"; (4) the notion that either of the two natures in Christ was not real; (5) the suffering of the divine logos during the Incarnation; and (6) the idea of "two Sons" in Christ (Driver and Hodgson 1925: xxxii). Let us now analyze the key accusations against Nestorius with reference to his defense in the *Bazaar*.

Nestorius's Rejection of *Theotokos*

As noted above, Nestorius's rejection of *Theotokos* is seen by many as ignoring the importance of the *communicatio idiomatum* (the sharing of attributes between the divinity and humanity of Christ) and thus challenging the divinity of Christ. However, these accusations ignore several facts. First, Nestorius's objection to *Theotokos*, politically unwise as it was, was based on biblical statements that speak of Mary as the mother of "Jesus," "Christ," or "the Son of God," but not God. In contrast to those who viewed Mary "as in some kind of way divine, like God," Nestorius claimed to be following both "the holy fathers of Nicaea" and "the Scriptures" in his opposition to *Theotokos* (Bethune-Baker 1908: 17); indeed, he was on much more solid exegetical ground than Cyril and others who championed the term.

Second, although he preferred *Christotokos* to *Theotokos*, Nestorius did not completely exclude the use of the latter, as long as it was clarified. As he stated in a sermon: "If any of you or any one else be simple and has a preference for the term *Theotokos*, then I have nothing to say against it—only do not make a Goddess of the virgin" (Loofs 1914: 32; cf. Sellers 1940: 172–73). The subsequent growth of the cult of Mary in many parts of the Christian world, in which the "Mother of God" is referred to as the "Queen of Heaven" and treated virtually as a goddess, can be seen as a realization of Nestorius's fears. In particular, the later role of the *Theotokos* as "the special protectress of Constantinople" who "fought alongside them [the inhabitants] in the battle" during the Avar-Persian siege of the city in 626 (Cameron 1978: 78–79) would have made Nestorius turn in his grave.

Third, Nestorius's formula of "the divinity makes use of the prosopon of the humanity and the humanity of that of the divinity" essentially serves the same function as the *communicatio idiomatum* (Anastos 1962: 136; cf. Sellers 1940: 167–71), so that "the *Logos* shows himself in the form of a servant and the man in the form of God" (Loofs 1914: 83; cf. Bethune-Baker 1908: 95; Driver and Hodgson 1925: 190, 241). As Anastos notes, the difference between Cyril and Nestorius on this point concerned "their disagreement concerning the subject of the God-man's career and experience. Cyril . . . [following the Alexandrian Christology] preferred to begin with the divine Logos. . . . Nestorius . . . associates all these activities [suffering, dying, rising from the dead] with 'the prosopon of the union' (the Jesus Christ of the Gospels)" (Anastos 1962: 138; cf. Driver and Hodgson 1925: 141–48).

Finally, the equation of Nestorius's position on *Theotokos* with the heretical ideas of Paul of Samosata and Photinus (d. 376), both of whom denied the divinity of Christ, ignores that fact that Nestorius's motivation in opposing *Theotokos* was to protect the Godhead from being diminished, for "if the Godhead of the Son had its origin in the womb of the Virgin Mary, it was not Godhead as the Father's" and therefore was akin to Arianism (Bethune-Baker 1908: 19). In fact, Nestorius sought to avoid two erroneous ideas, that the Godhead had its origin in a human being (Mary) and that the manhood of Christ was somehow less real than that of humanity in general (Bethune-Baker 1908: 62).

A related charge that was made against Nestorius must also be mentioned here. He was accused in the Acts of the Council of Ephesus of having said "I could not give the name of God to one who was two or three months old," referring to the Christ child. This was accepted without further inquiry by Cyril as evidence of Nestorius's rejection of the divinity of Christ. However, based on Nestorius's own account in the *Bazaar*, it seems that his probable words were that "he could not bring himself to call God a babe. . . . He refused to predicate infancy of God, rather than Godhead of an infant," a crucial difference (Bethune-Baker 1908: 77; cf. Driver and Hodgson 1925: 136–41).

Nestorius's "Prosopic Union"

Although Nestorius's rejection of *Theotokos* was the flashpoint for the controversy (due largely to the popularity of the term), Cyril equally critiqued him over his notion of a prosopic union. Herein lies a key problem over which scholars continue to disagree: the nature of Nestorius's metaphysical system and its relation to the "orthodox" Chalcedonian view of two natures in one person (the latter represented by one *prosopon* and one *hypostasis* in the Chalcedonian definition). This is difficult to unravel, given the different ways that Nestorius, Cyril, and others in the fifth century used the relevant Greek terms. Following the differentiation between *hypostasis* and *ousia* introduced by Basil of Caesarea 50 years earlier, Cyril located the "person" of Christ in the *hypostasis*. Thus for him, the union of divine and human was a "hypostatic union."

In contrast, Nestorius generally used *hypostasis* in the older sense, as a synonym for *ousia*. For him, both the divine and the human in Christ each had not only their own nature, but also their own *hypostasis/ousia*. Since the Nicene Creed had declared the Son to be *homoousios* (of one *ousia*) with the Father, Nestorius was unwilling to distinguish the *hypostasis* (equal to the *ousia* in his mind) of the Son from that of the Father, a necessary requirement for a hypostatic union to take place (since it only took place in the Son, not the Father or the Spirit). Because the *ousiai* of Godhead (which Christ shared with the Father and the Spirit) and manhood (which he shared with all humanity) were completely different essences, they could not be combined with each other; "To Nestorius Godhead and manhood . . . were much too real to be able to lose themselves in one another; the unity must be found in something other than the 'substances' themselves" (Bethune-Baker 1908: 53).

Rejecting Cyril's "hypostatic union" (which in Cyril's terminology also implied a union of natures), Nestorius opted instead for a "prosopic union," different in kind from both the unity of *ousia* (substance) shared by the members of the Trinity and the involuntary natural unity of body and soul in humans, which was used by Cyril as a metaphor for the divine–human union in Christ (Driver and Hodgson 1925: 412–13; Anastos 1962: 126–27). "Nestorius rejected the idea of a substantial union [because] such a union would result in a confusion of God and man" (Braaten 1963: 260) in which "each loses its own identity and ceases to function as a self-contained unit" (Chesnut 1978: 403). His starting place was quite different from Cyril's, as he notes in the *Bazaar*: "It is not the Logos who has become twofold; it is the one Lord Jesus Christ who is twofold in his natures. In him are seen all the characteristics of the God-Logos . . . and also all those of the manhood" (Loofs 1914: 79–80; cf. Driver and Hodgson 1925: 145).

Nestorius's theory of the prosopic union suggests that "in the person of Christ, a union of two persons took place so that they exchanged what is each other's . . . the union takes place in the interchange of roles, the one making use of the *prosopon* of the other" (Braaten 1963: 261). Thus, "the Logos 'takes' the prosopon of the manhood . . . as his prosopon, and 'gives' His divine prosopon to the manhood" (Sellers 1940: 147; cf. Driver and Hodgson 1925: 69–70). Or again, "Christ is the union of the eternal Logos and the Son of Mary, the principle of the union being that the *prosopon* of each has been taken by the other, so that there is one *prosopon* of the two in the union." In contrast, Nestorius terms Cyril's hypostatic union as "unscriptural, unorthodox, destructive of true religion, and unintelligible" (Driver and Hodgson 1925: xxxii–xxxiii), realizing that, if "the divine Logos . . . took in his *hypostasis* a human body, soul and intellect . . . so that his human nature had, therefore, no *hypostasis*," the practical result was "a suppression of the manhood of Christ" (Loofs 1914: 72–73).

Although his critics, including Cyril, have typically rejected Nestorius's use of "conjunction" (Greek *synapheia*) as too weak to describe the relationship between the divine and human in Christ, Bethune-Baker notes that the word can also have the stronger meaning "contact" or "cohesion" and that Nestorius uses "united" and "union" more frequently in the *Bazaar* than "conjoined" or "conjunction." Throughout, Nestorius's main concern was to avoid "words like 'mixture', 'commingling', 'blending together', 'confusion' and . . . all ideas which would merge the two substances and natures of Godhead and manhood in one" (Bethune-Baker 1908: 91), resulting in either "an Arian doctrine . . . which makes of the Logos a creature [or] an Apollinarian doctrine . . . which renders the humanity incomplete" (Braaten 1963: 260). Thus, for Nestorius, "God the Word does not become in his very nature something that he was not before . . . [and] the man remains genuinely man within the incarnation" (Chesnut 1978: 407).

But what exactly did Nestorius mean by *prosopon*? Biblical and patristic writers before him had used it to convey the whole range of meaning noted above (face, mask, role, outward appearance, person), and three (Athanasius, Epiphanius, and Theodore of Mopsuestia) had used it to describe the Incarnation in ways that anticipated Nestorius's later use of the term (Driver and Hodgson 1925: 402–10). However, given this range of meaning and the fact that none of the terms Nestorius uses are exactly equivalent to our word "person" and the modern psychological framework it represents (Driver and Hodgson 1925: 412), it is misleading to automatically interpret *prosopon* in his works as "person." By doing so, we are in danger of evaluating him from our modern point of view, modified by nearly 1600 years of theological, philosophical, and psychological development since his time (Braaten 1963: 261).

Loofs suggests rather that "the main thing in his notion of *prosopon* . . . was the external undivided appearance" and specifically "the undivided appearance of the historic Jesus Christ" (1914: 76, 79), an idea expanded by Driver and Hodgson, who propose that "Nestorius analysed everything that exists into . . . essence [*ousia*], nature [*physis*] . . . and appearance [*prosopon*]," the latter being "a real element in the being of a thing." As such, the prosopic union was not merely a "moral union" but a "real metaphysical unity," although Driver and Hodgson suggest it was "not strong enough to bear the strain it was designed to meet," to explain the oneness of Godhead and manhood in Christ (1925: 414–17, 419).

Chesnut further observes that "to be the prosopon of God means to Nestorius to be the Image of God, and to be the Image of God is first and foremost to will what God wills, to have the will and purpose of God" (1978: 399; cf. Driver and Hodgson 1925: 59; Sellers 1940: 134). This aspect of *prosopon* reminds us of the Antiochene emphasis on the union being voluntary, requiring the active participation of Christ's human nature. As Turner notes, "the problem is vital for Nestorius but purely marginal for Cyril" (1975: 311). However, the presence of a human will in Christ does not jeopardize the will of God, for as Nestorius explains, "he

[Christ] acquired nothing else than to wish and to will whatever God willed in him. For this reason God became in him whatever he was in himself" (Chesnut 1978: 400; cf. Driver and Hodgson 1925: 251). Again, "he in nothing deviated from the purpose of God . . . his will was bound to the will of God" (Chesnut 1978: 401; cf. Driver and Hodgson 1925: 63–64; Sellers 1940: 138–40).

Nestorius and "Two Persons" in Christ

The contrast between Alexandrian and Antiochene thought outlined above was essentially a difference in emphasis, between the unity of the person of Christ (Alexandria) and the duality of his divine and human natures (Antioch). Both schools of thought tended to accuse the other of overstating their respective emphasis. That Nestorius and other Antiochenes were accused of preaching "two persons" in Christ is therefore not surprising; this misinterpretation typically occurs when "the context and characteristics of the Christological language of the Antiochene tradition are ignored" (Uthemann 2007: 477). One of the main problems seems to have been Alexandria's inability to accept the symmetrical Christology of Antioch, where divinity and humanity both played key roles, united in the person of Christ. By contrast, Cyril and other Alexandrians insisted on the subject of their Christology being the divine logos, with the result that Christ's humanity became less important. Any attempt by Nestorius or other Antiochenes to present a balanced picture was interpreted as "preaching two persons."

However, Nestorius expressly denies any belief in two sons or two christs, ascribing this view to the followers of Paul of Samosata ("They speak of a double son and a double Christ"). In an exposition of the introduction to John's gospel, which refers to the divine Word of God indwelling Christ, he says, "How then can we understand this to be one Son, and Christ to be another Son, and one that is man only?" Elsewhere, he remarks, "God the Word and the man in whom He came to be are not numerically two" and "He is a single (person), but . . . He is different in the natures of manhood and Godhead" and "I call Christ perfect God and perfect man, not natures which are commingled, but which are united" (Bethune-Baker 1908: 82–85; cf. Driver and Hodgson 1925: 45–46, 50).

Thus, judged by his own words, Nestorius comes across not as a heretic, but as orthodox, in agreement with the theology articulated at Chalcedon. Indeed, he was in complete accord with the Tome of Leo, commenting when he read it, "I gave thanks to God that the Church of Rome was rightly and blamelessly making confessions, even though they happened to be against me personally" (Bethune-Baker 1908: 191–92; cf. Driver and Hodgson 1925: 340). A letter of Nestorius to the inhabitants of Constantinople, probably from 449, further states: "It is my doctrine which Leo and Flavian are upholding. . . . Believe as our holy comrades in the faith, Leo and Flavian!" (Loofs 1914: 25).

Nonetheless, Nestorius's use of *prosopon* is sometimes confusing and undoubtedly supported his enemies' accusations. Besides describing the union occurring in one *prosopon*, he also refers in places to two *prosopa* in Christ, although the former use is much more common than the latter (Loofs 1914: 79). Anastos concludes that he used *prosopon* in two distinct senses: (A) "the exterior aspect or appearance of a thing" (as Loofs observed) and (B) "an approximate equivalent of our word 'person'." The first relates to the two natures of Christ, indicating "each had a substantive reality . . . which remained undiminished after the union," while the second relates to Jesus Christ as "the common prosopon of the two natures." Nestorius is then able to speak of the "two *prosopa (sense* A) . . . in the one *prosopon (sense* B) of Jesus Christ" (Anastos 1962: 129–30; cf. Chesnut 1978: 402; Uthemann 2007: 478).

Put another way, "Nestorius' theory was that the two distinctly existing persons combine to make a new person, who is called Jesus. Hence, Jesus is one person made up of two persons" (Braaten 1963: 258). Admittedly, this dual sense of the word, never clearly explained by Nestorius, is confusing and opens him up to criticism, but given the general fluidity in the terminology of "personhood" mentioned above, it is not surprising and should not be grounds for accusing Nestorius of heresy, especially when he openly said "I separate the natures; but unite the worship" (Sellers 1940: 196).

Based on this distinction in the use of *prosopon*, Anastos summarizes Nestorius's actual Christology as follows:

> Jesus Christ was the divine Logos incarnate, the Son of God in the flesh, the Lord whom his disciples knew as a man but recognized to be God. The unity of his "personality" was further guaranteed by the fact that it was the Logos who both "gave" his prosopon (sense A) to the human nature and "took" that of the human for his own. Moreover, the human will of Christ was always obedient to the divine, so that there never was any conflict or division between the two. (Anastos 1962: 132)

Anastos further comments that "Nestorius' Christology is not characterized by preoccupation with either one of the two natures to the exclusion or detriment of the other, but rather by uncompromising insistence upon the union of both of them in Christ, in their full totality, and unimpaired" (1962: 140).

The Aftermath

In 435, Theodosius had officially banned "the impious books of the said lawless and blasphemous Nestorius" and had forbidden his followers "all right of assembly," an edict that was reissued in modified form in 448, during the height of Theodosius's subsequent support for Eutyches (Millar 2006: 176–77, 186–87). Nestorius himself was banished to Arabia in 436, eventually ending up in the Egyptian desert. The deaths of John of Antioch (440) and Cyril (444) ended this chapter in church history. Although the Council of Chalcedon in 451virtually eulogized "the blessed Cyril" in its Definition document, it anathematized "those who feign that the Lord had two natures before the union, but . . . one after the union," a perfect description of Cyril's position (Stevenson and Frend 1989: 352). Nonetheless, for the sake of ecclesiastical unity, the rallying cry was "Cyril and Leo taught alike" (Frend 1972: 48), and Nestorius continued to be the scapegoat, even though the language of the Definition of Faith, "apart from the word '*hypostasis*'. . . was exactly that used . . . by the West and by Nestorius" (Gray 2005: 222). Indeed, paradoxically, "the essence of Nestorius' beliefs, without his name attached to them, came to be affirmed at the Council of Chalcedon under a Cyrillian guise" (Bevan 2007: 40). Again, although the Western position coincided theologically more with the Antiochene position, "tactically and emotionally Rome was the ally of Alexandria" (Frend 1972: 131–34), and in the end, tactics trumped theological consistency.

By this time, Cyril's status as the champion of orthodoxy had become virtually unassailable; "at Chalcedon and for the century after each party [Chalcedonian or Miaphysite] was able to claim Cyril for their own and set one quotation from his works against another" (Frend 1972: 23). This universally favorable view of Cyril after Ephesus has traditionally been interpreted as evidence of the superiority of his theological views over those of Nestorius, but some have suggested that it equally reflects his polished rhetorical skills: "Nestorius' homiletic discourse was pedantic and recondite in style, while Cyril's was lively" (Wessel 2004: 9). Although some in Constantinople were concerned over Cyril's references to "one incarnate nature" in Christ, especially in light of his equation of *hypostasis* with *physis* (so that his "one *hypostasis* in Christ" could easily be interpreted as "one nature in Christ"), these objections were overcome by "Cyril's mastery of rhetorical argumentation" (Wessel 2004: 298, 301). Throughout this time, up to his death sometime after 450, Nestorius remained in exile in Egypt, well informed of ecclesiastical developments, as we learn from his extant memoirs, to which we now turn.

Conclusion

In conclusion, a comment is necessary about the scholarly approach to Nestorius, especially in the 20th century. Several scholars have concluded that Nestorius was either entirely or nearly orthodox in his beliefs, including Bethune-Baker (1908), Loofs (1914), Sellers (1940), Vine (1948), and Anastos (1962). Indeed, after reading the *Bazaar*, it is clear that he was not guilty of the heresy he was accused of, namely preaching two persons in Christ. Again, note the almost Chalcedonian ring of his confession of "one Christ, one Son, one Lord," and "in one Christ two natures without confusion. By one nature . . .

of the divinity, he was born of God the Father; by the other . . . of the humanity, [he was born] of the holy virgin" (Anastos 1962: 128; cf. Driver and Hodgson 1925: 295–96). Both Loofs and Anastos conclude that, being in full agreement with the Tome of Leo, Nestorius would have wholeheartedly approved of the Chalcedonian confession (Loofs 1914: 99–100; Anastos 1962: 138; cf. Driver and Hodgson 1925: 388–89).

However, the a priori conviction of other scholars that Nestorius was a heretic no matter what he actually taught has made it impossible for them to revise their views: "The old notion that church councils cannot err seems to exercise a powerful influence on some scholars" (Braaten 1963: 254). For those who believe that all church councils have the same divine inspiration and authority as the first Council of Jerusalem described in the New Testament (Acts 15:28), the idea that the church fathers may have gotten it wrong is a threatening concept.

Such scholars dismiss statements by Nestorius that are in fact orthodox as "an emergency invention forced upon him by his adversaries" or as evidence that he "used orthodox phraseology to confound his readers, or he used the orthodox terms in an ambiguous sense, meaning something else by them" (Braaten 1963: 255). They tend to judge Nestorius "in terms of "orthodox christological categories which were made precise at a later date," one even suggesting that if the orthodox Catholic position on Nestorius is questioned, then "even the doctrine of the infallibility of the Pope is at stake" (Braaten 1963: 260). Such a subjective approach is intellectually dishonest and patently unfair to Nestorius.

In contrast, Nestorius's words in the *Bazaar* provide a fitting conclusion to this tragic chapter in church history: "The goal of my earnest wish, then, is that God may be blessed on earth as in heaven. But as for Nestorius, let him be anathema. . . . And would to God that all men by anathematizing me might attain to a reconciliation with God; for to me there is nothing greater or more precious than this" (Bethune-Baker 1908: 190, 198; cf. Driver and Hodgson 1925: 372).

References and Further Reading

Anastos, Milton V. "Nestorius Was Orthodox." *Dumbarton Oaks Papers* 16 (1962): 117–40.

Bethune-Baker, J. F. *Nestorius and His Teaching: A Fresh Examination of the Evidence.* Cambridge: Cambridge University Press, 1908.

Bevan, George A. "The Last Days of Nestorius in the Syriac Sources." *Journal of the Canadian Society for Syriac Studies* 7 (2007): 39–54.

Braaten, Carl E. "Modern Interpretations of Nestorius." *Church History* 32 (1963): 251–67.

Brock, Sebastian P. "The 'Nestorian' Church: A Lamentable Misnomer." *Bulletin of the John Rylands University Library* 78, 3 (1996): 23–35.

Cameron, Averil. "The Theotokos in Sixth-Century Constantinople." *Journal of Theological Studies* 29 (N.S.) (1978): 79–108.

Chesnut, Roberta C. "The Two Prosopa in Nestorius' *Bazaar of Heracleides*." *Journal of Theological Studies* 29 (N.S.) (1978): 392–409.

DelCogliano, Mark, trans. "Nestorius, 2nd and 3rd Letters to Pope Celestine." www.tertullian.org/fathers/nestorius_two_letters_01.htm (translated 2005, cited April 5, 2009) (accessed May 31, 1010).

Driver, G. R., and Leonard Hodgson, trans. *Nestorius: The Bazaar of Heracleides*. Oxford: Clarendon, 1925.

Frend, W. H. C. *The Rise of the Monophysite Movement: Chapters in the History of the Church in the Fifth and Sixth Centuries*. Cambridge: Cambridge University Press, 1972.

Gray, Patrick T. R. "The Legacy of Chalcedon: Christological Problems and Their Significance." In *The Cambridge Companion to the Age of Justinian* (pp. 215–38). Edited by Michael Maas. Cambridge: Cambridge University Press, 2005.

Loofs, Friedrich. *Nestorius and His Place in the History of Christian Doctrine*. Cambridge: Cambridge University Press, 1914. (Reprint: New York: Burt Franklin Reprints, 1975).

Loofs, Friedrich, ed. *Nestoriana: Die Fragmente Des Nestorius*. Halle: Max Niemeyer, 1905.

McGuckin, J. A. "Nestorius and the Political Factions of Fifth-Century Byzantium: Factors in His Personal Downfall." *Bulletin of the John Rylands University Library* 78, 3 (1996): 7–21.

Millar, Fergus. *A Greek Roman Empire: Power and Belief under Theodosius II (408–450)*. Berkeley: University of California Press, 2006.

Nau, François, trans. *Nestorius: Le Livre d'Héraclide de Damas*. Paris: Letouzey et Ané, 1910.

Russell, Norman. *Cyril of Alexandria*. London: Routledge, 2000.

Sellers, R. V. *Two Ancient Christologies*. London: SPCK, 1940.

Stevenson, J., and W. H. C. Frend, eds. *A New Eusebius: Documents Illustrating the History of the Church to AD 337*. 2nd ed. London: SPCK, 1987.

Stevenson, J., and W. H. C. Frend, eds. *Creeds, Councils and Controversies: Documents Illustrating the History of the Church AD 337–461*. 2nd ed. London: SPCK, 1989.

Turcescu, Lucian. "Prosōpon and Hypostasis in Basil of Caesarea's 'Against Eunomius' and the Epistles." *Vigiliae Christianae* 51, 4 (1997): 374–95.

Turner, H. E. W. "Nestorius Reconsidered." In *Studia Patristica XIII* (Texte und Untersuchungen 116) (pp. 306–21). Berlin: Akademie-Verlag, 1975.

Uthemann, Karl Heinz. "History of Christology to the Seventh Century." In *The Cambridge History of Christianity*, Vol. 2: *Constantine to c. 600* (pp. 460–500). Edited by Augustine Casiday and Frederick W. Norris. Cambridge: Cambridge University Press, 2007.

Vine, Aubrey R. *An Approach to Christology*. London: Independent Press, 1948.

Wessel, Susan. *Cyril of Alexandria and the Nestorian Controversy*. Oxford: Oxford University Press, 2004.

CON

There were dramatic changes in the Roman world during the fourth and fifth centuries. In the western empire, invasions from cultures as diverse as the Visigoths, Vandals, and Huns marked this time period as extremely unstable. The eastern empire, however, weathered the storm slightly less dramatically. Because of the strategic location of the eastern capital of Constantinople, a wealthier agricultural base, and fewer vulnerable frontiers, the eastern empire was able to survive for another thousand years. Yet even the eastern empire experienced episodes of instability, and these periods of unrest are mirrored in church history.

The church of the fifth century was organized into a patriarchate model, with three bishops serving as patriarchs of the church. These patriarchs were more powerful than other bishops in the church, and they included the bishop of Rome, the bishop of Alexandria, and the bishop of Antioch. The bishop of Constantinople and the bishop of Jerusalem were in the second tier and were elevated to patriarch status by the Council of Chalcedon in 451, leading to something called the pentarchy. Eventually, the capital cities of Rome and Constantinople featured the two principal bishops.

Throughout the fifth century there were arguments about the definition of acceptable and unacceptable belief systems for the developing Christian religion. One of a series of recurring questions concerning the Christology of Christ was: Was Christ human, divine, or both? There were several church councils called to debate this important issue, including the Council of Nicaea (325) among others. One of the principal participants in the controversy was Nestorius (ca. 381–ca. 451), the bishop of Constantinople. We know little about Nestorius's early life, but according to the theological historian Friedrich Loofs, Nestorius was born in Syria and became a monk at an early age. He studied under Theodore of Mopsuestia (ca. 350–428) for a time. Nestorius was living as a monk when he was chosen by the weak leader Emperor Theodosius II (Flavius Theodosius II [401–450]) to become the bishop of Constantinople in 428 (Loofs 1914: 7).

Nestorius was a controversial figure from a very early age. As a young man, he was well known for his ascetic practices and for his public speaking ability. As a result of a power struggle, he was selected to be the bishop of Constantinople by Theodosius II. Even after his promotion to bishop, Nestorius maintained strong ties to Antioch. Immediately upon assuming his new leadership position, Nestorius began a series of reforms to make certain parishioners in Constantinople practiced Christianity correctly. As one of his first acts as bishop, he expelled several groups from Constantinople, including Arians and Novatianists. Then, he took disciplinary actions against a number of monks, including those who were not associated with particular monasteries, wandering monks, and monks who were acting incorrectly (Caner 2002: 212–15). Next, in one of his first sermons, Nestorius preached against the popular practice of referring to the Virgin Mary as *Theotokos* (which means "God-bearer" or "Mother of God"). According to Nestorius, the problem with calling the Virgin Mary the "God-bearer" was that Mary was human and therefore could not have been the mother of the divine nature of Christ (Nystrom 2003: 94). He worried that by using the term *Theotokos* the full humanity of Christ might be compromised. All of these actions served to bring him to the attention of rival bishops in the area.

The controversy concerning the correct title for the Virgin Mary actually had its beginnings in Nestorius's hometown—the city of Antioch. According to historian Philip Rousseau, Antioch was the one city that represented the new Christian world and was quite famous as the first place that followers of Christ were called "Christians." Through the years, Antioch housed a number of famous theologians including John Chrysostom (Rousseau 2002: 349–407) and Nestorius. Antioch was famous for the number of theological disputes that arose there as well. Additionally, Antioch was an important region politically, acting as a border between the eastern empire and the Sassanian Persians. Because of its historical and political position, Antioch became a central clearinghouse for new ideas concerning the changing views of Christianity. Unfortunately, failure to resolve the controversies concerning these shifting ideas eventually drove a wedge between Antioch and other Christians in the east (Rousseau 2002: 191–92).

Mosaic of Virgin Mary and Jesus Christ, Hagia Sofia, Istanbul. (Pavle Marjanovic/ Dreamstime.com)

Historical Background

Most of the conflicts concerning Christianity within the city of Antioch resulted from a dispute that had arisen over 100 years earlier in nearby Alexandria concerning the divinity of Christ. This argument was known as the Arian controversy, which developed into one of the most long lasting of all the Christian heresies. We know little about the founder of this debate, because it is difficult to reconstruct the life and writings of many early Christian writers, since they were later deemed heretical and their writings destroyed. Most of the information on Arius can be found in the writings of Athanasius (ca. 293–373) and the church historians Rufinus, Socrates, Sozemen, and Philostorgius. Beginning around 318, a priest named Arius clashed with Alexander, the bishop of Alexandria, over the interpretation of the divinity of Christ. This debate focused on the identity of Christ, centering on the first chapter in the Gospel of John. Arius claimed that the Son of God was less divine than God but was created by God before time began and was therefore a creature of God. For Arius, the Son was not made of the same divine "essence" of the Father and was less divine than God, but the Son still was divine. This argument was problematic because it seemed to indicate the existence of two gods. Arius also argued that the Son had a diminished role and that God had produced the Son "in time"; therefore, the Son was noneternal, and susceptible to change. If the Son was created "in time," then, at least in theory, the Son would be capable of change because nothing created in time can be expected to last indefinitely. The prospect of a changing Son was extremely troubling because it seemed to threaten the concept of eternal salvation (Nystrom 2003: 90).

Arius's teachings spread rapidly throughout the region; assisted no doubt by an Arian saying that appeared in popular culture as a song. By the time Bishop Alexander condemned his teachings and excommunicated him (ca. 320), Arius had gone into exile. While exiled, Arius's influence grew and he won new adherents, including several powerful eastern bishops. Despite efforts by various bishops to quell its popularity, the Arian movement continued to spread and eventually became powerful enough to threaten a permanent division between Christian factions. In order to maintain peace in the recently fused empire, the Emperor Constantine called a General Council at Nicaea in 325. It was here that the opponents of Arianism, led by the deacon Athanasius, succeeded in defining the coeternity and coequality of the Father and the Son, using the term *homoousios* to describe their sameness of substance. They also decided that the Son was not created, but instead was begotten, and that the Son had always existed. These beliefs were woven into the Creed of Nicaea and were explicitly included as a reaction to Arian beliefs. At the conclusion of the Council at Nicaea, Arius and several of the bishops who supported him were banished.

Unfortunately, the Council and Creed of Nicaea did not put an end to the controversy surrounding the relationship of the Father and the Son. After the death of Constantine in 337, the disagreements resumed. The Arian movement was still strong enough to sway the opinion of the general population, some of the eastern bishops, and even the new emperor, Constantius II (337–361). These bishops made the argument that the term *homoousios* did not allow enough distinction between the Father and the Son, because of its emphasis on the Father and the Son's sameness of substance. The bishops argued that *homoiousios*, "of similar substance," was a better definition. The eastern bishops lined up against the Nicene bishops, led by Athanasius until he died in 373. After his death, three great theologians from Cappadocia (northern Turkey) continued to speak for the decisions that were reached at Nicaea. Basil (the Great), Gregory of Nyssa, and Gregory of Nazianzus became known as the Cappadocian Fathers. They wrote their opinions in Greek and argued that it is the nature of divinity to express itself as a triune entity, and that the Father, Son, and Holy Spirit were equal in divinity, yet at the same time were distinctly individual. This equality eventually became the idea of the Trinity, which was accepted as orthodox at the Council of Constantinople in 381. Because of this council, Arianism was declared a heresy and eventually died out.

After defining the relationship between the Father and the Son, the Christian theologians tackled issues relating to the nature of Christ and his role in salvation. This question was no less problematic than that of defining the Trinity. There were two schools of thought regarding the idea of the nature of Christ. The Antioch theologians suggested that Christ had two completely separate natures, both human and divine. The Alexandrian theologians took a different approach, choosing to emphasize only the divine nature of Christ. In order to solve the dilemma of which school of thought was correct, the Council of Chalcedon was called in 451. Unfortunately, this council did not fully solve the dilemma of the nature of Christ, and because they were unable to come to a conclusion, a Syrian bishop by the name of Apollinarius (ca. 310–ca. 390) began to teach that the Son's body was human but his mind was divine. For Apollinarius, this solution made perfect sense, as it demonstrated that humanity and divinity could be present in the same body.

Of course there were many reactions to the Apollinarius theory. The Cappadocian Fathers said that Christ had to become human so that individuals might be saved. Because Apollinarius said that Christ's mind and body were not of the same nature, it implied to the Cappadocians that Christ had not become completely human. Theodore of Mopsuestia (ca. 350–428) was also a critic of Apollinarius. He argued that Christ must have had a completely human mind because of his experiences of emotion and intellectual growth. Apollinarius was discredited in the Council of Constantinople in 381.

Theodore of Mopsuestia was from Antioch and had his own theory about the nature of Christ. He posited that Christ was the only person who had two complete natures. Each of the natures was clearly distinguishable from the other, and this could be demonstrated from passages in the New Testament scriptures. According to Theodore, Christ's human nature was present when he wept or hungered—clearly physical manifestations of his human nature—and his divine nature was demonstrated when he performed miracles or taught parables. The focused emphasis on Christ's human nature allowed theologians to highlight the reality of Christ's human suffering, an emphasis that the Antioch school believed was often minimized by the Alexandrian school.

As discussed above, Nestorius was a student of Theodore of Mopsuestia, and because of this close association he carried Theodore's logic to the next step. According to scholar John McGuckin, Nestorius believed that the divine and the human parts of Christ were represented by two distinct natures—the divine nature demonstrating itself in divine works and the human nature as revealed by his earthly limitations (McGuckin 1994: 134–36). There was a popular custom of calling the Virgin Mary the "God-bearer" or "Mother of God," and Nestorius argued the imprecision of this designation. Since Christ experienced a human birth, this part of his nature should be categorized with physical characteristics like weeping or hungering. And since Mary could not be the mother of the divine nature in Christ—that part certainly came from the Father—Nestorius felt that it was not correct to call her *Theotokos*. A better title for the Virgin Mary, according to Nestorius, was *Christotokos* or "Christ-bearer/ Mother of Christ." This title recognized Mary as the mother of the human, though not of the divine nature of Christ.

Of course there was much controversy surrounding Nestorius's approach. Many Christians felt that Nestorius was attacking the cult of the Virgin Mother, and the acceptance of the title *Theotokos* became a sort of litmus test for faith. By 429 Nestorius had decided to bring his argument to the people by giving a series of public lectures at the cathedral. The first one of these sermons was given by a chaplain named Anastasius. In order to make sure Mary was not viewed as a sort of goddess figure, his lecture portrayed Mary as fully human, and he noted that it was impossible for God to be born from a mere woman. This sermon received very negative reviews, and another clergyman, Bishop Proclus (d. ca. 447) answered it with a sermon of his own on the Virgin Mother of God, which reiterated the popular view of the Virgin Mary. Since Proclus's sermon was greeted with loud applause, Nestorius decided to take matters into his own hands and answered the criticism with a series of his own sermons. The church historian Socrates suggests that by this time Nestorius saw this discussion as an underlying rebellion, symptomatic of those in Constantinople who resisted his reforms.

Nestorius's series of sermons at the cathedral did nothing to improve his standing in the theological community. Because of his stance on the *Theotokos* title, his opponents compared him to an ancient heretic Paul of Samosata (200–275), who taught that Jesus was only a God-inspired man. Rumors flew, claiming that Nestorius was teaching a theory of "two sons" rather than the orthodox belief in one son, and bishops from surrounding areas began to take notice of the tumult.

The issue of whether or not to grant Mary the title of *Theotokos* continued as part of the controversy; but another issue, concerning the nature of the union between God and man in Christ, soon became more important. Nestorius taught that there were three *prosopa* (persons) living in Christ. These persons included a divine *prosopon*, a *prosopon* of the human nature or substance, and a union *prosopon*. For Nestorius, if Jesus was wholly God and completely human, there must be a *prosopon* of each nature and also a *prosopon* of the union. This third type of *prosopon* was theoretically defined by Nestorius as a sort of "conjunction" to describe the union of God and humanity (Urban 1986: 85–86). It was this third idea of the "union" person living in Christ that would prove to be Nestorius's undoing.

Historical Evidence

It is impossible to trace the life and ideas of Nestorius without also examining the life of Cyril of Alexandria (378–428). Cyril was one of the finest Christian theologians of his day, and he also stands out in the ranks of the greatest patristic writers (McGuckin 1994: 1). We know there were difficulties between Cyril and Nestorius because we have fragments of Nestorius's writings and sermons as well as Cyril's correspondence from the surviving Acts of the Council of Ephesus. Cyril decided it was time to intervene when Nestorius began to make imprecise statements. Prior to the Council of Ephesus in 431, Nestorius had announced to a group of bishops that God was not an infant two or three months old. What he had meant to say was that human suffering should be attributed to Christ's human nature, not his divine nature. Unfortunately, the bishops believed Nestorius meant that God could not have appeared in human form. Cyril did not hesitate to take full advantage of this and arranged for a public sign to be carried around town printed with Nestorius's words "Jesus was not God," openly accusing Nestorius of heresy (Wessel 2004: 140–42). In addition to the placard, several ascetic monks wrote a series of letters to the emperor asking for a trial for Nestorius on the charge of heresy and negligence toward church affairs. Since several of these monks were part of his own church, Cyril considered it his right to get involved.

Cyril was certainly brilliant, ruthless, and quite politically savvy. Even though Nestorius held the powerful office of bishop and had a reputation as a gifted speaker, he could not compete with Cyril. Beginning with a letter to monks in the area, Cyril began his crusade against Nestorius. This letter, in turn, elicited a response from one of his Nestorius's colleagues in order to answer to the points raised by Cyril. The correspondence continued between Nestorius and Cyril over the next two-and-a-half years.

In order to decide the matter, both Cyril and Nestorius appealed to Pope Celestine I (422–432). In August 430, Celestine called a church council in Rome and heard the case. The council ruled that *Theotokos* was the correct designation for the Virgin Mary, and that Nestorius should renounce his former views on the subject. Nestorius and his allies rejected the ruling and asked that the emperor Theodosius organize a general church council.

By the end of the summer of 431, Theodosius convened the Council of Ephesus to resolve the problem. Theodosius believed that Ephesus was a neutral site, and expressly desired Nestorius to be present at the meeting. Unfortunately for Nestorius, Cyril began the proceedings without waiting for either Nestorius or the bishops from Antioch to appear. When Nestorius and his allies arrived, they were met by a mob of irate monks organized by Cyril. Because of Cyril's skillful leadership, it only took one day to condemn Nestorius as the new "Judas," strip him of his authority as bishop, and defend the concept of the *Theotokos* as Mother of God. Nestorius was ostracized and banished into Egypt. He died in 451, always claiming that he had been misunderstood and that his downfall had been orchestrated by Cyril.

Religious fervor in Constantinople calmed down considerably after Nestorius's dismissal in 431, but divisions remained between Antioch and Alexandria. The Antioch school of theology continued to defend Christ's distinct humanity, and the Alexandrian school continued to teach that there was no distinction between the human and divine natures of Christ. Pressure was placed on Cyril to moderate his position in order to restore good relations with the church at Antioch. Accordingly, Bishop John of Antioch (428–441) wrote a compromise known as the *Formula of Reunion* (433), which described Christ as a union of both natures: divine and human. Cyril was later able to describe Christ as having one nature (hypostasis) arising out of two distinct natures. These ideas became known as the *communication idiomatum*—a sharing or imparting of particular qualities—and helped explain that Mary had given birth to a human being and had borne divinity as well.

The *Formula of Reunion* compromise remained in effect while Cyril and John of Alexandria were alive, but after they died conflict broke out again between Alexandria and Antioch. This time the disagreement concerned a theory by a monk from Constantinople named Eutyches. He maintained that Christ had two natures before the incarnation but claimed that they were so well blended in their union that afterward Christ only had a monophysite (one) nature. By this time, Dioscorus had taken over Cyril's post as bishop of Alexandria. He called another Council at Ephesus in 449 that verified Eutyches's theory of Christ's single nature and prohibited anyone from mentioning the concept of Christ's two natures. In order to back up his prohibition, Dioscorus brought a group of fanatical monks along to intimidate dissenters. This second Council at Ephesus was considered a travesty and was nicknamed the "Robber Council" by Pope Leo I (440–461) and appealed mainly to monophysite

The Canons of the Council of Ephesus

At the first Council of Ephesus in 431, Cyril of Alexandria was able to push through a series of holy laws, or canons, to ensure that Nestorianism would be considered a heresy, and all who subscribed to it heretics.

Canon II. IF any provincial bishops were not present at the holy Synod and have joined or attempted to join the apostasy; or if, after subscribing the deposition of Nestorius, they went back into the assembly of apostates; these men, according to the decree of the holy Synod, are to be deposed from the priesthood and degraded from their rank.

Canon III. IF any of the city or country clergy have been inhibited by Nestorius or his followers from the exercise of the priesthood, on account of their orthodoxy, we have declared it just that these should be restored to their proper rank. And in general we forbid all the clergy who adhere to the Orthodox and Ecumenical Synod in any way to submit to the bishops who have already apostatized or shall hereafter apostatize.

Canon IV. IF any of the clergy should fall away, and publicly or privately presume to maintain the doctrines of Nestorius or Celestius, it is declared just by the holy Synod that these also should be deposed.

Canon V. IF any have been condemned for evil practices by the holy Synod, or by their own bishops; and if, with his usual lack of discrimination, Nestorius (or his followers) has attempted, or shall hereafter attempt, uncanonically to restore such persons to communion and to their former rank, we have declared that they shall not be profited thereby, but shall remain deposed nevertheless.

Canon VI. LIKEWISE, if any should in any way attempt to set aside the orders in each case made by the holy Synod at Ephesus, the holy Synod decrees that, if they be bishops or clergymen, they shall absolutely forfeit their office; and, if laymen, that they shall be excommunicated.

Source: *Nicene and Post-Nicene Fathers*, 2nd series, Vol. 14, edited by Henry R. Percival. Peabody, MA: Hendrickson Publishers, 1885.

Christians. To answer the monophysites, another council was called at Chalcedon in 451. This council adopted a definition of Christology positing that Christ was one person possessing two natures, both human and divine, and each shared characteristics of the other. They also put forward that Christ was of one substance with the Father, thus silencing the Arians. The Council of Chalcedon was considered a success because it defined Christology in a way that most Christians consider orthodox even today. Those churches that were unhappy with the compromise position joined the monophysite churches, a tradition that remains today in the Coptic Christian communities of Egypt and Ethiopia. Other followers of Nestorian founded a group called Nestorianism. It managed to continue by expanding eastward into Mesopotamia, Persia, and China. Nestorian communities can still be found today in Syria, Iraq, and Iran (Nystrom 2003: 94–96).

Historical Interpretation

Scholars who have analyzed the Nestorian controversy during the fifth century have questions about what the central question really is. As early as the fifth century an ecclesiastical historian named Socrates, in his *Ecclesiastical History*, viewed Nestorius as a victim of political pragmatism. He explained that even though Nestorius might be guilty of pride and ignorance, he was not guilty of heresy. Socrates restated Nestorius's view that the term *Theotokos* was problematic, as it might give rise to a goddess/virgin mythology. He also reiterated that Nestorius did not deny Christ's divinity. Martin Luther also examined the writings of Nestorius. In his book *Von Conciliis und Kirchen*, Luther notes that he did not understand the nature of Nestorius's error. After doing his own research on the matter, Luther found that Nestorius had been wrongly accused of teaching that Christ had two persons (Braaten 1963: 252–53).

Modern Historiography

There have been a number of texts published in the 19th and 20th centuries that served to reopen the question of Nestorius's orthodoxy. The first of these texts was Friedrich Loofs's edition of the *Nestoriana* (1905) in which he collected all of the previously known works of Nestorius as well as approximately 100 newly discovered fragments. The second important factor was the 1895 discovery of Nestorius's book called *Bazaar of Heracleides*, in a Syriac translation. This text was translated into English in 1925. In this text, Nestorius claimed that his words were misinterpreted, and that he believed that Christ had two natures, both human and divine, but in only one person. Scholars, however, are still divided as to whether Nestorius engaged in heretical rhetoric.

Historians began to examine the problem of Nestorius and his orthodoxy. The issues concerning Christ's divinity–humanity seemed to expand far beyond the *Theotokos* issue. Since there was serious contention between Alexandria and Constantinople throughout this time period, several scholars see friction as the real problem—both in the political realm and among the strong personalities of the era. For instance, Friedrich Loofs maintains that Cyril's interest in negating the teachings of Nestorius was a result of political maneuvering on Cyril's part, in order to avert attention away from his own teachings. G. L. Prestige argues that political and personal factors were certainly part of the problem, but that misunderstanding about language was a bigger issue (Prestige 1940: 264). According to Robert Sellers, both sides had a difficult time understanding the terminology used by the other side, but in essence were saying the same thing (1940: 208–14, 233).

More recently, scholars have examined the controversies and put forward the idea that while the differences in politics were significant, theological differences were more important. These historians argue that the fundamental issue centered on the view that Christ could only be depicted fully with a dual nature, according to boundaries set forth in scripture. Since the West adopts a use of concrete terms to describe the humanity of Christ, these academics generally view Western Christology to be closer to Nestorius's ideas than to Cyril's view.

A third group of scholars asks whether or not Nestorius believed that God was present at all in the incarnation, and to mixed results. Bethune-Baker posited in 1903 that Nestorius had taught two persons in Christ. However, after reading the *Bazaar of Heracleides* he changed his mind and agreed with Grill-meier that the Antioch bishops correctly identified the full humanity of Christ; but they did not go far enough in emphasizing the idea that God had become fully human (Bethune-Baker 1903: 274–76; Grillmeier 1975: 465–77). In contrast to these scholars, Donald Fairbairn argues that, on the one hand, the Nestorian dispute was not about the idea that there were two persons in Christ, or whether Christ was a single person, but instead the controversy was really about the identity of one personal subject. According to Fairbairn, Nestorius saw the *prosopon* of Christ as a unique hybrid of the divine and humanity. On the other hand, Cyril viewed Christ as a composite *prosopon*, as God himself who had become human and come to earth in order to provide humanity with a fuller communion. For Cyril, it did not matter how poorly Nestorius explained the composite notion of union in Christ, if there was a composite unity, then Christ was not divine and it might as well be the case that there were two sons of God (Fairbairn 2003: 130–32).

Conclusion

From the moment of Nestorius's excommunication until now there have been expressions of uncertainty as to whether he truly taught and believed what was later defined and condemned as Nestorianism (Braaten 1963: 251). The concept that became known as Nestorianism maintained that Christ was divided into to two persons, one human and the other divine, which denied the incarnation. The specific nature of Nestorius's belief system is still disputed, and until recently historians tended to view Nestorius from Cyril's point of view. Some scholars suggest that a mistranslation of the word *prosopon* caused most of the difficulties. The discovery of the text of the *Bazaar of Heracleides* has caused other scholars to reexamine the issues raised by the Council of Chalcedon and has convinced many that Nestorius was an orthodox theologian who was merely striving to negotiate a compromise between Antioch and Alexandria.

The theology of Nestorius continues to be problematic for historians. Nestorius was condemned and exiled as a heretic during the fifth century because of his beliefs. After the Council of Ephesus in 431, however, the Assyrian church of the east (eastern Iraq and Iran) refused to condemn Nestorius as a heretic. This rejection eventually led to a split known as the Nestorian schism, which separated the Assyrian church from the Byzantine church. Nestorianism was condemned and eventually stamped out in the Roman world, but because of missionary activity it spread into the Arabian Peninsula, India, and China. There are a few Nestorian communities remaining today, mostly in the Arabian Peninsula, but also in India and the United States.

References

Bethune-Baker, J. F. *Early History of Christian Doctrine*. London: Metheun, 1903.

Bethune-Baker, J. F. *Nestorius and His Teaching: A Fresh Examination of the Evidence*. New York: Cambridge University Press, 1908.

Braaten, Carl E. "Modern Interpretations of Nestorius." *Church History* 32 (1963): 251–67.

Caner, Daniel. *Wandering, Begging Monks: Spiritual Authority and the Promotion of Monasticism in Late Antiquity*. Berkeley: University of California Press, 2002.

Cross, F. L. *The Oxford Dictionary of the Christian Church*. New York: Oxford University Press, 2005.

Evans, G. R. *The First Christian Theologians: An introduction to Theology in the Early Church*. London: Blackwell, 2004.

Fairbairn, Donald. *Grace and Christology in the Early Church*. New York: Oxford University Press, 2003.

Ferguson, Everett. *Encyclopedia of Early Christianity*. New York: Garland, 1997.

Frend, W. H. C. *Encyclopedia of the Early Church*, Vols. I and II. New York: Oxford University Press, 1992.

Grillmeier, Alois. *Christ in Christian Tradition*. Louisville, KY: John Knox Press, 1975.

Hastings, Adrian. *The Oxford Companion to Christian Thought*. New York: Oxford University Press, 2000.

Kelly, J. N. D. *Early Christian Doctrines*. London: Adam and Charles Black, 1978.

Loofs, Friedrich. *Nestorius and His Place in the History of Christian Doctrine*. New York: Cambridge University Press, 1914.

McGrath, Aliester E. *Christian Theology: An Introduction*. London: Blackwell, 2007.

McGuckin, John A. *St. Cyril of Alexandria the Christological Controversy: Its History, Theology and Texts*. Leiden: Brill, 1994.

Nystrom, Bradley P., and David P. Nystrom. *The History of Christianity: An Introduction*. New York: McGraw-Hill, 2003.

Olson, Roger E. *The Story of Christian Theology: Twenty Centuries of Tradition and Reform*. Downers Grove, IL: InterVarsity Press, 1999.

Pelikan, Jaroslav. *The Christian Tradition: A History and the Development of Doctrine*. Chicago: University of Chicago Press, 1971.

Prestige, G. L. *Fathers and Heretics: Six Studies in Dogmatic Faith with Prologue and Epilogue*. New York: Macmillan, 1940.

Rousseau, Philip. *The Early Christian Centuries*. New York: Longman, 2002.

Russell, Norman. *Cyril of Alexandria*. New York: Routledge, 2000.

Sellers, Robert. *Two Ancient Christologies: A Study in the Christological Thought of the Schools of Alexandria and Antioch in the Early History of Christian Doctrine*. London: Society for Promoting Christian Knowledge, 1940.

Urban, Linwood. *A Short History of Christian Thought*. New York: Oxford University Press, 1986.

Wessel, Susan. *Cyril of Alexandria and the Nestorian Controversy: The Making of a Saint and of a Heretic*. New York: Oxford University Press, 2004.

9

The Celtic Church that arose after 400 CE as distinct from Roman Catholicism is a modern construct, rather than a historical reality.

PRO   Michael Greaney
CON   Joseph P. Byrne

PRO

During the reign of Charles I Stuart (1600–1649), there were two "parties" in the Church of England. The Puritans, or "Low Church," rejected anything that hinted of "Roman" control or influence. The "High Church" preferred to retain the outward forms of Catholic worship, as well as most of the doctrines apart from papal supremacy. Puritans asserted that adopting the outward forms of Catholic worship made one a "papist," whether or not the worshiper acknowledged papal supremacy. This presented the Stuart state, actually three different kingdoms with wildly divergent interests and strong mutual antagonisms, with a serious problem. Beginning with James I (1566–1625), the aim of the king was not so much to rule well, but to rule at all. Religion being the most volatile issue, the Stuarts pursued a policy of general toleration among the four main religious groups: Catholics, Puritans, the Scottish Kirk (Covenanters), and the Established Church.

Charles I's idea of governance was to achieve unity as one of the highest priorities and to enhance royal power at the same time. Because religious differences were believed to be at the bottom of much of the political discontent, imposing uniformity of practice became crucial. In this, Charles was strongly influenced by William Laud, archbishop of Canterbury (1573–1645). It was Laud's views that would go a long way in convincing Charles that the Celtic Church was a separate and threatening religious body. Laud had a great attachment to the "externals" of Catholic worship, but had to tread very carefully with respect to doctrine, because the Puritans regarded Laud as a virtual "papist" on account of the Catholic forms he preferred and tried to impose on the Church of England. This came into conflict with Laud's goal of a unified, national church to support a unified state. Laud believed he could only unify the Church of England by imposing externals and a uniform prayer book. In Laud's eyes and his intellectual and religious successors', form became everything, substance nothing.

Laud's sophistry would reach its ultimate expression in the Oxford movement of the early 19th century and its development of "Branch theory." In the eyes of Laud and his descendants, external practices, not adherence to specific doctrines, determine whether an organization is part of a universal church. Since the Celtic Church differed from the universal church on the continent on matters of form, it must, therefore, be a distinct and separate visible church, although part of the invisible church. The Catholic position (shared by the Orthodox and many Protestant churches) is that adherence to essential doctrines—most notably papal supremacy—makes a rite Catholic, not outward forms or liturgical practices. The issue, then, is whether the differences in liturgical practice that characterized the Celtic Church were "substantial" or merely "accidental," that is, involving only outward forms and not touching essential doctrine. The evidence of history supports the conclusion that the Celtic Church from the earliest time was, and always considered itself to be, in union with Rome. It was not a separate entity from the rest of the church in England, and thus, the idea of a distinct Celtic Church is a modern construct rather than a historically supported reality.

Palladius and Patrick

Contrary to popular belief, there were Christians in Ireland (called Scotia in late imperial and early medieval times) before the advent of Patrick, the "apostle of the Irish." Prosper of Aquitaine (ca. 390–455, 460, or 465, depending on the source consulted), recorded in his *Epitoma Chronicon* that Pope Celestine I (422–432) made deacon Palladius (ca. 408–ca. 460) a bishop and sent him on a mission "to the Scots believing in Christ" in the eighth year (431) of the reign of the Emperor Theodosius II (401–450).

The Palladius the pope commissioned as his first official representative to Ireland may be the same Palladius who recommended to Pope Celestine that Germanus be sent in 428 to dispute with adherents of "Pelagianism" in Britain where the heresy was particularly strong. Pelagianism denied original sin and Christian grace. Contemporaries disagreed as to Pelagius's country of origin. Augustine, Orosius, Prosper of Aquitaine, and Marius Mercator asserted that the cognomen "Brito" or "Britannicus" indicated that Pelagius was from Britain. Jerome, however (at odds with Augustine on most nondoctrinal matters), called Pelagius "a stupid fellow, stuffed with the porridge of the Scots," and claimed that the Irish diet affected the heresiarch's memory and reasoning power (Praef. in Jerem., Lib. I, III).

Jerome stated that Pelagius came from Ireland, staying in Britain only long enough to spread his doctrines there before traveling to Rome where he briefly succeeded in persuading Pope Zozimus of his orthodoxy. Augustine and Jerome put personal differences aside and convinced Zozimus to condemn Pelagianism.

The appointment of a bishop to an area outside the classical world bounded by the limits of the Roman Empire demonstrates the importance that Rome put on refuting and countering the heresy and in securing the orthodoxy of all believers in matters of essential doctrine. The civil unrest prevalent at this time throughout the empire had serious effects on the church as well. Sending a mission to "the Gentiles" (as those who lived beyond the boundaries of the empire were termed) should have had a very low priority. There was a desperate need to provide bishops and priests to meet the needs of existing believers within the empire, with nothing to spare for spreading Christianity into new areas. Clearly, however, Pelagianism was considered so dangerous that all possible sources of Pelagianism were to be identified and the heresy extirpated. Consequently, the pope decided that the best and most effective response was to send official missions to both Britain and Ireland, thereby making certain that Pelagianism had no hidden base from which it could reemerge and endanger the church.

Unfortunately, Palladius was not equal to the task. As effective as he evidently was within the world of Romanized Britain and Gaul, Palladius seems to have lacked the necessary background for dealing with a people outside that particular milieu. The culture and society of Ireland were significantly different from that of the classical world and constituted what was, effectively, an alien environment. Within a year, Palladius was recalled and Patrick replaced him.

According to his "Confession," Patrick was born somewhere in Roman Britain, the son of a Decurian, a civic official, but was captured at an early age and sold as a slave in Ireland. After years in captivity, Patrick escaped and made his way to Gaul, where he studied for the priesthood and was ordained. Patrick claimed he heard the Irish calling to him in his dreams, urging him to return to Ireland and convert them to Christianity. It is not clear how Patrick was selected to replace Palladius, but his superiors were evidently aware that Patrick was the ideal candidate to send on a mission to the Irish.

Consequently, Patrick was named a bishop and sent to Ireland. He made a number of important converts almost immediately, and eventually set up an administration based on the Roman model, headquartered in the ancient cultic center of Armagh. Most importantly, Patrick, whatever his perceptions of his own inadequacies or lack of learning, seems to have been outstandingly successful at completely eliminating Pelagianism among the Irish Christians that he found and in inculcating orthodox Christianity among his converts.

Patrick's success seems to have been recognized in Rome for, according to the Annals of Ulster, Rome sent three "auxiliary bishops" to Ireland to assist Patrick in 439, and in 441 Pope Leo the Great confirmed Patrick as head of the church in Ireland. Possibly realizing that outward forms and customs are not as important as adherence to sound doctrine, Patrick was less successful in grafting the traditional administrative structure and liturgical practices of the Western Church onto the unique culture in Ireland.

Concerned more with preventing the spread of a heresy, Patrick would likely have been somewhat lax in building a foundation of support for outward forms in contrast to the effort he put into making certain the Irish were orthodox. For a missionary operating in an alien environment, the important thing was the unity of belief in essential doctrines, not uniformity of outward practices.

Specific Differences

In the decades following Patrick's missionary effort, the Church in Ireland adapted to the unique conditions in that country. The most significant difference was that the Church in Ireland centered on monasteries instead of cities. The Irish tribal structure seemed particularly suited for this arrangement, with control of the local monastery often vested in the same family for generations. The abbot, not the bishop, became the most important administrative individual in the Irish Church. A bishop was doctrinally necessary in order to maintain the "apostolic succession" and the tie to the rest of the church. Politically and administratively, however, the bishop was of minor importance.

The style of "tonsure" was also different in the Irish Church. Tonsure is a rite in which a baptized and confirmed Christian is received into the clerical order by shaving all or a portion of his head. It was not universally practiced in the early church. Jerome disapproved of the practice. On the continent, the style of tonsure was adapted from that of slaves, whose heads were shaved in order to facilitate identification as social and legal inferiors. The tonsuring of a new cleric presumably symbolized the submission of the cleric as a slave of God. The practice was to shave the crown of the head, leaving a ring of hair. This led later commentators to suppose (erroneously) that the Western style of tonsure was in imitation of Jesus's Crown of Thorns.

In Ireland, however, monks were almost immediately esteemed as scholars and learned men, supplanting the Druids. Most authorities thus believe that the unusual style of Irish tonsure, in which the entire front of the head was shaved, leaving the hair in back to grow freely, was derived from a presumed Druidic tonsure. If true, this helped shift the veneration accorded to the old order of scholars and holy men to those of the new religion. Whatever the source, the style of tonsure practiced or lack thereof anywhere in the church did not affect doctrinal orthodoxy or the church's essential unity.

There were other variations that grew up in Ireland, such as from where in the sanctuary of the church the Gospels and other selections from the Bible were read, as well as the then-innovative practice of "private auricular confession" (i.e., confessing one's sins in private to a priest, instead of proclaiming them to the congregation). These, too, were administrative in nature and did not involve doctrinal matters. The practice of confessing sins in private was considered so beneficial in encouraging penitents to make good confessions that it was eventually adopted throughout the church.

The most important difference between the church in Ireland and the rest of the church on the continent, however, was in the method for calculating the date for Easter each year. Ireland used a method of calculation introduced by Patrick, formerly used in Rome, while Rome continued to use the same method, but changed to a different cycle of years. Although nondoctrinal, differences in the calculation of the date for Easter often caused people with an inadequate understanding of the issue to accuse those whose practice differed from their own as being heretics or dissenters. That these and similar accusations are without foundation is demonstrated by the fact that differences in the calculation of the date of Easter were never considered an impediment to the admittedly transient reunions of the Western and Eastern Churches in 526, 681, 787, 869, 1274, and 1439.

Columbanus

The strongest evidence for the unity of the Irish Church with that on the continent is given by Columbanus, considered by many authorities to be the greatest and most influential monk from Ireland. Columbanus was born in Leinster in or about 540. Becoming a monk at an early age, it was not until he was about 35, in or about 575, that he requested permission from his abbot, Comgall, to go to Gaul. With a dozen companions (personally selected by Comgall both for experience and for the symbolism of the number 12) Columbanus established monasteries following Irish practices in Annegray, Luxeuil, and Fontaine.

Royal favor shown to Columbanus seriously undermined the support previously enjoyed by the native Gaulish bishops, many of which were members of the nobility and who, despite the prevalence of simony (buying and selling church offices) and other sins, were Columbanus's nominal superiors. A Gaulish Church Council had, a few years before Columbanus's arrival, enacted decrees such as: no monastery or hermitage could be founded without the consent of the local "ordinary" (bishop); no abbot could rule more than one community; each abbot had to report yearly to the local ordinary; no abbot could absent himself from his monastery, make important decisions, or accept gifts of landed property without the permission of his ordinary; and that the monks' fasts and liturgical practices had to be approved by the local ordinary.

Columbanus, coming from the Irish culture in which the bishop was a minor, if necessary figure, violated every one of these ordinances. More concerned with unity of belief and doctrine, he likely gave no thought to the possibility that he was deeply offending some very powerful political opponents.

Nevertheless, the Gaulish bishops had to be cautious in how they handled the Irish interloper. Columbanus enjoyed a significant measure of royal support, while the bishops' credibility, if we can believe the conditions described by Gregory of Tours (ca. 539–595), was virtually nonexistent due to the decay of the local churches under their control. The Gaulish bishops therefore took the extremely dangerous and, for them, questionable step of accusing Columbanus of heresy or, at least, schism.

The native bishops based their accusations on the fact that, in the matter of tonsure and the calculation of the date of Easter, Irish practice differed from that of Rome. The facts that tonsure was hardly a doctrinal issue and that the method of calculating Easter used in Gaul also differed from that of Rome were ignored. The value of these issues in the eyes of the Gaulish bishops was that they were in an area in which the civil authorities had no power, and thus they could not interfere.

Faced with this difficult situation, Columbanus appealed to Rome. He wrote a series of letters to Pope Gregory, presenting his case and requesting that the pope issue a judgment in the matter. This was a bold step that put a stop to the Gaulish bishops' accusations. The letters are not only masterpieces of strategy and diplomacy, but they contain clear and unequivocal statements that Columbanus considered the pope the head of a universal church, that the pope was the obvious judge in a dispute of this nature, and, finally, that the Irish Church was in full communion with the church on the continent, headed by the pope, and not a separate entity: "All we Irish, inhabitants of the world's edge, are disciples of Saints Peter and Paul and of all the disciples who wrote the sacred canon by the Holy Ghost, and we accept nothing outside the evangelical and apostolic teaching; none has been heretic . . . none a schismatic; but the Catholic Faith, as it was delivered by you first, who are the successors of the holy apostles, is maintained unbroken" (Columbanus 2008: *Epistola* III).

Columbanus's concern was more for the unity of the church than in preserving the unique Irish liturgical heritage. He expresses a willingness to abide by the pope's decision, but it is plain that the real issue is not a difference in liturgical practice, but the underhanded tactics employed by the Gaulish bishops to rid themselves of a political rival.

Columbanus's concern for the unity of the church expressed itself a few years later in another letter he wrote to Pope Boniface IV, after Columbanus's expulsion from Gaul in 610 due to his refusal to retract his condemnation of the grandson of Queen Brunhild, Thiery II of Burgundy, for licentious behavior and loose living. The letter resulted from the Irish monk's concern for the schism over the "Three Chapters Controversy." This was a complex and extremely esoteric argument rooted in disagreement over the interpretation of the writings of three eastern theologians. The argument over whether writers were or were not orthodox was tearing the church apart. Several areas went into schism for a number of years, while others were close to a break.

Columbanus admitted that he did not understand the controversy, but he considered the unity of the church paramount. A theological argument on such abstruse matters could hardly, in his opinion, be so important that it was worth destroying the church. He urged the pope to take the lead in settling the question and to bring the church back together. The pope, the head of the universal church, was the obvious person to act as judge and to settle the matter.

It is thus reasonable to conclude, based on the statements and beliefs of one whom many authorities consider the quintessential Irish monk and the strongest defender of specifically Irish liturgical practices, that the Irish Church was an integral, even critically important, part of the universal church, as the widespread missionary efforts of the following two centuries were to demonstrate.

Irish Missionary Effort

Many authorities credit the Irish missionary effort in Europe from the 6th to the 11th centuries not only with reviving Christianity in areas where it had decayed, but with preserving and spreading what remained of classical learning after the implosion of the classical Roman Empire and the shift of the imperial "regnum" (rule) to Constantinople.

Despite—or, possibly, because of—the liturgical differences that characterized the Celtic rite, Irish influence was pervasive throughout Europe. Comparing the rigor and asceticism of the Irish missionaries with the (possibly exaggerated) laxity of the local clergy (Gregory of Tours lists clerical crimes and failings in his *History of the Franks*), kings and nobles preferred the advice and counsel of Irish monks. They made grants of land and wealth, providing the financial means for the establishment of the vast number of monasteries for both men and women that flourished throughout the Middle Ages, many of which are still in existence today.

Taking account only of the major institutions, these Irish "foundations" on the continent ranged from Ghent and Köln in the north, to Vienna and Salzburg in the east, and Tarentum and Naples in the south, and included such notable centers of religion and learning as Fulda, Paris, Lexeuil, Saint Gall, Berne, Milan, Bobbio, and even Rome itself. All the *Schottenklöster* ("Scottish" monasteries) eventually adopted the Benedictine "rule" to replace that of Columbanus.

The shift from the rule established by Columbanus to that of Benedict was gradual, resulting in the "Iro-Frankish" tradition, and eventually complete integration into the regular practices of the church on the continent. There are no recorded instances of violence or rebellion resulting from the change, although local rulers were known to evict Irish-born monks, as Brunhild did to Columbanus and his companions, but leaving the native-born Irish-trained clerics in place.

Such expulsions, however, were clearly political acts by the civil authorities, not religious matters, doctrinal or administrative. The peaceful and gradual integration of the Irish foundations, together with the vast number of them, even in the center of power of the Western Church, Rome, offers convincing proof that the Celtic Church was never considered a separate establishment, however much it might have differed on nondoctrinal liturgical practices. The form of religious belief and practice was different, but the substantial nature of the universal church remained fully intact.

The Venerable Bede and the Synod of Whitby

In his *Ecclesiastical History of the English People* (1994), the Venerable Bede supplies strong evidence that the Celtic Church was an integral part of the universal church. In the approximately 54 references to the Irish Church and its unique liturgical practices, there are no hints that Bede considered the Irish, whom he clearly admired, anything other than orthodox and in full communion (union) with the universal church headed by the pope. Bede's concern was not heresy or schism, but that differences in practice might eventually lead to conflict between members of the same church.

Bede's account of the Synod of Whitby, in which the issue was settled for England, is revealing. As Bede relates, the kingdom of Northumbria at the time had corulers, each trained in a different tradition. Oswiu, the father, had been taught the Irish tradition out of Lindisfarne, while his son, Alhfrith, had been rigorously instructed in the Latin tradition by a tutor, Wilfrid of Ripon, trained in Rome itself. The court and the people were split in their observances, with the most obvious being the celebration of Easter. Half the people would be celebrating the risen Lord, while the rest were still keeping the Lenten fast.

Matters came to a head when Ronan, an Irishman trained in the Latin tradition (whom Bede describes as a "violent defender of the true Easter," and "a man of fierce temper") caused the co-kings, Oswiu and Alhfrith, to request a synod in 664 to discuss the issues and decide on one, uniform practice for the kingdom. Because Northumbria exerted influence far beyond its own borders, the decision would determine which rite would predominate and, eventually, exclude the other throughout England.

King Oswiu opened the conference by stating its purpose: that all who served the one, true God should have a uniformity of observance, and that they were called together to determine which of the usages was the "truer tradition." Colman, selected to present the Irish argument, opened the

A page from the Anglo-Saxon theologian Venerable Bede's *Historia Ecclesiastica Gentis Anglorum*, (A History of the English Church and People), completed around 731. His most famous work, the History traces the events from the time of Roman Britain through the establishment of Roman Christianity in England. (HIP/Art Resource, NY)

The Synod of Whitby: The Roman vs. the Celtic Church

The Venerable Bede, the great English church historian, recorded the proceedings of the Synod of Whitby, held in 664 CE, during which time the date of Easter was debated between those holding to the Roman Catholic tradition and those holding to the Celtic tradition. The debates may have centered on Easter, but had ramifications for the practice of Celtic Christianity.

"You certainly sin if, having heard the decree of the apostolic see, and of the universal Church, and that the same is confirmed by Holy Writ, you refuse to follow them; for, though your fathers were holy, do you think that their small number, in a corner of the remotest island, is to be preferred before the universal Church of Christ throughout the world? And though that Columba of yours (and, I may say, ours also, if he was Christ's servant) was a holy man and powerful in miracles, yet should he be preferred before the most blessed prince of the apostles, to whom our Lord said, 'Thou art Peter, and upon this rock I will build my church; and the gates of hell shall not prevail against it. And I will give up to thee the keys of the kingdom of heaven'?"

When Wilfrid had spoken thus, the king said, "Is it true, Colman, that these words were spoken to Peter by our Lord?" He answered, "It is true, O king!" Then said he, "Can you show any such power given to your Columba?" Colman answered, "None." Then added the king, "Do both of you agree that these words were principally directed to Peter, and that the keys of heaven were given to him by our Lord?" They both answered, "We do." Then the king concluded "And I also say unto you, that he is the doorkeeper, whorl I will not contradict, but will, as far as I know and am able in all things obey his decrees, lest when I come to the gate of the kingdom of heaven there should be none to open them he being my adversary who is proved to have the keys." The king having said this, all present, both great and small gave their assent and, renouncing the more imperfect institution, resolved to conform to that which they found to be better.

Source: Bede. *The Ecclesiastical History of the English Nation*. London: J. M. Dent; New York: Dutton, 1910.

debate. Wilfrid followed, defending the observances of the Latin rite. Wilfred won the debate when he related Christ's institution of the papacy: "Thou art Peter and upon this rock I will build my Church and the gates of hell shall not prevail against it, and I will give unto thee the keys of the kingdom of heaven" (Matt. 16:18–19). Questioned by Oswiu, Colman admitted in effect that the popes, the heirs of Peter, were, in his opinion, the supreme authority in the church, whereupon Oswiu decided in favor of the Roman observances.

The terms of the synod and the manner in which the matter was settled clearly establish the fact that both sides believed themselves to be members of a universal church. The issue was whether unity of form should match unity of belief and doctrine, or whether such differences in form could be tolerated in the name of a deeper unity. It was never a conflict between two separate churches, a concept that Bede, as well as the participants in the synod, would have found incomprehensible.

Charlemagne

When Charlemagne assumed the *regnum* of the western portion of the Roman Empire, he made immediate opponents of the Byzantine rulers who also claimed the right to rule the entire ancient territory once governed by Rome. To bolster his claim, Charlemagne needed the support of the pope who, in return for the protection given to him by the Frankish ruler, vested Charlemagne with the imperial crown on Christmas Day in 800. The need to collect allies against Byzantine claims is amply demonstrated by the embassy sent to the Frankish court by the legendary Haroun al Raschid (of "Arabian Nights" fame), which included among the gifts the first elephant seen in Europe in centuries.

While acclaimed as the ruler of a reformed Roman Empire in the west, Charlemagne was still very much a barbarian, albeit an extremely self-conscious one. Despite continuing efforts, he never learned to read or write, and he tended to rely on forcible conversion of recalcitrants and pagans to Christianity as a means of unifying his new empire. Charlemagne's "horrific" conversion of the Saxons on threat of extermination is an example of his slightly misdirected enthusiasm for political and religious unity.

Despite his personal illiteracy (or possibly because of it), Charlemagne had great respect for scholarship and sponsored what became known as the "Carolingian renaissance." To revive learning, Charlemagne imported monks from Ireland. Given Charlemagne's need to retain the support of the pope against the rulers of Constantinople and the Eastern Church that had their support, it is extremely unlikely that the straightforward and somewhat literal-minded new Roman emperor would have relied on monks from a rival church. This, while not conclusive, adds circumstantial evidence that the Celtic Church was, despite differences in liturgical practices, an integral part of the Western Church.

Malachy of Armagh and Bernard of Clairvaux

Two reasons are generally given to justify the Norman invasion of Ireland in or about 1169. One was to stop the slave trade between the western coast of England and the eastern part of Ireland. The other was to halt the decay of the Irish Church and reform it in order to bring it more into line with the continental norm.

Contradicting the alleged religious motives for the conquest, the holiness of the Irish clergy and the effectiveness of their pastoral care were known throughout the entire Western world. Bernard of Clairvaux, one of the strictest and most rigorous reformers of the medieval church, was greatly impressed with the Irish priesthood. His best friend was Malachy O'More, archbishop of Armagh,

Primate of Ireland, who died in Saint Bernard's arms and was buried in Bernard's habit. When Saint Bernard's time came to die, he was in turn buried in the archaic habit of the Irish archbishop.

These endorsements negate the claim that the Irish Church was in need of reform, or that the Celtic Church was a separate establishment from that of the rest of the church in Europe.

Laudabilitur

While the authenticity of *Laudabilitur*, the Papal Bull allegedly issued to Henry II Plantagenet by Pope Hadrian IV permitting an invasion of Ireland and a transfer of the temporal rule to the English Crown, has been called into question, the fact that the argument was used at all indisputably establishes the fact that the people of the 12th century—both Irish and English—believed the Irish Church to be under the authority of Rome.

The story is that Henry II, seeking to add the country to his domains, went to the pope with a proposal that he, Henry Plantagenet, be given a papal mandate to bring about civil and ecclesiastical reform in Ireland. According to the protestations of the English king, the condition of the island was such that drastic action had to be taken or absolute chaos would soon take over, to the detriment of civil order and the people's immortal souls. The pope then issued a Bull that granted Henry II the temporal lordship of Ireland, to be held in fief from the pope. In return, Henry was to effect the necessary reforms and also pay a "Peter's pence" tribute annually to the Holy See, one penny for every house in Ireland. Letters in the royal archives, purported to be from Alexander III, Hadrian IV's successor, make mention of the Bull and confirm its provisions.

None of this makes any sense unless it is accepted as a given that people of the time believed that the pope had such power, and that the Church in Ireland and the Church in England were both integral parts of the universal church.

The Norman Invasion

The Norman invasion of Ireland offers further proof that the Celtic Church was considered in union with the universal church. While the Normans carried out a reform of sorts, as presumably permitted by *Laudabilitur*, it was not based on any desire to establish uniformity of religious practices or raise the moral tone of the Irish clergy. Instead, it was a campaign to destroy native institutions, seen as strange and alien, and replace them with a more familiar liturgical tradition.

Geraldus Cambrensis (Gerald of Wales), a chronicler of the conquest, gave high praise to the Irish clergy in *The History and Topography of Ireland* (1983). He described at some length their virtues (especially chastity), their strict observance of all rules and regulations, as well as the rigor of their fasts and other austerities.

How the actual reform was carried out may be demonstrated by taking the activities of John de Courcy, Lord of Ulster, and his Manx wife Affreca as typical. A number of history books credit the pair with making several religious foundations, but fail to mention how they carried these out.

The Irish Church had an overwhelmingly monastic character. Where other churches concentrated on enriching the episcopacy, the Irish expended their wealth on the monasteries. Consequently, those institutions that had escaped the inroads of the Danes had been accumulating the donations of the faithful for centuries. Irish monasteries were a favorite Viking target, as their store of wealth was well known. What the Danes overlooked, the Normans would soon gather in. When the de Courcys located a richly endowed native Irish monastery in or near their territory, they would expel the Irish monks or nuns, confiscate all the moveable wealth, and attach the lands to their own desmene.

The de Courcys would then reestablish the monastery, endow it with a token amount of land, and staff it with a few Norman monks. The remarkable thing about these maneuvers is that the native Irish did not resist, but accepted them as if de Courcy had a right to do as he did. The Irish clearly did not discern any substantive change in religion, only in administration.

The Tudor Reformation

Matters were different during and after the Reformation. Unlike the situation following the Norman Conquest, the religious changes of the Reformation were widely regarded as affecting the substantial (doctrinal) nature of the Church in Ireland. "Defend the faith" became the rallying cry of the resistance to the English, which succeeded to some degree in uniting the Irish, both native and Norman, against a common foe, who was perceived as attacking the true church. This had not been the case in previous invasions, which were often seen as personal quarrels of those directly involved, resulting in a lack of unified efforts to drive out the invaders.

Conclusion

There thus exists a great deal of evidence, both direct and circumstantial, that the church in Ireland was founded by missionaries sent from the pope and has always maintained union with the bishop of Rome as the recognized head of a universal church. There is, on the other hand, no evidence to suggest, directly or indirectly, that the church in Ireland was ever construed as an independent body, whether its presumed foundation is traced to apocryphal missionaries from Egypt who founded a "Coptic-Celtic Orthodox" Church, or to Joseph of Arimathea who allegedly established Christianity in Britain after traveling to Marseilles with the apostle Philip, Lazarus, and Mary Magdalene, leaving Mary Magdalene to stay in Gaul.

References and Further Reading

Attwater, Donald. *The Avenel Dictionary of Saints*. New York: Avenel Books, 1965.

Bede the Venerable. *The Ecclesiastical History of the English People*. New York: Oxford University Press, 1994.

Bernard of Clairvaux. *The Life and Death of Saint Malachy the Irishman*. Kalamazoo, MI: Cistercian Publications, 1978.

Bieler, Ludwig. *The Works of Saint Patrick*. Westminster, MD: Newman Press, 1963.

Bieler, Ludwig, ed. *Four Latin Lives of St. Patrick, Colgan's Vita Secunda, Quarta, Tertia, and Quinta*. Dublin, Ireland: Dublin Institute for Advanced Studies, 1971.

Columbanus. *Letters of Columbanus*. Cork, Ireland: University College, 2008.

Columbanus. *Sancti Opera Columbani*. Dublin, Ireland: The Dublin Institute for Advanced Studies, 1970.

D'Arcy, Mary Ryan. *The Saints of Ireland*. St. Paul, MN: Irish American Cultural Affairs Institute, 1974.

Einhard and Notker the Stammerer. *Two Lives of Charlemagne*. London: Penguin Books, 1969.

Geary, Patrick J. *Before France and Germany: The Creation and Transformation of the Merovingian World*. New York: Oxford University Press, 1988.

Geoffrey of Tours. *The History of the Franks*. London: Penguin Books, 1974.

Gerald of Wales. *The History and Topography of Ireland*. London: Penguin Books, 1983.

Lonigan, Paul R. *The Early Irish Church*. Woodside, NY: Celtic Heritage Press, and the Aodh Ruadh Ó Domhnaill Guild, 1988.

Martin, F. X., and Moody, T. W. *The Course of Irish History*. Boulder, CO: Roberts Reinhart Publishers, 1967.

Reilly, Robert T. *Irish Saints*. New York: Avenel Books, 1964.

Scholz, Bernhard Walter. *Carolingian Chronicles: Royal Frankish Annals and Nithard's Histories*. Ann Arbor: University of Michigan Press, 1970.

CON

Christianity was an offshoot of Judaism that developed in the cultural and political matrix of the first four centuries of the Roman Empire. As missionaries carried the religion throughout the empire, they found converts among people of various classes and ethnicities, virtually all of whom had experience of Roman life, imperial government, and Latin (or Greek) letters. Celtic peoples were scattered across the empire from Galatia (in Asia Minor) in the east to Wales in the west, and many of them were drawn to the gospel. By the later fourth century, Christianity dominated the Western empire, but the region itself slowly slipped away from Roman imperial control as pagan Germanic peoples forcefully migrated through Gaul, into Spain, and eventually into a Britain that had been largely abandoned by the Roman military after 410. Before the 430s, Irish people who had never known Roman rule became Christian, though nothing is known of this process nor of the contours of Christianity in Ireland before the arrival of Saint Patrick (ca. 432).

Cut off in many ways from the Christian sources of church administration and culture in the Mediterranean, Christian Celts, especially in Britain and Ireland, developed distinctive forms and practices that may have differed enough from those of the Roman Catholic Church to warrant labeling theirs a "Celtic Church." At distinct points in the 12th, 16th, 18th, 19th, and 20th centuries, historians and historically minded clerics have emphasized these differences. Yet there is not a shred of evidence that Celts of the era considered their church to be distinct from Christ's church (Jesus spoke of only one), though they (and others) clearly recognized often-important differences between themselves and *Romani*. In fact, from the early 1960s, historians of medieval Ireland and other Celtic areas have ceased discussing a "Celtic" Church altogether, emphasizing the differences among the Celt-Iberians, Welsh, Irish, Gauls, and Britons, rather than similarities that clearly distinguished them from emerging Roman Christianity or Catholicism. Dominating the concept of "Celtic," however, were always the Irish, the survival of whose records and whose peculiar position as a non-Romanized people had always made them the historiographical core of any "Celtic Church." And so today the term "Irish Church" generally replaces "Celtic Church" in genuinely historical discussions.

Most contemporary medievalists downplay the distinctiveness of even the Irish Church, however, either avoiding the label or qualifying it as not indicative of a church apart from that of Rome. In some ways, then, the controversy is settled, and not in the favor of this side. But historians are not the only ones with a stake in the matter. At various points in history, pointedly since the early 1960s and certainly since the early 1980s, some Christians and those drawn to Christian spirituality have discovered and explicated a distinctively "Celtic" Christianity or spirituality that they interpret as more "Jesus-like" and authentically Christian than Catholicism, Orthodoxy, or various expressions of Protestantism. Their books on Celtic Christianity or spirituality often play with very modern concerns over personal spiritual journeys, feminism, environmentalism, and patriarchal authoritarianism. Though harnessing historical figures, artifacts, writings, and events, modern Celtic Christians are far less interested in accurately interpreting the past than in providing a Christian alternative to traditional Christianity.

So, even discounting pan-Celtic and Celtic spirituality issues, the Irish Church in the early Middle Ages was distinctive enough from the Roman church on the continent to warrant calling it a separate church. In order to prove this point, we first need to examine the roots and expressions of that distinctiveness, and then provide a reasonable definition of "church" that allows for its application.

That the Celts Were Different

The Jesus movement, or Christianity, emerged out of first-century Judaism in a matrix of Greco-Roman culture set in an empire dominated by Rome at the height of its power. Its earliest missionaries spread the gospel among Jews and Gentiles in the Roman Empire, with only dimly understood efforts in non-Roman lands such as Ethiopia and India. As the movement developed into a church from the later first through fourth centuries, it adapted itself to the world Rome had built. Its holy scripture, or Bible, was available in Greek (both Old and New Testaments), with unofficial Latin versions preceding the "official" production of the Latin Vulgate by Saint Jerome in the late fourth century. Its organization evolved from small congregations huddled for worship in private house churches to a well-developed, hierarchical structure that borrowed freely from the declining Roman state. Regional leadership was provided by five patriarchs (father-rulers) who settled in the great cities of Constantinople, Antioch, Alexandria, and Jerusalem in the East and Rome in the West, while local administration was handled by bishops (overseers) and archbishops (leading overseers) whose seats (sees) were in the second tier of imperial cities and whose dioceses extended across the *civitates* (administrative districts) of the empire. These leaders had benefited from classical educations and often years of experience as civil or imperial officials. Christian intellectuals, or theologians, who had also benefited from secular Greek and Roman educations, developed intricate interpretations of the Hebrew and Christian scriptures as they sought to apply God's Word imbedded in them to social, political, cultural, and personal matters. They taught, wrote, and sometimes became bishops themselves.

Great stone basilicas built in the monumental Roman style replaced simple house churches, and these became home to broad fields of fresco and mosaics that pictorially proclaimed the Christian messages. Specially appointed (ordained)—and usually trained—priests aided the bishops or themselves led worship services or liturgies (including the Mass) in these grand spaces, using vessels and implements beaten and molded of precious metals and studded with jewels for the service and glory of God. At smaller local churches in towns and scattered across the countryside, and at shrines to heroes of Christian history (usually martyrs), priests also said the Mass, which combined the reading of scripture and preaching with the re-presentation of the Last Supper of Jesus and his apostles (the Eucharist with its bread and wine) as recorded in the New Testament and commanded by Jesus.

Along with teaching, preaching, and directing the liturgies, the priesthood, or clergy, was also responsible for an emerging set of rituals that bound the believer to the church and aided life in this world and the next. At birth or the point of formal conversion, the new Christian was baptized by either being immersed in water or by having water poured or sprinkled over his or her head by a priest or bishop, who also "sealed" the person with blessed olive oil (chrism). The spiritually purified new member of the church might over time, however, succumb to human weakness and Satan's temptations and sin by breaking God's moral law. For these people there was an evolving practice known as the Sacrament of Penance, which combined personal spiritual sorrow and repentance for disobedience to God and his church with a public, physical manifestation of that sorrow and desire to be forgiven in the form of actions ranging from prayer to pilgrimage. Christian rituals, or sacraments, also evolved around marriage and death and burial, and so Christianity came to envelope the believer from cradle to grave. The church proved a powerful mediator between innately sinful humans and a divinity who was seen as paradoxically both just and merciful. Like the emperor in the physical world, the Christian God wielded arbitrary power of spiritual (and eternal) life or death, focused in the act of final judgment and relegation of every person to the delights of heaven or the torments of hell.

Finally, both Eastern and Western Christianity developed monasticism for those who sought a spiritually focused life away from other social obligations. Beginning with hermits and later monastic communities in Egypt, this important institution spread north through Greek-speaking territories and north and west into North Africa, Italy, and Gaul. Eventually the sixth-century Italian hermit St. Benedict devised the rule (*Regula*) according to which most Western monasteries (Benedictine) organized and ran themselves.

It was Saint Paul himself who first preached and wrote to the Celts of Galatia in northern Asia Minor within a couple of decades of the Crucifixion. He had longed to go to Spain, whose inhabitants included many Celt-Iberians, though the gospel would arrive there in the hands of other missionaries. Celts of Gaul (Gauls) and of Britain (Britons) welcomed the new religion as its messengers sailed up the Rhone River and its sister streams and across the English Channel with merchants or soldiers. As part of the Roman Empire, all of these regions enjoyed regular commerce and communication with the Roman Mediterranean heartland. Latin, if often in a debased form, replaced or supplemented local Germanic and Celtic tongues, and some level of cultural integration aided Christianity's spread wherever Roman roads stretched. Without a doubt, Christian communities of Celtic Romans began to appear in the Western empire by the end of the first century CE.

The date of Christianity's first appearance in Ireland is lost to history, but surely there were Irish Christians before Bishop Palladius was dispatched to serve them in 431. The Romans had never controlled the island, nor had they ever tried. Pagan Irish people interacted with Christians in Britain, Gaul, and probably Spain through trade, piracy, and perhaps in service as mercenaries. Saint Patrick was a Christian Briton who was captured by Irish pirates and served as a shepherd. Escaping, he returned to Britain, then traveled to Gaul, where he prepared for a clerical life. Although the date 432 is usually given for his return to Ireland as a missionary, this is uncertain. Unlike Palladius, Patrick spread the gospel among nonbelievers, establishing a lasting Christian presence in north-central Ireland.

Despite Patrick's successes, and whatever those of Palladius, Christianity remained a minority religion for quite some time, and pagan worship and culture remained visible for nearly two centuries. Pagan Celtic culture centered on the Druids, who served their society as priests, healers, and scholars. Their mainte-nance of ritual and sacrifices kept the many Irish gods content and promised suc-cess to the leaders of Irish society. The *filid* was both a spiritual seer and poet who traveled among Irish settlements, bringing news of both the physical and spirit worlds and entertaining high- and low-born alike. Usually called "*brehon* law," after the law-speakers who maintained the society's legal framework, Irish secular law and its processes were well developed. After the arrival of Christian-ity and Roman writing technology it was recorded along with church laws (canon law). The Irish people were organized into small kingdoms called *tuatha*, each of which was led by a king or *rí*, and kinship groups formed the basic building blocks of the *tuatha*. A warrior elite maintained its social position by raiding and fighting battles for the *rí*. It is impossible to speak of Irish towns before the 10th century, when Viking trading posts like Limerick, Cork, and Dublin began to evolve. The Irish lived close to nature in small-scale settlements that knew little of stone construction and nothing of monumental architecture. They did, how-ever, possess skills and traditions in the decorative arts of metalwork and sculp-ture and recorded their thoughts in a rune-like written alphabet known as *ogham*, which consisted of one or more perpendicular and diagonal strokes arranged in sequence along a horizontal line, not unlike the teeth in a comb.

When Christianity established roots in this society it began a process of social and material change that eventually transformed Irish society, but in the process Christianity had to adapt in many important ways. What follows is a detailed list of some of the principal issues that set the Irish Church apart from that being hammered out in Rome.

How the Celts Were Different

Having never bent the knee to imperial power, the Irish seem to have experienced little contact of any sort with the earthly head of the Roman Catholic Church. Bishop Palladius may have been deacon to Pope Celestine I, but his mission seems to have originated in Gaul, not Rome. Patrick's mission had no roots at all in Rome and established no apparent ties to the apostolic see. In fact, the later

The Deer's Cry, or The Breastplate of Saint Patrick

Though its attribution to Saint Patrick is dubious, this most popular of Celtic hymns, dating from the late seventh or early eighth century, certainly reflects many of the themes of the Celtic Christian tradition.

I arise to-day:
vast might, invocation of the Trinity,—
belief in a Threeness
confessing of Oneness
meeting in the Creator(?).

I arise to-day:
the might of Christ's birth and His baptism
the might of His Crucifixion and Burial
the might of His Resurrection and Ascension
the might [of] His Descent to the judgement of Doom.

I arise to-day:
might of gradeso of Cherubim
in obedience of Angels
[in ministration of Archangles[*]]
in hope of resurrection for the sake of reward
in prayers of Patriarchs
in prophecies of Prophets
in preachings of Apostles,
in faiths of Confessors
in innocenceo[*] of holy Virgins
in deeds of righteous men.

I arise to-day:
might of Heaven
brightness of Sun
whiteness of Snow
splendour of Fire
speed of Light
sweiftness[*] of Wind
depth of Sea
stability of Earth
firmness of Rock.

I arise to-day:
Might of God for my piloting
Wisdom of God for my guidance
Eye of God for my foresight
Ear of God for my hearing

Word of God for my utterance
Hand of God for my guardianship
Path of God for my precedence
Shield of God for my protection
Host of God for my salvation
against nares of demons
against allurements of vices
against solicitations of nature
against every person that wishes me ill
far and near
alone and in a crowd.
I invoke therefore all these forces to intervene between me and every fierce
merciless force that may come upon my body and my soul:

against incantations of false prophets
against black laws of paganism
against false laws of heresy
against deceit of idolatry
against spells of women and smiths and druids
against all knowledge that is forbidden the human soul.

Christ for my guardianship to-day
against poison, against burning,
against drowning, against wounding,
that there may come to me a multitude of rewards;
Christ with me, Christ before me,
Christ behind me, Christ in me,
Christ under me, Christ over me,
Christ to right of me, Christ to left of me,
Christ in lying down, Christ in sitting, Christ in rising up
Christ in the heart of every person, who may think of me!
Christ in the mouth of everyone one, who may speak to me!
Christ in every eye, which may look on me!
Christ in every ear, which may hear me!

I arise to-day:
vast might, invocation of the Trinity
belief in a Threeness
confession of Oneness
meeting in the Creator.

Source: *The Irish Liber Hymnorum*. Ed. and trans. J. H. Bernard and R. Atkinson.
London: 1898.

Book of the Angel (seventh or eighth century) claimed that an angel, rather than the pope or other bishops, was responsible for "bishop" Patrick's ordination. In what were or had been Roman territories, universal authority vested in an emperor or pope was understood and acceptable, but in Ireland this was an alien concept. As the great monastic missionary Columbanus related to one pope, in Ireland, Rome was only "great and famous" for "that chair" of Saint Peter the apostle. The Irish Church recognized the popes who served as Peter's successors as advisers and judges of last resort, as clearly outlined in several collections of Irish ecclesiastical law (canons). The *Liber Angueli* (book of the angel), which sought to support the authority of the bishop of Armagh over all of Ireland, makes the same statement, referring to the pope as merely "having authority over the city of Rome." According to an imperial rescript, the popes had authority over all Western bishops; though, of course, the imperial arm had never touched Ireland. In the mid-seventh century, Irish clerics sought guidance from Rome as to the correct date on which to celebrate Easter each year (see below), but over the next four centuries there is no evidence of any other appeal (true also of the "Celtic" churches in Scotland and Wales). Popes sent no representatives (legates) to Ireland, and no Irish bishop traveled to Rome for his pallium (a wool stole that symbolized his office). Only pilgrims traveled from Ireland to Rome to pray at the shrines of Saints Peter and Paul; in fact, *róm* in Old Irish came to mean "burial place." Saints were more powerful and respected than popes, as Columbanus made clear to Pope Gregory I around 600. The pope had tried to force Irish missions in Gaul to adopt the Roman calculation of Easter: "don't make us have to choose," Columbanus warned, between Gregory and Saint Jerome (on whose purported authority Irish custom rested), for to abandon Jerome would be heretical. It seems clear that while the Irish Church never repudiated the Roman pontiff in the way Protestant churches of the Reformation era did, it certainly drew on a very different model of hierarchical administration.

The Roman Christian bishop, with his urban seat, cathedral church, and platoon of clerics and bureaucrats, was modeled on the Roman provincial governor, a model unfamiliar to the Irish. He also traced his lineage back to one of Jesus's apostles through the ritual of ordination—a problem for "Bishop" Patrick. The earliest Irish Christians lacked such leaders (hence Palladius's mission), but after the 430s bishops appear, with the *tuatha* as their dioceses. This meant that the organizational church had a structure that was directly blended into that of Irish society, rather than running parallel to it. This was reflected in the facts that the clergy as a whole came to be treated in Irish law as a separate kin group, and that bishops had the same "honor price"—the penalty due for a transgression against the person—as the *rí* (and the *filid* and *brehon*). This resulted in what historian Dáibhí Ó Cróinín (1995) labels a "tribal church" as opposed to the diocesan Roman model. Although continental rules prescribed that three bishops ordain a new one, the evidence suggests that it was rare in the early Irish Church for more than one to participate, a complaint of the English archbishops of Canterbury Lanfranc and Anselm as late as the early 1100s.

By the early 600s, Ireland saw the rise of the native monastic system (see below) and the concomitant decline in episcopal (bishop's) authority. The abbots (*coarbs*) who ran the monasteries came to manage Irish religious society as well, and bishops were relegated to sacramental functions such as ordinations of priests and other bishops. The evidence suggests that many bishops, if not most, came to be directly connected to the monasteries, and that some were even hermits, such as Cuthbert of Farne, or wanderers, an abuse complained about by Archbishop of Canterbury Theodore of Tarsus in the later seventh century. By the eighth century, Irish abbots, who were usually appointed members of the kin groups that patronized the monasteries, absorbed the managerial, administrative, governing, and disciplinary powers associated with continental bishops. Abbots who were not priests and had none in their monasteries needed bishops for saying Mass, hearing confessions, and baptizing infants, but many abbots were priests, and some had been raised from the episcopacy to the abbacy, a process opposite to that found among the Romans.

Irish abbots ruled monasteries that were peculiar in the Christian world, and uniformly so. The origins of Irish monasticism are unclear, but the practice as it emerges into the historical record by the sixth century is more closely related to that practiced in Egypt under the fourth-century rule of Pachomius than that found in much of Gaul or Italy. It may have derived directly from the travels of Athanasius, the fourth-century biographer of Saint Anthony, the archetypal Egyptian hermit. Interestingly, Anthony appears in Irish art, such as sculpted crosses, long before he does in Roman art. Monasteries were founded by the leaders of kin groups, and they and land donors retained the right to determine the abbots for generations, with the position being essentially hereditary. In a very real sense they were familial institutions, generally associated with lay settlements, and bishops had no jurisdiction over them. Local churches were administered from the monasteries and these could be strung out and geographically intermixed, forming "families" of the individual monasteries known as *paruchiae*. Scholars have found this system of quasi-familial organization to be related to the increasingly visible system of clientage, whereby weaker individuals sought more powerful ones to serve in return for protection. In society, this began to weaken ties of kinship, while in the *paruchia* system the more powerful kin groups gained in strength by their extended ecclesiastical associations.

In a society without towns, monasteries even replaced iron-age hill forts as geographic centers of political power. Following the plague years of the mid-660s, the bishop or abbots of Armagh, a seat that claimed Saint Patrick as its founder, contended with that of Kildare, associated with the estimable female Saint Brigid, for supremacy over the Irish Church in the sense that Canterbury had over the English. In so doing, the leaders at Armagh gathered a wide and numerous string of associated churches and monasteries, the "*Paruchia* of Saint Patrick," though they did not achieve their goal. By the 700s much of Irish Christian life was organized by and around the monasteries, which had also become the centers of Christian culture, including education, painting, metalwork, biblical study, and explication, in a world still peopled—if ever more lightly—by pagans and their Druids. But this intertwining of monasticism and the wider society may also be seen as a secularization of monasticism. Feuding clans meant feuding monasteries, and Clonmacnois fought two violent battles with Birr in 760 and Durrow in 764; after its battle, Durrow counted 200 of its own dead. From 697 to 780 the leaders of the Irish Church held no general meetings (synods), a sign of the failure of any central ecclesiastical authority, whether internal or foreign.

Irish spirituality was heavily invested in its monks, who became renowned for piety, asceticism, and learning, even in the Greek and Latin classics. After the flood of pagan Germanic peoples in Gaul and Britain from the early fourth century came Irish missionary monks, like Saint Columban, who founded the monastery at Iona, and Columbanus, who founded a *paruchia* of monasteries across Gaul and into northern Italy. Some modern commentators who have studied the written remains of Irish monks find a strain of naturalism that is largely absent from continental monastic writing of the period. Roman Catholic monks, influenced by the thought of Saint Augustine and Plato, are considered to have been opposed to nature, finding it alien to the spiritual life, and to have sought to deny or suppress even their human nature, because they considered it damaged by sin. Irish monks, on the other hand, are thought to have considered God-created nature inherently good and welcoming, perhaps since sin only affects the human spirit. It is this "dignity of nature," as expressed in poetry and prayer, that modern environmentalists and New Agers find so attractive. Yet Irish monks are also known for their self-denying asceticism, which sometimes seems downright masochistic. Early Christian Ireland produced no known martyrs, and this may have heightened the tendency to self-sacrifice among

Iona Abbey on the Scottish Isle of Mull is a Christian pilgrimage site dating from 600 CE. The island was the site of the monastery established by Saint Columba, who actively converted Picts to Christianity during the sixth and seventh centuries CE. (Corel)

those who wanted to witness to Christ with a full measure. This may have been behind the impulse to self-imposed peregrination or exile spent in wandering and missionary work, an impulse rarely if ever found among continental monks.

It was the tendency to piety and asceticism that fueled the eighth- and ninth-century monastic reform movement known as Céli Dé (or Culdee: servants/clients/serfs of God). Begun at Tallaght monastery by Mael-ruain in the 750s, it remained rooted at Tallaght and Finglas monasteries, but spread across much of Ireland. Like later continental reform movements, the Culdees sought to isolate monks from secular contamination, emphasizing prayer, personal labor, and a hermetic ethos rather than the communal cenobitic one. It died out by the later 800s, perhaps under the pressure of the Viking raids.

Peregrination and asceticism in general were forms of self-sacrifice made in the light of the individual's sin and the need for propitiation of a just God. Pilgrimage and prayer, especially that recited while in very uncomfortable positions (e.g., with arms outstretched for hours [*crucifigium*] or standing barefoot on gravel or thorn branches) were well-recognized forms of penance and reflected in Christendom's first penitentials (books of recommended penance). In the developing Roman church, penance remained public and after Saint Augustine the church emphasized the believer's total dependence on God's grace freely given for forgiveness and ultimately for salvation. Augustine and other early theologians condemned the Celtic (Irish? Welsh? Briton?) theologian Pelagius who taught that human repentance and efforts to follow God's law were rewarded with the requisite grace. Though formally condemned by the Roman church in 418, Pelagian influences are clearly evident in Irish theology and biblical commentary. This may have been the impetus for stressing the technicalities of penance and of shifting it from a public matter to a much more private one of confession to a "soul friend" (*anamchara*) and penance being carried out in isolation. If spiritual and physical exertions could satisfy a just God, then exert themselves they would. There were even special monasteries (for example at Tiree and Hinba) for monks undergoing periods of imposed penance. While the Catholic Church eventually picked up the Irish personal confession and penance, Pelagianism remained a heresy, providing critics of the Irish Church a clear target.

The peculiarities of the Irish Church became an active issue not in Ireland or Rome, but in Britain, where Irish missionaries had planted many churches and monasteries. During the early seventh century the southern Anglo-Saxon church had been organized by Catholic bishops centered in and stemming from Canterbury. The two Christian cultures clashed along their borderline at a synod held at Streanoeshalch (Whitby) under the gaze of King Oswiu of Northumbria in 664. One issue was the way in which the monks shaved their heads (as a sign of their religious calling) known as the tonsure. The Roman Benedictines left a ring of hair, while the Irish shaved from the forehead back, leaving the sides long. Though seemingly a minor matter of taste, the Benedictines demanded uniformity, but the Irish claimed that the Benedictine style was that of the arch-heretic Simon Magus and, therefore, utterly unacceptable.

The various methods of the annual dating of Easter, dated from the fact that Passover, which necessarily preceded Easter, was determined by the Jewish lunar calendar, as opposed to the Julian calendar solar method used by Christians, were not in synch. Early in the fourth century the Christian church decided that it would not follow the Jewish calculation but would determine it according to its own rules. These computational rules were complex, however, and resulted in three different systems. As in many matters, the Irish Church followed an older, 84-year cycle that they claimed had its roots in the Gospel of Saint John the evangelist. The flaws in this system were addressed in 475 by a Roman named Victorius of Aquitaine, who produced the "Victorian" calculation system, which proved to be more regular. Later, in 525, the Roman monk Dionysius Exiguus developed an even more refined system. Although the English monks pressed for the acceptance of the Dionysian tables at Whitby, it is not clear that Rome itself had accepted them in place of the Victorian. It is clear that Oswiu accepted the "Roman" tonsure and dating system for his churches, while the Irish were left with theirs, a further symbol of their independence (though in fairness, the Irish had consulted with the pope over the appropriate system).

Modern proponents of a "Celtic Christianity" often stress that the Irish viewed Christ as far more personal and close to humankind than Roman Christians did. They note the rationalism of the Greco-Roman culture, the transcendence of the Roman Emperor (a convenient mental model for the divine), and the monumental churches with their apse mosaics of Christ as ruler and judge. For the Irish, Christ was *ard-rí*, High King, in a society where kingship was local and approachable. Graydon Snyder (2002) finds that the Celtic "I" replaces the Roman, communal "we" as Christians approach their God in prayer and meditation, and that the Jesus who rewards effort and piety directly challenges the far more distant and ineffable God of the Romans.

Irish church structures were often very small, and some believe that the Eucharist was actually prepared in the structure while the congregation stood outside; a far cry from the great basilicas and churches of the continent. Services seem to have been in Latin, but from an out-of-date version of scripture, the *Vetus latina* rather than Saint Jerome's *Vulgate*, and followed the older Gallican liturgy rather than the newer Roman forms. Other historians have stressed the degree to which Irish canon law is intertwined with secular and political concerns, a development far less noticeable among "Roman" collections. The distinctive nature of Irish or Hiberno-Saxon art, with so little classical influence, is also considered a distinguishing feature of Irish church culture.

Traditions of an Irish Church

Bede, the eighth-century English Benedictine who related the issues and outcomes of the Synod of Whitby, may be said to be the earliest historian who recognized an Irish Church with characteristics distinctive from the Roman. These were noted again by reform-minded clerics in Rome and England in the 11th and 12th centuries, who sought to bring all Christian outliers under Rome's direct control, a move that lost the orthodox churches to the Schism of 1054. Irish ecclesiastical leaders complied, such that an Irish Church may be said to have disappeared by ca. 1100. Even so, the English Pope Hadrian (Adrian) IV recognized enough differences to allow a reforming "crusade" by the English around 1170. Interest in the early Irish (Celtic) Church was revived with the Anglican Reformation of the 16th century. Anglican Reformers who had split from Rome saw the early Celtic Church as purer than its Roman counterpart, and thus a model for the reformed one in England and Ireland. Archbishop of Canterbury Matthew Parker wrote in 1572 of the superficiality and vain ceremonies brought by his predecessor Augustine of Canterbury in 600 to the "pure and immaculate" British (Celtic) church. For these clerics, the Celtic Church was surprisingly Anglican. Eighteenth-century Romantics who sought the purer, noncivilized roots of Western culture in the "folk" of the past and present began interpreting the remains of the Irish Church in cultural (more primitive is better) terms rather than confessional ones. In the later 19th and early 20th centuries, it was Irish nationalist scholars like Douglas Hyde who found the distinctively Irish spirit in literary and spiritual works of early medieval Ireland. For them, the Irish Church was distinctive from that of the despised English, and from that of the overly clerical Catholic Church whose hierarchy often clashed with the nationalist aspirations. Finally, Celtic Christianity emerged as a romantic alternative to Catholicism or Protestantism in the wake of the early stages of religious feuding in Ireland. In the early 1960s, publication of a cheap version of Alexander Carmichael's collection of Scots folklore, *Carmina Gadelica* (Gaelic Songs) fueled popular interest in both pagan and Christian Celtic antiquity, and a fascination with Celtic Christian spirituality has grown up alongside neo-Druidism, neo-paganism, and Wicca. It was also the early 1960s when medieval scholars began to downplay the differences between Celts and "Romans" and emphasized the similarities between the two.

Conclusion

Clearly, differences between the Roman Church and the Church in Ireland were substantial. Whether they were distinctive enough to define two churches is a matter of how one defines "church." Since the Reformation Westerners have become used to accepting multiple Christian churches and have ceased (for the most part) from hurling changes of heresy and schism. Early Christians, on the other hand, recognized that Christ had established a single church, and all other facsimiles—such as Gnostics or Arians—were something else. If one can speak today, however, of a Lutheran church, a Presbyterian church, and a Methodist church and see the differences (and similarities) as something other than historical, then recognizing the Irish Church as distinct from that which developed under the direction of Rome and the "Romans" is eminently reasonable.

References and Further Reading

Bitel, Lisa M. *Isle of the Saints: Monastic Settlement and Christian Community in Early Ireland*. Ithaca, NY: Cornell University Press, 1990.

Bradley, Ian. *The Celtic Way*. London: Darton Longman and Todd, 2003.

Cahill, Thomas. *How the Irish Saved Civilization*. New York: Doubleday, 1995.

Charles-Edwards, Thomas. *Early Christian Ireland*. New York: Cambridge University Press, 2000.

Corning, Caitlin. *The Celtic and Roman Traditions: Conflict and Consensus in the Early Medieval Church*. New York: Palgrave, 2006.

Cronin, Deborah. *Holy Ground: Celtic Christian Spirituality*. Nashville, TN: Upper Room Books, 1999.

Davies, Wendy. "The Myth of the Celtic Church." In *The Early Church in Wales* (pp. 12–21). Edited by Nancy Edwards and Alan Lane. Oxford: Oxbow, 1992.

Dáibhí Ó Cróinín. *A New History of Ireland*, Vol. 1. New York: Oxford University Press, 2005.

Dáibhí Ó Cróinín. *Early Medieval Ireland: 400–1200*. New York: Longman, 1995.

De Paor, Máire and Liam. *Early Christian Ireland*. New York: Thames and Hudson, 1958.

De Waal, Esther. *A World Made Whole: The Rediscovery of the Celtic Tradition*. London: Fount, 1991.

Friesen, Milton J. "Monasticism in Fifth to Seventh-century Ireland: A Study of the Establishment of Christianity in Irish-Celtic Culture." *Religious Studies and Theology* 23 (2004): 79–98.

Gougard, Louis. *Christianity in Celtic Lands*. Dublin: Four Courts, 1992 (orig. 1932).

Herren, Michael W., and Shirley Ann Brown. *Christ in Celtic Christianity: Britain and Ireland from the Fifth to the Tenth Century*. Rochester, NY: Boydell, 2002.

Hughes, Kathleen. *The Church in Early Christian Society*. Ithaca, NY: Cornell University Press, 1966.

Hughes, Kathleen. *Early Christian Ireland*. Ithaca, NY: Cornell University Press, 1972.

Hughes, Kathleen, and Ann Hamlin. *Celtic Monasticism. The Modern Traveler to the Early Irish Church*. New York: Seabury, 1981.

Hull, Eleanor. *Poem Book of the Gael*. London: Chatto and Windus, 1913.

Jestice, Phyllis G. *Encyclopedia of Irish Spirituality*. Denver: ABC-CLIO, 2000.

Joyce, Timothy J. *Celtic Christianity: A Sacred Tradition, a Vision of Hope*. Maryknoll, NY: Orbis, 1998.

Kerr, W. S. *The Independence of the Celtic Church in Ireland*. London: SPCK, 1931.

Low, Mary. *Celtic Christianity and Nature*. Edinburgh: University of Edinburgh Press, 1996.

Mackey, James. *An Introduction to Celtic Christianity*. Edinburgh: T&T Clark, 1989.

Mac Niocaill, Gearóid. *Ireland before the Vikings*. Dublin: Gill and Macmillan, 1972.

McNeill, John T. *The Celtic Churches: A History A.D. 200 to 1200*. Chicago: University of Chicago Press, 1974.

Meek, Donald E. *The Quest for Celtic Christianity*. Edinburgh: Handsel Press, 2000.

Moorhouse, Geoffrey. *Sun Dancing: Life in a Medieval Irish Monastery and How Celtic Spirituality Influenced the World*. New York: Harcourt Brace, 1997.

Mytum, Harold. *Origins of Early Christian Ireland*. New York: Routledge, 1992.

O'Loughlin, Thomas. *Celtic Theology*. New York: Continuum, 2000.

Olsen, Ted. *Christianity and the Celts*. Downers Grove, IL: InterVarsity Press, 2003.

Pierce, Susan. *The Early Church in Western Britain and Ireland*. Oxford: British Archeological Report, 1982.

Rees, R. B. *Pelagius: Life and Letters*. Rochester, NY: Boydell Press, 1998.

Roy, James Charles. *Islands of Storm*. Dublin: Dufour, 1991.

Scherman, Katherine. *The Flowering of Ireland: Saints, Scholars and Kings*. New York: Little, Brown, 1981.

Sellner, Edward. *The Wisdom of the Celtic Saints*. Notre Dame, IN: Ave Maria Press, 1993.

Snyder, Graydon. *Irish Jesus, Roman Jesus: The Formation of Early Irish Christianity*. Harrisburg, PA: Trinity Press, 2002.

10

The inhabitants of Easter Island who erected the monoliths were from South America, not from Polynesia.

PRO   Chris Howell
CON   Harald Haarmann

PRO

Thor Heyerdahl's 1950 assertion that Easter Island (Rapa Nui) was also settled by pre-Columbian South Americans was based on his archaeological work on both the island and mainland South America as well as on his experimental voyages on the *Kon-Tiki* rafting expeditions. While much of his data are still utilized by researchers today, most of his conclusions about prehistoric civilizations in Polynesia and South America have since been discarded based on more recent research that points to a primarily Polynesian settlement of Easter Island. However, new archaeological findings have researchers revisiting Heyerdahl's general idea that contact indeed took place between Polynesia and South America, with Easter Island a likely central point between the two regions.

Two recent archaeological finds have forced researchers to reevaluate when Easter Island was settled and what regions Easter Islanders were in contact with. The first involves new radiocarbon dating on initial human activity on Easter Island's main canoe landing area at Anakena beach to around 1200 CE, or almost 800 years later than the normative view held based on previous radiocarbon dates from bulk organic material in the three volcanic cones of the island. Archaeology professor Terry Hunt (2007) conducted the radiocarbon dating and excavations at Anakena beach while leading a University of Hawaii at Manoa research team in 2006.

The second find involves the excavation, radiocarbon dating, and DNA testing of Polynesian chicken remains from the pre-Columbian archaeological site of El Arenal on the Aracao Peninsula in Chile. These were discovered and tested by Alice Story and Elizabeth Matisoo-Smith, a biological anthropologist from the University of Auckland in New Zealand. The DNA tests reveal genetic ties to Polynesian chickens from Tonga, and the radiocarbon dating placed those remains in South America between 1300–1420 CE. These chickens may be related to the Araucana chicken of South America known on both Easter

The Columbian Exchange Reaches Easter Island

One of the most insightful historical arguments relating to the Americas during the 1970s and 1980s was the rise of what Alfred W. Crosby coined the "Columbian Exchange," or the biological relationship between Europe and the Americas. Crosby later expanded his theory worldwide, showing that the flora and fauna of the continents were transported across the oceans, often with unforeseen ramifications. In his 1986 book, Crosby explained his theory this way:

> Back in the Old World, most particularly in the densely populated areas of civilization, many organisms had taken advantage of contiguity with humans and their plants and animals to become their parasites and pathogens. These freeloaders often were slower to emigrate to the Neo-Europes than were humans and the organisms that humans intentionally brought with them. For example, Europeans brought wheat to North America and created the first of their several wheat belts in the Delaware River valley in the eighteenth century where the plant thrived in the absence of its enemies. Then its old nemesis, the Hessian fly, unjustly blamed on George III's mercenaries, who supposedly brought it across the Atlantic in their straw bedding, arrived and obliged farmers of the valley to find a new staple. (1986: 281)

This idea plays into the debate about the native people of Rapa Nui in that the existence of sweet potatoes and chickens on the island seems to defy the traditional Polynesian explanation, as both were not native to the Pacific islands, but rather to the Americas.

Source: Alfred W. Crosby. *Ecological Imperialism: The Biological Expansion of Europe, 900–1900.* Cambridge: Cambridge University Press, 1986.

Island and South America but not necessarily from Eurasia. A debate over the research data has emerged in 2008 in the journal of the *Proceedings of the National Academy of Sciences*, with Story et al. (2007) answering critics satisfactorily so far concerning issues of dating and genetic testing interpretations.

The presence of Polynesian chickens in a pre-Columbian archaeological context may help answer one of the great mysteries associated with eastern Polynesia. How did the world's greatest seafarers set out on purposeful expeditions and find some of the most remote islands in the world, especially Easter Island and the Hawaiian Islands, and yet miss the Western Hemisphere or the Americas entirely? Maybe they didn't. And if so, this calls into question not only the nature but also the directions of such contact, assuming the chickens did not engage in maritime navigation.

Taken together, these finds challenge the traditional questions of when Easter Island was settled and who the Easter Islanders were in contact with. Further, such finds call into question the nature and direction of previous research and normative interpretations of Easter Island history. It may become necessary for the academic and research community associated with Easter Island to redirect questions, hypotheses, and research away from issues of earliest or first and toward the nature of human behaviors like contact and exchange if we are to become a more informed community on Easter Island human history.

Perhaps the basic questions, though not necessarily the conclusions developed by Thor Heyerdahl so long ago, are not dead at all. Was there contact between the Polynesian and South American worlds? If so, what was the nature and direction of that contact? How was Easter Island or Hawaii involved? Because so much evidence is missing from the past, can the research community really ever rule out the presence of South American Amerindians in Polynesia or vice versa? Are singular explanations and cause and effect really useful models for a better understanding of the past?

The idea of singular explanations for complex interactions between humans and environment is again at the forefront of research into the Easter Island mysteries. Researchers like Jerod Diamond (2005) have popularized an "ecocide" model for Polynesian settlers on Easter Island but have been contradicted by researchers such as Terry Hunt (2007), Paul Rainbird (2002), and Alice Story and her colleagues (2007) who suggest a more complex explanation is at work concerning human–environmental interactions. Essentially Diamond suggests humans were the problem in terms of collapse of Easter Island civilization while Hunt, Rainbird, and Story et al. suggest the Polynesian rat and European contact greatly complicate affairs for those interpreting human history associated with the island. According to the normative model, only Polynesians settled the island, only their impact on the environment created the ecocide, and only European historic descriptions later of a desolate island should be utilized to support that view. However, Hunt points out that early European seafaring visits to the island on Easter of 1722 CE by the Dutch captain Jacob Roggeveen actually describe it as lush and productive, with bananas, potatoes, sugarcane, chickens, coconuts, and remnants of decaying palm forests still visible. Archaeological and oral history data, however, suggest the island had undergone a human catastrophe by that time. Rainbird suggests that the arrival of European diseases, flora, and fauna, as was the case on other Polynesian islands, more likely created the ecocide. What are we to make of the contradictory interpretations and evidence? Perhaps that is just the nature of Easter Island research, a far more complex and contradictory world than singular interpretations might suggest.

Hunt and Orliac (2000) have both noted that linguistic evidence and radiocarbon dates from organic material in the craters were used to support an early occupation model of Easter Island between 300–800 CE. However, dated archaeological contexts definitely associated with human activity all point to a much later human presence and impact on the island, probably between 1200–1650 CE. It was the vague early dating evidence that lead Thor Heyerdahl to postulate that possibly two groups, with one from South America, helped settle Easter Island. Now that new dating strongly suggests a later arrival, at least for Polynesians and the Pacific rat, we need to rethink much of the island's interpreted history. Such redating of Polynesian colonization of eastern Polynesia includes Easter Island, and the Hawaiian, Marquesas, Society, Austral, and New Zealand islands. In other words, researchers are now reinterpreting the historical context of Polynesian settlement all across eastern Polynesia and not just at Easter Island. The arrivals of Polynesians are later, usually around 1200 CE, and the interaction suggested between islands is far more planned and more frequent than had previously been thought. The same may be true for interactions with the Americas. Before examining these reinterpretations and their ramifications in reference to the general questions explored by Thor Heyerdahl concerning Rapa Nui or Easter Island, a brief review of some relevant data associated with Easter Island is in order.

Easter Island (Rapa Nui)

Easter Island is a remote volcanic landform of 171 square km in the Pacific Ocean over 2,300 miles from South America and over 1,200 miles from its nearest Pacific Island neighbor, the Pitcairn Islands. Before human arrival, it was rich with trees, birds, and marine species that could help support human settlement. Fresh water was available though not plentiful in the three volcanic craters of Terevaka, Poike, and Rano Kau, in the water table, and in low tide freshwater springs along the coast. Early Easter Islanders relied heavily upon local, wild animals for their food supply, such as porpoise and sea and land birds, in what Jerod Diamond describes as the richest bird species nesting ground in the eastern Pacific. Canoes were made from giant Easter Island palms (*Paschalococos disperta* or *Jubaea* subspecies), similar to the Chilean palm (*Jubaea chilensis*), which were utilized both as a food supply with palm hearts and as a raw material for tools. Two other giant trees *Alphitonia zizyphoides* and *Elaeocarpus rarotongensis* grew to 100 feet tall and to 50 feet tall, respectively. Both were ideal candidates for constructing the large canoes utilized by Polynesian seafaring expeditions. Dransfield suggests there may be interesting connections between the Easter Island palms and those in Chile but believes the paleopollen and seed evidence on Easter Island is not sufficient to explore the nature of those relationships as they might address human contact between the two areas.

Human Impact

At least 21 species of trees and 31 species of bird (including six land bird taxa) went extinct after human arrival by a combination of human settlement and introduced flora and fauna species, especially Pacific rats (*Rattus exulans*) and foodstuffs, according to Diamond. Important foodstuffs introduced by humans included the sweet potato (*Ipomoea batatas*), the chicken (*Gallus gallus*), and bananas, sugarcane, coconuts, taro root, and the ti bush, though droughts and salty winds are

Moai on Easter Island. The staggering architectural achievement of the people of Easter Island was the creation, especially the transportation and erection, of hundreds of *moai* monoliths. (iStockPhoto)

problematic for much of the Polynesian agricultural plants. Interestingly rat bones on Easter Island are far more common in trash midden sites than are fish bones. This suggests, according to researchers Barnes, Matisoo-Smith, and Hunt (2006), that rats may well be an intentional food resource for Polynesian expeditions.

Fascination with the Easter Island civilization that built the more than 800 monumental carved, stone heads (*moai*) has led to much scholarly debate and speculation as to who founded and settled it over 1,000 years ago. Traditional interpretations have favored the Polynesian seafarers from the western Pacific as the first and only settlers, while a few researchers associated with Thor Heyerdahl believe an additional group of South American origin also settled on Easter Island. Research in the past decade has focused more on the ecocide issue on the island. A few researchers such as Heyerdahl at Tucume in north Peru and Matisoo-Smith and Storey at El Arenal in Chile have been looking for South American connections with Easter Island.

Traditional Interpretations

The normative interpretation of Easter Island history based on academic research was that Polynesian seafarers who were spreading across the Pacific Ocean from west to east over the past two millennia settled Easter Island. New Zealand, Easter Island, and the Hawaiian Islands were the last places reached as they were so far east and distant, toward the Americas or Western Hemisphere. Archaeological information, including radiocarbon dating of excavation layers, indicated that Easter Island was first settled by 400 CE. Easter Islanders settled the small island and lived in balance with the environment for perhaps 500 years or more, utilizing the island palms, dolphin, turtle, and marine resources, three freshwater volcanic lakes, and colonizing resources brought along in the outrigger canoes such as sweet potatoes, chickens, and maybe pigs and breadfruit. Then, almost suddenly, they began construction of monumental stone heads, not unlike those found on some other Polynesian occupied islands. This was followed by deforestation and soil erosion, loss of navigational ability, and eventually internal warfare that left the island civilization devastated and isolated until European ships arrived in 1722 CE and again in 1786 CE.

Critique of Traditional Interpretation

Interpreting human history even with well-researched and thought-out historical data is often a difficult proposition. Easter Island is certainly such a case. When the first Europeans came ashore in 1722 CE, the Dutch captain Jacob Roggeveen noted islanders of several classes and skin colors as did Captain Cook on a 1774 CE visit. Modern genetic testing of the few Rapa Nui left in modern times (Easter Island's indigenous inhabitants) revealed the presence of Polynesian ties. Genetic evidence was derived from select samples of modern Rapa Nui and also from burials in one of the prehistoric platforms on the island. So, clearly a strong Polynesian presence is associated with Easter Island both in the past and present. However, as human genetics researcher Cavilli-Sforza and his colleagues (1993) have noted, the limited sampling and strong evidence of historic bottlenecking or mixing of Easter Island populations due to slavery, disease, and deportation means that Thor Heyerdahl's 1950 hypothesis of Amerind genes influence cannot be rejected. Cavilli-Sforza et al. also note the unusual distance Easter Islander genetic data has with all other regions as compared even to other eastern Polynesians probably due to a founder effect and historic mixing. For instance, the Easter Islander genetic dataset's average distance from select South American and Southeast Asian groups is numerically 1,511 but other eastern Polynesians average genetic distance from those groups is only 1,031. As Cavilli-Sforza et al. suggest, Easter Island genetic history is greatly skewed due to historic processes and mixing. Without more sampling of the ancient Easter Islander remains we cannot be certain of past genetic relationships, especially if samples include modern islanders and migrations to the island.

Even the often-cited work by Erika Hagelberg (1994) that DNA extracted from 12 Easter Island skeletons from one platform shows the closest relationship with Polynesians is open to critique. There are numerous platforms on the island, and sampling only one can hardly be representative of the multiple groups noted by Roggeveen in his 1722 CE visit to the island. The central Mexican site of Teotihuacan in Mesoamerica is a classic example of why this sampling can be problematical, though certainly understandable when dealing with the limited resources of archaeology. It was not until full-scale excavations by archaeologist Renee Millon (1966), that the multiethnic nature of the densest city in the pre-Columbian Americas was revealed. The planned city in central Mexico contained a number of trade barrios that indicated populations from and exchange networks with other Mesoamerican peoples, including distant Oaxaca and the Mayan city–state of Kaminaljuyu. Further explorations at Kaminaljuyu confirmed the strong ties, including marriage alliances with Teotihuacan. Had a sampling strategy been employed, many neighborhoods at Teotihuacan, comprised of local populations, would be the most likely sampled, and the connections with the rest of Mesoamerica might not have been fully understood. We must be careful in the case of Easter Island to avoid the assumption that because it is a small island, we somehow have a firm grasp on its ecological and human history. Current research certainly suggests otherwise.

Of course we cannot know or even sample a majority of the original Easter Islander inhabitants and thus could never conclusively test all past Easter Islanders for ties to their ancestral lands before arriving on Easter Island. Cavilli-Sforza et al. suggest this simple fact makes it difficult to ever conclusively answer the origins question from past genetic samples, though we can feel confident that a significant component is Polynesian in nature. But what about modern Rapa Nui? Why are modern Rapa Nui on Easter Island so problematical in genetic studies? Just looking at historic estimates of population gives us a clue. Captain Cook in 1774 CE estimated about 700 individuals on the island. The Spanish expedition of 1770 CE mentions between 900–3,000, La Perouse in 1776 estimated 2,000. Modern researchers also oscillate. Prehistoric estimates from Diamond could be as high as 30,000, from Hunt 6,000, and as low as 500 from Cavilli-Sforza et al. In 1862 slavers took 1,000 Easter Islanders to Peru where 900 died. Only 15 made it back to Easter Island, albeit bringing back with them smallpox or cattlepox. By 1877 only 110 Easter Islanders remained! What are we to make of such fluctuations in genetic and population data? That Easter Island history is indeed a complex affair not easily interpreted or understood, either by Heyerdahl or by modern researchers. Interestingly the 90 percent die-off rate of the islanders taken to Peru is very similar to that noted for Native American communities from the time of the Columbian exchange, though it should be noted that western Pacific peoples also suffered from introduced diseases at lesser rates.

The typical story of European colonial interaction on Easter Island led to the death of most Rapa Nui and mixed genetic background for the 110 who survived into modern times and genetic testing, as Rainbird has argued. This would call into question the assumptions built into the early historic observations of class and caste as well as the validity of modern genetic studies. Just who were the Easter Islanders in the 1700s? How much interaction was already taking place with the outside world? What was the genetic background of the modern Easter Islander who were tested? Even the Easter Island script, known as RongaRonga, appears to be generated in the historic contact period as no evidence of the script can so far be dated in prehistoric archaeological contexts. In other words, historic impact on Easter Island has so skewed the record of the anthropological present and even the archaeological record via looting and disturbance, it is difficult to feel confident about research on Easter Islanders when it is applied to the past.

New Evidence

New evidence is emerging, however, that sheds further light on the prehistoric Eastern Pacific world and maybe on Easter Island itself. Both are archaeological finds. First, University of Hawaii at Manoa excavations into the island's only sand dune system and major canoe landing beach have produced consistent radiocarbon dates of human occupation no earlier than 1000 CE and more likely to 1200 CE. Exactly the time the palm forests were depleted, the stone statues (*moai*) were being erected, and environmentally the Polynesian rats were contributing to environmental imbalance. Reevaluation of Polynesian settlement of Hawaii and New Zealand dates also places their first human settlements to these times. Thus we might now see purposeful Polynesian expeditions all across the eastern Pacific for purposes of migration, settlement, and trade at much later dates than in the traditional interpretation. This is important and it may be related to the second find.

The second archaeological find of relevance involves Polynesian chickens in Chilean archaeological sediments dated between 1300 and 1420 CE. The dates fit well with later settlement of Easter Island and the eastern Pacific in general. Although debated, the published finds of New Zealand researchers Alice Storey, Elizabeth Matisoo-Smith, et al. (2007) at the El Arenal site in Chile appear legitimate. These dates are well before the Pizarro's expedition that conquered the Inca Empire and sent raiding parties down to Chile in the 1530s CE period. The expedition noted the presence of chickens in the Andes, but we cannot be sure of this description as camelids like the llamas were described as sheep. In any case, the Spanish introduced chickens into what became the viceroyalty of Peru, but their presence in modern Chile was quite light until later times. So history can shed little light on the presence or absence of prehistoric chickens in the Andes. However, archaeology can. Since no other domesticated chicken or fowl from pre-Columbian archaeological contexts have been found to date, we can suggest for now that the Chilean finds might well stem from Polynesian voyages that continued to the Americas in an easterly direction as they settled the eastern Pacific Ocean after 1200 CE.

Storey, Matisoo-Smith, et al.'s claims, of course, were controversial and the implications far reaching. A critique of those claims by Gongora et al. in 2008 was published in the same journal as the original claims. Storey, Matisoo-Smith, et al. reexamined their work and produced even stronger evidence for Polynesian chickens in prehistoric South America at El Arenal in Chile. The site was definitely abandoned before European contact and had no European artifacts. Two more chicken remains were uncovered from El Arenal and further support the original DNA analysis of these chickens as Polynesian. The dating of these remains to the late prehistoric or late pre-Columbian period (late 14th century CE median date) was not contaminated by marine deposits or food supply for the chickens. Their diet was terrestrial, not maritime. Further, Storey, et al. asserted that Cooper's study showed the drawback of using only modern DNA for ancient relationships when ancient DNA was also available. This refutal is probably also relevant for Easter Islander genetics studies as well. For the moment, the idea of Polynesian chickens in a pre-Columbian site in Chile seems well supported.

Our domesticated chickens also fit well with another domesticated food mystery, one that Thor Heyerdahl used to support his claims of South Americans on Easter Island. Sweet potatoes were first domesticated in the Americas but eventually showed up even on Easter Island. Though their seeds can germinate in salt water and they are found in some Polynesian settlements in the western Pacific, it seems also possible that Polynesian seafarers who brought the chicken to South America could also bring back the sweet potatoes to Easter Island. Claims that the Humboldt current do not allow such return voyaging except in El Niño storm years are problematic, as it has not been demonstrated that today's climate and weather patterns are the same as those 800 years ago.

The background of domesticated chickens could also support ties between Easter Island and South America. The wild ancestors of chickens are thought to derive from several varieties in Southeast Asia. Chickens may have been domesticated several times in Asia, perhaps independently. However, the archaic breed known as the Green Junglefowl and the Araucana chicken of Chile as well as Easter Island chickens show some affinities. Often tailless and laying blue-colored eggs, ties between these chickens suggest, along with giant palm trees and sweet potatoes, ties to Easter Island. But again, due to the nature of historic contact, these issues are presently difficult to explore further.

We would tend to expect chickens to come from Easter Island, as there were apparently no chickens in the pre-Columbian world before the plausible Polynesian contacts in South America, and chickens were the only major food supply animals brought by the early expedition(s) to settle Easter Island. No pigs or dogs have been found in a prehistoric context on Easter Island, and only the Polynesian rat may have been an additional food supply animal. This differs from other Polynesian settlement expeditions in the Pacific where pigs were a common food supply, such as in the Hawaiian Island settlement expeditions. Chicken pens in archaeological contexts can be found all over Easter Island and were noted by European explorers including the 1774 CE Captain James Cook expedition. Assuming that no other Polynesian domesticates show up in South America, Easter Island is the closest and most likely source for Polynesian chickens arriving at El Arenal in Chile.

Finally, increased research in the past two decades in South America points to a much richer seafaring tradition than was previously assigned to pre-Columbian South Americans. In Inca times, that highland civilization, with little seafaring background, helped sponsor expeditions that led to Inca pottery on the Galapagos Islands. The Inca relied upon a 2,000-year-old seafaring tradition on the coast not unlike the Persian relationship with the Phoenicians in the Mediterranean Sea. The 2,000-year-old Moche civilization was known to bring in whales on their watercraft, but it is the later coastal civilizations who would have most likely interacted with incoming Polynesians, groups like the Inca in the south or the Chimu in the north of Peru. Several origin myths even indicate the founding of these civilizations by legendary seafaring leaders who came by boat, including Taycanamu, Naymlap, and Chimo Capac. Taycanamu, according to Spanish chronicles, arrived by sea with a large fleet, established the Chimu dynasty, and left his son in charge before heading back across the sea to the west. Even the legendary god figure Viracocha is said to have left the Andes by going across the sea.

Such myths are similar to the founding myths associated with Easter Island (also known as *Te Piti* or navel of the world). These suggest the founder Ariki Hotu Matua sent out an exploratory canoe expedition before arriving on the island in his own expedition at Anakena beach after leaving "Hiva" possibly from the Marquesas and perhaps Mangareva to the west. The expedition was well planned with various flora and fauna brought along for settlement and with multiple waves of settlers to increase the chances of success.

It was into this rich seafaring trade zone of the eastern Pacific that Polynesian traders would have arrived in the late pre-Columbian times in South America. Trade took South American metallurgical items as far away as west Mexico and had Spanish chroniclers describing merchant seafaring communities with 6,000 members and craft that held 30 people and utilized triangular sails. If indeed these civilizations encountered each other, then there are many possibilities concerning flow of people, direction of trade, and more that need to be reexamined.

Conclusion

The traditional interpretation of Easter Island human history, while based on high-quality research, like all research into a distant past where most of the evidence has disappeared to the ravages of time, is in constant need of reevaluation and reinterpretation. This was true for Thor Heyerdahl's ideas, and it is true for today's research. New views that push the settlement of eastern Polynesia forward, especially Easter Island, New Zealand, and the Hawaiian Islands to around 1200 CE, challenge the traditional, established chronology and history for those islands and fits well with possible Polynesian contacts in the Americas after that time. These adjusted chronologies, historical descriptions of a still fertile Easter Island in the 1700s, and the role of the Polynesian rat, both as ravager of islands and as food source, also challenge traditional interpretations of the collapse of Easter Island. An Easter Island civilization that emerges later and survives longer than the traditional interpretations suggests is more likely to carry out expeditions for trade and contact with South America and elsewhere, contact that likely led to Polynesian chickens in pre-Columbian El Arenal in Chile. Chickens are exactly what we would expect to have come from Easter Island, as there were apparently no chickens in the pre-Columbian world before the plausible Polynesian contacts in South America, and chickens were the only major food supply animal brought by the early expedition(s) to settle Easter Island. This differs from other Polynesian settlement expeditions in the eastern Pacific where pigs were a common food supply, and this makes Easter Island by far the closest and most likely source for those chickens.

Such contact would also explain how South American-descent sweet potatoes show up on Easter Island. Dare we bring up the taboo subject of contact in both directions? Polynesian seafarers could have navigated their way back to Easter Island, especially in El Niño years, bringing South American foodstuffs such as sweet potatoes and even possibly, pre-Columbian South Americans. The research of Marshall Weisler (1995) on the Pitcairn Islands supports such an exchange model used by Polynesians to settle and create exchange systems on new islands. Resources and people were moving between the Pitcairns (Henderson and Pitcairn the nearest neighbors to Easter Island) and the Marquesas Islands, and such a model might well have connected Easter Island and South America. Because we can never genetically test all ancient populations on Easter Island or anywhere else, this can only be a suggestion. In other words, even if it is only Polynesians that settled Easter Island as part of an explosive push across the eastern Pacific, this could be seen as part of a larger interaction network, bringing up the question of trade and exchange with Easter Island's nearest large geographic resource, South America. The El Arenal chickens are strong evidence for something more than accidental contact, and the question can now be asked, what was the nature and extent of that contact?

Admittedly, we are dealing with a few chicken bones, hypothetical seafaring activities, and interpretation of data toward a set of historical events we may never be able to fully understand. We might ask ourselves—as researchers and interested parties on the subjects of Easter Island, contact, and issues of diffusion and exchange—if similar research scenarios existed in the past. What was the outcome of continued research into such controversial areas? We need look no further than the case of Scandinavian seafaring Vikings and contact with North America in the pre-Columbian period. Historic Viking sagas known as the "Icelandic Sagas" suggested contact and settlement might have taken place in areas referred to as Greenland, Markland, and Vinland near North America. However, the normative interpretation was that the Vikings went no farther than Iceland in the North Atlantic. Then came the 19th-century findings of significant Viking settlements on Greenland where 3,000 to 5,000 Vikings settled with cattle and more on over 400 farms during the period of 980–1430 CE. Complex trade with both Europe and the native peoples of North America was a hallmark of Greenland. Expeditions to explore the mainland of North America from nearby Greenland took place as early as 985 CE. Even Vinland turned out to be real as 1960s excavations at an actual Viking longhouse and settlement located at L'Anse aux Meadows in Newfoundland proved. The settlement may not have been the only one, as other contacts and expeditions from Greenland are mentioned, but this one is archaeologically verifiable and dates to around 1000 CE. Will the chicken bones of El Arenal turn out to be part of a much larger story of contact and exchange, two classic hallmarks of human civilization, as was the case with Native Americans, Vikings, and North America? With only oral traditions, historic accounts, and archaeology to guide us in South America, it may not be possible to elucidate the Polynesian and South American contact, as was the case with the Vikings and Native Americans. New finds are always just over the next wave of evidence interpretation.

References and Further Reading

Barnes, S. S., Elizabeth Matisoo-Smith, and Terry Hunt. "Ancient DNA of the Pacific rat (Rattus exulans) from Rapa Nui (Easter Island)" *Journal of Archaeological Science* 33 (2006):1536–1540.

Barthel, Thomas. *The Eighth Land: The Polynesian Settlement of Easter Island.* Honolulu: University of Hawaii Press, 1978.

Cavilli-Sforza, Luigi, P. Menozzi, and A. Piazza. *The History and Geography of Human Genes.* Princeton, NJ: Princeton University Press, 1993.

Diamond, Jerod. *Collapse: How Societies Choose to Fail or Succeed.* London: Penguin, 2005.

Dransfield, John. Palm and Cycad Societies of Australia. "Palms: *Paschalococos dispertab.*" Available at www.pacsoa.org.au/palms/Paschalococos/disperta.html (accessed June 4, 2010).

Gongora, Jaime, et al. "Indo-European and Asian origins for Chilean and Pacific chickens revealed by mtDNA," *Proceedings of the National Academy of Sciences* 105:30 (July 29, 2008), 10308–10313.

Hagelberg, Erika. "DNA from Ancient Easter Islanders." *Nature* 369 (1994): 25–27.

Heydon, Doris, and Paul Gendrop. *Pre-Columbian Architecture of Mesoamerica*. New York: Rizzoli Publications, 1988.

Hunt, Terry L. "Rethinking Easter Island's Ecological Catastrophe." *Journal of Archaeological Science* 34 (2007): 485–502.

Matisoo-Smith, Elizabeth, and J. H. Robins. "Origins and Dispersals of Pacific Peoples: Evidence from mtDNA Phylogenies of the Pacific Rat." *Proceedings of the National Academy of Sciences* 101 (2004): 9167–72.

Matisoo-Smith, Elizabeth, R. M. Roberts, G. J. Irwin, J. S. Allen, D. Penny, and D. M Lambert. "Patterns of Prehistoric Human Mobility in Polynesia Indicated by mtDNA from the Pacific Rat." *Proceedings of the National Academy of Sciences* 95 (1998): 15145–50.

Millon, Rene. *Teotihuacan: Onceava Mesa Redonda*, Vol. I. Mexico City: Sociedad Mexicana de Antropologia, 1966.

Orliac, C. "The Woody Vegetation of Easter Island between the Early 14th and the mid-17th Centuries A.D." In *Easter Island Archaeology: Research on Early Rapanui Culture*, edited by C. Stevenson and W. Ayres. Los Osos, CA: Easter Island Foundation, 2000.

Rainbird, P. "A Message for Our Future? The Rapa Nui (Easter Island) Eco-disaster and Pacific Island Environments." *World Archaeology* 33 (2002): 436–51.

Storey, Alice, J. M. Ramirez, D. Quiroz, D. V. Burley, D. J. Addison, R. Walter, A. J. Anderson, T. L. Hunt, J. S. Athens, L. Huynen, and E. A. Matisoo-Smith. "Radiocarbon and DNA Evidence for a Pre-Columbian Introduction of Polynesian Chickens to Chile." *Proceedings of the National Academy of Sciences* 104, 25 (2007): 10335–39.

Urton, Gary. "Inca Myths." In *World of Myths*, Vol. II, edited by Felip Fernandez Armesto. Austin: University of Texas Press, 2004.

Weisler, Marshall. "Henderson Island Prehistory: Colonization and Extinction on a Remote Polynesian Island." In *The Pitcairn Islands: Biogeography, Ecology, and Prehistory*, edited by T. Benton and T. Spencer. London: Academic Press, 1995.

White, Nancy. "Late Intermediate Peru: Chimu and Other States A.D. 900–1400." Available at http://www.indiana.edu/~arch/saa/matrix/saa/saa_mod08.html (accessed August 3, 2010).

Early American Impressions of Rapa Nui

The following account, written by U.S. Navy Paymaster William J. Thompson, was included in the 1889 Annual Report of the Smithsonian U.S. National Museum, and presents some of the earliest reports of European and American reaction to the native peoples of Rapa Nui.

The native character and disposition has naturally improved as compared with the accounts given by the early navigators. They were then savages wearing no clothes, but with bodies painted in bright colors. The women are said to have been the most bold and licentious in Polynesia, if the reports are correctly stated, but we found them modest and retiring and of higher moral character than any of the islanders. The repulsive habit of piercing the lobe of the ear and distending the hole until it could contain bone, or wooden ornaments of great size is no longer practiced, but there are still on the island persons with earlobes so long that they hang pendent upon the shoulder. In disposition the natives are cheerful and contented. Our guides were continually joking with each other, and we saw no quarreling or fighting. They are said to be brave and fearless of danger, but revengeful and savage when aroused. They are fond of dress and ornaments. Very little tappa cloth is now worn, the people being pretty well equipped with more comfortable garments, obtained from the vessels that have called at the island. . . . Straw hats are neatly braided by the women and worn by both sexes. The women wear the hair in long plaits down the back, the men cut the hair short and never discolor it with time as is the custom in many of the islands of Polynesia. The hair is coarse, black, and straight, sometimes wavy, but never in the kinky stage. The beard is thin and sparse. Gray hair is common among those beyond middle life and baldness is very rare.

Source: William J. Thomson. *Te Pito te Henua; or, Easter Island*. Washington DC: Government Printing Office, 1891.

CON

Thor Heyerdahl's expedition that he and his crew undertook with the balsa raft *Kon-Tiki* (an old name for the pre-Columbian Andean sun god Viracocha) in 1947 was not the first voyage with a traditional vessel in the Pacific Ocean. Heyerdahl had been inspired and challenged by the seafaring explorations carried out by the Frenchman Eric de Bisschop in the 1930s. De Bisschop's first voyage in a Chinese junk took him from Taiwan to Australia. Another, more spectacular voyage was undertaken shortly before the outbreak of World War II, this time from Hawaii to France in a Polynesian double-hulled vessel that de Bisschop named *Kaimiloa*.

While de Bisschop's intention was to demonstrate that seafaring in a west-east direction into Polynesia and within its vast expanse were possible in prehistoric times, Heyerdahl set out to prove the possibility of east-west seafaring (i.e., from South America into Polynesia). The *Kon-Tiki* expedition was repeated almost 60 years later, in 2006, when Torgeir S. Higraff set out with his crew in a balsa raft called *Tangaroa* (which is the name of the Maori "God of the Seas"). The *Tangaroa* expedition was intended predominantly to carry out investigations of the ecological conditions of the Pacific fauna.

The *Kon-Tiki* expedition in turn challenged de Bisschop to navigate a route from west to east (from Tahiti to South America) in a bamboo raft named *Tahiti Nui* (Great Tahiti). It is noteworthy that both Heyerdahl (in 1947) and De Bischoff (in 1957) lost their vessels because they shipwrecked, *Kon-Tiki* in the Tuamotu Archipelago and *Tangaroa* near the Juan Fernandez Islands off the coast of Chile. But both voyages proved that seafaring in traditional vessels was possible in either direction.

Although the *Kon-Tiki* endeavor stirred up much debate about American-Polynesian contacts in prehistory, it is De Bischoff's merit to have directed attention to a topic that was gaining in momentum, namely the investigation of possible landings of Polynesian seafarers on the shores of South America. The recent find of a bone of a Polynesian chicken in Chile may provide a lead for such investigation.

The *Kon-Tiki* expedition has remained the most spectacular of the Pacific explorations in rebuilt traditional vessels. This is also true for the conjectures and speculations about seafaring in the Pacific and about the peopling of the Polynesian islands that Heyerdahl publicized with his famous book *Kon-Tiki* (1950). Half a century ago, it may have still been possible to take Heyerdahl's claim about a migration from South America to Easter Island at face value. Then, the *Kon-Tiki* expedition could be categorized as an exercise in applied oceanographic science, with the weight to mark, in reality, the sea route where theory had it. However, nowadays, after decades of research in the prehistory and human genetics of Polynesian populations, Heyerdahl's enterprise has lost its validity as proof for prehistoric voyages from America to the West. In the history of Polynesian studies, the *Kon-Tiki* expedition will always retain its value as a demonstration of what is technically possible, although the insights from modern research do not back up Heyerdahl's claims.

Heyerdahl had tried to substantiate his claim about an alleged American population transfer to Polynesia with a serological study, comparing data from Peruvians and Polynesians. The invalidity of that study was convincingly proven by R. C. Suggs already in 1960. In view of the heated debate that arose in American academic circles in the 1950s and early 1960s, one cannot but admit "Heyerdahl's role as a pleasant *advocatus diaboli* who has provoked a mighty upsurge of archeological field-work in the Pacific area" (Barthel 1963: 422).

In 1956, Heyerdahl impressed the public with another exercise of applied science, this time with his demonstration how the *moai*, the large memorial stones on Easter Island, could have been erected. With traditional technical equipment, Heyerdahl and his crew succeeded in hauling several of the stones that had been lying on the ground, into an upright position, thus restoring a state of the cultural space prior to the arrival of Europeans.

What was demonstrated by this spectacular action were the possibilities of traditional engineering. Heyerdahl presented the world with a technical demonstration of how the stones could have been transported and hauled. In his book *Aku-Aku* (1958), the endeavor of 1956 is documented and recorded. From the standpoint of history, however, Heyerdahl's reconstructions fall short of a proper cultural embedding. Heyerdahl's technical action is no proof that the islanders did so in historical times. Modern anthropological research has produced insights that speak in favor of the *moai* as having been transported in an upright position straight from the quarry on the slope of Rano Raraku, one of the volcanoes, down to the lowland.

Kon-Tiki and *Aku-Aku* were illustrative demonstrations of modern Euro-American problem solving. In both enterprises, technical possibilities were explored to the fullest by the determined mind, without properly relating them to the conditions set by local cultural history. These conditions can be reconstructed to form an overall picture of Easter Island and the culture of its inhabitants, which is Polynesian to the core. Easter Island is called Rapa Nui (Flat High Plateau) by the islanders, and their Polynesian ties will be highlighted in the following for several domains, reconciling data from human genetics, biology, linguistics, cultural anthropology and the study of mythology, and popular beliefs.

Polynesian relationships are evident on Easter Island, not only with respect to human ecology (i.e., colonization, cultural history, and language) but also concerning environmental ecology (i.e., transfer of plant and animal species). Within the Polynesian network, the culture of Rapa Nui is most closely affiliated to that of the Marquesas Islands, at a distance of some 3,400 km to the northwest.

The Polynesian Genetic "Footprint" on Easter Island

On the genetic map of human populations in the Pacific region, Easter Island is the easternmost outlet in a wider, uniform landscape of a Polynesian gene pool. Although the dynamism of genetic expansion throughout the Pacific is still a matter of debate, there is consensus that the genomic profile of the Rapa Nui islanders is affiliated to the Polynesian ethnic stock.

Together with the Society Islands (including Tahiti), the Cook Islands, and New Zealand, the Rapa Nui genome forms part of "a cluster that is at a considerable distance from the rest of the Pacific islands" (Cavalli-Sforza et al. 1994: 364). The position of Easter Island as a genetic outlier conforms with the history of Polynesian migrations. Easter Island was reached by migrants coming from the northwest at the beginning of the fourth migration wave in the Pacific region (CA. 300 CE).

If there had been a pre-Polynesian population of American descent on Easter Island, then one would expect traces of ancient genetic mixing in the islanders' gene pool. The genetic admixture that is found in the genome of some islanders dates to the 19th and 20th centuries and is due to their descent from ethnically mixed marriages (i.e., of Rapa Nui people with Chilean immigrants to the island).

Plant and Animal Import from Polynesia to Easter Island

The history of human settlement on Easter Island is the history of the genetic drift from the center to the periphery of Polynesia. The same west–east drift can be established for the species of nonindigenous flora and fauna that were imported to the island by the early settlers. The origin of all those species has yet to be found in the ecological environment of Polynesia.

- Imported plants (with their names in Rapa Nui and in Latin for botanical identification):

  Kumara: various species of batatas (sweet potatoes; *Ipomoea batata*);

  Taro: the roots of which are edible (*Colocasia esculenta*);

  Uhi: various species of yams (*Dioscorea* sp.);

  Kaha: pumpkin (*Lagenaria siceraria*);

  Maika: banana (*Musa sapientum*);

  Toa: sugarcane (*Saccharum officinarum*);

  Ti: species of agave (*Cordyline terminalis*);

  Pua: Curcuma/yellow root (*Curcuma longa*);

  Mahute: species of mulberry (*Broussonetia papyrifera*) whose bark were worked to obtain fibers for making textiles (*tapa*);

  Marikuru: a tree species with fruits containing a soap-like syrup (*Sapindus saponaria*);

  Mako'i: a tree species whose wood was used for carving (*Thespesia populnea*);

  Naunau: a species of santel wood.
- Imported animals: The only two animal species that were not indigenous and came with the migrants were the Polynesian chicken (*moa*) and—unintentionally imported—the Polynesian rat (kio'e—*Rattus concolor*).

The history of spread of these various species provides evidence for Polynesian origins of the settlers and stands against speculations of an American colonization of Easter Island. Imports from America date to modern times. For instance, in the caves on the island, the poisonous spider, whose popular name is "black widow," finds its habitat. It is assumed that this spider species reached Easter Island in the 20th century with ship cargo from Chile.

Rapa Nui as a Polynesian Language

The indigenous language spoken by the islanders, Rapa Nui, is affiliated with the Oceanic subgroup of Malayo-Polynesian languages which are a branch of the Austronesian phylum. Rapa Nui shares all the major features of its linguistic structures with the other Oceanic languages. The sound system is extremely simple. It consists of five vowels and nine consonants (as opposed to eight in Tahitian or Hawaiian). A glottal stop may separate vowels, and its occurrence causes semantic change, that is words with an identical sound sequence have different meanings in case the glottal stop occurs: compare *pua* "flower": *pùa* "to cover oneself"; *hau* "string": *hàu* "hat." Word formation is limited to the use of some prefixes and suffixes. The grammatical structure is predominantly analytical. For instance, to mark the cases in noun inflection, prepositions are used that precede the noun (*o tou* for the genitive, *i tou* for the accusative); for example, *o tou poki* "of the boy."

The vocabulary of Rapa Nui shares, with other Oceanic languages, basic terminology in various domains such as seafaring (vessels and sailing), pottery for cooking and storage, horticulture (e.g., banana, yams), domesticated animals (i.e., fowl), constructions (e.g., housepost), weaving (e.g., weaving spindle), religion, and ceremonial traditions. Modern language use includes numerous lexical borrowings from Spanish and various English internationalisms. Bilingualism of the islanders (with Rapa Nui as first, and Spanish as second language) has produced patterns of interference of the linguistic systems, including code-switching.

If Heyerdahl's claim of American origins had any factual background, then the language of Easter Island would be somehow affiliated to the linguistic landscape of South America. In other words, if the islanders' ancestors had been migrants from America, they would have brought their language with them to Easter Island. Regarding any kind of relationship with American languages, the record for Rapa Nui is negative, no matter how "linguistic affiliation" is defined:

• As a member of the Oceanic group of the Malayo-Polynesian branch of the Austronesian phylum, Rapa Nui is genealogically distinct (and separated) from languages in the Americas, and from those in South America in particular.

• Rapa Nui is a genuinely Polynesian language without any admixture of an American language. This would be recognizable in its sound system, its grammatical structures, and its vocabulary. Such admixture would point in the direction of a fusion (or mixed) language, which Rapa Nui is not.

• In Rapa Nui, no ancient relics of a non-Oceanic language can be identified that would be evidence for a pre-Polynesian speech community. No language vanishes from the record without leaving traces in the region where it was spoken, regardless of how many other languages may form an overlay. If there had been any American language spoken on the island, its prehistoric presence would be recognizable in the form of a substratum (a Latin compound word: sub- "under" + stratum "layer"), that is, as elements of an underlying residue.

- The consequences of intense language contact have been studied for many settings throughout the world. The findings from extensive comparative research show that the interference of a language (Language A) that is overformed by another (Language B) may continue for a prolonged period, even if the overformed languages becomes extinct. This is a reflection of a stage of bilingualism when speakers of Language A transfer certain habits (e.g., of pronunciation or phraseology) to Language B to which they eventually shift. An illustrative example of such conditions is the prolonged influence of Etruscan (the pre-Roman language of Tuscany in Italy) on Latin in antiquity and on the local Italian dialect (i.e., Tuscan). The aspiration of certain consonants in Tuscan is a regular phenomenon in the habit of pronouncing sounds, which has been perpetuated over many generations and is explained as a long-term influence from Etruscan, still recognizable 2,000 years after Etruscan became extinct.

- The relevance of substratum influence is true also for naming. Although on a relatively small scale, there is much variation of the landscape on Easter Island. Natural formations include prominent markers such as volcanoes or high cliffs, in addition to plains and shallow beaches, crater ponds, springs and caves, and some offshore islets. All these parts of the landscape were integrated into the cultural ecology of the islanders through a process of name-giving, and the linguistic structures of those names are purely Polynesian. On Easter Island, no traces of pre-Polynesian names can be identified that would reveal any kind of linguistic affiliation with Amerindian languages.

- The perseverance of older names is a typical phenomenon of substratum continuity in all parts of the world. For example, there are many names of places, rivers, mountains, and of entire regions of Native American origin in the United States that bear witness to the former presence of Amerindians (e.g., Manhattan, Mississippi, Massachusetts). If there had been any Amerindian colonization of Easter Island, a distant memory of this would be reflected in name-giving. However, no such linguistic reflection exists.

- The maintenance of Rapa Nui is amazing since this language had been on the verge of extinction in the 19th century when only a few hundred indigenous inhabitants of Easter Island were left. Thanks to the resilience of the islanders, Rapa Nui has survived and is today spoken by some 3,000 people, of whom the majority live on the island. Some outgroups of Rapa Nui speakers are found in Chile and Peru.

The Cultural Heritage of the Rapa Nui Islanders

In addition to the local language, there is the web of Polynesian traditions that make up the cultural heritage of the islanders. The most visible of these traditions are the *moai* ("statue holding the spirit of an ancestor"), and they, literally, provide "massive" evidence for cultural ties with other regions of Polynesia. The *moai* were erected on ceremonial platforms (called *ahu* in Rapa Nui) near the beach and they faced inland, "looking over" the village community. Those *moai* that can still be seen today in an upright position in their original space were all reerected in the course of restauration of the island's cultural heritage.

Some 300 ceremonial platforms have been identified, and there may have been more than 1,500 *moai* standing at sites scattered throughout the island. In the main quarry, on the slopes of Rano Raraku, where the lava blocks were obtained from which the statues were carved, as many as 400 *moai* in various stages of their carving can be seen. The average height of the *moai* is 4 meters and the average weight is about 50 tons. The tallest statue that was ever erected on an *ahu* is 10 meters high and weighs 80 tons. It stood on the Ahu Te Pito te Kura in the northeast. The biggest and heaviest *moai* that was ever carved on Easter Island remained unfinished and is still fixed to the rock in the quarry. Its length is 22 meters and its weight has been estimated at 250 tons. Some *moai* were adorned with an additional (separate) headpiece (*pukao*) which most probably imitated the traditional headdress of the islanders.

The *moai* were the visible expression of a vivid ancestor cult among the islanders. The ceremonial reverence for the ancestors is an ancient custom widespread in Polynesian cultures. On Easter Island, *moai* were erected during a period that lasted for some 800 years, from CA. 700 CE to the beginning of the 16th century. During the long span of time, the outer appearance of the statues experienced changes, in the proportions of body parts, of facial features as well as regarding their stylistic realization.

The types of *moai* exhibit stylistic resemblances with statuary known from other parts of Polynesia. The most striking similarity lies with statues from the Marquesas Islands. Legend has it that the early migrants came from the direction

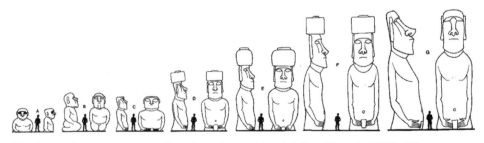

Typology of ancestor statues (*moai*) on Easter Island. (after Charola 1997: 60)

of the Marquesas (see below for mythology), which would explain how the artistic and aesthetic memory of the migrants' homeland (i.e., the Marquesas) was transmitted to and revived on Easter Island. The types of *moai* show different degrees of a local development of statuary, culminating in the most deviant types.

The cult of the *moai* experienced a decline in the early 16th century, as a consequence of the turmoil of intertribal clashes. It has been estimated that, at the dawn of prolonged conflicts among the clans over shortening natural resources, the population of the island may have counted between 7,000 and 10,000 individuals. The subsistence crisis put an end to activities relating to the carving and erecting of statues and to ceremonial services at the *ahu*. Possibly, the economic crisis triggered a crisis in the belief system. The revered ancestors, whose spirits had been watching over the daily affairs of the living members in the community for generations, seemed to be helpless in a time of conflict. Eventually the lack of trust in the protective capacities of the ancestor spirits may have led to the abandonment of the *moai* cult.

Community life on Easter Island continued, although it was overarched by a new worldview, the birdman cult (see the section below "Specifically Local Cultural Innovations on Easter Island").

Mythology and Popular Beliefs

From the beginnings of social relations among modern humans, oral tradition has been a prominent source for organizing the collective experience of the community in the cultural process. Arguably, the oldest text genre that developed was the explanation of the world within the framework of mythopoetic conceptions. "The myth is the prototypal, fundamental, integrative mind tool" (Donald 1991: 215). The most elementary layer of mythopoetic experience that we find in the world's cultures are myths of origin, usually explaining, in ethnocentric terms, how a certain group of people (a clan or kin group) is in the focus of historical events.

The myth of origin the inhabitants of Easter Island have created for themselves is a prominent marker where their cultural identity crystallizes. According to myth, the ancestors of the islanders came from the Marquesas Archipelago, in particular from Hiva Island. The legendary hero who led the colonizers to their destination was King Hotu Matu'a. In the mythical tradition, one single enterprise of colonization is recorded. The insights from modern anthropological and genetic research confirm that the settlement of the island was a onetime event.

After Hotu Matu'a and his followers had set foot on the Easter Island, the newcomers lived in isolation until the arrival of the Dutch captain Jacob Roggeveen, who discovered the island on Easter Sunday in 1722. The island, named Te Pito o te Henua ("the navel, center of the earth"), was divided by Hotu Matu'a into two parts, which were called Kote Mata Nui (in the north and west) and Kote Mata Iti (in the east and south).

The northern region was inhabited by the clans of Tu'uaro, the southern region by the Hotu'iti. The son and the nephew of Hotu Matu'a were revered as the founding ancestors of the clans. The internal structure of a clan was based on the units of *ure* (lineage) and *ivi* (extended family). The royal family (*ariki paka*) and the priesthood (*ivi atua*) represented the social elite.

The myths and popular beliefs among the islanders are permeated by Polynesian interconnections, and there are no clues as to early contacts with America. If there had been several waves of colonization, including one directed from South America, the memory of such events would have been crystallized in oral tradition and imagery. However, the Polynesian heritage is all there is in Rapa Nui mythology.

Specifically Local Cultural Innovations on Easter Island

It would be a misconception to perceive human ecology of Easter Island as a mere distant outlet of the Polynesian cultural network. In the course of time, Rapa Nui culture has produced its own local innovations, which are as significant for its fabric as are the traditional features the islanders share with other Polynesian societies.

The Birdman Cult

After the demise of the *moai* cult, a new worldview emerged amid continuous intertribal conflict. In the strive for a unifying symbol that could be shared by all islanders beyond clan rivalry the cult of the birdman was formed. This mythical being (Tangata Manu)—with a bird's head and human limbs—was identified as the representative on Earth of the newly established creator god Makemake. Images of the birdman are especially numerous in the area of Orongo on the slope of the volcano Rano Kau at the southwestern tip of the island. The motif of the birdman is mostly depicted in rock carvings (i.e., petroglyphs).

Motif of the birdman from Easter Island. (after Lee 1992: 1)

Orongo is a sacred site where an important annual ceremony was held. From a high cliff, with a wide view over the ocean, one can watch the arrival of the sea birds in spring. Among them is the manu tara ("sooty tern" in two subspecies, *Sterna fuscata* and *Sterna lunata*) that nests on three small islets (i.e., Motu Kaokao, Motu Iti, and Motu Nui) off the southwestern coast of Easter Island. It was the eggs of this bird that played a central role in the spring ceremony.

The protagonists of this ceremony were birdman contestants, aides (*hopu*) to the chiefs of the clans. They had to swim—in shark-infested waters with strong currents—to cross the strait that separates the small islets from Easter Island. The purpose of the contest was to retrieve an egg from the nest of a sooty tern and transport it safely back to the main island. The most difficult part of the contest was the task of climbing up the steep slope of the cliff on whose top the chiefs of the clans had gathered. The swimmer who arrived first and gave the intact egg to his chief was the winner.

Winning the birdman contest was not only a matter of individual bravery but it also meant the concession of privileges to the clan of which the contestant was a member. The winner, as the personification of the birdman, had to lead a secluded life for the rest of the year and live in a cave or ritual house, near the ancient quarry of Rano Raraku or near the northern coast at Anakena, which is the place where Hotu Matu'a landed according to the myth of origin. For one year, the winning clan ruled over the island and took care of the islanders' affairs.

The birdman cult fell into decline after Christian missionaries exerted their influence to convert the indigenous population. And yet, Christianity in its Catholic version never succeeded in erasing the memory of the birdman and its popularity. Symbolic of this is the imagery in the main church on the island at Hangaroa. Near the entrance door stands a large figure of the birdman, who is integrated into the local Christian canon and venerated as a saint. The motif of the bird is also present in the Christian imagery itself. In the sculptures—of the Virgin Mary holding her child and of the adult Jesus—that serve as altar pieces, the bird crowns the headdress of the human figures.

Writing Technology

Among the innovations that Rapa Nui culture experienced in precolonial times is the elaboration of a script. Documentation of the Rapa Nui writing system is found on the *Rongorongo* ("wood tablets/boards with incised script signs"). The *Rongorongo* script is the most elaborate of all the systems of notation in Polynesia and the only form of systematic sign use that meets the requirements of writing technology. Of the Polynesian languages, only Rapa Nui was written. The other speech communities of Polynesia were illiterate before the advent of the Europeans. During colonial times, the Latin alphabet was introduced to write the major Polynesian languages, among them Tahitian, Fijian, Maori, Hawaiian, and others.

The Latin script was also adopted to write Rapa Nui in the 20th century. Then, the knowledge of how to write and read *Rongorongo* texts had already been lost. The keepers of this knowledge were the priests (*ivi atua*), who were called *taula* in other parts of Polynesia. In the 1860s, Easter Island was depopulated by raids of slave traders who deported the majority of the islanders to Peru to work as laborers in the mines. Among them were the last of the priests, and the secrets of *Rongorongo* writing vanished with them.

The *Rongorongo* tablets were kept in caves, at sacred sites. Many of these tablets got lost, they were burnt by Christian priests, or they decayed under the weather conditions. How many *Rongorongo* might have ended up in private collections will remain a secret. Less than 30 texts are known to have survived. In some of the legends of the islanders the *Rongorongo* are described as "talking boards." Most probably, the contents of the *Rongorongo* texts was ceremonial (containing recitations, prayers, ritual chants, incantations, and mythical narratives) to serve the priest in his role as master of ceremonies and keeper of sacred knowledge. The cultural embedding of the *Rongorongo* tradition points at it being a sacred script, but it did not serve the purposes of practical writing in daily affairs.

Several attempts have been made to decipher the script. Although progress has been made with the identification of the principle of writing and with the identification of individual signs, it is not yet possible to read or translate entire text parts. There is consensus that the *Rongorongo* script is logographic, that is, based on whole-word writing. This means that one sign stands for an entire word (or idea, respectively). As for the association of the sign system with the sounds of the Rapa Nui language, this may not have been realized at all or, if so, on a minimal scale. *Rongorongo* signs, therefore, may stand for Rapa Nui words of different length (i.e., from one to four or even five syllables) without rendering individual sounds as phonetic units. This kind of writing was typical

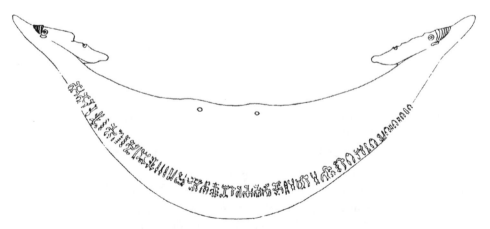

Rongorongo text from Easter Island (inscription as an adornment on a ceremonial pectoral, or *rei miro*). (after Haarmann 2000: 204)

of the early stages of writing technology, in the Old World (i.e., Danube script, ancient Sumerian pictography, ancient Indus script, Chinese writing of the oracle bone inscriptions) and in pre-Columbian America (i.e., Olmec writing).

The sign inventory is comprised of several hundred units. The visual forms of the signs show clear resemblances with the motifs in the rock art of Easter Island (e.g., images of the birdman, of vulvas, of pectorals, of geometrical motifs). The visual impression of the signs and the text corpus leave no doubt that *Rongorongo* was a genuine innovation of Rapa Nui coinage. When we ask for the motivation to elaborate such a script, then we find clues in an ancient Polynesian memorizing technique.

Sacred chants, incantations, and genealogies were important throughout Polynesia, and these had to be recited exactly in order for the desired result to take place. Accordingly, priest-chanters on Easter Island used rongorongo tablets as mnemonic devices. These tablets probably were related to the chanting staves used in Mangareva and the Marquesas. (Lee 1992: 126)

References and Further Reading

Barthel, Thomas S., Review of *Archaeology of Easter Island.* Edited by Thor Heyerdahl and Edwin N. Ferdon, Jr., *American Anthropologist* 65:2 (1963), 421–425.

Cavalli-Sforza, L., P. Menozzi, and A. Piazza. *The History and Geography of Human Genes.* Princeton, NJ: Princeton University Press, 1994.

Charola, A. E. *Isla de Pascua. El patrimonio y su conservación.* New York: World Monuments Fund, 1997.

Donald, M. Origins of the Modern Mind. *Three Stages in the Evolution of Culture and Cognition.* Cambridge, MA: Harvard University Press, 1991.

Ferdon, E. N. *Science* 142 (December 1963):.

Fischer, S. R. *Rongorongo: The Easter Island Script—History, Traditions, Texts.* Oxford: Oxford University Press, 1997.

Du Feu, V. *Rapa Nui (Descriptive Grammar).* London: Routledge, 1995.

Haarmann, Harald. *Historia universal de la escritura.* Madrid: Gredos, 2000.

Heyerdahl, Thor. *Aku-Aku: The Secret of Easter Island.* London: Allen & Unwin, 1958.

Heyerdahl, Thor. *Kon-Tiki Expedition: By Raft across the South Seas.* Translated by F.H Lyon. London: Allen & Unwin, 1950.

Langdon, R., and D. Tryon. *Language of Easter Island. Its Development and Eastern Polynesian Relationship.* Laie, HI: Institute for Polynesian Studies, 1983.

Lee, G. *The Rock Art of Easter Island. Symbols of Power, Prayers to the Gods.* Berkeley: University of California Press, 1992.

Pawley, A. The Austronesian Dispersal: Languages, Technologies and People. In *Examining the Farming/Language Dispersal Hypothesis* (pp. 251–73). Edited by P. Bellwood and C. Renfrew. Cambridge, UK: McDonald Institute for Archaeological Research, 2002.

Suggs, R. C. *The Island Civilizations of Polynesia.* New York: New American Library, 1960.

Van Tilburg, J. A., and J. Mack. *Easter Island: Archaeology, Ecology, and Culture.* Washington DC: Smithsonian Institution Press, 1995.

11

The Roman Empire's collapse was primarily due to social and political problems rather than the Barbarian invasions.

PRO   Heather Buchanan
CON   László Kocsis

PRO

Arguably the greatest empire of the ancient world, the Roman Empire eventually declined and collapsed. Exactly how the end came is still a matter of great debate today. At its height, the Roman Empire's reach was vast, extending from the Atlantic Ocean to the Euphrates River and from Britain to the Sahara. One thing appears clear: the barbarian invasions from without that ensued were the final blow to an empire already in the throes of collapse. At the core of the decline was the fact that the ideal of democracy was never truly realized in the Roman Empire; power always lay in either the hands of the few (as with the aristocrat-dominated senate) or in the hands of an emperor with absolute authority. Depending on the strength or weakness of a given emperor, so too went the internal stability of the empire. From a modern vantage point, Rome teaches how government can succeed and then fail due to the gradual internal crises left unchecked. The ensuing bureaucratic, political, social, and economic problems from the early days of the empire grew too numerous and too complex to be resolved in the end. Class conflict, constitutional flaws, and endless wars of conquest all contributed to the demise of the Roman Empire. Long before barbarian invasions came from without, Rome was collapsing from within.

Class Conflict

Stratification of Roman Society

Rome's first political and social steps after its transformation into a republic were problematic from the outset. Rome's humble beginnings was as a small Italian city–state consisting of an early Indo-European monarchy as the form of government until the early fifth century BCE. Around the sixth century BCE, the kings of the city–state were overthrown, and an aristocratic government was set up in place of the monarchy. In a true republic, power is concentrated in the hands of the people, but in the case of the Roman republic, however, the power was concentrated within a small landholding nobility. In turn, these aristocratic families, the *patricians*, set themselves apart from the commoners, the *plebeians*. The patricians were primarily the members of the senate. After the establishment of the early republic, Rome became mired in its own bureaucratic machine.

The division of Roman society guaranteed that the mass poor remained at the bottom ranks. The division between the patricians and plebeians (who outnumbered the patricians) would serve to hurt the empire from within, as the plebeians were determined to gain political social equality. A military crisis with outside invaders around 450 BCE forced the patricians to ask for the plebeians' help, and only then were important concessions made in favor of the plebeians. A new Roman army was formed comprising plebeians, and soldiers were grouped into centuries, or hundreds, which created a new lawmaking body, the *comitia centuriata* (Assembly of the Centuries) (Jones 1989: 215–19). While the *centuriata* gained voting rights in the Roman republic, the resulting laws and officials needed to manage the new government brought problems. The growth of administrative business within the government required the creation of additional offices, such as *quaestors* (tax collectors and army administrators) and censors (assigned citizens to the new classes and the determination of senate membership). The first codification of Roman law, known as the Law of the Twelve Tables, became binding over all Roman people, aristocrats and commoners alike.

By 265 BCE (after its emergence from Etruscan dominance and an early sack by Gauls in 390 BCE), Rome dominated the Italian peninsula. The government at that time consisted of two elected patrician magistrates who had military and administrative powers, including oversight of the senate. This monopoly of the government by the patricians caused a rift with the plebeians, who threatened to secede from the government.

An unequal division of classes continued into the third century. The Punic Wars (264–149 BCE) led to the formation of new political factions in Rome: the senators, equestrians, and proletarians. The senators had great wealth but were prohibited by law to engage in trade or industry. These landholders tended to monopolize the senate. The equestrians were a monied class that had made its fortune in war contracts from the Punic Wars. The proletarians were primarily the landless poor and unskilled laborers, but they were citizens with voting privileges.

Originally, the republic consisted of small grain farmers; after the wars, however, these farmers were ruined by the influx of a million bushels of grain brought in from conquered Sicily in tribute. The grain, produced on large slave plantations, was sold in Rome at lower prices than that of the Italian farms. As a result, displaced farmers went to Rome in search of work. Their abandoned farms fell to the senatorial, aristocratic class; these landholders then invested in slaves and produced pricey products such as wine and olive oil, which were profitable until the later years of the empire.

Slavery

Slavery had always been a part of ancient civilization, with the leisure class forcing the multitudes to work their lands. Rome, becoming rich after the destruction of Carthage and Corinth in 146 BCE, took slavery to its extremes, with thousands of slaves bought and sold within the same day. The Romans had little regard for human life, and the exploitation of the peasantry was justified to sustain and support the landed class, which was regarded as the highest and noblest rank in society. As a result, cheap slave labor would lead to slave gang revolts, and by the time of Spartacus's revolts (73–71 BCE), the empire nearly fell. A large rural and urban slave population remained. The identity of what it meant to be "Roman" changed by the last two centuries of the empire, because emancipated slaves of Greek and Asian origin became Roman citizens.

Bureaucratic Corruption

The creation of a bureaucratic farm tax collection system led to corruption, which weakened the empire, for it corrupted officials and further demoralized the lower class. Between 265–133 BCE, Rome made imperial acquisitions outside of Italy: Spain, Africa, Macedonia, and Asia. This growing empire had to be administered, defended, and taxed. Each new province needed a Roman representative, a magistrate, to govern it. In the early provinces, Rome created

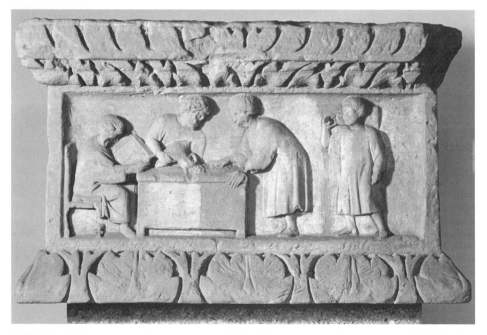

Relief depicting a tax collecting scene, Gallo-Roman, second century CE. (Rheinisches Landesmuseum, Trier, Germany/Giraudon/The Bridgeman Art Library)

praetorships with the power to rule. Each *praetor* was then given an assistant, a *quaestor*. Praetors made a fortune from their provincial commands: they accepted "gifts" from grateful subjects and made illegal assessments. A particularly lucrative method was to extend arbitrarily the limits of a given province through warfare; as the praetor was commander-in-chief of that region, he received a large share of the plunder from any and all subsequent conquests.

Like the praetors, tax collectors benefited from an inefficient and corrupt system. A curious feature of the Roman government was that tax collection was not one of the praetor's powers; instead, *quaestors* received the taxes from *publicani*, tax farmers. The *publicani* were Roman citizens organized into companies that bid for the right to collect taxes in a certain province for a set number of years. The system enabled the *publicani* to make a considerable profit above and beyond what was owed to the government. This system was without supervision, and the government appeared indifferent to the abuse of provincials by the tax collectors.

The growing class of businessmen took notice of the wealth to be gained and began taking their portion of the spoils of the empire. However, the rivalry between their greed with the public officials led to conflict. In Rome's capital, the poorer citizenry wanted some of the imperial wealth as well. Political machinations with the goal of imperial wealth added to the problems within the republic. Rome became the financial capital of the world. The new wealth, however, led to a Roman extravagance for the upper class that compromised the morals of a once dignified and rational society and left the landless poor with nothing.

Civil Unrest

Prior to the late second century BCE, disputes between the plebeians and patricians had always been resolved by negotiation and political reforms. The following century, however, saw partisan violence and civil wars that paved the way for the rise of military dictators such as Caesar, Antony, and Octavian.

Rome faced challenges from its landless citizens. Senators illegally claimed forfeited lands, and the proletarians were overrunning Rome itself. Senators were also creating scandals in the courts. Since all senators were jurors in court cases dealing with administrative scandals in the provinces, they rarely brought their fellow senators to trial for their crimes, particularly crimes they'd committed themselves. The Gracchus brothers, Tiberius and Gaius, came to political leadership in 133 and 123 BCE, respectively, and they tried to institute democratic reforms. In an attempt to help the proletarians gain land, Tiberius sponsored colonization programs that would distribute unassigned public lands in Italy to the landless citizens. However, senators fought this, and street riots broke out in the city. Tiberius himself was killed in street fighting. Ten years later, Gaius revived and expanded his brother's colonization program and went so far as to form a coalition of proletarians and equestrians to combat the senators. Then, Gaius made the fatal move to extend citizenship to Italian allies. Unwilling to share citizen rights with anyone else, all three classes, the senators, equestrians, and proletarians turned against Gaius and he eventually killed himself after being hunted down.

By 90 BCE, Roman allies were demanding full citizenship or complete independence from the empire. Greek and Asian provinces were on the brink of revolt because of mistreatment and neglect of the Roman fleet, which was leading to piracy. A social war (90–88 BCE) took place between Rome and her allies. Rome was unprepared and had to quickly grant citizenship to stop the fighting. However, the citizenship was in name only, for the allies could not vote or take office. For 60 years after the social war, Rome was awash in riots, political assassinations, civil war, and general collapse in government. Crime became rampant, and criminal elements carried out bribery, blackmail, and assassination.

Constitutional Flaws Support the Aristocracy, Then Lead to Absolute Authority

The Roman constitution, though a great achievement, contained many serious flaws that contributed to the empire's demise. In addition to failing to give equal protection to all Roman citizens (thereby upholding the aristocratic class), it provided a pretext for senatorial corruption, set the stage for military coups, and allowed the appointment of dictators for extended periods of time.

Ten years after the deaths of the Gracchus brothers, the senate declined further. A war with North Africa found senatorial commanders being defeated on the field, then taking bribes to accept humiliating peace terms. Gaius Marius, a respected equestrian military leader, was elected consul and went to Africa, where he defeated the Numidians within two years and brought their king to trial and execution in Rome. Marius became a hero, and senatorial prestige took a severe blow. Marius then went on to save Italy from a barbarian invasion from two Germanic tribes, which made him even more popular (233). Marius had successfully combined military and political power. Marius reformed the Roman army into a professional one that served the interests of its commanders rather than the state, making way for the army to be used as a tool of politicians. To deal with the barbarian threats, Marius was elected consul six times, which violated the constitution.

War within the Senate

Internal war in the senate ensued. Cornelius Sulla, the quaestor of Marius, one of the best generals of the social war, became Marius's rival for leadership. Sulla's own followers in the senate had since outmaneuvered Marius and seized control again; this was to Sulla's advantage, but there was a larger problem looming: senators were falling into debt because of their own excesses, and according to law, expected to face expulsion. In 88 BCE an activist tribune tried to expel those senators and bring the new allied citizens into power and substitute Marius for Sulla. Meanwhile, a revolt in Asia Minor had spread to Greece, with Athens and other towns threatening to break away from Rome. Dissatisfied subjects in the provinces joined the Asian revolt, and 80,000 Romans were massacred in a single day (in 237). Sulla had to put the domestic matter on hold until after he stopped the revolts in the provinces. After four years, Sulla put down the resistance and hurried back to Rome, but while he was away, his then-rival Marius had captured Rome and massacred Sulla's senatorial supporters.

Rise of a Dictator

Arguing that Rome had no legitimate government, Sulla made a plan to recapture Rome by declaring himself dictator, an emergency position appointed with the power to enact laws and take the necessary steps to end a crisis. When the danger passed, however, the dictator was expected to resign his office and restore normal government after six months. Sulla, however, was dictator for three years. He removed the equestrians from power, confiscated their lands, and killed many. He also increased the size of the senate and restored senators to the jury courts.

Rise of the Emperors

Sulla's opponents formed a government in exile in Spain and fought Rome on several fronts. After Sulla's death in 78 BCE, the senatorial, equestrian, and proletarian factions continued to fight. Ambitious generals from fights on all fronts sought power for themselves, including Julius Caesar, a supporter of Marius. In 60 BCE, Caesar, a former praetor of Spain, formed a triumvirate with the two other powerful generals at the time, Pompey and Crassus, to control Roman politics. Caesar became consul within a year and then added all of France, invaded Germany and Britain, and made a fortune in plunder with a five-year command. Caesar's victories in these regions provided him with a loyal army of soldiers more devoted to him than to the republic.

The rivalry between Caesar and Pompey led to Caesar becoming dictator. Pompey allied himself with the senate against Caesar. The senate moved to block Caesar's second five-year command in Gaul, as well as a consulship. Caesar refused to give up his command and a civil war broke out. Caesar captured Rome and ran out Pompey to Egypt, where he was assassinated. Within less than five years (49–44 BCE), Caesar extended his term as dictator to 10 years, then to life, and also served as the highest-ranking religious official as well. Although he instituted a beneficial tax reform and sponsored a successful colonization program for the proletariat, Caesar irrevocably harmed the empire by claiming absolute power.

In what appears to have become an established practice by that time, Caesar was assassinated and a new civil war ensued. A second, but equally flawed, triumvirate was formed, and a battle ensued between two of the three, Antony, a general, and Octavian, Julius Caesar's grand-nephew and appointed successor. The empire was split for a time between the two men, but that process failed. Octavian eventually defeated Antony in the Battle of Actium in 31 BCE, and the civil war was ended. Octavian returned to Rome in 30 BCE and replaced the republic with a new form of government, the principate. Within the principate, the senate gained importance as a lawmaking entity with the power to elect officials. When Octavian named himself Emperor Caesar Augustus, a damaging turning point in the Roman Empire took place from which there was no turning back. From Augustus's time onward, many incompetent and ineffectual emperors would emerge to hasten the fall of the empire.

The danger of an emperor with absolute power was evidenced in the reigns of Caligula (41 BCE) and Nero (54 BCE). Caligula declared himself divine in 40 CE (Wise Bauer 2007: 725). The madness of Nero served as a dire turning point for Rome in particular. In 64 CE, a fire started in Rome, which quickly spread. Nero is rumored to have started the fire to make way for a new palace or just for his own amusement (Wise Bauer 2007: 729). Beyond the devastating destruction of Rome, Nero made another critical move that weakened the empire: he gave away Armenia. After allowing 3,000 victorious parthians, enemies of Rome, to march through the city to witness him hand over the Armenian crown, Nero lost the confidence of the Roman people. This disgrace, in addition to a series of gruesome personal atrocities carried out by Nero, emboldened the Praetorian Guard to carry out Nero's assassination.

The emperors were often mired in ceremony and grandeur, which served to isolate them from their subjects; this effect was "another of the fatal disunities that brought the Empire down" (Grant 1990: 100). Another intrinsic failure of the emperor model of government was the idea of "favor." The idea of a good emperor was one of a paternal patron. Subjects were expected to reciprocate in the form of deference, respect, and loyalty (Garnsey and Saller 1987). The emperor distributed benefits to favored groups, namely the aristocrats and the army. In the late first and second centuries, a growing number of officials served as mediators to the emperor, which was advantageous to the local elites. Collusion between imperial officials and local landholders allowed them to exploit the tenant farmers.

The late emperors were constantly surrounded by an extensive court that cut them off from the outside world. Proximity to the emperor meant great influence for members of the Imperial Court, which included a cabinet or council at its center; the aristocracy felt hostility toward the ruler's personal assistants. Wherever they were stationed, emperors were cut off from the world by scheming courts. When the empire was split, the western emperors did not go out of their palaces, nor commanded the Roman army in wars. Both Honorius and Valentinian III preferred to remain in Ravenna, the new capital. This disconnect from the rest of the empire left the impression of a distant, absent government.

The army's entanglement in politics determined the outcome of a considerable number of emperors. Even after their arguably justifiable deposing of Nero by the Praetorian Guard, the guard capriciously switched allegiance seven months later to another potential emperor. At the same time, the army stationed at the Rhine River wanted yet another emperor, Vitellius, the commander of the forces in Germany (Wise Bauer 2007: 732). In the fourth century CE the army placed Valentinian I in power, and immediately afterward the soldiers demanded that he share power with a co-emperor. Fearing the possible death of a single emperor, the troops wanted to avoid chaos in that event. Valentinian took the western provinces and granted to his brother Valens the eastern provinces with equal legislative powers. All of the court services were duplicated in both capitals, a further drain on the economy.

The sense of a "unified" Rome with equal parts was shattered upon the death of Valentinian in 375. Valentinian's son Gratian failed to come to the aid of Valens, who was killed in battle against the Visigoths. Gratian made the critical decision of conceding Valen's successor Theodosius I most of the former western provinces in the Balkan peninsula. There had been an ongoing rift between the Latin West and the Greek East; Emperor Caesar Augustus believed that the Romans should maintain political supremacy over the Greeks (Grant 1990: 115). When Constantine the Great founded Constantinople as his capital in modern-day Turkey, it ushered in a new era where the East rediscovered its Greek heritage. From then on, the relations between the two empires unraveled and should be considered a major factor in the destruction of the weaker half, the West.

It can also be argued that due to a weakness in the imperial system, there was a break with tradition in the fifth century CE with the placement of a Hun into the highest command in the army, which led to civil war. By this time, Rome was dependent on barbarian soldiers for its defense, and this military had considerable influence on policy. Stilicho, appointed by Theodosius, was proof that "the Empire had to be defended not only against Germans without but against a German nation which had penetrated inside" (Bury 1992: 25). Stilicho's placement as the western empire's Master of Solders, or commander-in-chief, meant civil war, leading to the rebellion from the east.

The arrival of Hunnic tribes on the fringe of Europe in the fourth century who asked for asylum was a precipitous moment. Gratian unwittingly recruited these Huns into the army in 378 (Heather 1995). As a terrible result of the rift between the two governments, the Visigoth Alaric was able to enter Greece. Next, the eastern emperor Rufinus was assassinated, and suspicion fell on Stilicho. Stilicho was later assassinated at the request of senators to then western emperor Honorius.

The civil war between the western and eastern empires overshadowed the steady Hunnic penetration into the west. Civil war within the Hunnic empire left a final crisis for the western empire. Other barbarian groups broke free from the Huns after Attila the Hun's death in 453, and they started to press demands upon the western empire. Up to that point, Hunnic military power was being used by the western empire to contain immigrants on the borders. Cash-strapped, the western empire was unable to meet the barbarian army's demands. The eastern empire was both unable and unwilling to stop the ensuing invasions of the west; its provinces were doomed to become German kingdoms.

Imperialism Strains the Empire

The Military

In spite of the small proportion of power-holding aristocrats in comparison to the masses of poor commoners, the ruling class was able to maintain power practically in perpetuity; this hegemony was made possible by the military. Formal laws solidify the exercise of authority, and in the case of the early Romans, this power lay with the military-backed aristocrats. By the third century CE, internal instability led to 20 emperors recognized by the senate and 20 others laying claim to the throne with military support. The military became a destructive force in service to politicians.

Bureaucracy in Rome first appeared as a routine of the military discipline for which the Roman army was famous (Gibbon 1996: 10–17). The maintenance of the ancient world's most powerful army was the responsibility of a bureaucratic system able to recruit and financially care for it. The Roman military was hierarchical in structure, each with a fixed jurisdiction and a chain of command supported by tons of documentation. A Roman soldier was a professional who was specially trained, disciplined, and career minded. By the late republic, barbarians were allowed to serve and earn high rank, adding greatly to the number of soldiers to provide for.

As the bureaucracy advanced, emphasis was placed on merit and advancement. Dutiful soldiers could earn tenure, receive a bonus at retirement, and receive veterans' benefits. Along with the opportunities afforded Roman soldiers came the need for thousands of staffers, including accountants to handle payroll and messengers to check the ranks in the field.

An increasingly barbarian army irrevocably changed the social order of the Roman Empire. The civil strife weakened the empire and forced the emperors to resort to terror and compulsory laws. A new aristocracy emerged,

> which sprang up from the rank and file of the army . . . gradually produced a slave state with a small ruling minority headed by an autocratic monarch, who was commander of an army of mercenaries . . . the new army of the

second part of the third century was no longer the army of Roman citizens recruited from Italy and the Romanized provinces. . . . No sooner had this army recognized its own power at the end of the Antonine age, than it was corrupted by the emperors with gifts and flattery, and familiarized with bribery. (Rostovtzeff 1992: 31)

Each successive body of troops served completely at the pleasure of the emperor in power at the time. Eventually, the privileged classes found themselves at the mercy of a half-barbarian army. Later, in remote parts of the empire, the army served as the representative of Roman civilization. If a province was attacked, a soldier led the local defense and mobilized arms, men, and money (MacMullen 1992: 90). Civil authority was sanctioned by the government. Army garrisons often turned into cities themselves, but that extension would then require the building of official roads and bridges and require more troops, which was costly.

During the imperial era, the Visigoths became Rome's most successful enemy. The superiority of the Roman army was the result of the harnessing of military might for political purpose (Luttwak 1979). Having mastered large-scale warfare during the Punic Wars, Rome could not turn back to simpler times. Rome, embroiled in international warfare from then on, "never found the strength of will to lay down the sword. Her endless wars of conquest depleted her coffers, decimated her population, made enemies far and wide" (Bonta 2005).

Augustus's Pax Romana ended the war "industry." After he came to power, the army was supported by the considerable favor of the emperor. In the years of peace that followed, however, the army became a drain. The army rarely fought then, only in small barbarian skirmishes, leaving 250,000 to 400,000 idle mouths to feed. Augustus's division of the empire into armed and unarmed provinces weakened the empire, which left the region prone to social disorder and invasion.

By the end of the western empire in the fifth century, Rome had basically stopped producing its own soldiers. Conquered peoples enlisted in the Roman army as mercenaries. This practice was initially beneficial to the army, but when the soldier received his pension, he returned to his own nation, taking the pension with him, which would then contribute to the enrichment of peoples who would later sack Rome. Moreover, residents in "unprotected" provinces learned to defend themselves and became less reliant on the empire.

Later Negative Economic Effects Contribute to the Collapse

As previously mentioned, the ruling class objected to other forms of industry and discouraged the development of new technologies, which led to stagnation. For the wealthy, this land-based economy had to be maintained at all costs; any other economic improvements and innovations were viewed as a threat.

Competing industries such as mining were quickly shut down (Walbank 1992: 43), which would add to Rome's failure in later years. The economic market was locked in a limited circle of the upper and middle classes and the provincial armies, and the wider market of the peasantry was never tapped. In addition, the nobility's contempt for the artisan class (made up of primarily slaves and foreigners) overlooked a potentially lucrative part of the economy.

The end of slavery during Octavian's reign led to a shift in capitalistic activity within the empire. Freed slaves became citizens earning pay on village farms, which would eventually lead to urbanization. The gradual transfer of industry from the cities to the villages of former slaves with farming and other skills led to the decentralization of production. There were Romans "who preferred impoverished freedom to being anxious taxpayers" (Moorhead 2001: 27).

On the issue of taxes, one of the main concessions the patricians made to the plebeians was a tax reform that slightly reduced the impact of inherited status, which led to the rise of a capitalist class (Antonio 1979). However, the tax-paying proletariat saw no economic gains. A few hundred years after the republic was formed, Rome had gained control of the eastern Mediterranean. After the Punic Wars (264–149 BCE) with Carthage, the sea power, relegated to North Africa, the empire was extended to the eastern Mediterranean basin; this massive border expansion strained the republic. Higher taxes were required for the maintenance of the empire, and tax penalties crushed the poor.

There was little room for social mobility within the empire. Formal laws emphasized the nobility's exercise of authority over the poor. There were regulations regarding who qualified as having inherited status, and laws such as the Law of Debt required slavery for the poor (and their children) for failure to pay taxes. In contrast, aristocrats' tax delinquencies were overlooked or forgiven altogether. Poor farmers either abandoned their land or went to work for larger landholders, which reduced agricultural production, having a destructive effect in the later years of the empire. By the fourth century CE, the empire's ability to maintain its army was solely dependent on taxation. With taxes going directly to the military, the state was unable to benefit financially. A silver shortage also crippled the economy.

As Rome was primarily a land power, the maintenance of commerce over land was difficult. The upkeep of roads and the housing of traveling officials was expensive. A drop in long-distance trade occurred because products could be produced locally instead. At its height, the Roman Empire had nearly destroyed the local skilled networks and was relying on high-quality mass-produced goods such as pottery, boats, and wagons ordered from specialists hundreds of miles away. With the decline of the army and the lack of tax money to maintain roads, production and delivery were disrupted. The empire was reduced to that of "pre-Roman times, with little movement of goods, poor housing, and only the most basic manufactured items" (Ward-Perkins 2005: 137).

The End of the Empire

Rome, already collapsing from several internal problems, was unprepared and unable to regroup once the barbaric waves began. Roman civilization had kept Europe, the Middle East, and Africa cultured and prosperous for centuries, so it was a great loss when the western empire faced its demise. Other issues, such as the rise of Christianity and the growing power of the Holy Roman Church, played significant roles in the fall as well, but the larger issues already discussed are at the core of Rome's decline.

The civilized world could have possibly survived if the western and eastern empires had cooperated with each other, but the split between their governments was irrevocable. The resulting depopulation in the cities in the west was in part due to the artificial "newness" of the western way of living, compared to the east's longstanding traditions and agricultural practices long before they became romanized. The differences between west and east reached its apex in 476 CE when the last emperor of the west was deposed and his power fell to barbarian kings. After conflicts in the eighth and ninth centuries, the Christian churches split in 1054, when the pope excommunicated the patriarch of Constantinople and declared the Eastern Orthodox Church as heretical. The east was stronger than the west because wealth was more evenly distributed among its citizens, and there were fewer aristocrats (Ferrill 1992: 166).

No other empire since Rome has so fascinated the modern mind, due to its status as a forebear of modern civilization. The empire had unwittingly closed

---

Edward Gibbon and the Roman Pagan Ethic

One of the earliest and the best-known writers on the fall of Rome is British historian Edward Gibbon. Gibbon published his mammoth *The Decline and Fall of the Roman Empire* between 1782 and 1788. In it, Gibbon argued that Rome had become weakened over the centuries, as evidenced by the hiring of mercenaries to defend the empire, and thus had become too enamored of pleasure and the good life. Controversially, Gibbon argued that civic virtue fell out of favor with the rise of Christianity in the empire. Christianity's argument that life after death was more important than life on this Earth and its emphasis on pacifism weakened the traditional Roman emphasis on the military and the duty of its citizens to support the preeminence of Rome. Because of his assertions, and the prominence of church historians at the time, Gibbon was called a "paganist" and was accused of disputing the doctrine of the Roman Catholic Church, whose history is intimately tied with that of the Roman Empire after the Emperor Constantine. Some have argued that Gibbon's writings were the beginnings of the professionalization of historians, as he looked to the contemporary sources to shape his interpretations rather than to accepted church interpretations to shape his recounting of the events and their meanings.

in upon itself, subjugated its allies, and then presented to its democracy the contradictory idea of an emperor's authority. The legacy of the rule of Roman dictators and emperors will live in perpetuity, leaving the world forever changed. The governmental and architectural achievements of Rome teach us much, but the failures of Roman society teach even more.

References and Further Reading

Antonio, Robert J. "The Contradiction of Domination and Production in Bureaucracy: The Contribution of Organizational Efficiency to the Decline of the Roman Empire." *American Sociological Review* 44, 6 (1979): 895–912.

Bonta, Steve. "Lessons of Rome: the Rise and Fall of the Roma Republic Provides Lessons that Hint at Flaws in Modern Political Policies." *New American* (2005). Available at http://findarticles.com/p/articles/mi_m0JZS/is_4_21/ai_n25105131/ (accessed August 3, 2010).

Bury, John B. "Decline and Calamities of the Empire." In *The End of the Roman Empire: Decline or Transformation?*, 3rd ed., edited by Donald Kagan. Boston: Heath, 1992.

Ferrill, Arther. "The Empire Fell." In *The End of the Roman Empire: Decline or Transformation?*, 3rd ed., edited by Donald Kagan. Boston: Heath, 1992.

Garnsey, Peter, and Richard Saller. *The Roman Empire: Economics, Society and Culture*. Berkeley: University of California Press, 1987.

Gibbon, Edward. *The Decline and Fall of the Roman Empire*. Edited by David Widger. Salt Lake City, UT: Project Gutenberg, 1996.

Grant, Michael. *The Fall of the Roman Empire*. New York: Collier Books, 1990.

Heather, Peter. "The Huns and the End of the Roman Empire in Western Europe." *English Historical Review* 110:435 (1995): 4–41.

Jones, Tom B. *From the Tigris to the Tiber: An Introduction to Ancient History*. Belmont, CA: Wadsworth, 1989.

Luttwak, Edward N. *The Grand Strategy of the Roman Empire: From the First Century A.D. to the Third*. Baltimore: Johns Hopkins University Press, 1979.

MacMullen, Ramsay. "Militarism in the Late Empire." In *The End of the Roman Empire: Decline or Transformation?*, 3rd ed., edited by Donald Kagan. Boston: Heath, 1992.

Moorhead, John. *The Roman Empire Divided, 400–700*. New York: Longman, 2001.

Rostovtzeff, Michael I. "The Empire during the Anarchy." In *The End of the Roman Empire: Decline or Transformation?*, 3rd ed., edited by Donald Kagan. Boston: Heath, 1992.

Walbank, F. W. "Trends in the Empire of the Second Century A.D." In *The End of the Roman Empire: Decline or Transformation?*, 3rd ed., edited by Donald Kagan. Boston: Heath, 1992.

Ward-Perkins, Bryan. *The Fall of Rome and the End of Civilization*. New York: Oxford University Press, 2005.

Wise Bauer, Susan. *The History of the Ancient World: From the Earliest Accounts to the Fall of Rome*. New York: Norton, 2007.

CON

Although many causes can contribute to the fall of an empire, which is in fact the result of a process, even recent historical evidence shows that empires lose momentum when their territorial expansion is over, and that gives way gradually to territorial contraction or internal collapse. The collapse of the Soviet Union was preceded by losing the war in Afghanistan, which was its first loss during its history of unabated growth in political influence and military might. In the case of the British and French empires, the world wars contributed to weakening of their control, and the rise of nationalism and anticolonial movements were spurred by the nationalism of the empire-building nations. The German Third Reich came to an end after losing World War II, and the circumstances weren't very different in the case of the Roman Empire.

Some argue that the Roman Empire lived on as the Frankish king Charles the Great (Charlemagne) declared himself to be Holy Roman emperor in 796, but the same could also be said about the German–Roman Empire of the Middle Ages, with their desire to legitimize power in the name of antiquity, historic rights, or even divine rights. But the empire ended when none claimed or was able to claim the title, and this is valid for any empire since (Chinese emperor, Russian czar, Ottoman sultan, German kaiser, Austro-Hungarian monarch), whether there was a military defeat or not. The formal end of the Roman Empire corresponds with the time in which the empire and the title "emperor" no longer had value, therefore rendering it senseless in practice. We can rightly assume that a decisive military defeat and the occupation of the capital, Ravenna, and the complete partition of the former territory are decisive in defining the end of an empire. This may lead to the abolition of the main social–political features of the empire for a time, but its political existence is over forever.

The Beginnings of the End

The empire reached the peak of its territorial expansion in 106 CE, by conquering Dacia, but due to the military pressure of the barbarian tribes and peoples coming from the east, it had to give up and evacuate it in 271 CE, only after 160 years of conquest. The first signs of its impending collapse were shown during the so-called crisis of the third century (234–284), a period of political anarchy. The empire almost collapsed due to the greatest Gothic invasion seen to date, which hit the Balkans. The Goths' seaborne allies, the Heruli, supplied a fleet, carrying vast armies down the coast of the Black Sea, where they ravaged coastal territories of Thrace and Macedonia, while land forces crossed the Danube in Moesia (roughly modern-day Bulgaria). Similar Gothic invasion was hitting the province of Pannonia, which lead to disaster. The empire struck back in 268, with Emperor Gallienus wining some important victories at land and sea, but it was his successor Claudius II who finally defeated the invaders at the Battle of Naissus (modern-day Nis,

Erennio Etrusco, son of Decius and leader of the Roman army in the battle against the Goths at Abrittum in 251 CE. (Vanni/Art Resource, NY)

in Serbia) in 268. This was one of the bloodiest battles of the third century; the Goths allegedly left 30,000 to 50,000 dead on the field. The reign of Emperor Diocletian (284–305) regained control and saved the empire by carrying out substantial political and economic reforms, many of which would remain in force in the following centuries.

But by fourth century the heyday of the Roman army was almost over. Two main forces started to shape the destiny of the western empire: the Huns and the Germanic tribes. The main Germanic tribe, that of the Visigoths, who had fled from the Huns, at first had been allowed to settle within the borders by Valens, to become peasants and soldiers of the empire. As is usual they were mistreated by the local Roman administrators and rebelled, leading to the first war with the Visigoths (376–382). The Goths crossed the Danube again in 378 and defeated the Roman army at Adrianopole and subsequently settled in the Balkans, becoming known as eastern or Ostrogoths. This battle was of great political and strategic importance and the heaviest defeat of the Romans for four centuries. The Roman defeat left a large and hostile foreign force within the frontiers of the empire. This was followed by the reorganization of the army under the reign of Theodosius I (379–395), the last emperor succeeding to reunite under his authority the western and eastern halves of the empire. By doing so he outlawed paganism and made Nicaean Christianity the state religion, a move that also contributed to the collapse of the empire, lowering the fighting spirits of the troops.

Even before this event, the penetrations of barbarian forces was not uncommon, but after it, it became almost permanent. After the Goths, the Huns also crossed the Danube many times, and Attila the Hun conquered among others Naissus in 443, with battering rams and rolling towers, his military sophistication showing that his army had also adopted Roman methods of warfare.

The fall of the west wasn't without long lasting consequences, and that was the weakening of the east. The east also started to fall during the Gothic war launched by the eastern emperor Justinian in the sixth century, which aimed to reunite the empire again, but that eventually caused the most damage to Italy and strained the eastern empire completely in military terms. Following these wars, the Italian cities had fallen into severe decline, Rome itself being almost completely abandoned. A last blow came with the Persian invasion of the east in the seventh century, immediately followed by the Muslim conquests, especially of Egypt, which curtailed much of the key trade in the Mediterranean, on which Europe depended. Byzantium became a Greek empire, centered mostly nowadays in Greece and Turkey (Anatolia), and finally shrunk to the city of Constantinople itself, which fell ultimately in 1453.

Causes Leading to the Weakening of the State Supporting the Army

The first major problem that caused the weakening of the state supporting the army comprised the collapse of the Roman tax system; the looting economy ended with the territorial expansion and the weakening drive of military glory due to the lack of military successes. The first major reduction of real income appeared after the Sassanid wars in the third century, which stabilized the borders on the east, but also led to two negative long-term impact trends. First, the incentive for local officials to spend their time and money in the development of local infrastructure disappeared. Public buildings from the fourth century onward tended to be much more modest and funded from central budgets, as the regional taxes had dried up. Second, the landowning provincial literati shifted their attention away from provincial and local politics to the imperial bureaucracies, where tax money was concentrated. As archaeological evidence shows, the Germanic tribes on the empire's northern border increased their material wealth, due to their contact with the empire, and that in turn had led to disparities of wealth sufficient to create a ruling class and oligarchs capable of maintaining control over far larger groupings of their people than had previously been possible, therefore becoming significantly more formidable adversaries. The settled barbarians, however, due to high taxes, Roman prejudice, and government corruption, gradually turned against the empire and began looting and pillaging throughout the eastern Balkans.

Disease, Causing Population Decline

Archaeological evidences show that Europe continued to have a steady downward trend in population, starting as early as the 2nd century and continuing until the 7th century. This is largely due to the epidemics of smallpox and measles, which swept through the empire during this period, ultimately killing about half of the entire population. The severe drop in population left the state apparatus and army too large for the population to support; therefore, the depopulation of Italy favored Germanic expansion. The eastern half survived, however, due to its larger population, which was sufficient for sustaining an effective state apparatus. The European recovery may have started only once the population had gained some immunity to the new diseases. The ravages of disease didn't end with this. Later, the plague of Justinian may have been the first instance of bubonic plague, and it was so devastating that it helped in the effort of the Arab conquest of most of the eastern empire and the whole of the Sassanid Empire (most of modern Iran, Iraq, and Afghanistan).

The empire underwent major economic transformations. The economy of the empire was a kind of complex market economy in which trade was relatively free. Tariffs were low and laws controlling the prices of foodstuffs and other commodities had little impact because they did not fix the prices significantly below their market levels. On the other hand, the Romans had no budgetary system and thus wasted whatever resources they had available. The economy of the empire was basically a plunder economy, based on looting existing resources rather than producing anything new. Material innovation and technological advancement all ended long before the final dissolution of the empire, and as a consequence few exportable goods were produced. The economy, based upon slave labor, was inefficient and precluded having a middle class with purchasing power that could support local businesses. Roman territorial expansion was also a consequence of decreasing Roman agricultural output and increasing population. By conquering their neighbors, the Romans appropriated their energy surpluses (metals, grain, slaves, etc.). The booties stopped with the end of territorial expansion, but the large empire was costly to uphold, in order to maintain communications, garrisons, and civil government on a functional level. With the cessation of tribute from conquered territories, the full cost of the Roman military machine had to be borne by the citizenry, and this was increased even more by the pomp costs of the emperors. Eventually this cost grew so great that any new challenges such as invasions and crop failures could not be solved by the acquisition of more territory, and at that point, the empire fragmented into smaller units and became ripe for collapse.

By the third century beginning with the reign of Nero, the monetary economy of the empire had collapsed, because Roman mines had peaked and output was declining and territorial expansion stopped. Since mines of all commodities were being depleted, this led to the debasement of the currency and subsequent inflation. The lack of metals caused a decline of Roman technological and economic sophistication, while the inflation required that emperors adopt price control laws that resulted in prices that were significantly below their free-market equilibrium levels, transforming the empire into a kind of state socialism. These artificially low prices led to the scarcity of foodstuffs, particularly in cities whose inhabitants depended on trade in order to obtain them.

To counteract the effect of inflation on state revenues, the monetary taxation was replaced with direct requisitioning from the farmers. Individuals, most of them slaves, were forced to work at their given place of employment and remain in the same occupation. Farmers became tied to the land, as were their children, and similar demands were made on all other workers and artisans as well. In the countryside, people attached themselves to the estates of the wealthy in order to gain some protection from state officials and tax collectors. These estates, the beginning of feudalism, operated as much as possible as closed systems, providing for all their own needs and not engaging in trade at all. Workers were organized into guilds and businesses into corporations called *collegia*, and both became de facto organs of the state, producing for the state. There was a decline in agriculture, and land was withdrawn from cultivation, in some cases on a very large scale, sometimes as a direct result of barbarian invasions. However, the chief cause of the agricultural decline was high taxation on the marginal land, driving it out of cultivation. High taxation was spurred by the huge military budget and was thus indirectly the result of the barbarian invasion.

Environmental causes also played a significant role in the weakening of the state. The complex Roman society depleted its resource base beyond levels that are ultimately sustainable. The existence of large nonproductive masses, such as the army and bureaucracy, its establishment and running of infrastructures, which require substantial "energy" subsidies, overburdened the tax base, which collapsed as gradual environmental degradation caused crop failures and subsequent population decline. Deforestation and excessive grazing led to erosion of meadows and cropland. Deforestation had significant military causes as well, ensuring that the forests could not provide cover and camouflage for the enemies, usually attacking in smaller and less organized groups but using the advantages of the terrain. Shipbuilding was also a major contributor to deforestation. At times of war, hundreds of ships could be built within a month, leading to scarcity of timber in the immediate areas of shipbuilding centers.

The intensive agriculture needed to maintain a growing population required irrigation, which in turn caused salinization, resulting in fertile land becoming nonproductive and eventually increased desertification in some regions, mainly in Africa, Hispania, the Balkans, Anatolia, and in the Middle East. Many animal species became extinct, as the empire practiced large-scale and systematic environmental destruction. At shows held at the Coliseum in Rome there may have been up to 5,000 lions, bears, and wolves killed annually, leading to their extinction in all of western Europe and even in northern Africa and the Middle East (the Atlas lion being the favorite beast of the gladiator shows).

Lowland areas and areas close to water transports were highly urbanized first, but as population increased along merchant routes, the environment underwent drastic degradation as pollution from the burning of fuel wood filled the air and smelters that used wood as fuel transmitted heavy metals into the atmosphere. Urbanization and the resulting degradation of the environment ultimately weakened the Roman Empire, reducing its capacity to supply the necessary raw material and money for defense, which in turn resulted in the considerable weakening of the army.

The Weakening Army

The Roman military can be viewed as one of the greatest armies ever. However, from around the end of the fourth century, the military began to deteriorate continuously and irreversibly. Its causes are manifold. Perhaps the most important was the abundance of internal conflicts in which the military fought, split between rival contenders to the throne of the empire. The endless civil wars between factions of the Roman army fighting for control eroded the political capacity to maintain the army at superior organizational, tactical, and armament levels. On the contrary, some argue that the army still remained a superior force compared to its civilized and barbarian opponents, as is shown in its victories over Germanic tribes at the Battle of Strasbourg in 357 and in its ability to hold the line against the Sassanid Persians throughout the fourth century.

In spite of these instances, the prevalence of civil wars during the fourth and fifth centuries, when the Roman army was forced to fight, caused a constant drain of resources that might have been used against external enemies.

Treason and the killings of army generals, always a decisive factor in military defeat, became omnipresent. A critical event was the murder of Majorian (457–461) in 461, denying him the chance of recapturing Africa and holding the western empire together. After Majorian's murder, western imperial unity finally dissolved. Aegidius in Gaul and Marcellinus in Dalmatia refused to accept the new Emperor Libius Severus (461–465), who rose to power thanks to Ricimer's murder of Majorian. Another reason the army was weakened was the mixing of the ranks of the legions with barbarian mercenaries, with the army becoming basically a mercenary army recruited mainly from neighboring Germans. These barbarians were willing to join the army, either to stop the Romans from invading their territory or because they wanted Roman citizenship if they served for a certain number of years, as is also the case in modern mercenary armies, such as the French foreign legion.

The process of admittance was started by the emperors Diocletian (284–305) and Constantine I (305–337), who split the army into border and mobile components. The border troops became soldier-farmers and declined rapidly in efficiency, though they were still paid. The weakness of the border troops meant that emperors needed more mobile troops, so they expanded the army. This in turn increased the number of recruits needed, while the simultaneous reluctance of landowners to lose scarce workers led to the recruitment of the militarily inferior barbarians. The funds for the army were low; therefore, it had problems in recruiting Roman citizens, resorting rather to the cheaper but less trained and conscious barbarians, which had the result of decreasing its fighting efficiency. The military hired barbarians because Romans were unwilling to join, some even willingly cutting their fingers to avoid being drafted. As a result, the senate made service compulsory, but even this did not help. As a result, there were more Germans in the army then Romans, and this is why the barbarians were able to control the army. This Germanization and the resultant cultural dilution or barbarization led to lethargy, complacency, and loyalty of the legions to the Roman commanders, instead of the Roman government, and a surge in decadence among Roman citizenry.

The government promised higher cash rewards to those who joined the army, necessary to render the service attractive, but as the army became dominated by its commanders, which formed militias, one of them of Orestes, they became crucial in destabilizing the empire. The setup of a mercenary army was a direct consequence of the decline in military spirit and of depopulation in the old civilized Mediterranean countries, and the moral decay was due to the affluence experienced before, including a decline in patriotism and loyalty among soldiers. The Germans in high command had been useful, but they were also dangerous as the case of Odoacer has shown clearly. Since the barbarians could not be trusted, any successful army tried to avoid too much interaction with the enemy since its influence would become subject to collapse. The barbarians realized the importance of the army, started to take advantage of its unorganized nature, began to infiltrate the empire, and finally took over the empire.

The Romans could maintain their power only by continuously making and changing alliances with their enemies, pursuing a *divide et impera* (Latin for divide and rule) politics among the barbarians. In fact the Roman army wasn't able to destroy the barbarians that were attacking, and they couldn't keep other tribes out. These frequent alliances with the barbarians convinced the latter of the vulnerability of the empire and of any of its emperors. As Alaric was used against the western Romans, Maximus, the main plotter against Aetius, disillusioned by the emperor and his former ally Heraclius, used the Huns to get revenge on them, so two Hun friends of Aëtius, Optila and Thraustila, assassinated both Valentinian III and Heraclius in 455. Since most of the Roman soldiers present at the scene of stabbing were faithful followers of Aëtius, none made an attempt to save the Roman emperor. Prior to that, for example, by the time of emperor Caligula's assassination in 41 CE, his loyal Germanic guard responded with a rampaging attack on the assassins, conspirators, innocent senators, and bystanders alike.

Constantine I built the new eastern capital of Constantinople and transferred the capital there from Rome in 330, the east being promoted to the core of the empire. This occurred because Greek-speaking Christians—after years of persecution—had taken over the Roman Empire. Thus, what little available resources of metal they had were used to save the new capital city of the Roman Empire and its adjacent provinces of Greek-speaking Christian Anatolia. As a result, the Greek-Christian Romans drove all the Germanic invaders toward the Latin West, which had been demoted to the periphery. If the capital of the Roman Empire had not been transferred, then the authorities would have driven the Germanic invasions toward Anatolia, and the west could have been saved. Although the institution of the empire itself was not at fault, poor leadership played a significant role in the military failure of the empire.

The impact of Christianity was significant in other ways. Not upheld by conscious warriors, no longer proud of their cause and virtues, the army's morale had inevitably fallen, leading to a decrease in fighting virtue. The many losses the Romans had suffered further decreased the morale among soldiers. Christianity transformed its status from an oppressed and brutally persecuted religion into the official dominant religion of the empire, during the reign of Constantine. Consequently, most of the people became Christians, including all the Roman emperors after Constantine, except Julian. As the Christian philosophy favored pacifism, Christians were unwilling to fight, expecting rewards in heaven rather than from their daily lives. The more Christian the soldiers became, the more they lost their martial virtue, which was considered a sin in itself, and resulted in the lack of moral superiority.

The lack of technical superiority of the Roman army was another evident cause of the empire's collapse. The Roman army, based on infantry, lacked mobility and the adequate cavalry capable of securing that. Although it had cavalry, it could not match the completely mobile armies of their enemies on horseback. The horseshoe was invented by the Barbars, and their mobile army altered warfare from infantry to cavalry dominance for the next thousand years, a trend marked by the second Adrianople defeat in 378 CE. The lack of funds led to an ever-poorer quality of the weaponry and armor supplied to the troops, which in the end became so obsolete that enemies had better armor and weapons as well as larger forces. The decrepit social order offered so little to its subjects that many saw the barbarian invasion as liberation from their onerous obligations to the ruling class.

The Unfavorable International Situation

The empire faced ever growing external threats. The first was the emergence of the Sassanid Persian Empire in Iran (226–651), which resulted in the withdrawal of the Roman legions from the line of the Euphrates and also from much of Armenia and Kurdistan. Indeed, 20–25 percent of the overall military might of the Roman army and up to 40 percent of the troops under the eastern emperors confronted the Sassanids for about half a century. The constant pressure exerted by invading people caused a domino effect—the pressure on people who are living far from the empire resulted in sufficient pressure on people who lived on the empire's borders to make them contemplate the risk of full-scale immigration into the empire. Thus the Gothic invasion of 376 was directly attributable to Hunnish advancements around the Black Sea in the previous decade. In the same way the Germanic invasions across the Rhine in 406 were the direct consequence of further Hunnish incursions into Germania, so the Huns became deeply significant in the fall of the western empire long before they themselves became a military threat. The 395 division of the empire, between Arcadius and Honorius, the two sons of Theodosius, was also very unfortunate, since it ended the strategic depth of the empire, allowing fewer transfers of money and troops between the two parts. With longer borders to defend and fewer resources, some historians argue that the western collapse was inevitable after 395.

Evidence that Supporting the Military Causes Lead to the Fall of the Empire

The previous military defeats were a prelude to the final collapse of the empire. Its major landmarks are the battle of Adrianople with the Goths in 378; the crossing of the Rhine by the Germanic tribes and Alans in 406; the first sacking of Rome after 800 years in 410 by the Goths; the loss of Africa in 426 to the Vandals; the battle of Catalaunum in 451 with the Huns and the subsequent Hunnish incursion into Italy; the second sacking of Rome by the Vandals in 455; and the final push by Gothic leader Odoacer in 476 CE.

At the second Battle of Adrianople in 378, some 10 km from Edirne in modern Turkey, though the Roman army had a clear numerical superiority (20,000–40,000 opposed to 12,000–15,000 of Goths, according to estimates) and also had Emperor Valens on the battlefield, their effort was disorganized and undisciplined. This Roman army consisted of heavy infantry, various archers, and cavalry, but it attacked the circular Gothic coach camp (wagon lager) too late and in disarray. In the meantime, the Gothic heavy cavalry encircled the Roman infantry, and with its Gothic and Alan infantry pushing from the front, it caused the whole Roman army to fall into a disorganized rout, leading to the massacre of two-thirds of it, including the emperor himself. The causes of the defeat were manifold, including redeployment problems and simultaneous attacks on other fronts, leading to insufficient number of troops in the three Roman armies, which theoretically fought together.

A peace agreement was forged with the Goths in 382, in which the new eastern emperor, Theodosius I, had recognized their claim to the province of

Thrace. The eastern emperors, as would be the rule in the Byzantine Empire, used deception and lies to weaken their enemies, since they no longer had adequate military fighting power. As an example of this tactic the invader Visigoths became allies and used this against the western Roman army under Eugenius and Arbogast, which were supporting the western contender that had been rejected by Theodosius. Alaric the Visigoth accompanied Theodosius's army in invading the west in 394. At the Battle of the Frigidus, Theodosius had explicitly ordered the Goths to charge the usurpers army before he engaged his soldiers, with the intent of weakening both the Visigoths and the western Romans. This led to the sacrifice of the Visigoths with approximately half of them dying, which enabled Theodosius to win the battle. This convinced Alaric that the Romans sought to weaken the Goths by making them bear the brunt of warfare in order to completely subjugate them after Theodosius died in 395. Alaric soon resumed hostilities against the eastern empire.

Fearing the Visigoths, Emperor Diocletian moved the capital of the western empire from Mediolanum (modern Milano) to Ravenna in 286, which was better located strategically. In the meantime, Alaric made several attempts at invading Italy, but was halted by Flavius Stilicho and decisively defeated at the Battle of Pollentia and later in the Battle of Verona, but the west was unable to succeed alone, so it finally proposed an alliance with the Visigoths to help reclaim Illyricum. However, when the Vandals and Sueves crossed the Rhine and invaded Gaul, the invasion was called off and Alaric was left with the expense of preparations for the campaign. Stilicho persuaded the Roman senate to reimburse Alaric, but the fiasco had sown resentment in both the Romans and in Alaric's Goths. These events were followed by more violence on the part of the Roman army, this time aimed at the barbarian soldiers and slaves in Italy, many of them who had been captured by Stilicho in his earlier wars. Around 30,000 escaped Italy and fled to strengthen Alaric's army. This was paralleled at the end of the fourth century when small barbarian tribes who had opposed the early empire now banded together to form more powerful confederations such as the Goths, Franks, and Alamanni. The Danube had been crossed many times before 406, but the Rhine had never been, at least decisively. When the Huns arrived in 360 and drove the Goths into the empire, the Roman army near Constantinople, the capital, was defeated. From then on, the Romans could not destroy these Goths, and after one group of barbarians had entered the empire, the Romans could not muster the military strength to keep others out. So on December 31, 406 (or 405, according to some historians), a mixed army of Vandals, Suebi, and Alans crossed the frozen river at Moguntiacum (modern Mainz) and began to ravage Gaul, some moving on to Hispania and Africa, with the empire losing de facto control over most of these lands forever. These invaders went on to settle all over the western empire: the Visigoths, Alans, and Suevi took land in Spain; the Vandals in Africa; and the Burgundians, the Visigoths and Franks in Gaul. Some historians are doubtful about the increased power of these nations and claim that emperors like Diocletian, Constantine, Constantius II (337–361), and Valentinian I (364–375) kept the barbarians beyond the borders. But the process continued after the fall of the empire, such as the Saxons invading Britain and at the end of the fifth century, while the Ostrogoths occupied Italy.

The sieges and sackings of Rome proved to be the decisive military weakness of the empire. The decisive Visigoth political interfering at the highest level became visible soon after they invaded Italy and laid the first siege to the city in late 408. Rome was being affected by starvation and disease and became desperate, so the senate sent several envoys, including the pope, to Ravenna to encourage Emperor Honorius to strike a deal with the Goths. When this didn't happen, the Roman senate offered Alaric a nice amount of gold, silver, silk, and pepper in exchange for lifting the siege. This showed that the Romans lacked a sufficient army to defend even the heartland of the empire. This military weakness proved decisive for Alaric, who wanted the provinces of Rhaetia and Noricum (roughly present-day Austria, Switzerland, Slovenia, and southern Bavaria) as a home for the Visigoths, and the title of Magister Militium, but the emperor refused this and tried to sneak a force of Illyrian soldiers into Rome. The army was intercepted by Alaric and, outraged by the insult, besieged Rome for a second time, destroying the granaries at Portus. Faced with the return of starvation, the senate surrendered again, this time under pressure from Alaric, who appointed Priscus Attalus as a rival emperor. So the barbarians actually decided who would be the emperor. Alaric was made Magister Utriusque Militium and his brother-in-law Ataulf, the commander of the cavalry, Comes Domesticorum Equitum. They marched toward Ravenna to depose Honorius, who was ready to surrender when an army from the eastern empire arrived to defend Ravenna. As another blow, Heraclian, the governor of the African coasts, cut off Rome's grain supply, threatening the city with another famine. Alaric wanted to send Gothic troops to invade Africa and secure food for Rome, but Attalus refused, probably fearing that the Goths would seize Africa for themselves. In response, Alaric ceremonially deposed Attalus and reopened negotiations with Honorius.

When Alaric was on the verge of an agreement with Honorius, his forces were attacked by Sarus, a fellow Gothic commander who was allied to Honorius and who had a blood feud with Ataulf. Alaric returned to Rome and laid siege to it a third time. On August 24, 410, the slaves opened Rome's Salarian Gate, and the Visigoths poured in and looted for three days. Because they had already been converted to Christianity, it was not a particularly violent looting, but it still had a profound effect on the city, since it was the first sack after almost 800 years of successful defense, after the victory of the Gauls lead by Brennus in 387 BCE. This sack proved to be a major historical landmark, as many great edifices were ransacked, including the mausoleums of earlier Roman emperors. As a result, tens of thousands of citizens fled, many into Africa. After raiding Greece and invading Italy, the Visigoths settled elsewhere in the empire, founding the Visigoth kingdom in southern Gaul and Hispania.

Although Roman and most Western sources claim that the Roman–Visigoth army defeated the Hunnish alliance on the fields of Catalaunum in 451, the battle was rather indecisive. The Romans built on an alliance with the Visigoths, whom they had defeated earlier under the leadership of Aetius in the Battle of Narbonne in 436. This conclusion of indecisive outcome in 451 is supported by the facts that the Huns left the fields the second day completely organized, the king of the Visigoths was killed during the battle, and the Romans did not pursue them. Aetius himself had grown up among the Huns as a royal hostage and knew better than anyone else that the victory, if we may call like that, wasn't decisive. This was also reinforced by the fact that shortly after the battle, in 452, Attila again entered Italy itself looking to marry the daughter of the emperor. Attila's friendship with Aetius and his respect of his enemies and for the Roman culture caused him to behave extraordinarily civilized, even more than other Roman commanders of the time, and he withdrew from the gates of Rome, probably under some Christian influence but specifically on the request of pope who was absolutely mesmerized by this behavior and conferred him the title of "Scourge of God." It is evident that the Huns could have ransacked Rome in 452 as they did in other Roman towns because Roman defense was nowhere to be found. But what was delayed for the time would eventually happen.

The Vandals invaded the African provinces of the western empire (Mauretania) in 429, mostly completing it by 439. This had severe financial and strategic consequences; it not only ended the western control of these wealthiest provinces, but it also exposed the Mediterranean to pirate raids. This was shown clearly during the second sack of Rome, which was performed by the Vandals in 455, when a Vandal fleet led by King Geyserik could sail up the Tiberis from Carthage, showing that there was no Roman navy present or capable of fighting, nor any field army to resist it. In opposition to the forgiving Huns or moderate Visigoths, the Vandals had been looting the city for 14 days, taking also shiploads of slaves, giving birth to the term "vandalism," meaning useless and senseless destruction. The Vandals then moved to Africa, but the western emperor Majorian was unable to retake it in 461. During his preparations, the news got out to the Vandals, who took the Roman fleet by surprise and destroyed it. A second naval expedition against the Vandals, sent by Emperors Leo I and Anthemius, was defeated in 468.

In 476, Odoaker, a leader of the Germanic *foederati* was promised land in Italy by militia leader Orestes for fighting against Nepos, the emperor. The *foederati* were Germanic troops under their chieftain's commands. Julius Nepos was nominated emperor by the eastern emperor Zeno and considered to be the legitimate emperor by Zeno's rival Basiliscus. As Nepos fled to Dalmatia, the promissor Orestes placed his son Romulus on the throne, naming the emperor Augustus, but failed to keep the promise he had made to Odoacer. Outraged by

A Philosopher-Solider Views the End of His Son and the Empire

Written in 413 CE, this letter by Synesius of Cyrene, a philosopher-soldier, demonstrates his view that Christianity did not weaken the Roman military ethic, but, in the life of his son Marcellinus, enhanced it.

To the General

Praise is the reward of virtue, which we offer to the most illustrious Marcellinus at this moment when he is leaving his post, at this moment when suspicion of every flattery is in abeyance. When he arrived here, he found our cities attacked from without by the multitude and rage of the barbarians, from within by the lack of discipline of the troops and the rapacity of their commanders. Marcellinus appeared in our midst as a god. He vanquished the enemy in a single day's fighting, and by his continual alertness he has brought our subjects into line. He has thus out of both calamities brought peace to our cities.

Nor did he claim any of those profits that usage has made to appear lawful; he has not plotted to despoil the rich or ill-treat the poor. He has shown himself pious towards God, just towards his fellow citizens, considerate to suppliants.

On this account a philosopher priest is not ashamed to praise him, a priest from whom no one ever received a testimonial bought by favor. We wish that the courts of law also were present with us, so that, collectively and individually, all we inhabitants of Ptolemais might have presented him in return with such a testimonial as is in our power, however inadequate, for words are somehow far inferior to deeds. I would most willingly have made a speech on the occasion in behalf of us all.

But since today he is beyond the frontier, we wish at all events to dedicate to him our testimony in the form of a letter, not as those from whom a favor is solicited, but as those who have solicited one.

Source: "Letter 62: To the General: a Farewell." *Letters of Synesius of Cyrene*, translated by A. Fitzgerald. London: 1926.

this, Odoacer defeated him in the Battle of Ravenna and entered the capital and forced the child emperor, Romulus Augustus, to abdicate and killed Orestes. Although Odoacer recognized Nepos until its death in 480, he put an end to the western Roman empire by sending the imperial insignia to Constantinople. The significance of this is reinforced by the fact that he didn't proclaim himself as an emperor, although he could have. Strictly speaking he wasn't allowed to hold the title of emperor because he wasn't a Roman citizen, therefore he asked Zeno to become formal emperor of the entire empire, and in so doing he legalized Odoacer's own position as imperial viceroy of Italy. Odoacer could also have chosen himself a puppet, since he legally kept the lands as a commander of the eastern empire, in the name of Zeno. Zeno recognized him as imperial viceroy, deposing at the same time Nepos, the last legitimate western emperor, who was murdered by his own soldiers in 480, putting an official end to the already defunct western empire.

By keeping the Roman administration, senate, and most of the taxes in place for a time, Odoacer was accepted for good not only by his conational Germans, but also by the neo-Latin speakers, becoming the first German-Italian king of Italy. The Germanic *foederati*, the Scirians, the Heruli, as well as a large segment of the Italian Roman army, proclaimed Odoacer "king of Italy" (*rex Italiae*). Later, Zeno, concerned with the success and popularity of Odoacer, started a campaign of slander against him, inciting the Ostrogoths to conquer and take back Italy from him, which happened with Zeno's approval, but instead of returning the western empire, they founded their independent Ostrogothic kingdom in Italy in 493, under the rule of their king Theodoric the Great.

Although there were other troublesome changes that took place in the Roman Empire during the fourth and fifth centuries, the true cause of the empire's downfall was primarily military in nature. The empire had reached its military and territorial zenith, but had become so overburdened by its own needs in terms of soldiers (necessitating the heavy use of mercenaries), material (greatly impacting the Roman civilian population), and political influence (becoming part of the imperial intrigue rather than separate from it) that it essentially collapsed upon itself, allowing the barbarian armies an opportunity of which they took full advantage. With the influx of Germanic tribes in the western empire, the age of Roman power truly had come to an end.

References and Further Reading

Cameron, Averil. *The Mediterranean World in Late Antiquity, CE 395–600.* London: Routledge, 1993.

Davis, Paul K. *100 Decisive Battles from Ancient Times to the Present. The World's Major Battles that Shaped History.* New York: Oxford University Press, 1999.

Elton, Hugh W. *Warfare in Roman Europe: CE 350–425.* New York: Oxford University Press, 1996.

Ferrill, Arthur. *The Fall of the Roman Empire: The Military Explanation.* New York: Thames and Hudson, 1986.

Galsworthy, Adrian. *The Complete Roman Army.* London: Thames and Hudson, 2003.

Gibbon, Edward. *The Decline and Fall of the Roman Empire.* Edited by David Widger. Salt Lake City, UT: Project Gutenberg, 1996.

Heather, Peter. *The Fall of the Roman Empire: A New History of Rome and the Barbarians.* New York: Oxford University Press, 2006.

Jones, A. H. M. *The Decline of the Ancient World.* London: Longman, 1966.

Jones, A. H. M. *The Later Roman Empire, 284–602: A Social, Economic and Administrative Survey.* London: Blackwell, 1964.

MacMullen, R. *Corruption and the Decline of Rome.* New Haven, CT: Yale University Press, 1989.

Mierow, Charles Christopher, trans. *The Gothic History of Jordanes.* English version with an Introduction and a Commentary. Princeton, NJ: Princeton University Press, 1915.

Nardo, Don. *The Decline and Fall of the Roman Empire.* World History Series, 27. San Diego: Lucent Books, 1998.

Potter, David S. *The Roman Empire at Bay.* CE *180–395.* Routledge History of the Ancient World. London: Routledge, 2004.

Procopius. "The Vandalic War." In *The History of the Wars*, Books III and IV. Trans. by H. B. Dewing. Cambridge, MA: Harvard University Press, 1916.

Ward-Perkins, B. *The Fall of Rome and the End of Civilisation.* New York: Oxford University Press, 2005.

12

The Hawaiian and other Polynesian seafarers developed navigation methods based on observation of constellations and currents, so that they could sail intentionally from Tahiti to Hawaii and back.

PRO   Harald Haarmann
CON   Claire Brennan

PRO

The exploration and colonization of the islands in the Pacific Ocean have puzzled generations of scholars and have spurred wide-scale speculation among a broader public. Over a span of more than 200 years, the debate about how the Pacific was settled has produced an enormous amount of literature, ranging from observations about the lives and customs of Polynesian islanders in voyagers' logbooks to scientific investigations about ancient seafaring, archaeology, and population genetics.

No other region in the world offers so many similarities among local cultures and so many resemblances among languages that are genealogically related, scattered, as they are, over thousands of islands over an extremely vast area called Oceania. The geographic distances in Oceania are enormous. It is some 6,000 nautical miles (or 10,000 km, respectively) from Australia or New Guinea in the west to Easter Island in the east and some 5,000 nautical miles (about 8,500 km) from the Hawaiian archipelago in the north to the South Island of New Zealand.

Seafaring in the western Pacific and on the Pacific Rim started at a very early time. Those who crossed the strait that separated Southeast Asia from New Guinea during the Ice Age were the first seafaring humans. They undertook their voyages in canoes or on rafts more than 62,000 years ago. At that time, New Guinea and Australia were still interconnected in the land mass known as Sahul. Those early seafarers did not have any technical devices for their navigation, but they certainly observed phenomena in their natural surroundings very carefully and learned how to respond to the impact of environmental factors on their living conditions. Most probably, the people who crossed the waters to reach Sahul had some, albeit rudimentary, experience with currents and star constellations.

For a long time, reliable information about seafaring and colonization in the Pacific was scarce, a condition that kept spurring speculation, often revealing a tendency to degrade the Polynesian ancestors' navigation skills and to underestimate their inventiveness. Most of this speculation originated at a time when the zeitgeist of colonialism favored a consciousness of superiority among Europeans and Americans, who saw those who did not work metal, did not possess writing, sailed without naval charts, and lived their lives without the blessings of the monopoly of a male god as primitive. Who would credit primitive islanders for sophisticated schemes of seafaring and specialized skills in navigation? It took well into the postcolonial era for the zeitgeist to shift from a marginalization of Polynesian achievements of seafaring to a genuine appreciation of their endeavors, untainted by old-fashioned misconceptions and worn-out prejudices.

Linked by Language

Those people who set out on their deep-sea voyages were members in sustained communities, united by the same language, rather than cast together by the vicissitudes of local conflicts and warfare. The history of the explorations of Oceania is the history of the eastward spread of Austronesian languages. The Austronesian family of languages (or phylum) is the second largest phylum (after the Niger-Congo language family) in the world, according to the number of genealogically related languages (i.e., some 1,230 individual languages). Most of the Austronesian languages belong to the Malayo-Polynesian branch. The cultural and linguistic unity of those Austronesians who colonized the Pacific islands is manifested in the fact that all languages of the Pacific form a homogeneous subgroup of Malayo-Polynesian: Oceanic (i.e., Hawaiian, Tahitian, Fidjian, Samoan, Maori, Rapanui, and other local varieties of Oceanic). Moreover, seafaring in the Pacific is just the eastern scenario of Austronesian migrations.

Impetus for Migration

Austronesian-speaking seafarers also sailed west and reached Madagascar off the coast of East Africa. The distance between that island and Southeast Asia is about 4,700 nautical miles (about 7,500 km). The true magnitude of the global endeavor of the Austronesian migrants can be seen in the extent of their western and eastern explorations. The overall picture of sea-bound movements of the Austronesians does not favor any speculation about their seafaring as being accidental.

If those who set sail for distant islands had been refugees and displaced people, leaving areas devastated by warfare between local clans, accounts about their rescue would have found their way into local myths of origin among the Polynesians. However, such sagas of alleged rescue operations are not typical of Polynesian mythology. Even if turmoil caused by warfare might have been the driving force for emigration in some cases, these are of rare occurrence and remain isolated in the long-term chronology of intentional and organized seafaring in Oceania.

For an understanding of the intentionality of the colonization movement in the Pacific region it is important to perceive the worldview of the Polynesians. This means that outsiders—whether Americans, Europeans, or people from Australia, Asia, or Africa—have to take into consideration the perception of Oceania in the cultural memory of the islanders. A modern observer who looks at a map of the Pacific region is impressed by the huge masses of water. This sort of vastness may evoke negative emotional associations such as emptiness of uncontrollable space, perils at sea, untraversable distances, vicissitudes of weather conditions, and the like. The mindset of a Polynesian, however, is differently tuned. An islander perceives the wholeness of Oceania in proportions different from outsiders. The many islands, scattered throughout the region, gain in profile as landmarks in a cultural landscape. The waters of the ocean are not perceived as unpredictable or even hostile. Instead, the ocean takes the role of a pathway connecting islands and communities, rather than functioning as a boundary to separate them. The vastness of the Pacific Ocean forms part of the islanders' cultural space, a space for interaction between nature and human beings. This mindset can be reconstructed from early maps that local guides drew for European sailors in the early days of contact. In these maps, the masses of water are drastically reduced, whereas the islands are given emphasis as spaces for human agency.

The Chronology of Migrations in the Pacific Region

The colonization of the Pacific Islands unfolded in a long-lasting process of several migratory waves, with intervals of stabilization of newly explored sea routes. It was mainly Austronesian-speaking people who explored and colonized Oceania. The migration of Austronesian populations begins with the second wave (starting around 1500 BCE). Those migrants profited from the experiences of seafaring of their predecessors who were not of the same ethnic stock as the Austronesians. The technology of building vessels apt for covering long nautical distances improved over generations, as did the methods of navigation, and it eventually enabled the Polynesians to explore the far-distant peripheries of Oceania (i.e., Easter Island, the Hawaiian Islands, and New Zealand).

The first migration (before ca. 40,000 BCE), coming from the mainland of Southeast Asia, to reach New Guinea more than 40,000 years ago were the ancestors of the modern Papuans, whose languages are unrelated to the Austronesian phylum. The first wave of migration proceeded as far as the Bismarck Archipelago and the Solomon Islands. The second migration (between 1500 and 1000 BCE) were Austronesian populations. It is still a matter of debate from where these people came: from the islands of Southeast Asia (west of New Guinea) or from their early settlements on the northern and eastern coasts of New Guinea. The Austronesian migrants reached the Carolines in the north, the Samoa group in the east, and New Caledonia in the south. The Fiji Islands are located in the central part of this area (i.e., Melanesia) that was colonized during the second migration. The Melanesian cultural complex, centered on Fiji, provides the foundation for the subsequently developing Polynesian culture, which proliferated into a wide array of local cultures during later migrations. The proliferation of cultures found its parallel in the direction of gene flow. The Polynesian lineages stem, genetically, from the gene pool of populations in western Melanesia. The third migration (starting ca. 200 BCE), starting from the Fiji group, was directed to the east. The settlements on the Society Islands, with Tahiti as their cultural center, date to the time of the third migration. The fourth migration (starting ca. 300 CE) saw the greatest distances in the Pacific Ocean traversed by migrants from Tahiti. The distant Easter Island was settled around 300. The sea route to the north of Tahiti brought settlers to the Hawaiian Islands.

The fifth migration (10th century) involved the exploration of the sea route to the southwest of Tahiti, and migrants reached the islands of New Zealand toward the end of the 10th century. The last of the bigger islands to be settled was the Chatham group, east of New Zealand. The first Polynesians to reach Chatham around 1000 most probably arrived there, not from New Zealand, but on an independent voyage from Tahiti. The Moriori culture of Chatham declined in the first half of the 20th century.

The time frame for the more recent migrations are conservative estimates. The more calibrated radiocarbon dates become available, the more accurate the association with the absolute timescale will be. It has been assumed that early

War canoe used by the Maoris, the indigenous people of New Zealand, 19th century illustration. (Gianni Dagli Orti/Corbis)

settlers may already have reached the Marquesas Islands in far east Polynesia at the beginning of our era (that is by 0 CE), several hundred years earlier than according to the conservative time frame.

Migrations Planned

It has been demonstrated by means of computer simulations of the migratory movements in space and time that the peopling of the Pacific Islands cannot have occurred as the result of accidental drifts. Such accidental drifts would have produced random patterns, with densely populated islands contrasting with widely unpopulated areas. The only explanation for the regularities and the emergence of the dense web of local settlements is that the migrations were carefully planned. Polynesian demography is the outcome of intentional seafaring. In time, the seafaring endeavors became more frequent and better organized. This was not only the result of farsighted planning of voyages but also the accumulation of knowledge about climatic conditions and the advancement of technological development. Each wave of migrants could profit from the experiences of previous generations to improve their know-how of seafaring. Many of the sea routes that had been explored in the course of colonization were already regularly frequented for trading more than 2,000 years ago. The migrants from the second wave onward who set out on their voyages were agriculturalists, and they transferred their knowledge of food production (as horticulture and full-scale agriculture, where this was possible) to newly explored islands. To establish new settlements at a distance from the existing ones, it was necessary to transport plants and

Nainoa Thompson and the Science of Polynesian Navigation

One of the most persuasive arguments in favor of Polynesian navigational techniques is the fact that they have been re-created and used in the modern era. Starting in the 1970s, Nainoa Thompson began to study the ancient Polynesian science of way-finding for long-distance ocean voyaging, and has since then engaged in several journeys without the benefit of modern navigational equipment. In 1980 Thompson, his mentor Mau Piailug, and their crew made the trip from Hawaii to Tahiti aboard their voyaging canoe, the *Hokule'a*. They completed the over 2,500-mile journey through open ocean without the aid of any modern navigational devices. During 1985–1987, Thompson took the *Hokule'a* on what he called the "Voyage of Rediscovery," navigating all over Polynesia, visiting Tahiti, the Cook Islands, New Zealand, American Samoa, and 250-island atoll of Rangiroa before returning to Hawaii. During the early 1990s, Thompson built another voyaging canoe, named the *Hawai'iloa*, this time using all native Hawaiian materials, rather than the modern materials used to construct the *Hokule'a*. However, the *Hokule'a* had one more important voyage to make, this time completing the so-called Polynesian triangle by reaching Rapa Nui, or Easter Island, on October 8, 1999.

livestock (i.e., pigs, fowls, and dogs). To safeguard the continuity of new settlements over generations, the migrant groups had to include both men and women.

Long-Distance Voyage Navigation Knowledge

The Polynesians did not have any technical devices to facilitate their navigation, and they did not possess systems of notation to draw charts of currents or of star configurations. What they definitely instrumentalized for their orientation at sea was their refined perception of natural phenomena. Over time, a vast amount of specialized knowledge about seafaring accumulated, and this knowledge was transferred, by means of oral memory, from master to disciple in the professional domains of specialized handicraft. The builders of canoes and catamarans profited from the experiences of seafarers to make their vessels apt for maneuvering against high waves and gusty winds. And the settlers who took livestock and provisions on their journeys learned from the stories that earlier migrants told to make improvements for their selection.

A crucial question that has puzzled many scholars is the proportional relationship between one-way voyages (go and no return) and two-way voyages (go and return). Trade and cultural ties can only be kept up under the condition that voyagers explored new terrain for settlement and returned to their base to report about their discoveries. There are areas in Oceania that were settled in one-way voyages and remained isolated. This is true for Easter Island and for New Zealand. Geographic distance, though, was not a decisive condition for either isolation or permanent contact with other islands. The Hawaiian Islands are located on the extreme northern periphery of Oceania, thousands of miles away from other major island groups. Nevertheless, a trade route existed between Hawaii and Tahiti. An experienced seafarer would certainly explore the chances for a safe return, especially when sailing out into unknown space. One method of safeguarding return was sailing upwind. Crosswind sailing is more adventurous, but this kind of movement "became more sure when expanding geographical knowledge allowed a return to land downwind of the point of origin" (Irwin 1992: 102). Computer simulations of far-distant voyages, undertaken by groups of migrants in several canoes, and their chances of two-way success show that the ratio for the loss of canoes and their voyagers was fairly low.

Three major factors used extensively by the Polynesians are essential for successful navigation under natural conditions: the knowledge of climatic conditions, experience dealing with currents, and the orientation at the position of major stars and star configurations in the nightly sky.

First, the knowledge of climatic conditions: In the tropical zone of Oceania, the air is heated up over the water masses and rises. This warm air drifts toward the north and south and cools down, and some of it streams back to the equator. Additional cold air streams down from the northern and southern latitudes, collides with the hot air, and causes turbulences, eventually producing tropical storms. Storms that originate over the ocean are called *taifuns* (a Japanese expression) in the Pacific, cyclones in the Indian Ocean, and hurricanes in the Caribbean. The streaming of the air follows regular movements, creating elementary patterns for the direction of winds, so that "air flowing toward the pole gives winds from the west and air flowing toward the equator gives winds from the east" (Irwin 1992: 9). The polarization of west-easterly winds was one of the cornerstones of observation on which the Polynesian seafarers built their navigation system. Local conditions produced further variations of wind patterns. For instance, experience taught seafarers that the winds in January are the most favorable for sailing east from the Solomon Islands. The observance of winds and their direction is one thing; exploiting such winds for the purpose of practical seafaring is quite another. An astounding level of sophistication of craftsmanship is revealed in the Polynesian technology of constructing vessels apt for long-distance sea traveling and in the sailing equipment of those vessels. These vessels were not built by unskilled craftsmen, and they were not built for random travel. They reflect the accumulated know-how of many generations of seafaring people. The big canoes for seafaring were outrigged in Micronesia and double hulled in Polynesia, with a length of up to 22 meters. They could sail at 8 knots and cover up to 150 nautical miles in a day. The aptness of the canoes for seafaring is manifested in every detail of the technical equipment. The most effective type of sail in Polynesia is the sprit sail, a "triangular sail mounted apex downward" (Finney 1977: 1278). In such vessels, provisions could be stored from one to three months. In a month's voyage, these canoes could traverse distances of several thousands of nautical miles. It is noteworthy that, from the beginning of the migration movement, the winds posed challenges rather than played the role of pleasant forces that could be exploited by Polynesians intending to set out to sea. During the early migrations, the seafarers had to sail against the prevailing winds. Later, the movement was across and down the winds. The conditions changed again when the migrations reached beyond the tropics into the zone of temperate climate.

Second, the knowledge of oceanic currents: The great and stable currents were known to the early seafarers because they had to maneuver within or across them. Both the north equatorial current and the south equatorial current stream from the east in a westerly direction. The equatorial countercurrent streams from the west to the east, from the Carolines to Central America, reaching the coast in the region of Panama. In the eastern Pacific, the circular anticlockwise movement of the waters caused by the Humboldt (or Peru) current has a bearing on the direction of local currents as far as the Marquesas. Traveling from Hawaii to Tahiti was a demanding endeavor, and such a journey required crossing easterly winds almost constantly. The easiest part was the final passage from Tuamotu to Tahiti. Sailing from Tahiti back to Hawaii might have been easier, with southeasterly winds taking vessels as far as beyond the equator.

Finally, the knowledge of star positions and of star configurations: Several factors make the observation of the nightly sky in the Pacific region more favorable and practical for orientation than in many other regions of the world. One of these factors is the weather conditions. Statistically, the tropical and subtropical zones offer more sunshine than the temperate zone, with its higher probability for cloudy weather. Comparatively, these favorable conditions made the observation of stars and their configurations a more practical means of orientation for Polynesian seafaring than for the Vikings in the Northern Hemisphere. Another factor is that air pollution caused by human agency is minimal in Oceania, so that different categories of brightness of stars can be discerned with the naked eye. The air is so clean that the contours of the Milky Way are visible. Consequently, star configurations gain in profile under these conditions.

Astronomers can tell from their experience that the Southern Hemisphere is "richer" in stars and star configurations than the Northern Hemisphere. Since a greater variety of star categories is visible in the clean air of Oceania, this also means that stars that are not bright are visible, providing a dim-light background for the bright stars. The verified constellations of stars in the Pacific region, however, revealed themselves to western seafarers as late as the 16th century. Before then the Europeans used stellar charts from antiquity. The best known of these are the compilations of charts in the work "Megale Syntax" (Great Syntax) of the astronomer Ptolemaeus (second century CE). The original Greek version got lost, but its contents were preserved in an Arabic translation, which, in turn, were retranslated into Latin in 1175.

The Polynesian seafarers were well acquainted with the star configurations of the Southern Hemisphere. Practically every major group of islands in Oceania has its own particular star configuration. Using the position of single bright stars and these configurations for navigation was not as easy as looking at the sky, because the constellations, forming sections in the bigger mosaic of visible heavenly bodies, may shift their relative position depending on the seasons. At times, certain configurations are invisible. The seafarers had to learn from the experience of earlier generations what stars and configurations to orient to where and when.

Navigators would rely on the observation "from the rising point and trajectory of a large number of familiar stars—steering by 'star paths' enables the skilled navigator to make allowances for the effects of drift by winds and currents" (Nile and Clerk 1996: 63). The knowledge of particular star configurations and their position in association with certain islands assisted seafarers in choosing and keeping direction to reach the intended goals of their voyages. Orientation at the stars alone would certainly not have sufficed for successful navigation. The navigation skills of the Polynesians were anchored in the interplay of all variables of seafaring, with the identification of familiar stars forming part of a web of orientation, also including the equally important observance of and interaction with currents and winds.

Importance of Regular Seafaring and Trading

Once sea routes had been explored, these were used not only for the transport of settlers and their livestock but also for the transfer of trade goods. The earliest evidence for overseas trading activities comes from Melanesia. The most important merchandise to be traded in early times was obsidian as raw material. In the course of time, a greater variety of goods were traded. Since sea routes for trading had already been explored in Melanesia before the colonization of the Polynesian islands, the history of seaborne trading is older than the Polynesian settlements, and the Melanesian tradition was inherited by the Polynesians.

The evidence documenting the existence of ancient trade routes—for short-distance as well as for long-distance trading—speaks in favor of organized seafaring. Seafaring in terms of frequenting certain sea routes in regular intervals without navigational skills is unthinkable. The simple opening of a trade route requires knowledge about the conditions of two-way voyaging. In concrete terms, this means that the traders have to know that there is a place out at sea where they will find buyers for their goods, and they also have to know how to get there and how to return. Seaborne trading grew in magnitude and importance for the interconnection of scattered settlements in Melanesia and throughout Polynesia.

According to the time depth of their appearance, a number of goods played a major role in sea trading. Obsidian is volcanic glass that was used in many parts of the world for tools. Obsidian flakes provide sharp cutting edges. This raw material was found at two sites on the island of New Britain in the Bismarck Archipelago off New Guinea. One is Misisil, where obsidian might have been obtained by the pre-Austronesian islanders more than 10,000 years ago. The other site is Talasea. Already around 4500 BCE, Talasea obsidian was transported to the neighboring island of New Ireland, at a distance of some 30 km from New Britain. In our era, Talasea obsidian found its way as far as New Caledonia, Vanuatu, and Fiji. Obsidian was not an isolated article for trade, but it often appeared together with *lapita* pottery, which is tempered with sand and hardened in open fires. It has produced a variety of forms such as cooking pots in a globular shape, bowls, and dishes with a flat bottom. The *lapita* pots were often decorated with geometric motifs, sometimes also with stylized naturalistic pictures of human beings. The earliest evidence for *lapita* production is known from the Bismarck Archipelago, dating to ca. 1600 BCE.

By the time *lapita* production declined (around 500 BCE), this type of pottery had spread throughout Melanesia, far beyond the area of settlements where the workshops for these goods were located. The evidence thus suggests "that early Lapita history was not one of isolated settler communities but, rather, involved continuing contacts and exchanges based on two-way voyaging in sailing canoes" (Nile and Clerk 1996: 55). The *lapita* voyagers traversed longer distances than the early obsidian traders (more than 1,600 miles, or 2,500 km).

Basalt (as raw material): Because of its qualities, this special stone was the preferred raw material for adzes. The earliest adzes were made of shells and later of local stone. The Tuamotu group of islands (to the northeast of Tahiti) offered a special variety of basalt that was traded over long distances. Since Tuamotu lies on the sea route from Hawaii to Tahiti, it is not surprising that Tuamotu basalt as a raw material for adzes is found both in Hawaii and in Tahiti. The distance between the two island groups is about 3,000 nautical miles (about 4,800 km).

A modern reconstruction of the Hawaiian two-sailed canoe, called *Hokule'a* in the Hawaiian language, was used in 1976 to make a voyage from Maui in the Hawaiian Islands to Tahiti. This voyage was made without the help of modern instruments of navigation, with star configurations and the observation of currents and winds as the only means of orientation. The voyage was successful and may serve as a demonstration to illustrate the possibilities of seafaring over long distances in historical times. Another voyage with the same vessel was undertaken from central Polynesia to New Zealand several years later, and this endeavor was also successfully concluded.

Ceremonial Voyages

Voyaging was not only regularly practiced for the transport of migrants, livestock, and trading goods but also for revitalizing social contacts between settlers and for reaffirming cultural relationships between settlements that were separated by the waters of the ocean. Traditions to conduct ceremonial voyages originated in many parts of Oceania. Perhaps the network of ceremonial voyages with the widest geographic range is the *kula* network of gift exchange in Melanesia. To perform the ceremonial voyages in connection with this gift exchange, relatively long distances have to be traversed in special ceremonial canoes. The settlements that participate in the *kula* network cover an area of some 250 nautical miles (about 360 km) in diameter, from the southeastern tip of New Guinea in the west, the Laughlan Islands in the east, the Trobriand Islands in the north, and the Louisiade Archipelago in the south.

The annual voyages of the *kula* gift exchange are performed in richly decorated outrigger canoes. The decorations are painted and worked with cowrie shells. The men in the village communities organize themselves in groups to visit their trading partners overseas. The ritual exchange of gifts includes shell necklaces (*soulava*), which move in a clockwise direction, and armshells (*mwali*), which move anticlockwise.

References and Further Reading

Conte, E. "L'homme et la mer." *Encyclopédie de la Polynésie* (Papeete, Tahiti), Vol. 5 (1990): 41–56 (including a series of illustrations of canoe types and sailing gear).

Finney, Ben R. "Voyaging Canoes and the Settlement of Polynesia." *Science* 196, 4296 (1977): 1277–85.

Garanger, J. "Le peuplement de la Polynésie orientale." *Encyclopédie de la Polynésie* (Papeete, Tahiti), Vol. 4 (1990): 41–56.

Irwin, Geoffrey. *The Prehistoric Exploration and Colonization of the Pacific*. Cambridge: Cambridge University Press, 1992.

King, Michael. *Moriori—A People Rediscovered*, 2nd ed. Auckland: Viking, 2000.

Kirch, P. V., and R. C. Green. *Hawaiki, Ancestral Polynesia: An Essay in Historical Anthropology*. Cambridge: Cambridge University Press, 2001.

Nile, Richard, and Christian Clerk. *Cultural Atlas of Australia, New Zealand and the South Pacific*. Abingdon: Andromeda Oxford Limited, 1996.

Oppenheimer, Stephen, and Martin Richards. "Polynesians: Devolved Taiwanese Farmers or Wallacean Maritime Traders with Fishing, Foraging, and Horticultural Skills?" In *Examining the Farming/Language Dispersal Hypothesis* (pp. 287–97). Edited by Peter Bellwood and Colin Renfrew. Cambridge: McDonald Institute for Archaeological Research, 2002.

Thornton, Agathe. *The Birth of the Universe—Te whanautanga o te ao tukupu*. Auckland: Reed Books, 2004.

CON

The debate over Polynesian migrations is a long running one. Early European voyagers in the Pacific were perplexed by the existence of people who were obviously culturally related but who inhabited the widely dispersed islands of the Pacific. European navigators were particularly confused as their own technology had only just allowed them to voyage to these islands, and yet on landing they seemed to be inevitably confronted by people using stone-age technology who had reached these small and widely scattered pieces of land well before them. Once appeals to divine intervention were no longer thought a sufficient explanation for Polynesian dispersal, speculation about their methods of finding and settling islands became widespread, and among the explanations proposed was that of accidental voyaging.

The area bounded by Tokyo, Jakarta, and Easter Island contains 80 percent of the world's islands. The islands of the Pacific region are generally grouped into the geographic regions of Melanesia, Micronesia, and Polynesia, and debates about navigation focus on Polynesia. The islands of Polynesia are generally described as being contained within a triangle, with the corners comprised of New Zealand, Hawaii, and Easter Island. The corners of the triangle are distant from everywhere. Hawaii is approximately 2,000 miles from the North American continent (it is about equally distant from California and the Aleutian Islands), and 600 miles from Johnson Atoll, a small piece of land. It is 2,400 miles from Tahiti, and 3,800 miles from New Zealand. Similarly New Zealand is about 1,300 miles distant from its nearest continent (Australia) and only slightly closer to Fiji, the nearest island group. Easter Island is often described as the most isolated place on Earth, as it is 2,400 miles west of South America and 1,200 miles east of Pitcairn, the nearest land. The region of central Polynesia contains islands much closer together; it is travel to these distant corners of Polynesia that is involved in this debate.

The debate over the navigational practices of Polynesians continues into the present because the existence of a recognizably single culture across this area of the world is an astonishing feat. The Pacific is vast—it is greater in area than all the world's land masses combined, and larger even than the rest of the world's oceans combined. The difficulty of settling Polynesia meant that it was the last region on Earth to receive humans. While Melanesia could be settled by a process of island hopping—moving from one island to another always within sight of land—settlement of Polynesia required new techniques as voyagers had to set out without being able to see their destination, and travel without land in sight for long periods of time. Melanesia was fully settled approximately 3,200 years ago, but Easter Island was only reached about 1,700 years ago, Hawaii 1,600 years ago, and people arrived in New Zealand possibly as recently as 700 years ago. Whether settlement of this region involved deliberate voyaging or contained elements of chance remains an open question.

The idea of regular deliberate voyaging between the far reaches of Polynesia has its problems. Certainly such voyages were not occurring when Europeans entered the Pacific, and the possible place of chance in Polynesian settlement should not be ignored. While the idea of Polynesian navigation across the vast Pacific is presently fashionable, older ideas about the role of drift voyaging in Pacific settlement deserve consideration. Before examining support for the theory of drift voyaging, it is worth noting what it is not: the idea that Polynesians discovered their islands by chance does not deny that Polynesians, when encountered by Europeans, used canoes and undertook ocean voyages. Instead the argument is over whether long-distance navigation—not observed by Europeans on contact—had occurred at some point in the past, and whether Polynesian people had deliberately voyaged between far-flung islands and had deliberately set off in quest of unknown land. Alternatively the drift voyage thesis maintains that the Pacific is a difficult environment and that some Polynesian settlement can be explained by voyages of chance when fishing parties or groups of refugees stumbled across islands when blown there by unexpected winds or pushed there by unknown currents.

Early Support for Drift Voyaging

As Europeans explored the Pacific they were fascinated by the people who lived there, recording observations of them and information gained from talking to them. Part of early European interest in Polynesian navigation was pragmatic—Europeans wanted help in navigating the vast Pacific, and they were eager for information that could be gained from Polynesians, Tahitians in particular. Thus the famous British navigator Captain Cook eagerly compared information about the location of Pacific islands with his passenger, the Tahitian navigator Tupaia, who joined Cook's *Endeavour* voyage in 1769. While Tupaia was able to add 80 islands to Cook's charts, he did not impart any information about lands as distant as New Zealand or Hawaii, indicating that voyaging between Tahiti and these places did not occur at that time and had not occurred for a long time, if at all. Similarly, when the Spaniard Andia y Varela visited Tahiti in 1774–1775 he, too, picked up a Tahitian navigator. Andia recorded the ability of the Tahitian to set courses to travel to islands that were not visible from Tahiti itself, but the islands known in this way were limited to those not too far distant, and such islands were in regular contact with Tahiti. The far corners of Polynesia were not known to Tahitians at the time of contact with Europeans, showing that long-distance voyaging was not occurring and had not occurred in the recent past.

This experience of a lack of knowledge of the far corners of Polynesia was not limited to Tahiti, but occurred throughout the islands of central Polynesia. While in Tonga, Cook collected information about other Pacific islands from his hosts. That list included 156 islands known to his Tongan informants, but despite this wealth of knowledge, islands that required open-water journeys of more than 30 miles from Tonga were not included. Thus large and significant island groups in the vicinity but more than 30 miles distant (such as the Cook Islands, Tahiti, and Niue) were not among those described to Cook. It would seem that Tongan navigation covered only limited legs of the ocean, although island hopping along chains of islands meant that Tongans were aware of many islands. However, the information collected by Cook indicated no knowledge in Tonga of the existence of Hawaii, Easter Island, or New Zealand, and again clearly indicated that regular voyages to any of those places did not occur at the time of contact and had not occurred in the recent past.

In this early period of contact there is no evidence that Tahitian navigators visited, or were even aware of, islands as far distant as Hawaii. Deliberate navigation took place, but it occurred only within limited regions, such as within the island groups of Tahiti, Hawaii, and Tonga/Samoa. Travel between these discrete groups, and between island Polynesia and New Zealand, was not observed and seemed not to have occurred at all recently. Tupaia was unaware of the location of Hawaii, and although Tupaia traveled with Cook on his first voyage, Cook did not visit the Hawaiian Islands until his third voyage to the Pacific. In Cook's observations the only indication of the existence of more distant islands were Polynesian stories of distant origins, but no voyages to the corners of the Polynesian triangle occurred. The mystery of Polynesian dispersal could not be easily solved.

As a result of the lack of any clear evidence of Polynesian long-distance navigation at contact, the first theorist to suggest that Polynesian navigators reached their islands by drift voyages was Cook himself. Cook regularly observed Polynesian canoes during his visits to island Polynesia, and he was impressed by the size, speed, and maneuverability of those that he observed in Tahiti and Tonga. However, even after extended contact with Tupaia, Cook argued that Tahitian navigation did not deal with very long voyages and did not have the tools to cope with long periods at sea out of sight of land. In addition to his observations of the limits of Tupaia's knowledge of Polynesia, Cook also observed evidence of drift voyages occurring across long distances. While in the southern Cook Islands he observed survivors of a drift voyage from Tahiti. A canoe had been blown off course, and although 15 members of the crew had died, five had survived and landed in Tahiti. Cook argued that such chance events accounted for the settlement of Polynesia, as people in canoes were blown away from known land, and some were fortunate enough to land on previously unknown islands and establish societies. No evidence of more deliberate long-range voyaging was found by Cook.

Postcontact Changes in Polynesian Traditions

The stories of distant origins noted by Cook at contact have led to speculation about repeated long-distance voyages, but such sources must be used with care. At the time of Cook's first voyage, closer connections were developing between the Pacific and Europe, muddying the waters of the Pacific as far as the extent of traditional navigational knowledge was concerned. Polynesians were eager to incorporate European geographic knowledge into their own, and Europeans were fascinated by Polynesian peoples and set about collecting their traditions. The transmission of Polynesian traditions into European language and culture, and then back again, inevitably altered them, and "pure" Polynesian traditions have been lost as traditions evolved in the face of new ideas. For example, Cook's use of Maori names for the islands of New Zealand, not available to Tahitians before his voyage there, were given to Andia in 1774–1775 as part of Tahitian navigational knowledge. The Maori names for the islands of New Zealand were not part of the traditional navigational knowledge of Tupaia. However, when Cook discussed his voyages with Tahitian navigators, he introduced them to the existence of New Zealand, using those names. That knowledge was adsorbed and quickly incorporated, and the names for New Zealand's islands became considered traditional knowledge and was not differentiated as originating from a later period than other navigational knowledge.

European fascination with Polynesian tradition only increased as Europeans came to settle in New Zealand and Hawaii. The first theorist to propose large-scale,

Captain James Cook Describes a Polynesian Canoe

The first European to voyage through Polynesia was the famous British captain James Cook. His writings formed the first notions the rest of the world would have of the Pacific as a whole and of its people. He wrote at length of Polynesian seafaring, and what follows is his description of the canoes the native people used.

The ingenuity of these people appears in nothing more than in their canoes: they are long and narrow, and in shape very much resemble a New England whale-boat: the larger sort seem to be built chiefly for war, and will carry from forty to eighty, or a hundred armed men. We measured one which lay ashore at Tolaga: she was sixty-eight feet and a half long, five feet broad, and three feet and a half deep; the bottom was sharp, with straight sides like a wedge, and consisted of three lengths, hollowed out to about two inches, or an inch and a half thick, and well fastened together with strong plaiting: each side consisted of one entire plank, sixty-three feet long, ten or twelve inches broad, and about an inch and a quarter thick, and these were fitted and lashed to the bottom part with great dexterity and strength. A considerable number of thwarts were laid from gunwale to gunwale, to which they were securely lashed on each side, as a strengthening to the boat. The ornament at the head projected five or six feet beyond the body, and was about four feet and a half high; the ornament at the stern was fixed upon that end, as the stern post of a ship is upon her keel, and was about fourteen feet high, two feet broad, and an inch and a half thick. They both consisted of boards of carved work, of which the design was much better than the execution. All their canoes, except a few at Opoorage or Mercury Bay, which were of one piece, and hollowed by fire, are built after this plan, and few are less than twenty feet long: some of the smaller sort have outriggers, and sometimes two of them are joined together, but this is not common. The carving upon the stern and head ornaments of the inferior boats, which seemed to be intended wholly for fishing, consists of the figure of a man, with a face as ugly as can be conceived, and a monstrous tongue thrust out of the mouth, with the white shells of sea-ears stuck in for the eyes. But the canoes of the superior kind, which seem to be their men-of-war, are magnificently adorned with open work, and covered with loose fringes of black feathers, which had a most elegant appearance: the gunwale boards were also frequently carved in a grotesque taste, and adorned with tufts of white feathers placed upon a black ground. Of visible objects that are wholly new, no verbal description can convey a just idea, but in proportion as they resemble some that are already known, to which the mind of the reader must be referred: the carving of these people being of a singular kind, and not in the likeness of anything that is known on our side of the ocean, either "in the heaven above, or in the earth beneath, or in the waters that are under the earth," I must refer wholly to the representations which will be found of it in the cut.

Source: James Cook. *The Three Voyages of Captain James Cook*. London: William Smith, 1842.

long-distance deliberate voyages by Polynesian navigators in the precontact period was Percy Smith, who was a keen early 20th-century collector of Maori traditions. However, Smith is now acknowledged to have fundamentally altered Maori traditions as he collected and recorded them, tidying and reinterpreting stories collected earlier to fit in with his expectation of a unified mythology. In an attempt to rationalize the stories available from Maori and earlier European sources and to create a coherent framework of tradition from which he could extract further information, Smith in effect grafted European myths about Maori onto Maori mythology. Many of his ideas about the arrival of Polynesians in New Zealand, including the figure of Kupe (a great navigator who made a return voyage between tropical Polynesia and New Zealand in ca. 750 CE) and the idea of the Great Fleet of seven canoes that arrived and settled New Zealand, were adopted by Maori themselves and have become accepted as prehistoric Maori traditions. These ideas were exposed as European rather than Maori myths by D. R. Simmons in 1969, and his work has subsequently been consolidated but not challenged, yet the myths involved have not been abandoned. While raising interesting questions about the extent of Polynesian voyaging, the work of collectors of tradition produced altered versions of Maori tradition and in the process destroyed the original. This means that stories such as those of the Great Fleet cannot be understood as unadulterated Maori tradition or as a record of previous periods of deliberate long-distance navigation.

Similar traditions were found or invented in Hawaii by Abraham Fornander (1878). In a manner very similar to the collectors of myths in New Zealand, Fornander was fascinated by the mystery of Polynesian origins, using an unsophisticated linguistic analysis to (wrongly) give them Aryan origins, with a further connection to the Mediterranean. Among the stories that he collected, and in writing down and editing unsuspectingly changed, was that of the great navigator Hawai'iloa who traveled from his homeland to Hawaii. Hawai'iloa was reported by Fornander to have returned home to collect his family, and then made a second successful landfall in the Hawaiian islands. Although 19th- and early-20th-century anthropologists might consider such stories to provide evidence of regular long-distance Polynesian voyaging, too many questions have been raised about the process of recording and then reremembering what was involved in their codification for weight to be placed on them as evidence of repeated long-distance voyaging.

Andrew Sharp and Drift Voyaging as an Explanation for Polynesian Distribution

While these adulterated traditions were seen as providing evidence of long-distance Polynesian navigation, questions about the feasibility of such voyages continued to emerge. While not necessarily promoting purely accidental voyaging, some commentators did question tales of repeated voyages between such distant points as Tahiti and Hawaii. For example, in 1924 John Bollons, an experienced sailor, wrote:

> It is amazing how boldly the landsman has launched the Polynesian out into the—at that time—infinite ocean; described the voyage, the seaworthiness of the canoes, the cargo carried, the manner in which the canoes were hove-to in bad weather, and the navigating by stars and the rising and setting of the sun. How simple it is, or seems to be, when one is living ashore" (quoted in Bellwood 1979: 301).

The distances proposed for deliberate and repeated navigation were immense, and Bollons was not the only sailor to point out that navigating the Pacific with modern tools was not always simple, and that doing so without the benefit of modern ship-building technology or navigational instruments was not as simple a task as it might seem to those who had never been in a boat out of sight of land with the sky clouded over and a shifting wind blowing.

Yet it was a landsman, Andrew Sharp, who launched the fiercest attack on the romantic myth of Polynesian navigation. In 1956 Sharp published the book *Ancient Voyagers in the Pacific* and challenged the notion that ancient Polynesians navigated the vast expanse of the Pacific easily and often. Sharp did not argue that all long-distance voyages in Polynesia were solely the result of aimless drifting, but he did argue that the notion of repeated navigations between the center and far corners of Polynesia was not clearly supported by tangible evidence. Sharp's attack on the romantic notion of a vast Pacific highway did not deny the possibility of Polynesian navigation in all its forms, but rather it questioned the regularity and control that Polynesian navigators could exercise over voyages more than about 300 miles in length out of sight of land—especially those thought to connect the corners of the Polynesian triangle to the center. While Sharp argued for "drift" voyages, his definition of drift is problematic. His book argued that when a destination is unknown, no course can be set for it—that navigation to an unknown place is by definition impossible. This is not quite the same thing as drifting directionless across the ocean, but it was enough to ignite fierce opposition, as it seemed to challenge ideas about Polynesian cultural development and to strike at a source of pride for indigenous Polynesians.

Despite the opposition that Sharp aroused, his book raised useful (and at the time unanswerable) questions about the nature of Polynesian navigation. Responses to his work were immediate and heated, and some involved projects to undermine his argument by establishing what traditional navigation entailed. Certainly early enthusiasts for traditional navigation did not specify what tools the Polynesian navigator had available, nor how it was possible to steer a reliable and repeatable course without a compass, out of sight of land or how to cope with the effects of currents whose influence would be essentially invisible. Essentially very little information was available on how to navigate sufficiently precisely to locate small islands in a vast ocean when failing to find them would mean dying at sea. Certainly such knowledge was not generally available in the middle of the 20th century, and it was Sharp's work that prompted attempts to save and revive such knowledge where it still existed. Before his publication, ideas of Polynesian navigation were based on vague ideas of using the position of the sun and stars without any clear indication of how this was to be achieved.

Sharp raised other useful questions that challenged unexamined assumptions about Polynesian long-distance navigation. He argued that the materials available to islanders when building their craft could not construct a craft capable of reliably sailing long distances. In particular, Sharp argued that the rope materials available within Polynesia were vulnerable to strain on long voyages and could not be relied on in rough conditions or when sailing against the wind. He also pointed to the seasonality of winds, and of stars, as guides to Pacific navigation. He noted that language differences had arisen within Polynesia, indicating a failure of continued communication. Similarly the incomplete distribution of Polynesian livestock (the dog, rat, pig, and chicken) throughout Polynesia argued against continuing, regular contact. Sharp also questioned the assumption that Polynesian canoe-building and navigational technology had declined by the time of Cook's first visit, arguing against the assumption that knowledge had previously existed and somehow been lost. And Sharp was able to produce evidence of well-documented cases of unintentional and unnavigated voyages across the Pacific in historic times. His book raised useful questions about the difficulty of long-distance navigation across the Pacific and about the role of drift voyages in the discovery of land, but they came under immediate attack because they contradicted those mythical ideas about Maori navigation and the settlement of New Zealand.

Sharp received some support for his ideas, notably from Kjell Akerblom in a 1968 Swedish publication. Such support was perhaps surprising as Sharp also challenged the notion that the Vikings had reached North America, considering the sagas provided unreliable evidence. (Subsequent archaeological discoveries have provided conclusive evidence for a short-lived Viking presence in North America.) Certainly Sharp's skepticism about Polynesian navigation was justified in terms of the material available to him. In response to his book much work was done on the ways in which Stone Age Pacific peoples might have navigated, including practical experiments recording the ways in which modern navigators still using traditional methods found their way between known groups of islands. It is worth noting that such material was mostly collected from Melanesia and Micronesia, as it had been lost in Polynesia when new navigational tools became available.

Thor Heyerdahl and the Implications of a South American Connection

However improbable, the most famous intervention in the argument about deliberate voyaging in the settlement of the Pacific involved a Norwegian. In 1947

Norwegian ethnologist Thor Heyerdahl and his balsa raft *Kon-Tiki* crossing the Pacific Ocean on his drifting expedition from Peru to Polynesia, 1947. (Keystone/Getty Images)

Thor Heyerdahl set off across the Pacific on the balsa-wood raft, the *Kon-Tiki*. The raft was towed about 50 miles offshore from Peru, and then drifted and sailed across the Pacific before reaching the Tuamotu Archipelago, a distance of approximately 4,300 miles in 101 days. The voyage seized the public's imagination and demonstrated that despite the vast size of the Pacific, it was possible to run into land by chance rather than design. Other raft navigators of the Pacific followed in Heyerdahl's wake, not always successfully. Eric de Bisschop died in the Cook Islands in 1956 after a long-distance rafting accident, and in 1974 the crew of a junk expedition was rescued after five months at sea far from land in the northern Pacific. Heyerdahl's expedition was intended to deal with questions of Polynesian origins rather than their means of migration, and it drew on the older idea that because the prevailing winds in the Pacific blow from the east, people were blown into the Pacific from South America. Heyerdahl's South American origin for Polynesians has generally been rejected—on the grounds of language, a cultural trail of artifacts on the western edge of island Polynesia pointing to island hopping and settlement, and on physical characteristics—but his expedition indicated that long-distance voyages guided by luck rather than design could succeed and so produced evidence to support the possibility of significant drift voyages in the settlement of the Pacific.

Heyerdahl was not the only scholar interested in South American influences in the Pacific. Robert Langdon (2009) spent his career pointing out that the idea of Asian origins cannot account for the spread of plants and animals throughout the Polynesian islands, as a number of significant species are of South American origin. The South American origin of species such as the *kumara* (sweet potato) cannot be denied, and the presence of such species again points to the possibility of drift voyages by South American rafts. Langdon argued that rafts that became dismasted were likely to drift west across the Pacific, and pointed to historical examples of such voyages, including that of Heyerdahl. He added the idea that weather patterns in the Pacific are not constant, and that El Niño weather patterns might have facilitated such drift voyages from South America, again citing voyages within recorded history, this time of two European vessels. The first was the voyage of an English pirate in 1687 who drifted from the coast of South America to an island that Langdon identifies as Easter Island. The second, more convincing, example was that of the HMS *Chanticleer* in 1870, which was carried into the Polynesian triangle while attempting to navigate between Panama and Callao. It stopped at Easter Island on its way back to the South American coast. Thus, evidence of South American influences within the Pacific has links to the question of the role of drift voyages in establishing Polynesian culture.

The Problem of Evidence

The major difficulty in this debate is the lack of solid evidence for either position. By the time written records began in the Pacific, with the arrival of Europeans in the 16th century, any period of navigated voyages to the corners of the Polynesian triangle was past. Instead of Polynesian canoes navigating the far reaches of the Pacific using traditional methods, Polynesian people quickly began traveling on European ships and adopting European ship technology and navigational instruments. In particular, Hawaiian men traveled the world on European and American whaling ships and also participated in inland fur expeditions in North America. In 1834 a federation of chiefs from the northern regions of New Zealand registered a flag in order to identify ships originating in New Zealand. Such a flag was useful to them because they owned and operated a fleet of European-style trading ships. This quick adoption of new materials and their associated technologies meant that the building of large traditional canoes was quickly abandoned throughout Polynesia, and information that might shed light on the abilities of those canoes was lost with them.

In terms of the larger question of Polynesian origins, the pathway of Polynesian migrations tends to be reconstructed through linguistic analysis and archaeology of pottery and stone tools, rather than direct evidence of surviving canoes. This is because the Pacific is a difficult environment for wood to survive in. Canoes in particular were faced with the rot inherent in wet surroundings and also with various burrowing creatures such as the Teredo worm. As a result, other than images made by Europeans at the time of contact, no direct evidence remains of canoes even at that time. No direct evidence is available, or can reasonably be expected to have survived, from earlier periods. As a result, ideas about possible navigated long-distance voyages are based on speculation, not material evidence.

Reconstructed Voyages and Their Connections with the Present

The reemergence of indigenous cultural identity in the Pacific has clouded the issue further. Islanders who had been colonized by European powers were rediscovering their political identities in the 20th century. As a result, reaction to Andrew Sharp's book was in part a reaction to what was seen as an insult to the ingenuity and navigational prowess of their Polynesian ancestors. An early example of reemerging pride in Pacific traditions can be found in the work of Te Rangi Hiroa (Sir Peter Buck), an anthropologist of Maori descent who worked as director of the Bishop Museum in Hawaii. As early as 1938, his book *Vikings of the Sunrise* was a clear statement of pride in ancestral achievements, including the navigation of the Pacific. Further cultural renaissance followed in New Zealand, and later throughout the Pacific, and this renaissance tended to draw on ideas of deliberate voyaging across the vast expanses of the Pacific.

The cultural renaissance in Hawai'-i that began in the 1970s was clearly associated with experimental canoe reconstructions and voyages. The establishment of the Polynesian Voyaging Society and the management of its canoe *Hokule'a* were largely concerned with the contemporary cultural revival of native Hawaiians. That canoe was reconstructed using historical images and modern materials and in 1976 successfully navigated the 2,250 miles between Hawaii and Tahiti using reconstructed navigational techniques. Between 1985 and 1987 the *Hokule'a* navigated a 12,000 mile course between Hawaii and New Zealand. However, a Hawaiian attempt in the early 1990s to construct a large voyaging canoe using only traditional materials was forced to compromise for reasons of scarcity of resources and time and for reasons of safety, as traditional sail and rope materials could not be processed in a way to make them work for such a large canoe. That project did lead to the voyage of a fleet of reconstructed canoes between Rarotonga in the Cook Islands and Hawaii in 1992. While the voyage of a fleet of reconstructed canoes was a remarkable achievement, it was a remarkable achievement in the present, rather than direct evidence of deliberate voyaging in the past. The use of reconstructed methods of navigation and of reconstructed canoe styles made an important statement about the value of Polynesian cultural traditions, but the voyage also exposed the failings of some of the vessels that attempted to join the fleet and the difficulties of navigating the Pacific. A Tahitian-built canoe was found to be unseaworthy and could not participate, and at various times the requirements of safety and of timetables meant that the canoes had to be towed by modern vessels. The voyage established both that Polynesian vessels and navigational techniques were well developed and worthy of pride, and that the Pacific is a difficult ocean that is not easily navigated and where winds are fickle, and the danger of capsize and destruction is prominent.

Recorded Drift Voyages

Such rediscovering of traditional navigation and voyaging methods was often an explicit response to the criticism felt to emanate from Sharp's work. However, while deliberate voyages in reconstructed canoes have been undertaken in recent years, accidental drift voyages have also occurred. These voyages have been unplanned, yet at times have covered extraordinary distances. Such an example was reported in 2001 by the BBC when a Samoan fishing boat was pushed out to sea by currents after losing the use of its motor. Of the four crew, two died during the journey, but two survived a 2,800-mile, 132-day voyage to Papua New Guinea. Similar long-distance drift voyages have been noted by all participants in the debate on Polynesian navigation, beginning with Cook and including numerous examples cited by Sharp. Drift voyages certainly occur within the Pacific, and some fortunately end in landfall. Whether this process could constitute a complete explanation for Pacific settlement is a separate question—that long-distance drift voyages have occurred and continue to occur is not in doubt.

Conclusion

The debate about navigation in the Pacific cannot be fully resolved. The evidence available is not conclusive—the watery environment means that physical remains of great voyaging canoes are unlikely to have survived to the present, and in the time since the settlement of the Pacific, particularly the past 200 years, remembered evidence has been distorted. In those past two centuries massive change occurred as a result of the availability of iron and other aspects of European material culture, and the ways in which Polynesians traveled underwent a fundamental transformation. Traditions have also been distorted in the process of collection and recording, making stories of repeated voyaging suspect. Current theories of the way in which Polynesians settled the Pacific and of long-distance navigation tend to reflect contemporary concerns. At present it is unfashionable to argue that drift played a prominent part in Polynesian settlement of the Pacific. However, despite the rediscovered skills of Pacific navigators and the impressive voyages of reconstructed canoes, the Pacific remains a difficult environment. The continued process of drift voyages across seemingly impossible distances cannot be dismissed, and the role of accident and drift in the settlement of Polynesia requires consideration. Polynesians were fine mariners and efficient navigators within island groups, but the Pacific is a vast ocean, and Polynesian canoes were certainly at times directed by wind and current rather than human will.

References and Further Reading

Akerblom, K. *Astronomy and Navigation in Polynesia and Micronesia*. Stockholm: Ethnographical Museum Monograph 4, 1968.

Belich, James. *Making Peoples: A History of the New Zealanders from Polynesian Settlement to the End of the Nineteenth Century*. Auckland: Penguin Press, 1996.

Bellwood, Peter. *Man's Conquest of the Pacific*. New York: Oxford University Press, 1979.

Buck, Peter H. (Te Rangi Hiroa). *Vikings of the Sunrise*. Philadelphia: Lippincott, 1938.

Finney, Ben. *Sailing in the Wake of the Ancestors: Reviving Polynesian Voyaging*. Honolulu: Bishop Museum Press, 2003.

Fornander, Abraham. *An Account of the Polynesian Race, Its Origins and Migrations and the Ancient History of the Hawaiian People to the Times of Kamehameha I*, Vol. I of III. London: Trubner, 1878.

Heyerdahl, Thor. *Sea Routes to Polynesia*. London: George Allen and Unwin, 1968.

Horridge, Adrian. "The Austronesian Conquest of the Sea—Upwind." In *The Austronesians: Historical and Comparative Perspectives* (pp. 143–60). Edited by Peter Bellwood, James F. Fox, and Darrell Tryon. Canberra: ANU E Press, 2006.

Howe, K. R. *The Quest for Origins: Who First Discovered and Settled New Zealand and the Pacific Islands?* Auckland: Penguin, 2003.

Langdon, Robert. *Kon-Tiki Revisited*. Melbourne: Australian Scholarly Publishing, 2009.

Sharp, Andrew. *Ancient Voyagers in the Pacific*. Wellington: Polynesian Society, 1956.

Simmons, D. R. "A New Zealand Myth. Kupe, Toi and the 'Fleet'." *New Zealand Journal of History* 3, 1 (1969): 14–31.

Simmons, D. R. *The Great New Zealand Myth: A Study of the Discovery and Origin Traditions of the Maori*. Wellington: Reed, 1976.

Smith, S. Percy. *Hawaiki: The Original Home of the Maori; with a Sketch of Polynesian History*. Auckland: Whitcombe and Tombs, 1910.

13

The Toltecs and Maya developed wheels for religious reasons, but not for wheelbarrows or other practical uses. The reason is that they had sufficient slave labor.

PRO   Talaat Shehata
CON   Harald Haarmann

PRO

Although the Toltecs and Mayans made use of the wheel in calendars and other religious symbols, they did not use the wheel for practical purposes, in the ways that the earliest Mesopotamian, Egyptian, Sumerian, and other Middle Eastern societies did. However, there were other widespread technologies for which they had no use. Archaeological evidence has proven that the Toltecs did not have a practical use for writing alphabetically, and neither the Toltecs nor the Mayans used any forms of metal tools until 800 CE, money for bartering purposes, or the use of ancient and well-recognized and regarded beasts of burden, as donkeys, mules, oxen, camels, or horses. They simply had a historically parallel and unique way of going about developing their civilizations. The Toltecs and Mayans have historically appeared to stand on their own separate and unique grounds. The facts inform us that the Toltecs and Mayans brought forth, separately, *authentic* and very dynamic and prosperous civilizations in what is regarded as Mesoamerica, or what are current central Mexico, Guatemala, and Honduras.

Wooden, stone, and obsidian tools were used, along with extensive human labor, to build the magnificent architectural and temple structures that have been left behind. The wheel, the central harbinger of other Mediterranean, Asian, and Old World European civilizations, was only to be found in Toltec and Mayan relics as symbolic religious and cosmological items, or as toy objects to be enjoyed by their young or young at heart, especially during their joyous days of festivities. Besides being made of clay and containing miniature clay-rollers; the wheels of the Toltecs and Mayans were not later created for any constructive technological purpose. The slave argument—that by having slaves, the Toltecs and Mayans did not need to be primarily focused on developing the dynamic, mobile, and progressive nature of the wheel—seems to not fare well with the fact that the other, mostly Middle Eastern civilizations that most heavily used the wheel also made extensive use of slaves. Therefore, historically, what we need to

Mayan wheeled animal toy, found near Vera Cruz, Mexico. (Private Collection/Boltin Picture Library/The Bridgeman Art Library)

focus on is not so much why the Toltecs and Mayans did not make use of the wheel, as other global civilizations had, but, instead, how they were able to create the magnificent civilizations they did without the use of the wheel and other known Old World metal tools. Finally, what does it tell us about how civilizations had evolved in parallel paths throughout history, and continue to do so? Was and is there a predetermined manner and pattern by which they needed to adapt themselves, or was it ultimately of any historical significance that they could achieve the magnificent scales they had attained in their precise "moment" in history?

From the 10th to the 12th centuries CE, the Toltecs had achieved relative dominance over their neighbors in the central highlands of Mexico. Their capital was located in Tula. The legend of Quetzalcoatl, an ancient prophet ruler and divine presence to be emulated by future generations of Toltecs, Mayans, and Aztecs who would later conquer and subjugate the Toltecs for a few long centuries *prior* to the arrival of the Spanish and Hernando Cortez, played an important role in these societies' collective religious beliefs, traditions, and practices. A divine personification of absolute love, Quetzalcoatl, or the Feathered Serpent as he was often called by his devoted followers, was later misrepresented by the Aztecs in their daily and ritual practices, with the wholesale slaughtering and sacrificing of captive elite and a few nonelite prisoners and members of their own expansive civilization. This perversion of the original message of Quetzalcoatl was similar in scope to the Spanish perversion of Christ's message of love; they put many of the Native American inhabitants they encountered in the Aztec kingdom and beyond to the sword, in the name of Christ and his followers' ultimate "salvation."

Regarded as a "white bearded man" (which explains why the Spanish did not experience *initial* resistance to their presence when they first made contact with the Aztecs and the Native American inhabitants), Quetzalcoatl, a divine man of love and wisdom, issued strict rules against blood sacrificial practices, which had been rampant among the Toltecs and other tribal groups within the central Mexican highlands for centuries *prior* to his arrival. He exalted the presence of a single all-encompassing supreme being and introduced the use of the calendar to the Toltecs to better help them maximize the annual yields from their staple crops, such as corn, squash, gourds, potatoes, and lima beans, to mention a few. A solar calendar of 365 days was put to use, and a lesser efficient ritual standard calendar of 260 days was also used.

From 1122 to 1150, the Toltecs were of the strong conviction that the reincarnation of Quetzalcoatl in the being of the son of Ce Tecpatl Mixcoatl, who had ruled Culhuacan during that period, had been realized in Ce Acatl Topiltzin. Topiltzin, within a few short years of his father's passing, gathered a small force and conquered the Toltec capital in Tula and publicly claimed that divine and royal title. During his reign, prosperity seemed to flourish throughout the land. The arts, extensive small metal industries, and diverse crafts took root and thrived in the larger society of around 120,000 inhabitants. Topiltzin, as the reincarnation of the divine presence of Quetzalcoatl, ceased the ritual practice of animal and human sacrifice. Most, if not all, domestic and neighboring violence by Toltecs was temporarily ended. But this unusual period of stability and peace would not last for long. By 1168, the Toltec civilization had reached its weakest point and gradually began to collapse. Folklore and the reputed *Annals of Cuauhtitlan* refer to sorcery being practiced on Quetzalcoatl, with the initial intent of getting him to change his policies regarding animal and human sacrifices. This included the uberdrive format by which a few imaginative members of the community, as in most other global cultures, identified Quetzalcoatl troubles with the "evil" deity Tezcatlipoca. As the story goes, since Quetzalcoatl refused to accede and return to the old bloody sacrificial practices of the magicians and priests that surrounded him, they were able to ally themselves with the powers of the "evil" deity Tezcatlipoca and have Quetzalcoatl escape Tula after being humiliated by Tezcatlipoca. How that humiliation was precisely undertaken is left conveniently "mysterious" in the *Annals* and the rendered folktales, which gives them the quality of gossip. To add more relish to the prefabricated tale, Quetzalcoatl, then in exile, decided to set himself on fire so that he would reemerge as Venus, the morning star. But, sadly, these elaborate tales never really established who the outside invaders were (though over time archaeologists, historians, and other scholars believe that the Toltecs were eventually conquered by the rising Mayan civilization) who actually contributed to the Toltec collapse. At that point in Toltec history, matters and events take on an ethereal appearance for any serious scholar or reader. It is for that precise reason that one can better understand how difficult it can be, unlike in researching and reflecting on Mediterranean historical issues, for one to gain a deeper understanding of the important realities and difficulties that scholars of Atlantic history have contended with. That is, while pursuing and researching the earliest stages of Atlantic history, as demonstrated in this latest Toltec example of how their civilization eventually collapsed, one needs to be able to gain a much deeper understanding of all the important individual pieces of the Mesoamerican and ultimately the earliest period of the Atlantic world.

The question that often imposes itself on scholars within the region concerns the primary interaction and convergence of the tribal groups, kingdoms, and civilizations within the central Mexican highlands, at the height of the Toltec, Mayan, and Aztec periods. Hundreds of languages abounded, and exact population sizes and the precise locations of these population centers are still unknown variables. This, of course, includes the lack of true historical knowledge of the exact time period that jurisdiction had been exercised by one people upon another, and what the ultimate definitive effect was to both the conquered and the conquerors. The interregnum between the collapse of the Toltec civilization and its eventual conquest by the Mayans, and the spotty, if not downright blotched, history as to what immediately followed, clear indications of such a very serious dilemma.

Despite their eventual collapse, Toltec religious beliefs, values, rituals, and traditions would conquer all future civilizations in the central Mexican highland region. As mentioned, the worship of Quetzalcoatl and the adoption and implementation of his precepts and teachings were of paramount significance. Similar to the taming nature of Islam on Genghis Khan's children, grandchildren, and great-grandchildren, and their Mongol hordes on the steppes of Southwest Asia, which contributed to the emergence of the artistic wonders and brilliance of the Mogul Empire, Toltec religious beliefs profoundly impacted the conquering Mayan forces and their daily, communal, spiritual, and artistic evolution. Being much more prone to very militaristic and aggressive violent tendencies, the Mayans gradually began to implement and place their unique stamp on their conquered subjects' art forms. The tendency in the beginning was to view more warrior elite-dictated art forms of military figures and the glorification of their achievements for the larger Mayan community. In time, militaristic propaganda began to give way to much more complex and stylistic art forms, intricate hieroglyphic texts, and the creation of more innate art works that glorified the beauty of this world which the deceased might take with them into the afterlife. This new trend for the Mayans only further emphasized the natural and newly acquired intellectual attributes of their larger culture, instead of the often prefabricated and self-aggrandizing achievements of the elite warrior class. Eventually, the Mayans, instead of maintaining their earlier militaristic autocratic ways, evolved into a much more peaceful theocracy. This new worldview would change in the early 1400s, once they encountered the conquering Aztec forces.

At the peak of their civilization, Mayans owed much of their adapted agricultural practices, growth of their cities, and the acquisition of writing tools to most of the surrounding areas of the geographic locales they had conquered. Squash, beans, and corn were raised in the low south and southwest coastland areas. They had been grown in those areas since 3000 BCE. The creation of pottery and wheel-shaped items among the pottery was attained by 2500 BCE. Between 1500 and 1200 BCE, in time, villages and cities emerged in those lowland areas. Between 800 and 600 BCE, writing emerged among the Zapotecs in the Oaxaca region. The first states evolved by 300 BCE. The Mayans were left with the simple task to either internalize, develop, envision, adapt, or customize the contributions that neighboring and surrounding groups had to offer them, or reject them and continue their earlier rigid militaristic mindset. They wisely chose the former. Archaeological evidence shows that *within* the Mayan areas proper, indications of the mastery of pottery and the emergence of villages began around 1000 BCE. Imposing architectural structures and designs began to take shape around 500 BCE. Finally, written texts began to appear in Mayan culture, around 400 BCE. With 15,000 inscriptions written solely on pottery and stone, and the sole mention of the role, deeds, and conquests of members of the royal and noble classes, very little knowledge is available to cast light on the daily lives and function of the average Mayan man, woman, and child.

The Mayan king donned the dual political role of head of state and the religious one of highest priest. He often presided over calendar and astronomical events, at which wheels were often used and exhibited as an important supplementary item, which established in its intricate design the cyclical evolution of the cosmos and in some cases the location of the morning star, Venus. By being capable of exhibiting to the Mayan nobility and population his mastery of the cosmic order, the Mayan king was able to convince the people that he was capable of guaranteeing their collective prosperity and well-being by his predictions of when and how much rain would fall to inundate the often potentially drought-stricken fields. In Mayan culture, therefore, the king was the critical medium through which the people could channel their hopes between themselves and the gods. In reality, as in any game of chance, the odds were greatly stacked against the player; in this case, the king. So, he spent most of his time thinking on his feet and guaranteeing that his nobles and military elites were loyal, consolidated, and forever showered with material and land ownership favors.

The large mass of the Mayan peasantry and population were only too happy to keep their king, his family, the advisers, and members of the nobility contentedly living in luxury. They not only built majestic architectural and often beautiful interior designed structures, palaces, and mansions for them, but also kept them well fed on venison meat, corn, squash, lima beans, and other assorted of beans and food items. But, curse the days that the king was unable to provide them with the much-needed rain for their crops and continue to maintain, if not increase, the prosperity that they felt was annually due them. This pattern of interaction between the king and his subjects, along with some very serious climatic change, extreme drought conditions, soil erosion, the significant increase in unusable fallow fields, and the profound increase in population as well as with some self-defeating ritualistic practices and outside foreign threats, led to instability. The Mayan civilization experienced a precipitous rise and fall, between the first empire, which lasted from 200 to 850 CE, and the second and last empire, which lasted from 1000 to 1350 CE. All this occurred with the internecine problems that

A Spanish Official Encounters the Mayan City of Palenque

Among the first Europeans to visit the magnificent Mayan city of Palenque was Antonio del Rio, who led an expedition there in 1784. Below is his description of the architecture he found there.

The interior of the large building is in a style of architecture strongly resembling the gothic, and from its rude and massive construction promises great durability. The entrance is on the eastern side, by a portico or corridor thirty-six varas or yards in length and three in breadth, supported by plain rectangular pillars, without either bases or pedestals, upon which there are square smooth stones of more than a foot in thickness forming an architrave, while on the exterior superficies are species of stucco shields, the designs of some of them, accompanying this report, are numbered 1, 2, 3, while, over these stones, there is another plain rectangular block, five feet long and six broad, extending over two of the pillars. Medallions or compartments in stucco containing different devices of the same material, appear as decorations to the chambers, . . . and it is presumable, from the vestiges of the heads which can still be traced, that they were the busts of a series of kings or lords to whom the natives were subject. Between the medallions there is a range of windows like niches, passing from one end of the wall to the other, some of them are square, some in the form of a Greek cross and others, which complete the cross, are square, being about two feet high and eight inches deep. . . . Beyond this corridor there is a square court, entered by a flight of seven steps; the north side is entirely in ruins, but sufficient traces remain to show that it once had a chamber and corridor similar to those on the eastern side, and which, continued entirely along the several angles. The south side has four small chambers with no other ornament than one or two little windows, like those already described. The western side is correspondent to its opposite in all respects, but in the variety of expression of the figures in stucco: these are much more rude and ridiculous than the others, and can only be attributed to the most uncultivated Indian capacity.—The device is a sort of grotesque mask with a crown and long beard like that of a goat, under this are two Greek crosses. . . .

It is by no means improbable that these fantastic forms, and others equally whimsical, were the delineations of some of their deities to whom they paid an idolatrous worship, consistent with their false belief and barbarous customs.

Source: Antonio del Rio. *Description of the Ruins of an Ancient City, Discovered Near Palenque, in the Kingdom of Guatemala, in Spanish America.* London: Henry Berthoud, 1822.

continued to plague them for over a millennium, which finally caught up with them and directly contributed to their collapse and defeat by the Aztecs, in the mid- to late 14th century CE.

Instead of simply viewing Mayan geographic conditions as being tropical or a rainforest, we need to understand that since much of their livelihood was only within a thousand miles of the equator, with 17 to 22 degree latitude readings during the first four months of the year (January to April), their homeland experienced regular very dry months. As for the rainy season, that usually arrived from May through October of each year, which would be the only time a neutral observer might accurately regard it as a "seasonal tropical forest." So, the reality of the Toltec and then Mayan civilizations was that they had to adapt themselves to the extremes of their environments. Often, one slight annual misstep would lead to disaster for their people. This was never made any clearer than when the first few early and larger classic Mayan civilization collapses occurred by the ninth century and continued into the tenth century CE. During that time period, the steep hills were used for planting, which in comparison with the earlier used valley soil, were much more acidic in composition, less fertile, and had a much lower yield in phosphate retention and production.

It is a well-known fact among farmers in the central Mexican highlands that corn and other vegetable yields in the fertile valley fields are much higher and richer in protein and fiber content than anything that could be grown on the hill slopes. This was the ultimate dilemma that the Mayans had to contend with during their civilization's growth over the millennia. This fact amazes many archaeologists, historians, and scholars as to the Toltecs' and Mayans' individual and collective abilities to create, innovate, and continue to maintain their civilizations under such dire conditions for such a prolonged period of time without making use of the wheel or any of its later contributing technologies as parallel civilizations in the Middle East, Asia, and the Old European World had done.

During each of the separate collapses throughout their protracted history, the Mayans built larger and more intricate structures, temples, and palaces. The idea that preoccupied them was that when times were hard, you just tried to build bigger and better edifices to please the gods. It is estimated that from 250 CE, when their dire water, irrigation, drought, and climate change conditions were evident, the Mayans increased the construction of their monuments, city structures, and temple sites with their increased amounts of wheel-shaped pottery for cosmological and ritualistic uses, in exponential proportions. The greatest

Disc with relief design representing a ball player. Around the edge of the disc are a series of dates including day and 20-day period signs. Mayan, 590 CE. (Museo Nacional de Antropologia, Mexico City, Mexico/ Giraudon/The Bridgeman Art Library)

amount of construction often occurred a few short years prior to the actual fall of either of the civilizations in question, (i.e., the first major fall in the 9th and 10th centuries, and during the second and final one in the mid to late 14th century). The Mayan population had grown exponentially during both periods. The demand on the shrinking agricultural land had grown vicious, especially on the relatively infertile steep hill soil, which seemed to be the only land left for Mayans to compete for. With increased construction projects, sediment erosion of the hill and valley fields increased. That only added more to the Mayans' troubles. The hill slopes had become so eroded that whatever nutrients they still had available for future farming were being eradicated. With the rainy season, much of these sediments, combined with the initial acidic nature of the soil in the hills, were washed down into the more fertile valleys, creating its own chaos. By 700 CE the soil in both the valley and the hill slopes had become relatively toxic, too toxic for any future agricultural benefits by the Mayan population. Added to the mix was the regular use of plaster for their building projects and as writing objects, which the Mayans stripped off the barks of the surrounding trees in the forest. This, in time, created a looming deforestation catastrophe. Pine trees that had been growing in the central Mexican highlands for eons within a few short centuries had been completely cleared from all the hill slopes. The trees were not only used for construction and plastering purposes, but also for their fueling needs. This in time contributed to the increased drought cycle, since the presence of trees had helped continue whatever increase they enjoyed in extra rainwater. Now, with the forests gone, less rain fell to help irrigate their field on the hill slopes and in the valleys.

From 760 to 910 CE the Mayan collapse spread throughout its different power centers throughout the region, incrementally and at different stages. But, the collapse of the civilization that the Mayans had known for over a millennium had arrived and was merciless. The results were so glaring that the overall impact on such a flowering and productive civilization was sobering to any serious reader or scholar's eyes. From what had been the most productive, overpopulated, artistic, and most vibrant regions of the Mayan civilization, the low southland area, during the period of the first Mayan civilization's fall, 99 percent of its inhabitants had disappeared. Most perished as a result of starvation, thirst, and regular killings of one another because of conflicts over continued limited resources. With increased warfare among themselves, the scarce resources growing scarcer, and shrinking land spaces surrounding them, the extremely valuable properties still available evolved into no-war parches of land that the different communities were forced to honor in the attempt to maintain a zone of insulation from one another. This continued the downward spiral of no further agricultural land to farm. Yet another important factor to keep in mind is that with the exponential increase in population and no more land to occupy once the old agricultural property had turned fallow or become drought-stricken, the Mayans found themselves with their individual and collective backs very seriously up the irascible wall. Each Mayan was forced into the unenviable position of making a last stand in order to survive. What's even more sobering was that they were faced with those deadly nonchoices, once again, by the time of the second major Mayan collapse, when the Spanish had made first contact with them in the first decade of their arrival in the early 1500s. A population of over 33 million Mayans had shrunk to a mere 30,000. Which leaves us with this very serious question: Could current postmodern and modernizing societies and future generations learn from this hard lesson and not allow it to happen to them? History will definitely keep us informed.

Besides all the unique and astounding features of both Toltec and Mayan civilizations, the important lesson that should be drawn from their existence and continued persistence over the centuries, against often insurmountable geographic, physical, and ecological odds, is not that they never "constructively" made use of the wheel or what different technologies it was able to spawn over the centuries in the early Middle East, Asian, and Old World societies; but, instead, could any of these wheel-driven societies have dealt with the internecine geographic, physical, and ecological problems that the Toltecs and Mayans daily dealt with and arrived at any better results? It's very doubtful. The wheel question, despite its importance in historical context when one looks at the larger landscape, seems quite trivial. In current postmodern advanced societies, it's sad to see that we are dealing with the same problems, if not much more serious ones, in matters as climate change, green-house gas emissions and their catastrophic impact on the Arctic region, the erosion and depletion of prime agricultural soil and land, a persistent exponential increase in the global population, dwindling water resources, an increase in the civil wars on a global basis over limited natural resources, and growing rates of domestic crimes, abuse, violence, and warfare throughout the world. The wheel, in perspective, hasn't really done anything to address, if not alleviate, any of these very serious problems. They continue with us today, as they did during the height of the Toltec and Mayan civilizations; except, today, and into the near and distant future, it has become much more magnified. If there's anything to be learned from the Toltec and Mayan civilizations, besides how were they able to create and maintain their separate civilizations for numerous centuries, without the use of Middle East, Asian, or Old World technologies, it is that we must avert the manmade and nature-created catastrophes that they dealt with before we find ourselves meeting the same ultimate fate that they met, after an extended flowered and magnificent period of existence.

References and Further Reading

Bailyn, Bernard. *Atlantic History: Concept and Contours.* Cambridge, MA: Harvard University Press, 2005.

Bentley, Jerry H. "Cross-Cultural Interaction and Periodization in World History." *AHR* 101 (June 1996): 749–70.

Demerest, Arthur, Prudence Rice, and Don Rice, eds. *The Terminal Classic in the Maya Lowlands.* Boulder: University Press of Colorado, 2004.

Fagan, Brian. *The Long Summer: How Climate Changed Civilization.* New York: Basic Books, 2004.

Gill, Richard. *The Great Maya Droughts.* Albuquerque: University of New Mexico Press, 2000.

Lentz, David, ed. *Imperfect Balance: Landscape Transformation in the Pre-Columbian Americas.* New York: Columbia University Press, 2000.

Lerner, Daniel. *The Passing of Traditional Society.* Glencoe, IL: Free Press, 1958.

Manning, Patrick. "The Problem of Interactions in World History." *American Historical Review* 101 (June 1996): 777–81.

Pilcher, Jeffrey M. *Food in World History.* New York: Routledge, 2006.

Redman, Charles. *Human Impact on Ancient Environments.* Tucson: University of Arizona Press, 1999.

Sharer, Robert. *The Ancient Maya.* Stanford, CA: Stanford University Press, 1994.

Turner II, B. L. "Prehistoric Intensive Agriculture in the Mayan Lowlands." *Science* 185 (1974): 118–24.

Organski, A. F. K. *The Stages of Political Development.* New York: Knopf, 1965.

Webster, David. *The Fall of the Ancient Maya.* New York: Thames and Hudson, 2002.

Whitmore, Thomas, and B. L. Turner II. "Landscapes of Cultivation in Mesoamerica on the Eve of the Conquest." *Annals of the Association of American Geographers* 82 (1992): 402–25.

Worster, Donald. "World without Borders: The Internationalizing of Environmental History." In *Environmental History: Critical Issues in Comparative Perspective.* Edited by Kendall E. Bailes. Lanham, MD: University Press of America, 1984.

CON

The web of ideas that are placed in opposition on whether the Toltecs and Mayan developed the wheel for religious reasons versus practical uses related to the presence or absence of beasts of burden or slave labor is highly arbitrary, and its logical foundation is disputable. What does the practical use of the wheel have to do with slave labor? Is it reasonable to explain the absence of the one (i.e., the wheel to facilitate labor) with the abundance of the other (i.e., slave labor)? No, it is not and there is good reason to reject this opposition as pseudological. In this context, the existence of the one factor cannot explain the absence of the other. This lack of explanatory potential can be illustrated by prominent instances of cultural history.

For example, to those who, in the early civilizations of the Old World, carried out the monumental building projects—of the ziggurats, the stepped temples in Mesopotamia, and of the pyramids of the Old Egyptian Kingdom—the wheel was known as a practical device, and it was used. The invention of the wheel in the Old World was an independent event, and this event was not related to the availability of a human workforce. The wheel had already been in practical use hundreds of years before the first monuments were erected.

The monumental structures in Egypt and Mesopotamia could have been erected with the exclusive help of manpower. The corresponding large structures (i.e., ceremonial platforms, pyramids, temples) of the pre-Columbian era in the New World demonstrate that the construction of large-scale architecture without the use of the wheel was possible. The fact that the workforce in the Old World civilizations that were communal or slave labor-oriented had the wheel at their disposal made work much more effective, but the completion of the projects, in theory and practice, did not require the interplay of the two factors (i.e., manpower + wheel) as a necessary precondition.

The Mesoamerican "Missing Link"

In the New World, too, the wheel could have been introduced as a practical device at any time. At least the preconditions for such a move were present. Inventive thinking had been widely applied for various technical skills (e.g., masonry, pottery-making, mining, the working of hard stone such as jade, and rubber production). The idea of a turning wheel or disk was known as a symbol from the American calendrical system. The historical stage was set for a combination of the idea of the wheel and the application as a device by technical skills (an option that did not materialize).

Is there something like a "missing link" between the idea of the wheel as a cognitive concept and its practical application as a device for transport, a clue that existed in the Old World but was missing in the New World? In terms of technical skills, the pre-Columbian Mesoamericans could compete with any of the other ancient peoples of the world. They even invented techniques to work the hardest stones that exist.

> Jade was the most highly prized mineral in Pre-Columbian Mesoamerica. . . . Jadeite is much harder than obsidian and slightly softer than quartz; because of its structure, it is the toughest and most durable of stones. . . . The ability to carve and polish extremely hard stones seems to have been known before

the introduction of the Olmec style . . . but the Gulf Coast Olmec may have perfected the skill. (Pohorilenko 1996: 120)

The synchronization of the invention of wheel and the mobilization of a large workforce would not need to be seen as working the same way in America as it did in the Old World. World history teaches valuable lessons, provided one opens one's mind to learn them. The lesson of the wheel is highly instructive in that it illustrates the fundamental insight that there is no automatism in cultural evolution. The processes of technical innovation that operated in the Old World did not operate in the same way in the New World.

A special challenge must have been felt when, in the second millennium BCE, a network of long-distance transport without wheelbarrows was established (see below). Nevertheless, the idea of the wheel was never explored in Mesoamerica for possibilities of its practical manifestation. There was a "missing link" in the chain from idea to application, and because there was something missing, this caused a blocking of practical application.

The wheel is not the only issue that may illustrate fundamental differences of development. Another issue is the absence of iron melting in pre-Columbian Mesoamerica. It may always remain a mystery why the Native Americans mined iron ore but did not process it by applying melting techniques to extract the metal. Instead, they worked the ore (i.e., magnetite) and molded and polished it to produce mirrors. There are reasons why the development of the wheel differed in America from Asia, Europe, and Africa. The question why the pre-Columbian Americans did not use the wheel for practical purposes is usually discussed in relation to the aspect of the use of the wheel, that is from a standpoint where "practical use" is placed in opposition to "nonpractical use." This approach is biased, because a mode of thinking that gives priority to considerations of utility and mundane functions of technical innovations is typical of our time, and of the Euro-American worldview in particular. Such thinking was definitely absent from life in the Mesoamerican communities of the pre-Columbian era.

To understand the ways of the pre-Columbian Americans and their worldview, we are advised to refrain from any projection of our modern views onto their world. What is called for is an internal reconstruction of pre-Columbian realities of community life, whereby paying due tribute to the conceptualizations of the American ancestors, as can be concluded from their cultural heritage. This means that the modern investigator has to make an effort to "stand beside him- or herself" and to become familiar with the mindset of those who created the pre-Columbian civilizations to avoid distortion by modern ideologies. Any discourse about the significance of the wheel in those remote cultures is only meaningful within the context of a reconstructed worldview.

Cultural Trajectories of the Mesoamerican Mindset in the Pre-Columbian Era

The discussion of differences of mindset may start with the most unifying of all cultural concepts—how human beings in different cultures perceive the idea of "community." According to the pre-Columbian mindset, the venerated ancestors as well as the representatives of the living generations were members of the community. The Maya buried their dead beneath their houses as an expression of a close relationship between the venerated dead and the living.

> The link between the community, Earth, and the ancestors was manifested in other ways too. The dead could be shown as trees planted in the soil, as on the sides of the sarcophagus in the Temple of the Inscriptions at Palenque. Here the ancestors of the ruler Pacal are shown as trees emerging from fissures in the earth. (Marcus 2000: 237).

Venerated ancestors were imagined as trees that were important for the Maya diet and economy. Cacao, chicozapote, avocado, guayaba, coyol, and mamey trees have all been identified as species of this category of "ancestor tree." As the reference to the tree spirits of ancestors illustrates, the Maya imagined their community as an extension of the space for the living, which also included spirited nature.

Since the times of the Olmec civilization, which had already emerged in the second millennium BCE, daily life of the pre-Columbian Mesoamericans unfolded under the auspices of a balance between the world of humans and that of the spirits. The cosmos of the inhabitants of the agrarian village communities comprised its own cultural living space; the surrounding nature, which was imagined to be spirited; the ancestors whose spirits were believed to advise and guide their living descendants in their mundane matters; and the supernatural beings (i.e., divinities and their various functions).

> For the indigenous person [i.e., the pre-Columbian Mesoamerican], the natural world was not something to be manipulated, exploited, and destroyed by humans at their pleasure, as it has been for Western culture. Rather it was a sphere populated by supernatural powers and forces with which people had to forge ties, necessary for the survival of humankind and for the conservation of nature, and as the context in which sacred beings manifested themselves. (de la Garza 2000: 70)

The balance between the worlds had to be maintained through rituals and ceremonies. The ceremonial traditions of the Mesoamericans are manifold, and many have persisted, in various transformations, over many hundreds of years to the present. A colorful example of the perpetuation of ancient beliefs is the tradition to celebrate the "Days of the Dead" in Mexico on the occasion of All Saints' Day at the beginning of November. People would visit the graveyards, decorate the graves, and leave food and drinks for the ancestors, and then they would invite the ancestors' spirits to their homes and organize a feast for them. After the celebration, they would escort the spirits back to the graveyard to their resting place.

The mindset of those people who lived in the spirited world of pre-Columbian cultures lacked something that is so typical of the Euro-American way of thinking: striving for innovations and inventions for the sake of progress in technology. When reference is made here to the absence of a quality of the mindset, this does not mean that the pre-Columbian Mesoamericans lacked inventiveness. On the contrary, those who crafted the ancient American civilizations possessed astounding skills and mental capacities as well as technical know-how. Their skills were embedded in a worldview in which all technical progress was measured in terms of its benefit for the ritual balance between humans and the spirit world. One aspect that was definitely negligible in the thinking of Mesoamericans was the idea to save energy and manpower through the introduction of technical innovations to make daily work more efficient.

A way of thinking without the monopoly of practical priorities did not support technical inventions of the kind that were made in the Old World, where a different mindset might have dominated. This mindset must have been more problem-oriented toward devising practical solutions for things and toward improving existing technologies. Such thinking was the mother of many inventions in the Old World, among them the use of the wheel for work and transport. The first wheeled wagons appear on the western periphery of the Russian steppe zone about the middle of the fifth millennium BCE. About that time, the potter's wheel was introduced in Europe (Ukraine) and in western Asia (Mesopotamia).

Cultural Relativity as to How the Abstract Mind Works

We modern people identify objects according to their form and shape, not necessarily according to their function. In this way, we perceive what is similar or identical from the outer appearance. An object that is round and has an axis hole in the middle is called a wheel. In English, the same term wheel is used, regardless whether we speak of a wheel on a car or as part of a motorcycle, of a potter's wheel, of a wheel-shaped part in any kind of machinery, or of the picture of a wheel. Since the same term is used for the most different contexts in which a wheel-shaped object may appear, our abstract mind easily perceives all these objects as similar or identical. When we look at whatever wheel-shaped object, we readily associate the practical use of the wheel in our daily life, and we do this because our minds are conditioned by knowledge about the practical functions of the wheel that has been transferred over many generations in our cultural memory.

Only if we inspect the relationship of wheel-shaped objects and the terminology that is associated with them in other languages will we notice differences in the perception of such objects in the minds of people who live in cultural environments distinct from the world of English. One such environment is Tibetan culture. The Tibetans adopted Buddhism in the early Middle Ages, and, together with the scriptures and the teachings, they became acquainted with the eight-spoked wheel, the sacred symbol of infinite spiritual power and energy. The term for the symbol of infinite spiritual energy is *chakra*, a word borrowed from Sanskrit that was introduced to Tibet as an element of Buddhist worldview. When Tibetans are asked how they perceive the meaning of *chakra*, their answers indicate that this religious symbol is stored in the minds of Buddhists in a "separate chamber" and that all possible connotations range in the domain of abstractness. This means that it is difficult for a Tibetan to think of this same wheel as being a practical device for transport. The conceptual difference between the religious wheel and the wheel for practical functions is anchored in the language. The expression for a wheel as a device for transport is completely different: *korlo*. In the marked difference of items of the linguistic matrix is reflected an equally marked distinction of concepts on the cognitive level (i.e., wheel 1 = religious symbol vs. wheel 2 = practical device). Such contrasts like those described for Tibetan culture and language also exist in other cultural environments. For instance, the term for a potter's wheel is *durgn* in Armenian. Since this expression deviates clearly from other words for wheel-shaped objects, it can be concluded that Armenians, guided by their language in their perception, do not necessarily identify all wheel-shaped objects as similar or identical.

For the pre-Columbian cultural horizon, such distinctions cannot be demonstrated for the simple reason that the wheel for practical functions was never introduced, and the only concept that was associated with a wheel-shaped object was the wheel in a religious context. In the ancient cultures of the Old World, the wheel as an abstract motif is known from imagery dating to periods before the invention and the introduction of the device for transport. Therefore, in the Old World, the conceptual spectrum for wheel-shaped objects was extended to its full range. In the New World, this range was not explored in its total extension.

The Wheel as a Religious Symbol in Pre-Columbian Mesoamerica

Like people all over the world, the Native Americans knew what wheel-shaped objects looked like because of their observations of natural phenomena. The most impressive wheel-shaped objects in the sky are the sun and the moon. The latter celestial body attracted special attention because of its shape-shifting rhythm: full moon, descending crescent after 7 days; ascending crescent after 14 days; full moon after 7 days. It is noteworthy that the motif of the disk (or wheel or circle) is among the oldest ornaments of Olmec art, and it had already featured on sculptures dating to ca. 1150 BCE. In numerous transformations, this basic concept persisted throughout the periods of pre-Columbian cultural development, and the disk/circle/wheel motif is, in manifold ways, combined with other motifs in Mesoamerican religious iconography. In the Mayan tradition, the icon for the sun was a four-petaled motif, which is known as the *kin* sign. *Kin* in Mayan means both "sun" and "day."

The sun and the moon were conceived as divinities, like other known celestial bodies. However, these two bodies, which impressed the Mesoamerican mind by their size and properties, held a prominent position among all the other gods. The sun was personified as a male god, perhaps because of the vigor and strength of the solar energy, especially when thinking of the power of the rising sun. Contrasting with this personification, pre-Columbian mythology and art identified the moon as feminine. The duality of the sun god and the moon goddess manifests itself in many monumental buildings dedicated to these divinities. Perhaps the most impressive ensemble is that which constitutes the two pyramids, the larger sun pyramid and the smaller moon pyramid, in the ancient town of Teotihuacan, which was called "city of the gods" by the Aztecs. The civilization of Teotihuacan, situated some 40 km to the northeast of Mexico City, flourished between ca. 100 and 600 CE. The city was abandoned, for unknown reasons, in the early ninth century, but it was later frequented as a center of pilgrimage by the Aztecs.

The name of the sun god in Mayan is *Kinich Ahau* ("sun-faced or sun-eyed lord"). In later Mayan iconography, "the sun god is closely identified with jaguars, and at times appears with a jaguar ear" (Miller and Taube 1993: 106). In the Aztec religion, the sun was personified as *Huitzilopochtli*. For the Aztecs, this male figure played the role of a supreme god, and his attributes, which he holds in his hands, are a petaled disk and the fire serpent. The Mayan moon goddess is often identified as *Ixchel*, a figure whose name can be translated as "Lady Rainbow." However, the image of the moon goddess shows a young and beautiful woman, while *Ixchel* was depicted as an old woman. The identification of the moon goddess with *Ixchel* may have resulted from confusion caused by the description of the Mayan gods in the early Spanish accounts of the native Mesoamericans in the sixteenth century. Then, *Ixchel* was the most prominent figure among the Mayan. The original name of the Mayan moon goddess is not known. She is usually depicted as sitting on the crescent, which is the glyph for moon in Mayan writing. Her typical attribute is a rabbit. According to classical Mayan beliefs, the picture of a rabbit becomes visible on the surface of the celestial body at the time of the full moon. The moon goddess was held in high esteem, and she was venerated as the patroness of pregnancy and childbirth, of weaving and divination, and also of fertility. In the Aztec mythical tradition, the moon goddess is called *Coyolxauhqui*, and she is identified as Huitzilopochtli's sister.

Extensive ceremonial services were carried out to worship both the sun and the moon with their prominent status in the Mesoamerican pantheon. In view of the sanctity of the two concepts of the sun and the moon and of the attention these two celestial bodies and their personifications enjoyed in the pre-Columbian communities, it is reasonable to assume that their visual images were also sanctified. Once the shape of the disk or circle is sanctified as an attribute of a prominent divinity, the cognitive path to imagine, any practical use for a device in the same shape as a divine attribute is most likely to be blocked. This blocking, postulated here as a psychological phenomenon, can hardly be evidenced with any certainty for the mindset of people living in bygone cultures. And yet this kind of psychological impediment to explore the benefits of wheel-shaped devices cannot be reasonably ruled out. In this context, it is amazing that some of the pre-Columbian imagery illustrates wheel-shaped motifs that spontaneously evoke the association with spoked wheels on wheelbarrows or wagons in the mind of Westerners.

The Role of the Calendar Wheel

The impression of the changing of the seasons of the year must have spurred reflections about the vegetation cycle among the pre-Columbian Mesoamericans in the early agrarian communities of the second millennium BCE. For the Mesoamerican calendar system, though, other aspects of cyclic events obviously had greater importance than the vegetation cycle. This can be conjectured from the number of days that were counted in the oldest known Mesoamerican calendar system, the so-called 260-day almanac. The specific number of 260 days is not associated with either astronomical or agricultural phenomena. This system "was probably devised by midwives to calculate birthdates, working from first missed menstrual period to birth, approximating the 9-month human gestation period" (Miller and Taube 1993: 48).

The oldest evidence for the pre-Columbian calendar system, which originated in the first millennium BCE, comes from the Olmec civilization in the coastal areas of the Gulf of Mexico. The earliest calendrical inscription dates to the sixth century. This calendar persisted in religious functions throughout the pre-Columbian period. Its name in Mayan has been reconstructed as *tzolkin*, and the Aztecs called it *tonalpohualli*. A civic calendar was used alongside the ritual calendar for daily use. This calendar counted 365 days and was called *haab* by the classical Maya. According to the Mayan tradition, dates were always given in the form of a double count, thus synchronically counting an event based on both calendars and their time measurements. The operation of the calendar was conceptualized in terms of the turning of a wheel. Since there were two parallel calendrical systems, there were two calendar wheels that turned synchronically. It would take a long span of time—or exactly 52 years of 365 days (= 18,980 days)—so that a given date would repeat itself. This period is called the calendar round.

A Mayan Wheel in England

One of the most interesting and controversial appearances of a Mayan wheel took place centuries after the decline of Mayan civilization, and thousands of miles away. During August 2–3, 2004, a large crop circle in the shape and design of a Mayan wheel appeared at Silbury Hill, Wiltshire, England. The wheel, used by the Mayans as a calendar, counts down to the year 2012, and some "experts" have ominously predicted that this seemingly supernatural apparition portends the end of the world. Of course, the fact that 2012 is the end point of the calendar is no surprise to anyone who has studied actual Mayan calendars, as they all indicate an end-of-time point in the year 2012.

The wheel as a visual icon to illustrate the proceeding of the time count according to the two calendars became a common motif in pre-Columbian iconography and architecture. Well known is the Aztec calendar stone in the form of a big wheel, and the archaeological record yields numerous disk-shaped stones with signs of calendrical notation. The familiar motif of the calendar wheel was also reproduced in some of the late Mayan books and in early Spanish manuscripts of the 16th century in which the Native American calendar system was documented at a time when it was still in use. In a highly pervasive way, the visual impression of the calendar wheel illustrates the closeness of ideas, of the abstraction of the cyclical movement of time counting, and of the wheel as a practical device. Despite the familiarity and the popularity of the calendar wheel as an (abstractly) turning device, this association never spurred the pre-Columbian mind to transfer the idea, in a process of cognitive analogy, and to make the device work for mundane purposes for transport and labor.

Trade Routes and Transport

The pre-Columbian civilizations all share basic properties—of cultural patterns (e.g., the calendrical system), of ornamentation in the visual arts and architecture (e.g., the jaguar motif), of belief systems (e.g., the cult of the rain god), and of ideas about life (e.g., the cosmic cycles of a renewal of life). Scholars have long wondered how cultural traditions and technical skills could have spread so widely over a large area and what the origins were. Modern research has produced insights that allow for the reconstruction of a sophisticated network of trade relations throughout Mesoamerica and of a web of idea diffusion. The Olmecs were the first Native Americans who explored trade routes leading from the Gulf Coast inland. These routes, which were traveled from the second millennium BCE, connected the coasts of the Atlantic with those of the Pacific. It is over this network of trade and communication that the foundations of the classical civilizations were established.

Manifold goods were traded, among them cacao (chocolate), mollusk shells, turtle shells (for making drums), fish, stingray spines, shark teeth, rubber, salt, tar, pottery, clay, obsidian, iron ore and pigments, turquoise, mica, and so forth. Among the luxury goods in the Olmec-controlled trade from coast to coast were spondylous shells, pearl oyster, jade, and alabaster. Trade was carried out between villages, but the routes that were regularly traveled also included connections with areas that were important for the exploitation of raw material such as obsidian (used for tools and ornaments), precious stones (e.g., jade, serpentine), and minerals (e.g., magnetite for making mirrors).

Manpower was the only resource throughout the pre-Columbian era to keep up trade relations and to guarantee the movement of materials and commodities. Beasts of burden were unknown as were wheelbarrows. Transporting raw material such as iron ore and stones (i.e., obsidian, jade), ceramic objects, shells, and foodstuff only by way of carrying everything on one's back must have been laborious. The lack of beasts of burden is no criterion to pervasively explain the lack of the wheel. Wheelbarrows can be drawn by humans, applying the principle of transport that is well known from Southeast Asia (i.e., transportation by means of rickshaw carts).

The light of adapting the idea of the wheel to make it work as a practical device obviously never flared up, because the incentive to surpass the impediment of a religious "blocking" was never activated. And yet, whatever approach may be chosen to explain the missing link, none of these approaches are ultimately satisfactory. So the absence of the wheel in practical functions may always remain a mystery of pre-Columbian history.

References and Further Reading

Adams, Richard E. W. *Ancient Civilizations of the New World*. Boulder, CO: Westview, 1997.

de la Garza, Mercedes. *The Mayas: 3000 years of Civilization*. Mexico City: Monclem Ediciones, 2000.

Diehl, Richard A. "Tula and the Tolteca." In *The Aztec Empire* (pp. 124–27). Edited by Felipe Solis. New York: Solomon R. Guggenheim Foundation, 2004.

Haarmann, Harald. *Foundations of Culture. Knowledge-construction, Belief Systems and Worldview in Their Dynamic Interplay*. New York: Peter Lang, 2007.

Marcus, Joyce. "Toward an Archaeology of Communities." In *The Archaeology of Communities. A New World Perspective* (pp. 231–42). Edited by Marcello A. Canuto and Jason Yaeger. New York: Routledge, 2000.

Miller, Mary, and Karl Taube. *The Gods and Symbols of Ancient Mexico and the Maya. An illustrated Dictionary of Mesoamerican Religion.* London: Thames and Hudson, 1993.

Pohorilenko, Anatole. "Portable Carvings in the Olmec Style." In *Olmec Art of Ancient Mexico* (pp. 119–31). Edited by Elizabeth P. Benson and Beatriz de la Fuente. Washington DC: National Gallery of Art; New York: Harry N. Abrams, 1996.

14

Native American languages can be traced to three grand linguistic roots.

PRO Harald Haarmann
CON Peter N. Jones

PRO

The history of surveys and classifications of Native American (Amerindian) languages reaches as far back as the 17th century. No other approach to a historical classification has spurred as lively a debate among linguists, anthropologists, and archaeologists as has the approach presented by Joseph H. Greenberg in 1987, who distinguished three macrophyla, or linguistic groups. First, the Amerind macrophylum, comprising the great majority of indigenous languages of the Americas, which are grouped in 11 subfamilies. The more than 900 individual languages of this macrophylum are assumed to be descendants of a common basis (protolanguage) that was transferred to America with the first wave of migrants from Siberia. The conventional date for that migration is given as some 13,000 years ago. Second, the Na-Dene languages, comprising the Athabascan language family (Navajo, Apache, etc.) and several language isolates (Eyak, Tlingit, Haida) in the northwestern part of North America. The common basis for the languages of this macrophylum (altogether 42 individual languages) was transferred to America by the migrants of the second wave who came some 11,000 years ago. Finally, the Eskimo-Aleut languages, comprising local variants of Eskimo (Yupik, Inuktitut, Inupiatun, Inuit, etc.) and of Aleut. These languages have derived from a common basis that is about 9,000 to 10,000 years old. The evidence presented here will prove that Greenberg's ideas on the basic macrophyla of Amerindian languages is correct.

This distinction of linguistic macrophyla is in accordance with the three major migrations in the course of the prehistoric peopling of the Americas that have been identified by archaeology and human genetics. While the historical relationships within the macrophylum of the Na-Dene languages (and of the Eskimo-Aleut macrophylum, respectively) are undisputed, most scholars in the field of linguistics oppose the higher-order classification of the Amerind stock and postulate a greater number of language families. In the ongoing controversy, marked positions of pro (represented by the "geneticists") and con (propagated by the "diffusionists") are taken.

The overall pan-American vision of the linguistic landscape as propagated by Greenberg has almost been buried under the critique of shortcomings of his methodology brought forward by the diffusionists. Despite a continuous dispute over the reliability of compared lexical items, reconstructed forms, and the classification of individual languages, the main issue has remained, in principle, one of perspective. If one follows the great currents of the early settlement of America and the early movements of populations that have been reconstructed by human genetics, then it seems conclusive to strive to reconcile findings of historical linguistics with these insights. That is Greenberg's perspective. What is reflected in the critique by diffusionists of Greenberg's comparisons and categorizations is the state of agony in which historical linguistics finds itself with its rather insufficient methodology to reach deep beneath the horizon of time, rather than the negation of sets of lexical equations that are historically related to certain postulated cognate words as their common basis. In the following outline, the emphasis is more on the relativity of perspective and methodology (linguistic versus nonlinguistic) and less on the discussion of details.

Anyone who engages in the debate about language classification in the Americas has to cope with natural limitations of the documentation of the subject matter, the some 1,010 native languages. Although the amount of data about the Amerindian languages is continuously growing, grammatical descriptions and dictionaries are, by far, not available for all languages. Also, for practical purposes any comparative study has to limit itself to a selection of analyzed languages and a selection of vocabulary. The some 2,000 words in Greenberg's catalog of cognates are but a fraction of the entire lexicon of any living language. Nevertheless, Greenberg's overview is the most comprehensive of all the lists that have ever been applied by comparative taxonomy. Greenberg has been criticized, notably by Ives Goddard (1987), for shortcomings in the reconstruction of historical protoforms of the Amerind languages. Here, the critique seems to be at odds with the possibilities to explore deeper chronological layers in the evolution of languages in convincing ways with comparative-analytical methods. In this context, it is worthwhile to stress the fact that documentation of Native American languages from older periods is scarce.

Historical Documentation of American Native Languages

The history of indigenous languages of the Americas had unfolded for many thousands of years before the earliest written records of them originated. The first known Amerindian community where the native language was written was that of the Olmecs in Mesoamerica. The central area of this oldest pre-Columbian civilization extended across the modern Mexican federal states of Guerrero, Veracruz, and Tabasco. The Olmec civilization developed the basic technologies and laid the foundations for institutions that were later adopted by the Mayans, Aztecs, and other civilized peoples of the pre-Columbian era: writing, a calendrical system, monumental architecture, and so forth.

Longer texts in Olmec and, later, in Mayan date to the first millennium BCE and are contemporaneous with Greek and Roman literacy in Europe. In a comparative view, the written documentation of Native American languages is much younger than the tradition of writing in the Old World, where the beginnings lie with ancient Egypt in the fourth millennium BCE and with the Danube civilization in the fifth millennium BCE. The documentation of languages in the Americas over some 2,500 years is therefore much more limited than the written record of languages in Africa and Eurasia, and this has a bearing on the approaches to trace the splitting of individual languages, their branches, and whole language families (phyla) in the horizon of absolute time.

For the longest span of time in the history of Native American languages, no empirical evidence is available to identify the spread of languages and their splitting processes. What can be reconstructed with the methods of historical-comparative linguistics for prehistory are theoretical constructs, that is, fabrics of protolanguages whose real value as a means of communication remains questionable. Linguistics proper and anthropology played the role of forerunners for the study of languages in the Americas for more than a hundred years and well into the second half of the 20th century. During the past few decades, more and more insights into the formation of language families, about their historical relationships, and about the contacts involving their communities of speakers have been produced by interdisciplinary research. In addition to linguists and anthropologists, the American linguistic landscape has been studied by archaeologists, ethnologists, culture historians, and, more extensively since the 1990s, by human geneticists.

The documentation of Native American languages began in the 16th century. Following the model of the first grammar of a European vernacular language, Spanish, in 1492, European missionaries wrote the first grammars and compiled the first dictionaries of Amerindian languages. The first grammar was that of Tarascan, spoken in western Mexico, written by Maturino Gilberti and published in Mexico City in 1558. The classical Nahuatl language, the lingua franca of the Aztec Empire, was described by Alonso de Molina. This work—still of historical value—was printed in 1571. Many of the Spanish missionaries were interested in Amerindian languages, and the first valuable accounts about the number of individual languages come from the region of the Spanish colonies in America. Lorenzo Hervás y Panduro (1735–1809), a Spanish Jesuit, provided the first survey of languages in South America. In his universal encyclopedia—an edition with 21 volumes in Italian appeared between 1778 and 1787, a Spanish version in 6 volumes between 1800 and 1805—one finds much valuable information about American languages and their grammar and vocabulary.

Another remarkable source with collections of vocabularies from various American languages, the biggest enterprise of language studies during the age of Enlightenment, is the monumental dictionary of Catherine II the Great, who ruled Russia from 1762 to 1796. The dictionary project (Vocabularium Catherinae) is associated with her name because she actively participated in the collection of its materials. As for the American languages, the czarina contacted representatives of American public life in personal letters, such as Benjamin Franklin and George Washington, to obtain data about indigenous languages. Benjamin Franklin, founder of the American Philosophical Society (1769), was perhaps the most knowledgeable American in matters of Amerindian cultures and languages at the time. Catherine's collections of linguistic data were organized by the German scholar Peter Simon Pallas in two volumes (1786–1789), published in Saint Petersburg. The collections of American languages are not included in this first edition of the *Linguarum totius orbis vocabularia comparativa*. The second, enlarged edition, which appeared in four volumes in 1790 and 1791, contains data from American languages.

In the early phase of data collection about American languages, the curiosity to explore the exotic world of indigenous cultures dominated over any systematic approach of their study. The two amateurs who published books about American languages in the 17th century—Roger Williams (*Key into the Language of America*, 1643) and John Eliot (*The Indian Grammar Begun: An Essay to Bring the Indian Language into Rules*, 1666)—had fanciful ideas about the relationship among individual languages. They thought that all Amerindian languages were more or less the same. Among the amateurs of the 18th century were the protagonists of the independence movement. Regna Darnell notes that Thomas Jefferson, "who devoted considerable energy to collecting Indian vocabularies in the years before his presidency," was one of these (Haarmann 2004: 780).

While in the context of language studies in Europe (especially relating to the Indo-European and Semitic languages) during the 18th century, knowledge was constantly accumulating about the historical relationships of language families, but the situation was much less promising with respect to languages in the Americas. The collections of linguistic data in the comparative enterprises of the 18th century, carried out by Europeans, did not yet allow a systematic approach to the genetic classification of American languages, although the encyclopedic work compiled by Hervás y Panduro is still of historical value. With an increase in the amount of data that became available about Amerindian languages in the course of the 19th century, reflections about their genetic classifications could be based on more solid grounds after that time.

The Linguistic Landscape of the Americas

Some 1,010 individual native languages are spread over the areas of the two Americas, the majority of them in South and Central America. This number is an approximation, because it gives an account of the present situation. The exact number of Amerindian languages will never be known, because there is constant fluctuation. A hundred years ago there were more languages than today, and in a hundred years there will be fewer. The weakening of language maintenance in Amerindian speech communities and the loss of indigenous languages produced a marked trend of decline by the 19th century, and this trend has been accelerating in the past decades.

The decline of the vitality in Amerindian speech communities has been monitored for some 150 years. When Franz Boas (1858–1942), the German-born father of American anthropology, set out on his monumental enterprise to map out the ethnographic landscape of North America, he perceived the threat to the survival of many native languages. The loss of indigenous languages is a continuous process, and, in many cases, the date of extinction can be determined with the death of the last speaker. Examples of such processes are Omurano (Peru; extinct since 1958), Chumash (U.S./California; extinct since 1965), Jorá (Bolivia; extinct since 1963), Tillamook (U.S./Oregon; extinct since 1970), Yamana (Chile/Argentina; extinct since 1978), Nooksack (U.S./Washington; extinct since 1988), Twana (U.S./Washington; extinct since 1980), Yavitero (Venezuela; extinct since 1984).

Systematic surveys about the rate of loss of languages are available only for some regions such as for Brazil. Of the 230 Indian communities that still existed around 1900, altogether 86 had become extinct by 1950, either as a result of total assimilation of speakers of native languages to Portuguese or because the community became defunct with the overaging and the death of its members. Still in our times, there is uncertainty about the fate of certain speech communities. Despite the general trend of a loss of native languages and humanitarian concerns about the disintegration of world cultural heritage, the modern observer has to be cautious not to get entangled in a web of disinformation about the current situation. A number of languages and the communities of their speakers have been reported as extinct, but deeper investigations produced contradicting evidence of their survival. The language of the Karitiana in the Amazonian region was classified by Ribeiro (1957) as extinct, although living speakers have been reported in recent years. Similarly, other Amazonian languages such as Aruá, Mondé, or Arara (at the mouth of the Gi-Paraná) were listed as extinct in the 1960s but were "rediscovered" in the 1980s.

Pitfalls and Quandaries of Historical Classifications

The history of the classification of American languages illustrates that there are two aspects of the concept of "historical" classification. First, there is classification associated with the linguistic infrastructure. This relates to the taxonomies of historical reconstruction of genetic relationships between languages as applied by historical linguistics. Here, the focus is on the identification of the time depth of the splitting of individual languages from a common basis by means of comparing cognate words and grammatical structures. Second, there is classification based on external factors that cause variation in the development of languages. External factors that shape the ecology of languages are manifold, and they may be environmental, social, cultural, or economic. The development of languages in contact may unfold under similar conditions of the landscape where they have spread (e.g., the Pueblo cultures in the arid zone in the U.S. Southwest). Certain social traditions may cause intense language contact and fusion of linguistic structures in certain areas (e.g., the custom of exogamy, that is marrying members of ethnic groups that are different from one's own, such as among many local communities in the Amazon region). The cultures of Amerindians (and their corresponding languages) may be (and have been) classified according to similarities of their socioeconomic traditions (e.g., grouping the Amerindian cultures in the U.S. Northeast according to the criterion of their common traditional system of subsistence: hunting in wooded terrain).

Historical classifications of American languages have been elaborated by focusing on both internal features (relating to the linguistic infrastructure) and external factors (ecological in a wider perspective). A general trend can be recognized in a retrospective of classification approaches. Purely linguistic taxonomies tend to produce a greater number of regional groupings (language families, or phyla) than those classifications that are more oriented at external factors of language ecology.

The first synopsis of northern Amerindian languages, based on observations of similarities (and dissimilarities, respectively) of lexical items, was accomplished by Albert Gallatin, Thomas Jefferson's secretary of the treasury, from a questionnaire he circulated starting in 1836. In his survey of 1848, Gallatin distinguished 32 language families. Information about Amerindian languages continually increased. A much more comprehensive survey of languages in the Americas originated in the late 19th century. In 1891 John Wesley Powell published his classification of Amerindian languages in which he distinguished altogether 55 independent stocks (later revised to 58). Powell had been director of the Bureau of Ethnology (under the auspices of the Smithsonian Institution, founded in 1846) since 1879 and had access to some 670 vocabularies that had been collected by the bureau. Powell's classification was mainly based on lexical comparisons and, given the lack of knowledge about historical sound changes at the time, it necessarily remained an analysis of surface value. Reliable information about the grammatical structures of Amerindian languages was still scarce at the time, so such data would not have sufficed for elaborating a survey.

Although deficient from the standpoint of modern linguistic taxonomy, Powell's classification, evaluated by himself as preliminary, nevertheless remained a yardstick for later conservative approaches to classification. Powell was concerned with the mapping out of local ecological conditions of neighboring speech communities, while the overall currents of cultural history of the Americas played no role in his perspective. The orientation at a broader perspective, however, also found its reflection in enterprises to classify Amerindian languages. In 1921 Edward Sapir published his classification, aimed at the reconstruction of cultural history rather than at taxonomic perfectionism. Sapir distinguished only six "super stocks" with various subdivisions. Greenberg, with his fundamental distinction of only three macrophyla, reaches out for the extreme orientation at reconstructions of cultural history of the Americas. His radical position is marked by the special reconciliation of the parameters of his classification scheme with the insights about genetic fluctuations among the Amerindian populations.

John Wesley Powell, U.S. explorer and scientist. The Smithsonian Institution, under his directorship, published the first classification of Native American languages. (Library of Congress)

In a way, the classifications of Powell and of Greenberg mark positions on the extremes of a continuum of scientific parameters that are available for taxonomic purposes. It would be futile to compare Powell's 58 groupings with Greenberg's distinction of three macrophyla without any reservation. That would be something like comparing apples to pears. The two approaches differ greatly with respect to the architecture of the featural grid that was applied for each classification. It would be as futile to evaluate one survey as "right" and the other as "wrong," because the two classifications represent different levels of methodology.

There is another aspect to working with classifications that has to do with the hierarchical order of units of applied taxonomy. In the various classifications of Amerindian languages, different terminologies are applied. Key concepts such as *language family, subfamily, phylum, macrophylum, stock, super stock*, and others—not to speak of the multitude of subdivisions—are not synonyms but rather associate different meanings. Some terms are more comprehensive than others. For instance, one of the largest groupings of languages in South America is classified by some linguists as the "Tupí language family," with various regional subdivisions. Others are inclined to emphasize the greater independence of the subdivisions, which are themselves categorized as "language families" and as belonging to a "Tupí macrophylum." Classifying the

Tupí languages as one macrophylum or eight language families is a matter of the relativity of perspective, not one of being right or wrong.

Any discussion about the classification of languages is confronted with certain methodological limitations. Among the fields of science that are associated with language studies, some can explore deep layers of human evolution, while others do not reach far back in absolute time. Human genetics is in a privileged position, because its scientific methods favor investigations into the depth of prehistory to trace the fluctuation of populations from the early settlement of America onward. The situation of archaeology is less favorable. Through their excavations, archaeologists may retrieve artifacts along the trails of the great American migrations and the spread of people. Some types of artifacts (e.g., spear heads) are interpreted as leitmotifs, as typical markers of different stages of cultural development. And yet archaeology has to do with fragments of material culture, without any overall picture of human communities in prehistory.

Native American Migration

Scholars agree that at some point during the last Ice Age, a group of nomadic hunters crossed from eastern Siberia to Alaska by means of what was then a strip of land across the Bering Strait, perhaps pursuing the megafauna (mammoths etc.) that then still thrived. Some scholars hold that this group was responsible for all of the early settlement of the Americas, that they followed their game as far as South America, and that they were the progenitors of the Inca and Maya as well as the Inuits.

The Clovis culture, named for artifacts found in Clovis, New Mexico, has often been considered the culture descended from these land bridge crossers and was believed to have spanned much of the Americas. For decades, the lack of strong evidence of pre-Clovis settlements helped to support this theory.

In addition to the Bering land bridge migration, other scholars posit human migrations along water routes, with South America often believed to have been settled earlier than North America. Some models have Siberians traveling to the Northwest coast by boats, usually used for river travel (aided by the low sea levels of the era), Southeast Asians crossing the Pacific to South America, and Oceanic peoples crossing the Antarctic coast on their way to the South American tip. One Atlantic coastal migration model even suggested a Cro-Magnon progenitor for the Algonquians. Originally proposed in the 1930s, that Atlantic model has been largely displaced by the Solutrean hypothesis, proposed by Dennis Stanford and Bruce Bradley in 1999. According to their theory, the Solutrean people of prehistoric Europe crossed the Atlantic on small watercraft, with the aid of ice floes. These Solutreans would have been the progenitors of the Clovis culture, and an ancient site in Virginia is claimed as an example of a transition between the Solutrean and Clovis cultures as the people moved west.

Linguistic reconstructions of genetic relationships between languages are hampered by limitations of the time depth, which can be reached by taxonomic methodologies. This factor makes the linguistic identification of language families a rather tedious business.

The Time Depth of Historical Linguistics and the Chronology of the Splitting of American Language Families

There is an ongoing debate about the validity of methods as applied by historical linguistics to estimate the time depth for the emergence of language families. Methodology is the furthest advanced in the field of Indo-European studies. The individual languages of the Indo-European phylum are the best known and the most broadly investigated. There are more linguistic data available about Indo-European languages than about any other language family.

Despite the favorable conditions to study these languages that are genetically related, the methods to analyze the time depth of their splitting from a reconstructed protolanguage are not generally accepted. Widely applied are lexicostatistical methods. Structural differences of cognate expressions that are historically related (e.g., English *mother*, German *Mutter*, Latin *mater*, Russian *mat'*, Sanskrit and Old Persian *matar*, Old Irish *mathair*, etc.) in a variety of Indo-European languages are projected onto a time scale of assumed rates for sound change. The crucial issue with linguistic dating methods is the operation with average dates for language change. In modern research, the role of language contacts and linguistic interference in linguistic structures has been emphasized as a factor that blurs average dates of sound change and the splitting of a common basis into individual languages.

Some historical linguists accept an early date for the formation of a common protolanguage from which all known Indo-European languages derived, setting the date of its emergence at approximately 7000 BCE. Others are much more skeptical about the reliability of comparative methods, and their estimates are much more cautious, ranging between 4500 and 4000 BCE. The application of lexicostatistical methods that allow for the comparison of a large number of languages has produced a scaling of the time depth for the formation of many other language families, and the scalings are as controversial as for the Indo-European phylum.

As for the language phyla of the Americas, only rough estimates for the periods of their formation are as yet available. In a general overview, the following major groupings are to be distinguished:

1. Era of Formation between 4000 and 3500 BCE: Algonquian (northeastern U.S.; individual languages: Micmac, Cree, Ojibwa, Blackfoot, Cheyenne, etc.), Oto-Mangue (Central America, predominantly Mexico; individual languages: Chinantec, Mixtec, Zapotec, etc.).

2. Era of Formation between 3500 and 3000 BCE: Uto-Aztec (southwestern U.S., Mexiko, El Salvador; individual languages: classical Aztec, modern varieties of Nahuatl, Shoshone, Sonora, etc.).

3. Era of Formation between 3000 and 2500 BCE: Chibcha (southern regions of Central America, northern regions of South America; individual languages: Aruak, Chibcha, Kuna, Rama, etc.), Tupí (lowlands of Brazil, Paraguay; individual languages: Tupí, Guaraní, Wayampi, etc.), Panoan (Peru, northeastern Bolivia, northwestern Brazil; individual languages: Capanahua, Nukuini, Karipuná, etc.)

4. Era of Formation between 2500 and 2000 BCE: Quechua (Andian region: Colombia, Ecuador, Peru, Bolivia, Chile; individual languages: Quechua of Cuzco, Ayacucho, Chimborazo, jungle Inga, etc.), Tucanoan (southern Colombia, Ecuador, Peru, Brazil; individual languages: Cubeo, Macuna, Secoya, etc.), Arawakan (Central America, northeastern regions of South America; individual languages: Guajiro, Carib, Taino, etc.), Mayan (southern Mexico, Guatemala, Belize, northwestern Honduras; classical Mayan languages are Chol and Quiché, modern languages are Tzeltala, Acatec, Ixil, Mopán, etc.).

5. Era of Formation between 2000 and 1500 BCE: Iroquoian (northeastern U.S.; Mohawk, Oneida, Seneca, etc.).

6. Era of Formation between 1500 and 1000 BCE: Athabascan (U.S./Alaska and southwestern regions; individual languages: Navaho, Carrier, Apache, etc.), Siouan (U.S./prairies of the Midwest; individual languages: Tutelo, Dakota, Crow, etc.), Mixe-Zoquean (Mexico/federal state of Oaxaca; individual languages: classical Olmec, Quetzaltepec, Popoluca, etc.).

The general impression of linguistic diversity in relation to the distinction of language families and their formation period is that even the maximum time depth of ca. 4000 BCE as reconstructed for Algonquian is fairly "shallow" when compared with the time depth of the early settlement of America. The span of time for which no historical-linguistic reconstructions are available ranges between 6,000 and 8,000 years, if not more. It must seem conclusive that the oldest dates for the formation of protolanguages come from North America, while those for language splittings in South America are considerably younger. These proportional differences in time scales can be reconciled with the migration movements of early settlers from north to south.

The time scales illustrate that, in the Americas, there are no old macrophyla like some found in Eurasia (i.e., the Indo-European, Uralic, or Afro-Asiatic language families, the protolanguages of which date to between 7000 and 8000 BCE). Even the oldest protolanguages that can be reconstructed for American phyla (i.e., the Algonquian and Oto-Mangue language families) are much younger. The era of the formation of protolanguages in America is comparable to some of the younger groupings in Eurasia (e.g., the Austronesian, Dravidian, and Altajic language families).

An Interdisciplinary Approach to Classification

Whatever positions geneticists and diffusionists may take in the ongoing debate about Amerindian languages, no one can bridge the time gap between ca. 11000 BCE (the conventional date for the beginning of the peopling of America) and ca. 4000 BCE (the approximate date of the separation of the Algonquian phylum from an assumed common Amerind basis) with any linguistic reconstruction.

It cannot be reasonably ruled out that those Americans who created the earliest rock art spoke languages whose historical relationships were still recognizable as stemming from a common protolanguage. In general, pictures engraved or painted on rocks in the Americas have been produced from the end of the Ice Age—some 12,000 years ago into the historical era. It is noteworthy that the oldest dates attributed to rock art locations are found in South America, not in the Northern Hemisphere, although the Paleo-Indians arrived from the north. The controversial dates for sites such as Goias in northern Brazil (ca. 43,000 years ago) and Pedra Furada in northeastern Brazil (between ca. 30,000 and 25,000 years ago) do not fit the conventional time frame for the earliest migrations of humans from Siberia to North America (between 13,000 and 11,000 years ago). Taima-Taima in northwestern Venezuela (ca. 13,000 years ago) and Monte Verde in central Chile (ca. 12,500 years ago) still predate the oldest sites in North America.

Whatever the date of the first settlement and of the oldest rock pictures, the traces of the languages spoken in those remote times are lost. In the course of the migration movement from north to south, the process of a branching out of the protoform that may be considered the ancestor of all recent Amerind languages started sometime and unfolded until the oldest phyla can be identified by historical linguistics.

As long as there is no documentation or reliable reconstruction of the splitting of linguistic phyla in remote times, there is no way to disprove the validity of Greenberg's pan-American vision, albeit there has been substantiated criticism of methodological flaws in the comparative methods that were applied to identify historical relationships. Instead of trying to dislodge the overall perspective of a distribution of languages in accordance with the three-wave migration that is firmly anchored in the findings of archaeology and human genetics, it seems more reasonable to clarify the internal groupings of the Amerind macrophylum, for instance, by investigating with more scrutiny than hitherto whether Algonquian is Amerind or not.

Clarification of the linguistic interrelations within the Amerind complex is also needed. To this end, it is essential to establish a comprehensive catalog of grammatical and lexical equations that can also be acknowledged by the diffusionists.

There is a whole network of undeniably pan-American (Amerind) equations. An example is the pronoun system. The lexical roots to mark the first person (i.e., *n-*) and the second person (i.e., *m-*) are found in Amerind language from Canada to Chile. If directed to fruitful goals, the ongoing debate might even take on a special challenge for all of linguistics, and that is the task to refine historical-comparative methodology.

The search for the common origin of the Amerind languages, descendants of the language(s) of the first settlers who reached America, is no unreasonable quest, although, for the time being, such a remote protolanguage—although attempted—cannot be reliably reconstructed with the methods currently applied. And yet the connections between the languages of the second wave to America, the Na-Dene languages, and Eurasian languages (i.e., Palaeoasiatic, Caucasian) can be demonstrated with some certainty. The linguistic relationship of the languages of the third wave is undisputed, because the interconnections between the local varieties of Eskimo in America and Siberia can be evidenced beyond doubt.

It is interesting to draw a comparison with an earlier stage in comparative linguistics, at a time when Greenberg's unconventional classification of *The Languages of Africa* (1963) was first published. His novel ideas about how to systematize the genetic relationships of African languages stirred up vigorous opposition among linguists then as did his pan-American vision in the late 1980s, but it was equally valid. It is noteworthy that it did not even take two decades before Greenberg's classification of African languages became widely accepted. Here, too, the great currents of African history are reflected in the grouping of macro. In the case of the current controversy about American languages, it might be advantageous to write about it from a neutral standpoint (as a European linguist) and to view the linguistic landscape of America from an eagle's perspective in order to see the validity of Greenberg's hypotheses.

References and Further Reading

Bellwood, Peter. "The Time Depth of Major Language Families: An Archaeologist's Perspective." In *Time Depth in Historical Linguistics*, Vol. I. Edited by Colin Renfrew, April McMahon, and Larry Trask. Cambridge: McDonald Institute for Archaeological Research, 2000.

Bright, William. "Review of Language in the Americas (Greenberg 1987)." *American Reference Books* 23 (1988): 440.

Cavalli-Sforza, L. Paolo Menozzi Luca, and Alberto Piazza. *The History and Geography of Human Genes*. Princeton, NJ: Princeton University Press, 1994.

Darnell, Regna. "Anthropological Linguistics: Early History in North America." In *International Encyclopaedia of Linguistics* (Vol. I, pp. 69–71). Edited by William Bright. New York: Oxford University Press, 1992.

Goddard, Ives. "Review of Language in the Americas (Greenberg 1987)." *Current Anthropology* 28 (1987): 656–57.

Greenberg, Joseph H. *Language in the Americas*. Stanford, CA: Stanford University Press, 1987.

Grimes, Joseph E., and Barbara F. Grimes. *Ethnologue Language Family Index*. Dallas: Summer Institute of Linguistics, 1996.

Haarmann, Harald. "Sociolinguistic Aspects of Cultural Anthropology." In *Sociolinguistics: An International Handbook of the Science of Language and Society*, 2nd ed. (pp. 769–85). Edited by Ulrich Ammon, Norbert Dittmar, Klaus J. Mattheier, and Peter Trudgill. Berlin: Walter de Gruyter, 2004.

Mithun, Marianne. *The Languages of Native North America*. Cambridge: Cambridge University Press, 1999.

Ribeiro, D. "Culturas e línguas indígenas do Brasil (Cultures and indigenous languages of Brazil)." *Educação e Ciencias Sociais* (Rio de Janeiro) 2 (1957): 1–102.

Ruhlen, Merritt. *On the Origin of Languages. Studies in Linguistic Taxonomy*. Stanford, CA: Stanford University Press, 1994.

Weltgeschichte der Sprachen. Von der Frühzeit des Menschen bis zur Gegenwart (World history of languages. From the times of earliest humans to the present). Munich: C. H. Beck, 2006.

CON

For well over 100 years, linguists, historians, and anthropologists have debated whether the diversity of Native American languages known to have prehistorically existed in the Americas can be reduced into just three grand linguistic roots, or whether the linguistic diversity is too great for such a reduction. The reasons behind this long-standing debate are complex and multifaceted, and over the years theories have been put forth that argue for one side or the other. Current empirical evidence indicates, however, that such a reduction is not possible and that Native American languages cannot be reduced beyond several dozen language roots, conclusively resolving the debate.

In fact, this is the only logical conclusion possible given the great linguistic diversity known to have prehistorically existed in the Americas, as well as the current physical anthropological and archaeological evidence. For example, over 300 distinct, mutually unintelligible languages are known to have been spoken north of the Rio Grande River before the arrival of Europeans. Likewise, over 1,500 languages were spoken in Central and South America before the arrival of Europeans; countless others disappeared before any documentation of their existence could be completed. Furthermore, the ones that we do know about and that have been adequately studied differ in fascinating ways not only from the better-known languages of Europe and Asia, but also among themselves in their sounds, in the concepts they package into words, in their grammatical categories, and in their larger patterns of expression. While it has been possible to classify the languages of Europe into just three roots—Indo-European, Finno-Ugric, and Basque—similar attempts to reduce the vast diversity of Native American languages into a similar tripartite classification scheme have been met with skepticism.

Attempts to Find Roots

Original attempts to find the linguistic roots of Native American languages began early in the 20th century with the work of Paul Radin (1919) and Edward Sapir (1912, 1917). However, it was not until James Greenberg (1987) published his highly contentious linguistic consolidation theory that the languages of Native Americans were reduced to just three grand linguistic roots. Although most linguists rejected this proposition, some physical anthropologists accepted it, as it seemed to fit with their data. For example, G. Richard Scott and Christy Turner II (2000) argued that such a reduction corroborated their evidence based on dental morphological characteristics of Native Americans and north and south Asians. Similarly, S. L. Zegura (1984) argued that this hypothetical tripartite linguistic classification scheme fit with early results obtained from genetic studies. However, as linguists examined Greenberg's theory and further evidence was gathered in other fields concerning the early prehistory of the Americas, this tripartite linguistic classification scheme became untenable. Rather, current empirical evidence conclusively demonstrates that it is impossible to reduce the languages of Native Americans beyond a few dozen linguistic roots.

Edward Sapir

In addition to his work with Radin and on the Athabaskan languages in general, Edward Sapir (1884–1939) was one of the most influential and accomplished linguists of his generation. Much of his work continues to polarize linguists in the 21st century, as the theories he set out formed a significant portion of early structural linguistics. In his landmark study *Language: An Introduction to the Study of Speech* (1921), he put forth an extensive grammar-typology, classifying the languages of the world according to their grammatical structures. Most famously, some of his ideas were incorporated by his colleague Benjamin Whorf into the Sapir-Whorf hypothesis (Whorf 1949), which states that the nature and structure of a person's native language determines (or put more weakly, affects) that person's experience of and interaction with the world. The Sapir-Whorf hypothesis has come under a great deal of criticism in the past few decades, and the debate has been one of the most important in linguistics and cognitive science.

Between the beginning of the 20th century and the present day, linguistic methods for reconstructing language affiliations through time have grown in rigor and sophistication. The first to classify Native American languages in some continental fashion was John Wesley Powell (1891a, 1891b). Powell's classification of languages north of Mexico included 58 roots (or "families") and became the baseline for subsequent work in the classification of Native American languages. As Sapir later expressed during his own work on classifying Native American languages, "the cornerstone of the linguistic edifice in aboriginal North America" was provided by the early work of Powell (Sapir 1917: 79). Before this, Spanish and French colonialists and early Euro-Americans such as Roger Williams (1973), Peter Stephen Duponceau (1819a, 1819b), Albert Gallatin (1973), and Robert Gordon Latham (1845, 1856) did work in the languages of Native America, but none had attempted to classify all the languages of the Americas on such a geographic scale.

Because Powell was the first to attempt a classification of Native American languages, the method he used was not very developed. Instead, it was a rather impressionistic inspection of rough word lists and vocabularies gathered from early encounters between Euro-Americans and Native Americans. According to Powell, "The evidence of cognation [that languages are derived from a common ancestral family] is derived exclusively from the vocabulary" (1891a: 11). Franz Boas (1911) subsequently took up the task of refining the linguistic understanding of Native American languages, building on the work of Powell. As has been well documented in the writings of Regna Darnell (1969) and Andrew Orta (2004), Boas came to be associated with a cultural particularist approach to language and culture, in which he compared and contrasted the typological traits of languages in a particular geographic area to determine how they might have been reshaped as a result of mutual influence in that limited area. Out of this work, Boas documented how difficult it was to distinguish linguistic traits that were the result of a genetic linguistic relationship from those that were a result of simple linguistic borrowing or cultural processes. Because of this work, Boas cautioned those attempting to reduce the diversity of Native American languages into only a few grand linguistic roots, because determining linguistic affiliation was extremely difficult.

Others working with Native American languages at this time, such as Alfred Kroeber (1909), Edward Sapir, and Paul Radin, also published influential work on the debate of how many linguistic roots were present in the Americas. Kroeber, for example, worked on the languages of California and the Great Basin, while Sapir worked on Plateau languages; both worked on historical-linguistic affiliations. Kroeber was not in favor of reducing the linguistic diversity of Native American languages beyond specific geographic areas, while Sapir became known as a strong advocate of distant hypothetical linguistic roots that combined all Native American languages. Radin, conversely, focused primarily on merging

Franz Boas, who helped spread the discipline of anthropology in the United States, was a scholar of broad learning, concerned with all aspects of humans and human culture. (Library of Congress)

all known languages into just a few roots rather than investigating specific languages or linguistic patterns of change. He argued that all Native American languages were genetically related and belonged to one large linguistic root. He saw in his colleagues' work (that of Alfred Kroeber and Edward Sapir) only 12 remaining independent roots and believed that merging them into one was "hardly so revolutionary." However, according to Lyle Campbell, most of Radin's contemporaries did not accept his attempt to unite all these languages, primarily because the evidence for such a unification was highly conjectural.

Today, Native American language classification has been greatly influenced by the opinions of these early linguists. As a result of these historical attempts to understand and document the relationships of Native American languages, two schools of thought developed over time, resulting in today's debate and its opposing sides. Those that followed the consolidation process of Sapir, Radin, and others continued to look for evidence that Native American languages could be reduced to just a few grand linguistic roots, while followers of Boas, Kroeber, and others maintained that such a reduction was overly simplistic.

Greenberg's Consolidation Theory

Over time the debate came to a standstill, because little evidence to resolve it was forthcoming and because linguists concerned themselves with other aspects of Native American languages. In 1987, however, Greenberg revived the consolidation theory with the publication of *Language in the Americas*, sparking renewed interest in the debate. In this book Greenberg argued that it was possible to reduce all Native American languages into just three grand linguistic roots, each of which represented a unique migration wave separated in both space and time. These three grand linguistic roots, dubbed Amerind, Na-Dene, and Eskimo-Aleut, were argued to represent the linguistic roots of all Native American languages and claimed to be the culminating results of Sapir's methods. As both

Victor Golla (1988) and Robert Rankin (1992) have independently pointed out, however, the methods of Greenberg and Sapir are fundamentally different, in spite of their shared interest in large-scale consolidation of linguistic roots.

A basic fact on which all linguists agree concerning Native American languages is that historically there was extensive linguistic diversity in the Americas and that within this diversity, various levels of inclusively existed, resulting in linguistic roots. Greenberg, however, went beyond this general consensus and claimed that the Americas were settled by three separate population movements, each of which contained a different linguistic root for a total of just three in the Americas. Historical linguistics, however, as Campbell (1997) and Mithun (1990) have noted, is only able to reliably reduce the diversity of Native American languages to approximately 55 genetic roots in North America, 10 in Central America, and more than 80 in South America, totaling approximately 150 distinct linguistic roots for all of the Americas. One of the central components behind this long-standing debate is the confusion stemming from the terminology used to argue each side. To clarify my side of the argument, it is important to briefly discuss some of the terms used within linguistics and the debate.

Linguistics and Debate Terms

The term "dialect" is generally used to mean only a variety (regional or social) of a language that is mutually intelligible with other dialects of the same language. "Language," conversely, means any distinct linguistic entity that is mutually unintelligible with other languages. A language *root* is a group of genetically related languages, ones that share a linguistic kinship by virtue of having developed from a common earlier ancestor. Thus, it is common to find linguistic roots being designated with the suffix *-an* (e.g., Algonquian, Athabascan, Uto-Aztecan). Furthermore, it is important to note that language roots can be of different magnitudes. That is, they can have different time depths, with some larger-scale roots including smaller-scale roots as their members or branches (e.g., Celtic is a language root that has a shallower time depth than the larger language root of Indo-European, of which Celtic is part). Within this basic terminological structure, linguists have used a wide array of confusing terms to distinguish more inclusive from less inclusive roots. For example, the term "subroot" (also termed "subgroup" or "branch") refers to a group of languages within a well-defined language root that is more closely related to each other than to other languages of that root; they constitute a branch of the phylogenetic tree of the language root (i.e., Numic is a subroot of the larger Uto-Aztecan language root).

Terms that have been used for postulated but undemonstrated higher order, more inclusive roots such as in the present debate (i.e., proposed distant genetic relationships) include stock, phylum, and the compounding element macro- (as in macroroot, macrostock, and macrophylum). These terms have become confusing and controversial, as might be expected when proposed names for entities that are not fully agreed to exist are at stake (such as Greenberg's Amerind). Stock is ambiguous in that in older linguistic usage it was equivalent to language family (a direct transfer of the common German linguistic term *Stamm* [or *Sprachstamm*]). However, the term has often been used in America to indicate a postulated but unconfirmed larger long-range grouping that would include more than one established language root or genetic unit, such as William Shipley's (1980) use of the proposal of macro-Penutian in the Plateau region of North America. Finally, the terms phylum and macro have also been used to designate large-scale or long-range proposed but unestablished language roots.

To avoid any misunderstandings in the argument being presented here, these terms will not be used, instead the term root is solely used, because it appears both sufficient and not as controversial. This is because if the entities called stock, phylum, or macro were found to be correct, they would in fact be roots. Therefore, such terms are spurious, and it is more parsimonious to simply refer to these proposed higher orders more inclusive groups as hypothetical linguistic roots.

Lack of Methodological Agreement

The tripartite linguistic classification of Native American languages (that is, Eskimo-Aleut, Na-Dene, and Amerind) is not new, but reflects the culmination of reductionistic methodological processes that began at the start of the 20th century. Beyond the general confusion surrounding the terminology of the debate, a more substantial critique for not agreeing with the tripartite linguistic classification is the fact that there is no agreed method of reconstructing linguistic genetic affiliations at a deep time scale. In fact, there is no agreed method of chronologically determining when various languages and language roots diverged from each other. This is particularly true when attempting to unite large geographic areas or reconstruct languages beyond a few thousand years such as in the Americas. In fact, Peter Forster and Alfred Toth have convincingly demonstrated that even within linguistic studies of Indo-European, the largest and best-documented language root in the world, "the reconstruction of the Indo-European [phylogenetic] tree, first proposed in 1863, has remained controversial" (2003: 9079). Furthermore, unlike languages from Europe or other parts of the world, Native American languages have no tradition of older written texts on which a study of their history can be based. This has resulted in skepticism concerning any conclusions reached in the study of Native American languages because the linguistic deductions are thought to not be as sound as those from other parts of the world. However, as Ives Goddard argued, just because "documents and documentation are rarely accorded the attention they receive in the traditional study of Old World languages" (1973: 728) does not mean that the conclusions reached by careful historical-linguistic work are of a spurious nature. Rather, because of this fact, historical linguistics has had to develop a sophisticated methodology for investigating language change and linguistic affiliation across space and time.

Methods to Investigate Linguistic Affiliation in the Americas

Two primary methods have been used when investigating the question of linguistic affiliation in the Americas: historical linguistics and multilateral word comparison. The method of historical linguistics is widely used and has been stringently developed for the past hundred plus years, ever since it was originally proposed by August Schleicher (1983). Contrary to this, the method of multilateral word comparison was developed only recently by Greenberg, who adapted principles from the glottochronology of Morris Swadesh et al. (1954) and Sapir's lexical, morphological, and phonological comparative method. According to M. Ruhlen (1986, 1987), in the method of multilateral word comparison, lists of words from the different languages under comparison are generated based on superficial similarities of sound and meaning, along with discursive considerations of similarities in grammatical morphemes. The primary aim of the method is classification, but the classification that results from it is simply a codified statement of the judgments of similarity that have been made in assembling the sets of words across the languages under comparison. Golla calls this method "the inspectional route to genetic classification" (1988: 93), while Calvert Watkins calls it "etymology by inspection" (1990: 293). The terms used by Golla and Watkins reflect the fact that this method depends essentially on lexical similarities determined largely by visual inspection.

The historical-linguistic approach, in contrast, dubbed "the major alternative" by Greenberg and colleagues (1986), employs standard techniques of historical linguistics to attempt to work out the linguistic history of the languages involved. Further, unlike the multilateral word comparison method, the approach of standard historical linguistics employs techniques for formulating and testing hypotheses about the undocumented history of languages. These techniques have been developed and refined over the past century on the basis of the study of the historical changes undergone by a wide variety of languages. The goal of historical linguistics, therefore, is to determine the principles and factors that govern language change. Once the principles of language change have been determined, it then becomes possible to investigate affiliations between languages across space and time.

Of primary concern here is the fact that after related languages have been separated for only a few thousand years, the resemblances between them resulting from their historical connections decrease through normal linguistic changes. The longer languages have been separated, the harder it becomes to develop a proper phylogenetic tree demonstrating the history of the particular language and how it relates to other languages. This is why it is important to follow the historical-linguistic approach of establishing principles of language change. Because the multilateral word comparison method skips this step, however, it suffers from potentially biased data through the comparison of words from possibly nonsynchonous languages.

This central limitation of the multilateral word comparison method is particularly evident in the data used to support arguments for the tripartite linguistic classification scheme. For example, the data Greenberg used to support his argument were of poor quality, often drawn from brief early notes made by explorers passing through an area for the first time rather than the rich, linguistically superior dictionaries and grammars now available for many languages. Furthermore, as discussed by Mithun, in an attempt to increase the compatibility of the lists generated through the multilateral word comparison method, Greenberg retranscribed many of the lexical items into his own phonetic system, apparently without knowledge of the actual phonetic systems of the languages under comparison. Thus, numerous errors were introduced into Greenberg's dataset, and the retranscription process used by Greenberg rendered it impossible to recover the original sources of the material, none of which were cited, because "listing all these sources in a general bibliography would have added greatly to the length and cost of the work" (Greenberg 1987: xv).

Not only is the method of multilateral word comparison of a dubious nature, but some of the languages used as data for comparison by Greenberg are also of a spurious nature. For example, Greenberg introduced some language names into his dataset that are not languages at all. Membreno, which Greenberg classified as a Lencan language from Central America, is actually the name of a person (Alberto Membreno), whose work contains several Lencan word lists from different Honduran towns. Similarly, in several instances Greenberg gave the names of towns where a certain language was spoken as names of distinct languages. For example, Greenberg lists six Lencan languages when there are currently only two known; the other four are towns where Lencan is spoken. Although these errors are unlikely to greatly affect the overall tripartite linguistic classification scheme developed by Greenberg, they do indicate that the tripartite linguistic classification is highly conjectural and rests on unsound evidence. Furthermore, while it is generally agreed that basic vocabulary is, on the whole, more resistant to replacement than lexical items from other sectors of the vocabulary, such basic words are, in fact, also often replaced, so that even in clearly related languages, not all basic vocabulary reflects true cognates. This was one of the valid insights of Swadesh's glottochronology, generally discredited as a method of dating, but nevertheless based on the valid observation that even basic vocabulary can be and is replaced over time. This is a fundamental problem in attempting to reconstruct languages and their linguistic roots far back in time.

Greenberg acknowledges that if Native American immigrants left no linguistic relatives in Asia and died out in the Americas, there would be no linguistic evidence of their presence in the Americas. It is quite possible that groups, particularly if they were small, speaking a particular language or dialect may have simply died off, and consequently there might be no linguistic connection between America's earliest colonists and contemporary Native Americans or indigenous Asian groups, complicating any attempts at reducing the languages of Native Americans to just three grand linguistic roots.

Empirical Evidence Argues against Language Root Reduction to Three

Not only does the linguistic evidence not support the reduction of Native American languages into just three grand linguistic roots, but as mentioned earlier, empirical evidence from other fields also argues against such a reduction. For example, the molecular genetic evidence, based on haplogroup frequencies of genetic markers found on both the mitochondrial DNA (mtDNA) and the Y chromosome, argue that early Native Americans originated from a broad geographic area in Asia, and that this area does not correspond to any of the linguistic roots proposed by Greenberg and those in favor of the tripartite linguistic classification scheme. The molecular genetic data indicate that the initial migration into the Americas originated in south-central Siberia between 35,000 and 20,000 years before the present. These early migrants are hypothesized to have followed the Northwest coast route until they were south of the glacial ice sheets, where they expanded into all continental regions and brought with them mtDNA haplogroups A–D and Y chromosome haplogroup P-M45a and Q-242/Q-M3 haplotypes.

The molecular genetic evidence further indicates that a later migration entered the Americas, bringing mtDNA haplogroup X and Y chromosome haplogroups P-M45b, C-M130, and R1a1-M17, possibly using an interior route. Because these haplogroup markers come from a wide area in Asia, and because the Asian languages represented within these areas cannot be reduced into just three linguistic roots, it is argued that early Native Americans had a wider linguistic base than just three grand linguistic roots. Other physical anthropological data, such as craniomorphology and dental morphology, also support the conclusion that early Native Americans came from a wider geographic area that included several dozen linguistic roots and that attempts to reduce the linguistic roots into just a few linguistic roots has not been possible for the area.

Conclusion

There is great linguistic diversity in the Americas. While some scholars debate how many linguistic roots Native American languages can be reduced to, most believe that there are approximately 150 different language roots in the

Americas that cannot be shown to be related to each other. In spite of this diversity, it is a common hope that future research will be able to demonstrate additional genetic relationships among some of these roots, reducing the ultimate number of genetic units that must be recognized. However, the linguistic diversity that currently must be acknowledged means that on the basis of language classification, as well as other empirical evidence, we are unable to reduce the diversity of languages in the Americas to just three grand linguistic roots.

References and Further Reading

Boas, F. *Handbook of American Indian Languages*, Vol. bulletin IX. Washington DC: Government Printing Office, 1911.

Bright, William. "On Linguistic Unrelatedness." *International Journal of American Linguistics*. 36 (1970): 288–90.

Campbell, Lyle. *American Indian Languages: The Historical Linguistics of Native America*. New York: Oxford University Press, 1997.

Darnell, Regna. "The Development of American Anthropology, 1879–1920: From the Bureau of American Ethnology to Franz Boas." Dissertation, University of Pennsylvania, 1969.

Duponceau, Peter Stephen. "A Correspondence between the Rev. John Heckewelder, of Bethlehem, and Peter S. Duponceau Esq., Corresponding Secretary of the Historical and Literary Committee of the American Philosophical Society, Respecting the Languages of the American Indians." Transactions of the Historical and Literary Committee of the American Philosophical Society, Vol. I, pp. 351–465, 1819a.

Duponceau, Peter Stephen. "Report of the Corresponding Secretary to the Committee, of His Progress in the Investigation Committed to Him of the General Character and Forms of the Languages of the American Indians." Transactions of the Historical and Literary Committee of the American Philosophical Society, Vol. I, pp. 14–46, 1819b.

Forster, Peter, and Alfred Toth. "Toward a Phylogenetic Chronology of Ancient Gaulish, Celtic, and Indo-European." *Proceedings of the National Academy of Sciences* 100, 15 (2003): 9079–84.

Gallatin, Albert. *A Synopsis of the Indian Tribes within the United States East of the Rocky Mountains and in the British and Russian Possessions in North America*. New York: AMS Press, 1973/1836.

Goddard, Ives. "Philological Approaches to the Study of North American Indian Languages: Documents and Documentations." In *Linguistics in North America* (pp. 727–45). Edited by T. A. Sebeok. The Hague: Mouton, 1973.

Goddard, Ives, and Lyle Campbell. "The History and Classification of American Indian Languages: What Are the Implications for the Peopling of the Americas?" In *Method and Theory for Investigating the Peopling of the Americas* (pp. 189–207). Edited by R. Bonnichsen and D. G. Steele. Corvallis, OR: Center for the Study of the First Americans, 1994.

Golla, Victor K. "Review of *Language in the Americas* by Joseph H. Greenberg." *American Anthropologist* 90 (1988): 434–35.

Greenberg, James. *Language in the Americas*. Stanford, CA: Stanford University Press, 1987.

Greenberg, J., C. G. Turner II, and S. Zegura. "The Settlement of the Americas: A Comparison of the Linguistic, Dental, and Genetic Evidence." *Current Anthropology* 27 (1986): 477–97.

Jones, Peter N. *American Indian mtDNA, Y Chromosome Genetic Data, and the Peopling of North America*. Boulder, CO: Bauu Institute Press, 2004.

Kroeber, Alfred Louis. "Paiute." *Notes on Shoshonean Dialects of Southern California* (pp. 256–62). Edited by A. L. Kroeber. Publications in American Archaeology and Ethnology, Vol. VIII. Berkeley: University of California Press, 1909.

Latham, Robert G. "Miscellaneous Contributions to the Ethnography of North America." *Transactions of the Philological Society* 2 (1845): 31–50.

Latham, Robert G. "On the Languages of Northern, Western, and Central America." *Transactions of the Philological Society* 14 (1856): 57–115.

Lightner, Theodore M. "On Swadesh and Voegelin's 'A Problem in Phonological Alternation'." *International Journal of American Linguistics* 37 (1971): 227–37.

Mithun, Marianne. "Studies of North American Indian Languages." *Annual Review of Anthropology* 19 (1990): 309–30.

Orta, Andrew. "The Promise of Particularism and the Theology of Culture: Limits and Lessons of 'Neo-Boasianism'." *American Anthropologist* 106, 3 (2004): 309–30.

Powell, John Wesley. "Indian Linguistic Families of America North of Mexico." In *Seventh Annual Report, Bureau of American Ethnology* (pp. 1–142). Washington DC: Government Printing Office, 1891a.

Powell, John Wesley. "The Study of Indian Languages." *Science* 17, 418 (1891b): 71–74.

Radin, Paul. *The Genetic Relationship of the North American Indian Languages*, Vol. XIV. Berkeley, CA: University of California Press, 1919.

Rankin, Robert L. "Review of *Language in the Americas* by Joseph H. Greenberg." *International Journal of American Linguistics* 58 (1992): 324–51.

Ruhlen, M. *A Guide to the World's Languages*, Vol. I. Stanford, CA: Stanford University Press, 1986.

Ruhlen, M. "Voices from the Past." *Natural History* 96, 3 (1987): 6–10.

Sapir, Edward. *Culture, Language and Personality*. Berkeley: University of California Press, 1949.

Sapir, Edward. *Language: An Introduction to the Study of Speech*. New York: Harcourt, Brace and Company, 1921.

Sapir, Edward. "Language and Environment." *American Anthropologist* 14, 2 (1912): 226–42.

Sapir, Edward. "Linguistic Publications of the Bureau of American Ethnology, a General View." *International Journal of American Linguistics* 1 (1917): 280–90.

Schleicher, August. "The Darwinian Theory and the Science of Language." In *Linguistic and Evolutionary Theory: Three Essays by August Schleicher, Ernst Haeckel, and Wilhelm Bleek* (pp. 1–70). Edited by K. Koerner. Amsterdam: John Benjamins, 1983/1863.

Scott, G. Richard and Christy Turner II. *The Anthropology of Modern Human Teeth: Dental Morphology and its Variation in Recent Human Populations*. New York: Cambridge University Press, 2000.

Sherzer, Joel. *An Areal-Typological Study of American Indian Languages North of Mexico*. Amsterdam: North-Holland, 1976.

Shipley, William. "Penutian among the Ruins: A Personal Assessment." *Proceedings of the Annual Meeting of the Berkeley Linguistics Society* 11 (1980): 437–41.

Swadesh, Morris, et al. "Symposium: Time Depths of American Linguistic Groupings." *American Anthropologist* 56, 3 (1954): 361–77.

Watkins, Calvert. "Etymologies, Equations, and Comparanda: Types and Values, and Criteria for Judgement." In *Linguistic Change and Reconstruction Methodology*. Edited by P. Baldi. Berlin: Mouton de Gruyter, 1990.

Whorf, Benjamin L. *Four Articles on Metalinguistics*. Washington, DC: Foreign Service Institute, Department of State, 1949.

Williams, Roger. *Key into the Language of America*. Detroit: Wayne State University Press, 1973/1643.

Zegura, S. L. "The Initial Peopling of the Americas: An Overview from the Perspective of Physical Anthropology." *Acta Anthropogenet* 8, 1–2 (1984): 1–21.

15

The historical Buddha was born in 563 BCE and lived to 483 BCE.

PRO   Anita Sharma
CON K. T. S. Sarao

PRO

Several methods have been employed by historians, archaeologists, and astrologers, among others, to calculate the lifespan of Buddha. But most of them are unreliable, especially those that either depend on very late materials or are of a dubious nature. The literary and archaeological source material available for the construction of ancient India's exact historical chronology is totally insufficient and unsatisfactory, and thus almost all the dates are quite tentative. However, we can look at the historical events surrounding Buddha's life and determine that the traditional dates of Buddha's life, 563–483 BCE, are valid. Buddha's dates are inextricably linked to the date of King Ashoka's accession. There are four reasons for this. First, no concrete date prior to Ashoka is available in ancient India, with the exception of the invasion of Alexander (327–326 BCE) and the beginning of Chandragupta Maurya's reign (calculated variously between ca. 321–313 BCE). Chandragupta, who began his reign a few years after Alexander's invasion, was Ashoka's grandfather and, according to the *Puranas* and the Sri Lankan chronicles, began his reign 49 years before Ashoka did. Second, almost all the textual sources that provide information relating to the date of the Buddha use Ashoka as a reference point. Third, according to A. K. Narain in *The Date of the Historical Śākyamuni Buddha*, both of the Buddhist sectarian traditions "are interested, and compete, in 'possessing' Aśoka in relation to the date of the Buddha *without* fixing a definite date for the latter first" (1994: 43). Fourth, Ashoka is the earliest historical personality who is intimately connected to Buddhism and provides epigraphical (thus more reliable than literary) information on the Buddha, including his birthplace, different holy books, and teachings. Thus, Ashoka appears to hold the key, and his lifespan needs to be determined first before any assumptions can be made on the lifespan of the Buddha.

On the basis of the names of various Greek kings (Antiochus, Ptolemy, Antigonas, Magas, and Alexander) mentioned in Rock Edicts II and XIII, the date of Ashoka's accession may be put at about 268 BCE and the coronation (*abhisheka*), which took place in the fourth year of his reign (that is, after three years), in about 265 BCE. These dates for Ashoka have been accepted more or less satisfactorily by modern scholarship.

Theories on Dating Buddha

The different hypotheses relating to the calculation of Buddha's dates fall within two categories that are based on ecclesiastical division in Buddhism: the northern Buddhist tradition and the southern Buddhist tradition. The calculations of the northern Buddhist tradition place the date of the *Mahaparinirvana* of the Buddha about 100 or 110 years before the coronation of Ashoka. The leading proponents of this date include H. Bechert (1982, 1991–92, 1995), K. T. S. Sarao (1989), and R. Gombrich (1991). This form of calculation, also known as short chronology, has been criticized on the ground that it appears to be "a fabrication by the monks of the Sarvāstivāda sect of Mathurā, who wanted to connect Upagupta with Aśoka. As a result of this device, the coronation year of Aśoka was moved to fit in with the years of Upagupta's life, i.e. around 100 years after the Nirvāna" (Yamazaki 2003: 147). This short chronology also fails to do justice by adjusting the periods of the Vinaya elders (who were guardians of the *Vinaya*) as well as the large number of kings who ruled in India and Sri Lanka between the period of the Buddha's time and that of King Ashoka.

Here we are concerned with the traditionally accepted date of about 483 BCE, the calculation of which is primarily done on the basis of the southern Buddhist tradition. The southern Buddhist legends contained in the *Dipavamsa*, the *Mahavamsa*, and the Pali version of the *Samantapasadika* place the consecration of Ashoka 218 years after the *Mahaparinirvana* (the Great Decease) of the Buddha. The best survey of the arguments that lead scholars to believe the calculation of Buddha's dates should be based on what is called the long chronology as found in Andre Bareau's research paper, "La date du nirvāna," published in 1953. The southern Buddhists had in the beginning adopted 544–543 BCE as Buddha's year of death. But this was later recalibrated by Geiger (1912) and others, who pointed out that 60 years extra had been added into the chronology of the kings of Sri Lanka and thus there was the need for a recalibration. One of the main arguments for the validity of Geiger's chronological calculations was a theory proposed by D. M. Z. Wickremasinghe (1904–12) in "Kiribat-Vehera Pillar Inscription" that a chronology starting from 483 BCE as Buddha's death date was known and had been used in Sri Lanka until the beginning of the 11th century and that the *Buddhavarsha* of 544 BCE was generally accepted at a later date. Indications are to be found that in earlier times, and indeed down to the beginning of the 11th century, an era persisted even in Ceylon in which 483 was reckoned as Buddha's death year. From the middle of the 11th century, the death year was presumed as 544 BCE, and this date is still in use.

As to Parākramabāhu I, we have information from inscriptions, confirmed and completed by literary data, that he was crowned 1,696 years after the Buddha's death, that is, in the year 1697 AB (after Buddha). Eight years later, in 1705 AB, a second coronation apparently took place. In the fourth year after that, when 1,708 years had gone by since the *Nirvāna*, that is, in 1709 AB, he held a Buddhist synod. According to the Ceylonese era, those are the years 1153, 1161, and 1165 CE (Ceylonese era). But this date for Parākramabāhu is supported by an entirely independent source, namely a South Indian inscription at the Temple of Tiruvālīśvara in Arpākkama.

According to Culavamsa, the six predecessors of Parākramabāhu, from Parākrama Pāndu onward, reigned for 107 years. Thus the accession of the last-named prince falls at 1590 AB, or according to the Ceylonese era, 1046 CE. Moreover, this date is confirmed by the south Indian *Manimangalam* inscription, which is dated in the same year. According to the latter, Parākrama Pāndu was conquered and killed in this year by the Cola king Rājādhirāja I. It is true that the Culavamsa gives Parākrama Pāndu a reign of two years, but we must rather take the accession and death of the king as falling in one and the same year, 1590 AB, that is 1046 CE.

But a date for Udaya III among the predecessors of Parākrama Pāndu can also be fixed from a south Indian inscription, which throws a completely new light on the whole reckoning of eras. Since, according to the Culavamsa, the time between the accession of Udaya III and that of Parākrama Pāndu amounts to 93 years and 8 days, and the latter ascended the throne in 1590 AB, we consequently have the date 1497 AB for the accession of this former king. But this year, according to the Tanjore inscription of King Rajendra Coladeva, must be about the year 1015 CE. The inscription gives an account of a military expedition to Ceylon. The details of the invasion by Cola correspond with one that occurred under Udaya III at the beginning of his reign. Udaya III's expedition falls between the fourth and sixth years of the reign, that is, between 1015 and 1018. This year must coincide with the years 1497 and 1498 AB. The difference between 1,497 years and 1,015 equals 482, which falls within pre-Christian times. This would mean Buddha died in 483 BCE.

Foundation of Long Chronology

The cornerstone of the long chronology is the number 218 mentioned repeatedly in the Sri Lankan chronicles: the *Dipavamsa* and the *Mahavamsa*. For instance, the *Dipavamsa* (VI.1) in this regard says, "218 years after the Sambuddha had attained Parinirvana, Piyadassana [Ashoka] was consecrated." Similarly, the *Mahavamsa* (V.21) goes on to say, "After the Conqueror's Nirvāna and before his [Aśoka's] consecration there were 218 years, this should be known." We are also told in the *Dipavamsa* and the *Mahavamsa* that the unrest that led to the Third Council arose at the Asokarama in Pataliputta 236 years after the death of the Buddha, and that this council was completed in the 17th year of Ashoka's reign. This also places the *Mahaparinirvana* 218 years before the consecration of Ashoka.

Since the date of Ashoka's accession is calculated to about 268 BCE, the Buddha's death may be computed to about 486 (268 plus 218) BCE. But if the three years above are not accounted for, the death of the Buddha is put in the year (218 plus 265) about 483 BCE. It may also be interesting to note that the length of Bindusara's reign in the Sri Lankan tradition is given as 28 years, as against 25 of the *Puranas*. In all probability, this was because the Sri Lankan tradition included the three years before Ashoka's consecration in the reign of Bindusara. But the total length of Ashoka's reign was not changed likewise in these records.

As pointed out by Andre Bareau, the *History of Khotan* places the start of King Ashoka's reign in year 234 of the Buddhist era (BE), which is not very different from the long chronology's 218 BE. The dates of the long chronology also appear to be supported by the events of contemporary political history. For instance, the lists of Magadhan kings in different sources, though showing discrepancies on many points, are nevertheless unanimous in placing several kings between Ajatashatru and Chandragupta, the grandfather of King Ashoka. These lists can only be adjusted satisfactorily between the Buddha and Ashoka by following the long chronology. Another important reason the long chronology appears to be more logical is that, instead of the suspicious number of 100 in the short chronology, the long chronology has the exact number of 218.

W. Geiger's discussion of the chronology of the Buddha in his *The Mahāvamsa or the Great Chronicle of Ceylon* played an extremely important role in getting acceptance for the long chronology as against the short chronology. Other scholars like Andre Bareau and P. H. L. Eggermont (1956, 1969) also followed suit, and thus the long chronology became the basis for the date of the Buddha. However, the biggest landmark that provided justification for the long chronology came in the shape of the *Dotted Record of Canton*. This record is contained in the *Li-tai san-pao chi* written by Fei Chang-fang in 597. This source, as discussed by W. Pachow in "A Study of the Dotted Record," mentions that, according to the famous Buddhist Master Samghabhadra:

> there is a tradition which had been handed down from teacher to teacher for generations, viz., after the passing away of the Buddha, Upali collected the Vinaya and observed the Pavarana on the 15th of the 7th Moon of the same year. Having offered flowers and incense to the Vinaya on that occasion, he marked a dot [on a record] and placed it close to the Vinaya text. Thereafter this was repeated every year. . . . In this manner the teachers in turn handed it down to the present master of *Tripitaka*. . . . Having observed the *Pavarana* and offered flowers and incense to the *Pavarana* at midnight (on the

15th) of the 7th Moon, in the 7th year of Yung-ming [AD 489], he added a dot [to the record]) as a traditional practice. The total amounted to 975 dots in that year. A dot is counted as a year. (1965: 343)

On the basis of the figures supplied in this record, we get 489 CE minus 975 years equals 486 BCE as the year of the Mahaparinirvana. But Pachow noted that three extra dots had been inadvertently added. The actual number of dots in the year 489 CE should have been 972 and not 975. In that case, he pointed out, the actual date of the *Mahaparinirvana* should be 489 CE minus 972 equals 483 BCE.

As the two independent sources of information, one from Sri Lanka (as mentioned in the *Dipavamsa* and the *Mahavamsa*) and the other from China (the *Dotted Record of Canton*), provided substantially the same information, about 483 BCE was accepted as the correct date of the *Mahaparinirvana* of the Buddha by Buddhist scholars.

Other Support for Long Chronology

The long chronology has also been supported on the basis of the so-called agreement of this chronology with the Jaina chronology as well as the *Puranas*. The Pali Canon points out clearly that the Buddha and the Mahavira were contemporaries. Since an apparently independent, although late, Jaina tradition states that the death of the Mahavira took place 155 years before the accession of Chandragupta, and since the accession of Chandragupta can be dated to about 317 BCE, Mahavira Jaina's death may be put in the year 317 plus 155 equals 472 BCE. But here the main difficulty is that the same Pali source, the *Digha Nikaya*, places Mahavira Jaina's death before that of the Buddha. Two separate answers have been provided for this contradiction. One, as pointed out by Hermann Jacobi (1879) in his introduction to *Kalpasūtra of Bhadrabāhu*, is that the Buddhist texts were confused by there being two places called Pava and were probably also confused by the relative dating. The second is that the southern Buddhists, as proposed by A. L. Basham (1951) in *History and Doctrine of the Ājivikās*, knew very little about other sects, and it was the Ajivika leader Makkhali Gosala who had died before the Buddha and not Mahavira Jaina.

The long chronology has also found strong support in the information available in the edicts of King Ashoka. For instance, the Minor Rock Edict (MRE) I of Ashoka, which refers to the date 256. As noted by G. Bühler (1877), this figure has been interpreted by these scholars to mean a time span of 256 years between the installation of MRE I and the *Mahaparinirvana* of the Buddha. A. K. Narain has discussed in detail the implications of the number 256 and has vigorously proposed that it is clinching evidence for proving that the Buddha's *Mahaparinirvana* took place about in the year 483 BCE. He has translated the relevant portion of the edict as follows: "This proclamation [was made] having given [that is, allowed or having past] two hundred and fifty-six [years] to

---

Mahavira Jaina

Also known as Vardhamana, Mahavira (599–527 BCE) was the central figure of Jain-ism, which grew and developed in parallel to Buddhism. Mahavira was said to be the 24th of the Tirthankaras, perfectly enlightened beings. The first 23 Tirthanka-ras may have been mythical or at least exaggerated by legend—they're described as hundreds of feet tall, living for thousands of years.

Mahavira taught that karma accumulates on the soul in response to good and evil deeds, and the soul responds by seeking the temporary pleasures of the mate-rial world. He taught the necessity of five vows in order to lead a life of right con-duct: nonviolence, truthfulness, abstinence from theft, chastity, and detachment from the material world.

---

elapse [after] the ascension of the body of our Buddha" (Narain 2003). The date of issue of this edict is hard to fix, and Narain feels that it must have been issued toward the end of Ashoka's reign, that is, in the 37th year. This means the edict was issued in the year 228 (265 minus 37) BCE. The upshot of this is that the *Mahapari-nirvana* of the Buddha took place about in the year 484 (228 plus 256) BCE. As months and days are not mentioned, about 484 can be recali-brated to about 483 BCE. A date for the Buddha calculated in this manner has its own merits. As pointed out by Narain, it "is independent of the so-called two Buddhist traditions as well as that of the *Dotted Record*, the amended version of which, inci-dentally stands not only substanti-ated now but also freed from its dubious association with the *later* Theravada tradition" (Narain 2003).

Dhamekh Stupa at Sarnath in Uttar Pradesh, India, is a stone and brick structure built during the reign of Emperor Asoka in the third cen-tury BCE. The stupa, constructed on the site where the Buddha (Siddhartha Gautama) preached his first sermon, is decorated with intricate floral patterns. (Philip Baird (http://www.anthoarcheart.org)

Archaeological evidence also ap-pears to support the long chronology. The Pali Canon gives clear evidence of Buddhism being an urban religion and the Buddha having preached in urban centers. A large number of the urban centers mentioned in the Pali Canon that have been identified have provided evidence of northern black polished ware (NBPW). Though the precise dates of the origin and spread of NBPW in the Ganges Valley are not without dispute, there is a general consensus that it had become fairly widespread by about 500 BCE. It would be fair to say that the urbanization of the Ganges Valley, also sometimes called the Second Urbanization, originated in the sixth century BCE. Buddhism can also be traced back to at least 550 BCE. Archaeological records relating to the excavation records of some of the urban centers in the Ganges Valley also tend to support this.

Here, it may not be out of place to look at the archaeological records of Kaushambi, the oldest city of the Second Urbanization. This city appears to have been established by at least the end of the Vedic period, though its excavator, G. R. Sharma, places it as early as 1000 BCE. According to the Buddhist canonical text, the *Digha Nikaya*, Kaushambi was a well-known capital city of the Vatsas/Vamsas and was one of the six major cities (*mahanagaras*) of India at the Buddha's time. Major trade routes of the time passed through this city. Kaushambi was perhaps one of the most important cities politically, religiously, and economically at the time of the Buddha. The Mathura sculpture from the Ghoshita Monastery of a *Chakravarti* Buddha of year two of Kanishka I, installed according to the inscription at the promenade of Gautama Buddha, is the oldest Buddhist relic from Kosam. With the help of an inscribed stone slab the monastery was identified with the well-known Ghoshita Monastery. The excavator, Sharma (1960), places the first phase of its construction in about 600 BCE.

Shravasti was perhaps the most important city for the Buddha, considering he delivered the largest number of his sermons in this town and spent most of his Rainy Retreats (*vassavasa*) here. Archaeologists, like K. K. Sinha (1967), who have either excavated it or who, like H. Härtel (1991), have studied the data available on this city, have pointed out that the origins of this city go at least as far back as the sixth century BCE.

Even the earliest portions of the Pali Canon presuppose the existence of a developed currency, and such a currency involving large transactions of gold and silver coins must have taken time to develop. Although it has been debated whether the earliest coins can be dated, as P. L. Gupta discusses, "coins . . . were current prior to the fifth century BC" (Gupta 1969: 11). Though no evidence of coinage can be found in later Vedic texts, measures of precious metals may have been used as payment. Discovery of 3,000 cowrie shells from the NBPW levels at Masaon-Dih throws interesting light on the use of currency before the introduction of coins. Without entering into discussion on the numismatic evidence, it may be reasonable to assume that coins made their beginning in India during the sixth century BCE. Thus the evidence of the existence of coinage also seems to support the long chronology.

Though the stratigraphical sequence of the cultures of the Ganga Valley is now well established, the absolute chronology still remains debatable. In "Radiocarbon

Dates from South Asia," G. L. Possehl (1987) notes that now quite a few radiocarbon dates from various sites are available. Though normally they should suffice for establishing the chronology of various cultures, the erratic nature of many dates (even after calibration) has divided archaeologists nearly as much as have the two traditions for the date of the Buddha. While dealing with C14 dates, we also have to bear in mind several associated problems, especially, as D. H. Thomas (1978) notes, that they are not precise statements of the age of samples but estimates of probability. It is unlikely that we will get uniform dates for the beginning and end of a culture from all parts of its geographic area. The Buddhist order depended on the existence of a strong economic base. The monks were supposed to spend the Rainy Retreat in fixed locations, and this would have been easiest near large urban settlements. The large cities were no longer mere administrative centers and sovereign residences. They had also become the nerve centers of economy and commerce. Uncertain and unsatisfactory as archaeological data still are in this context, they appear to lean toward supporting an early rather than late date for the *Mahaparinirvana* of the Buddha. There thus is at least a good case that can be made for the Buddha having lived in the sixth century BCE.

Ceylon-India Chronological Connections

In the chronological system, the succession of the great teachers from Upali onward plays an important role. There is a continuous synchronological connection between the history of Ceylon and that of India. The *Dipavamsa* and the *Mahavamsa* talk of five patriarchs (*acharyas*) who transmitted the *Vinaya* from the time of the Buddha's death until the days of Ashoka. These five elders were Upali, Dasaka, Sonaka, Siggava, and Moggaliputta Tissa. The *Dipavamsa* mentions: "Seventy-four of Upali, sixty-four of Dasaka, sixty-six of Thera Sonaka, seventy-six of Siggava, eighty of Moggaliputta: this is the *Upasampadā* of them all" (1958).

Though this verse mentions the years of *Upasampada*, in reality these are the ages at which these patriarchs died. This fact is borne out by the verses preceding as well as following this verse. For instance, the *Dipavamsa* mentions that Upali attained nirvana at the age of 74. Thus, the number 74 mentioned in the verse is the age at which Upali died and not the year or period of *Upasampada*. The same should be taken to be the case regarding the other numbers mentioned in connection with the other elders.

The other verse of the *Dipavamsa* says, "Learned Upali was all the years chief of the Vinaya, Elder Dasaka fifty, Sonaka forty-four, Siggava fifty-fifth year, the [elder] called Moggaliputta sixty-eight" (1958). This verse clearly implies the number of years for which the five elders were the custodians of the *Vinaya*.

It appears that Upali joined the order at quite a mature age. He was born in the family of a barber, later took up service with the Sakyan princes, and joined the order along with them. Even during the lifetime of the Buddha, monks considered it a great privilege to learn the *Vinaya* under him. He specialized in the study of the *Vinaya* and won the foremost place among the *Vinayadharas*. According to the *Dipavamsa*, he was renowned for having reached the pinnacle of the *Vinaya*, and it was in this capacity that Kassapa entrusted him with compiling the *Vinaya Pitaka* at the First Buddhist Council that took place at Rajagriha. We are further told in the *Dipavamsa* that when 16 years had elapsed after the death of the Buddha, Upali was 60 years old. This means that he was 44 (60 minus 16) years old when the Buddha died, that is, when he became the *Vinaya* custodian. But as mentioned above, he actually lived to be 74. Thus, Upali was the custodian of the *Vinaya* for 30 (74 minus 44) years. This is also supported by a direct statement in the *Dipavamsa* that Upali was the custodian of the *Vinaya* for 30 years.

Dasaka was a learned brahmana from Vesali. After meeting and holding a discussion with Upali, Dasaka entered the order to study the doctrine. He appears to have been fairly mature in years when he joined the order. He learned the whole of the Vinaya and became an *arahant*. As per the *Dipavamsa*, he was the custodian of the Vinaya for a period of 50 years and was followed by Sonaka, the son of a caravan leader from Kasi, who had joined the order at the age of 15 at Rajagriha. He saw Dasaka Thera, and, very pleased with him, entered the order after fasting for three meals until his parents would give their consent. He soon became an *arahant* and leader of 1,000 monks. Sonaka kept the *Vinaya* for 44 years.

Siggava, the son of a minister from Pataliputra, joined the order at the age of 18 along with his friend Chandavriji. As pointed out in the *Dipavamsa*, Siggava was the custodian of the *Vinaya* for 54 years (having died during the 55th year of custodianship). Siggava died when 14 years of the reign of Chandragupta had elapsed. As King Chandragupta Maurya had begun his reign in about 321 BCE, Siggava's death took place in about the year 321 minus 14, which is about 307 BCE.

Conclusion

The above-stated information based on various archaeological and literary sources may be summed up as follows.

The lifespan of the Buddha is arrived at by adding together two numbers, one being the date of the accession of Ashoka to the throne, the second being the length of the interval between that date and the date of the death of the Buddha. Upali, Dasaka, Sonaka, and Siggava kept the *Vinaya* for 30, 50, 44, and 54 years, respectively. The death of Siggava took place in about the year 307 BCE. Between about 307 BCE and the death of the Buddha, 178 years had elapsed. As the custodianship of these four patriarchs is mentioned only in years, and months and days are not mentioned, an error of a couple of years is possible. Considering this, it may not be out of order to adjust the figure of 178 to 176. This would mean that the Buddha's death may approximately be placed in about the year 483 BCE. This agrees with the date calculated on the basis of the popular number 218 as well as the *Dotted Record of Canton*. Thus the year 483 should be accepted as the year in which the death of the Buddha took place. However, this date should only be taken as a close approximation to the real date rather than an exact date for the reasons specified above.

References and Further Reading

Bareau, A. "La date du nirvāna." *Journal Asiatique* 241 (1953): 27–62.

Basham, A. L. *History and Doctrine of the Ājivikās.* London: Luzac, 1951.

Bechert, H. "The Date of the Buddha Reconsidered." *Indologica Taurinensia* 10 (1982): 29–36.

Bechert, H., ed. *The Dating of the Historical Buddha/Die Datierung des historischen Buddha*, 2 vols. Göttingen, Germany: Abhandlungen der Akademie der Wissenschaften, 1991–92.

Bechert, H., ed. *When Did the Buddha Live?* Delhi: Sri Satguru Publications, 1995.

Bühler, G. "Three New Edicts of Aśoka." *Indian Antiquary* 6 (1877): 149–60.

Dipavamsa, The. Edited and translated, with introduction, by B. C. Law as "The Chronicle of the Island of Ceylon or the Dīpavamsa." *Ceylon Historical Journal* 7 (1958): 1–266.

Eggermont, P. H. L. *The Chronology of the Reign of Asoka Moriya.* Leiden: E. J. Brill, 1956.

Eggermont, P. H. L. "New Notes on Aśoka and His Successors II." *Persica* 4 (1969): 97.

Geiger, W., ed. *The Mahāvamsa.* London: Pali Text Society, 1912. Translated by W. Geiger and M. H. Bode as *The Mahāvamsa or the Great Chronicle of Ceylon.* London: PTS, 1912.

Gombrich, R. "Dating the Buddha: A Red Herring Revealed." In *The Dating of the Historical Buddha/Die Datierung des historischen Buddha* (Vol. 1, pp. 238–59). Edited by Heinz Bechert. Göttingen, Germany: Abhandlungen der Akademie der Wissenschaften, 1991.

Gupta, P. L. *Coins.* New Delhi: National Book Trust, 1969.

Härtel, H. "Archaeological Research on Ancient Buddhist Sites." In *The Dating of the Historical Buddha/Die Datierung des historischen Buddha* (Vol. 1, pp. 61–89). Edited by Heinz Bechert. Göttingen, Germany: Abhandlungen der Akademie der Wissenschaften, 1991.

Jacobi, H., ed. "Introduction." In *Kalpasūtra of Bhadrabāhu.* Leipzig, 1879.

Mendis, G. C. "The Chronology of the Early Pāli Chronicle of Ceylon." *University of Ceylon Review* 5, 1 (1947): 39–54.

Müller, Max F. "The True Date of Buddha's Death." *The Academy* (March 1884): 153.

Narain, A. K. "An Independent and Definitive Evidence on the Date of the Historical Buddha." *Buddhist Studies Review* 6 (1994), 43–58.

Narain, A. K. *The Date of the Historical Śākyamuni Buddha*. Delhi: B.R. Publishing, 2003.

Pachow, W. "A Study of the Dotted Record." *Journal of the American Oriental Society* 83, 3 (1965): 342–45.

Possehl, G. L. "Radiocarbon Dates from South Asia," data list circulated by the author in September 1987.

Rhys Davids, T. W. "The New Aśoka Inscriptions." *The Academy* (July 1877): 37.

Rhys Davids, T. W., and J. E. Carpenter, eds. *The Dīgha Nikāya*, 3 vols. London: Pali Text Society, 1890–1911. Translated by T. W. and C. A. F. Rhys Davids as *The Dialogues of the Buddha*, 3 vols. London: Pali Text Society, 1899, 1910, and 1957.

Sarao, K. T. S. "Urban Centres and Urbanization as Reflected in the Pāli Vinaya and Sutta Pitakas." Ph.D. thesis submitted to the University of Cambridge, 1989.

Sharma. G. R. *The Excavations at Kausambi: 1957–59*. Allahabad, India: University of Allahabad, 1960.

Sinha, K. K. *Excavations at Sravasti: 1959*. Varanasi, India: Banaras Hindu University, 1967.

Stein, O. "The Coronation of Candragupta Maurya." *Archiv Orientalni* 1 (1932): 368.

Takakusu, J. "Pāli Elements in Chinese Buddhism: A Translation of Buddhaghosa's *Samantapāsādikā*, a Commentary on the *Vinaya*, Found in the Chinese *Tripitaka*." *Journal of the Royal Asiatic Society* (1896): 436.

Thomas, D. H. "The Awful Truth about Statistics in Archaeology." *American Antiquity* 43 (1978): 232.

Thomas, E. J. "Theravādin and Sarvāstivādin Dates of the Nirvāna." In *B.C. Law Volume* (Vol. 2, pp. 18–22). Edited D. R. Bhandarkar et al. Delhi: Poona, 1946.

Wickremasinghe, D. M. Z. "Kiribat-Vehera Pillar Inscription." *Epigraphia Zeylanica* 1 (1904–12): 153–61.

Winternitz, M. *A History of Indian Literature*, Vol. 2. Calcutta: University of Calcutta, 1933.

Yamazaki, G. "The Importance of the Dotted Record." In *The Date of the Historical Śākyamuni Buddha* (pp. 147–50). Edited by A. K. Narain. Delhi: B. R. Publishing, 2003.

CON

Though there is general agreement that the Buddha lived for 80 years, precisely when he lived is hard to pinpoint for three main reasons. First, the different texts that give information on the birth and death dates of the Buddha not only contradict each other, but they are also self-contradictory in most cases. Second, because of their religious character, most of these texts do not mention numbers in the sense in which they are understood in science. In other words, in most cases the numbers can only be used as approximations. In many cases the numbers are also given as rounded-off numbers and hence cannot be used for precise calculations. Invariably the Buddhist texts appear to exaggerate numbers, and in all Indian religions, there is always a tendency to claim antiquity for a religious leader. Moreover, as the textual sources mention, spans of time are given in years only, not months and days; the figures are not as precise as one would want them to be. Third, no useful date for calculating the lifetime of the Buddha is available in the history of ancient India before the arrival of Alexander the Great. Because of these factors, it is doubtful at best that the traditional dates for Buddha's life, 563–483 BCE, are accurate.

The calculation of the dates of the Buddha is inextricably linked to the dates of the Mauryan kings, Chandragupta and Ashoka. Therefore, these two dates need to be determined before any work can be done on the dates of the Buddha. It is more or less certain that Chandragupta started to rule in about 317 BCE, although some scholars have put it a little earlier. According to N. K. Bhattasali in "Mauryan Chronology and Connected Problems," "The murder of Poros by Endamos, and his retirement from India in 317 BCE are significant indications. The breaking out of the Indian revolt headed by Chandragupta does not appear to be possible before this date" (1932: 283), and, therefore, according to O. Stein in "The Coronation of Candragupta Maurya," it "is impossible to reckon with an acknowledged dominion of Candagutta before 317 BCE" (1932: 368). On the basis of the names of various Greek kings mentioned in the Thirteenth Rock Edict, the date of Ashoka's accession may be put in about 268 BCE and the consecration, which took place in the fourth year of his reign (i.e., after three years), in about 265 BCE.

Long and Short Chronologies

The sources used for the study of the dates of the Buddha may broadly be divided into two categories, depending on whether they support the so-called long chronology or the short chronology. These chronologies are based mainly on the southern and northern Buddhist legends, respectively.

The southern Buddhist legends contained in the *Dipavamsa* and the *Mahavamsa* place the consecration of Ashoka 218 years after the *Mahaparinirvana* (the Great Decease) of the Buddha. The date of the Buddha's death would therefore have taken place in about 483 (265 plus 218) BCE. The short chronology is based on the testimony of the Indian sources (*Vinaya Pitaka*) and their Chinese and Tibetan translations. In all the recensions of the *Vinaya Pitaka*, it is pointed out that the Buddha died 100 or 110 years before the consecration of Ashoka. In other words, the *Mahaparinirvana* should be dated in about 365 (265 plus 100) BCE or 375 (265 plus 110) BCE.

One possible important reason for the popularity of the long chronology is that, instead of the suspicious number of 100 in the short chronology, the long chronology has the exact number of 218. But this does not necessarily mean that 218 is a true number just because it does

A stone relief of the Buddha's footprints on a pillar of the stupa commissoned by the emperor Asoka in the third century BCE at Sanchi in present-day India. (Adam Woolfitt/Corbis)

not appear to be rounded off. It is also important to note that the weakness of the long chronology is that the *Dipavamsa* (fourth to fifth centuries CE) in which it is found was written two or three centuries later than the sources in which the short chronology first appears. The longer the interval between the time of the events and the time they were recorded, the greater the possibility of an objective error. The number 218 may not be acceptable on various other grounds too. For instance, it may have been inflated through additions to an originally much smaller number so that credence could be given to various personalities as well as events. As a matter of fact, the long chronology appears to have been developed in an attempt to adjust the traditional short chronology to the particular needs of the Sri Lankan historiography. Thus, as pointed out by E. J. Thomas (1946) in "Theravadin and Sarvastivadin Dates of the Nirvana," the relevant passages in the *Dipavamsa* actually point to the existence of the original short chronology, which failed to be assimilated into the long chronology of the final version of the *Dipavamsa*.

W. Geiger's (1912) discussion of the chronology of the Buddha appears to have been extremely influential in the acceptance of the long chronology over the short chronology. Other scholars like André Bareau (1953, 1995) and P. H. L. Eggermont (1956, 1969) followed suit, and thus the long chronology became the basis for the date of the Buddha. However, the biggest justification for the long chronology came in the shape of the *Dotted Record* of Canton (Guangzhou), contained in the *Li-tai san-pao chi*, written by Fei Chang-fang in 597 CE. According to this tradition of putting one dot on the Vinaya record every year resulted in 975 dots in the year 489 CE, as detailed by W. Pachow (1965) in "A Study of the Dotted Record." But Pachow believed that three extra dots might have been inadvertently added, and that the actual number of dots should have been 972 and not 975. On this basis, 483 BCE (i.e., 489 CE minus 972 years) was calculated as year of the *Mahaparinirvana*.

But this tradition from the Chinese sources is apparently not independent in origin. It has been maintained, for instance by A. Bareau and J. Takakusu (1896), that this tradition initially originated in Sri Lanka and hence cannot be used reliably. It appears thus that the dot is a later invention to dignify the *Vinaya*. Moreover, the very way in which it was preserved, handed down from generation to generation and carried from one country to another, appears rather mysterious and suspicious. We cannot but express doubts concerning its authenticity. Most important, the Sri Lankan chronicles and the *Samantapasadika* speak of the transmission of the *Vinaya* by the teachers initiated by Upali, but in them we do not come across any reference, whatsoever, to the practice of adding dots to a record every year after the Rainy Retreat (*vassavasa*). Such being the case, it is difficult, according to Pachow, to believe that the dotted record was initiated by Upali and handed down in succession by the *Vinaya* teachers. Moreover, if there was really a record initiated by Upali, when Mahinda, the sixth teacher of the *Vinaya* succession, came to Sri Lanka, he should have brought it with him and continued to add dots each year throughout his life. If so, such a record would have been safely preserved in Sri Lanka as a sacred object like the Bo-tree, or the Tooth Relic. But this was not known to writers of either the Pali or the Sri Lankan texts, nor was it noted in the *Travels of Fa-hsien*, when Fa-hsien (Faxian) visited Sri Lanka in the beginning of the fifth century. Thus one may pose the question whether Mahinda really brought such a thing to Sri Lanka. In case such a thing did not exist in Sri Lanka, then one may ask how it came to China, and from where. In any case, as no written record of the *Vinaya* existed until the time of Dutthagamani in the first century BCE, it is difficult to accept the authenticity of this tradition. Moreover, as Max Müller notes in "The True Date of Buddha's Death," "the process of adding one dot at the end of every year during 975 years is extremely precarious" (1884: 153).

The long chronology has also been supported on the basis of the so-called agreement of this chronology with the Jaina chronology as well as the *Puranas*. But the *Puranas* show so many disagreements among themselves that they are not really reliable for calculating the dates of the Buddha. The most important reason for not using the Jaina chronology for dating the Buddha, according to Bareau (1995), is that the Jaina chronology itself depends on certain Buddhist traditions, notably the Sri Lankan tradition. Thus, despite the fact that the two teachers were contemporaries, it is difficult to accept the Jaina chronology for its inherent snags. According to M. Winternitz (1933) in *A History of Indian Literature*, the tradition of the long chronology cannot be traced with confidence beyond the middle of the 11th century. Some scholars have supported the long chronology on the basis of three Ashokan edicts of Sahasaram, Rupanath, and Bairat, which refer to the year 256. This figure has been interpreted by such scholars as G. Bühler (1877) in "Three New Edicts of Ashoka" to mean a time span of 256 years between the installation of these inscriptions and the *Mahaparinirvana*. An attempt has also been made by scholars to present a date akin to the short chronology on the basis of these inscriptions. For example, T. W. Rhys Davids (1877: 37) provided "426 BCE, or perhaps a few years later" as the date of the *Mahaparinirvana* by pointing out that the number 256 represents the time span between the installation of these inscriptions and the Buddha's abandonment of his home. However, some scholars, like Hermann Oldenberg (1881), have pointed out that unnecessarily too much has been made of this figure not only because the inscriptions contain no word for years but also because they do not refer to the Buddha, but to 256 "beings."

The theory of 100 years is widespread throughout the world. Geiger notes that the Tibetan sources place the reign of Ashoka 100 to 160 years after the Buddha's death. Taranatha says that the Tibetan *Vinaya* gives 110 AB (after Buddha) as one of the dates for Ashoka. Similarly the Chinese *Tripitaka* gives 116, 118, and 130 AB as the dates for the consecration of Ashoka. In Vasumitra's account, Ashoka is also placed about 100 year after the death of the Buddha. According to Hsuan-tsang (also spelled as Xuanzang), as noted by S. Beal (1906) in *Si-yu-ki: Buddhist Records of the Western World*, at the time of his death, the Buddha had said "A hundred years hence there shall be a King Ashoka." Still at another place, Hsuan-tsang points out "the different schools calculate variously from the death of the Buddha. Some say it is 1,200 years and more since then. Others say, 1,300 or more. Others say, 1,500 or more. Others say that 900 years have passed, but not 1,000 since the nirvana."

The various dates here recorded would correspond with 552, 652, 852, and a date between 252 and 352 BCE. By the last date, Hsuan-tsang probably means to place the death of the Buddha a hundred years before Ashoka.

Case for a Later Date

Two important reasons, however, appear to favor a later date for the Buddha. They are the archaeological considerations and the lists of the patriarchs (*acariyaparampara*). The archaeological records in the Ganges Valley show (perhaps with the exception of Kaushambi) that even by about 450 BCE, the new urban settlements were indeed not those cities we might expect after reading early Buddhist literature. Extensive use of baked bricks for construction, a well-developed sanitation system, and so forth are not found in the excavations until later times. In early Buddhist literature, the existence of prosperous and fully developed urban centers is taken for granted. Though the roots of the Ganges urbanization may be traced back to about 500 BCE or so, the archaeological records clearly suggest that the sort of urban centers that are talked about in the earliest Buddhist texts could not have come into existence before the end of the fifth century BCE. Critics of this argument may say that such references are later interpolations or that certain portions of the canon are altogether late compositions. But such criticism appears superficial, because the whole material milieu reflected in early Buddhist literature is urban. Wherever we may look, Pali *Tipitaka* reflects a city culture and a faith laden with munificence by the city folks that included kings, their ministers, and business magnates.

As many as 173 urban centers (some undeniably being mythical or late) are mentioned in the first two *pitakas* and are evenly spread out in these texts. Here an argument may be made that perhaps the whole of Buddhist literature was grafted onto various urban settlements for prestige or other reasons, because terms associated with village (*gama*), such as *gamadhamma* (vile conduct) and *gamakatha* (village-talk, included in the list of foolish talks), are frowned on in Buddhist literature. But it is impossible to accept such an argument. It is not only the urban settlements but so much else that goes into making an urban civilization that is reflected everywhere in early Buddhist literature. Long-distance trade, a money economy, financial transactions, interest, usury, mortgages, the developed state and its paraphernalia, prostitution, and many other characteristics clearly point to the existence of a fully grown urbanization in Buddhist literature. There is so much urbane that is part and parcel of the life and activities of Gautama Buddha, it would be hard to imagine him living in a preurban society.

A part of the *Mahaparinibbana Sutttanta* of the *Digha Nikaya*, which mentions six *mahanagaras* (cosmopolitan cities), is dated by Winternitz as forming part of the earliest Buddhist literature. These *mahanagaras* were Champa, Rajagriha, Shravasti, Kaushambi, Saketa, and Benares. A look at the scanty evidence so far provided by the excavators of these cities clearly tempts agreement with the short chronology. If we are to accept the existence of these six settlements as *mahanagaras*, then that can be visualized perhaps by the end of the fifth century BCE at the earliest. The archaeological data available from the Ganges Valley show that even by about 500 BCE, the new urban settlements were indeed not those cities that may be expected after reading the early Buddhist literature.

Though scholars disagree as to when coins came into existence in India, it is reasonable to say they were introduced in India during the fifth century BCE. Even the earliest portions of the Pali Canon presuppose the existence of a developed currency, and such a currency involving large transactions of gold and silver coins must have taken time to develop. The Buddhist Sangha depended on the existence of a strong economic base. The monks were supposed to spend the Rainy Retreat in fixed locations, and this would have been easiest near large urban settlements. The large cities were no longer mere administrative centers and sovereign residences. They had also become the nerve centers of economy and commerce. Uncertain and unsatisfactory as archaeological data still are in this context, they appear to lean toward supporting a later rather than earlier date for the *Mahaparinirvana* of the Buddha. In other words, there is at least a good case that can be made for the age of the Buddha being about a century later than generally accepted.

As pointed out above, extensive use of bricks for construction works, including fortifications, well-developed sanitation, palatial buildings, a fully developed state system and its paraphernalia, an extensive interregional commercial network with powerful and influential business magnates, a well-developed currency and other financial institutions like usury, mortgage, and so forth, is well reflected throughout the Pali *Tipitaka*. The material milieu reflected in the early Buddhist literature is overwhelmingly urban. A collective analysis of the data available on the six *mahanagaras*, mentioned in the earliest portions of the Pali literature, shows that urban centers of this magnitude could not have existed before the end of the fifth century BCE. As compared to the later Vedic texts and their socioeconomic context, the early Buddhist texts depict a prosperous urban life, a flourishing interregional trade dominated by a new class of influential and powerful merchants, and the emergence of Magadha as the most powerful early state among a large number contesting *mahajanapadas* in the Ganges Valley.

The existence of fortifications around the various urban centers and their relationship with the Buddha's time constitute yet another problem difficult to resolve for an early date. The archaeological evidence does not support the fortification of any of the early Ganges cities, with the possible exception of Kosambï, even in the fifth century BCE, whereas fortified towns are frequently mentioned in the early Buddhist texts.

Political power, centered in the urban centers, and riches were accumulated in these cities. The emergence of these strong *mahajanapadas*, which is identifiable mainly in the early Buddhist literature, therefore would have to be dated in the fifth century BCE rather than in the sixth century BCE, as has been the custom in dating them until now. Furthermore, such an interpretation would provide the needed time for a gradual evolution of the urban settlements and their surrounding kingdoms. The same would be true with regard to the development of interregional trade and the rise of an urban merchant class. The latter, in particular, may have needed much more time than we have conceded to them in view of the early date of the Buddha and of the early Buddhist literature, which depicts an already flourishing merchant culture. Such a late date of the rise of urban centers, a merchant class, and its flourishing interregional trade may help to explain the lateness of the punch-marked coins.

Some scholars believe that a consideration of the probable distance between the Buddha and Ashoka in terms of doctrinal development of Buddhism, as L. Schmithousen writes, "would seem to render a somewhat later date more probable" (1992: 143). A study of Buddhist poetry also tends to show, as S. Lienhard writes, that the corrected long chronology "definitely seems to lie too far back in time" (1991: 196). "It would seem to be easily compatible with the assumption that Buddhism had not yet produced distinctive monuments and institutions, and that, instead, it was still rather young and not yet fully visible when Megasthenes visited Pataliputra around 300 B.C." (Halbfass 1995: 205). P. H. L. Eggermont, in his "New Notes on Ashoka and His Successors II," also feels that "Buddhism was still young at Ashoka's time" (1956).

In the chronological system upon which the *Dipavamsa* and the *Mahavamsa* are based, the succession of the great teachers from Upali down to Mahinda played an important part. This *acariyaparampara* is of interest because in it there is a continuous synchronological connection between the histories of Sri Lanka and India. Here the system appears to have been carried out in detail and completed. As is clear in the accounts of the *Dipavamsa* and the *Mahavamsa* there was a teacher–pupil relationship between them, and this continuity is of vital importance. The lists of *acariyas* that occur in the *Vinaya*, Sri Lankan chronicles, and elsewhere as *Vinayadharas* are more reliable and useful than any other form of information to determine the date of the Buddha. As most of the research was conducted in the light of number 218, it was given that the number of elders as the *Vinayapamokkhas* for the period between the Buddha and Ashoka caused a problem. There were not enough elders. Thus it was pointed out that to bridge the gap of 218 years, each of the elders had to be assigned too lengthy a period of time as guardian of the *Vinaya*. The statement in both the *Dipavamsa* and the *Mahavamsa* that the eight elders who considered the Ten Extravagances in the Second Council had all seen the Buddha was also seen as creating difficulties. These so-called *contradictions*, however, were regarded as faulty records on the part of the Theravadins. More weight was given to the chronology of the kings, even though this, too, posed difficulties. All these problems had come up because the number 218 was thought to be supreme.

In our calculation of the date of the Buddha based on the lists of patriarchs, we have used the beginning of the reign of Chandragupta as the base year as opposed to the year of Ashoka's coronation. This shortens the gap between the date of the Buddha and the base year, thus reducing the margin of error.

Patriarchs

According to E. Frauwallner (1956) in *The Earliest Vinaya and the Beginnings of Buddhist Literature*, northern sources (the *Divyavadana*, the *Ashokavadana*, and so forth) point out three generations of patriarchs, that is, Mahakassapa/

Ananda, Sanavasa, and Upagupta, dating from the Buddha's death to the time of Ashoka (excluding Madhyantika, whose name appears to have been inserted by the legend-teller monks). Sanavasa was a merchant of Magadha at the Buddha's time, who after the Buddha's death became a monk under Ananda's guidance, moved to Madhura (Mathura) later on, and introduced Upagupta into monkhood. Sanavasa must be Sambhuta-Sanavasi of Madhura/Ahoganga, who took part in the Second Council. As many different sects agree, it appears Sanavasa's participation in the Second Council is quite probable. Upagupta is said to have been a temporary advisory monk of Ashoka.

The southern sources relate that five patriarchs transmitted the *Vinaya* from the time of the Buddha's death until the days of Ashoka. These five elders were Upali, Dasaka, Sonaka, Siggava, and Moggaliputta Tissa. We are told in the *Dipavamsa* that when 16 years had elapsed after the death of the Buddha, Upali was 60 years old. This means he was 44 (60 minus 16) years old when the Buddha died, that is, when he became the *Vinayapamokkha*. As Upali lived to be 74, he was the custodian of the *Vinaya* for 30 (74 minus 44) years. This is also supported by a direct statement in the *Dipavamsa* that Upali guarded the *Vinaya* for 30 years.

When Upali died, Udaya had completed 6 years of his 16-year reign. This means during the last 10 (16 minus 6) years of Udaya's reign, Dasaka was the custodian of the *Vinaya*. But Dasaka died when 8 years of the 10-year reign of Susunaga had elapsed. As Anuruddhaka/Munda ruled for 8 years between Udaya and Susunaga, Dasaka appears to have been the custodian for a total of 26 years (10 plus 8 plus 8).

Susunaga ruled for 10 years and Dasaka died 8 years after the end of Susunaga's reign. After the death of Susunaga, the Ten Brothers reigned for 22 years, and Sonaka died when 6 years of their reign were over. This means Sonaka kept the *Vinaya* during the last 2 years of the reign of Susunaga and first 6 years of the reign of the Ten Brothers, making it 6 (2 plus 6) years.

Siggava was the custodian during the remaining 16 (22 minus 6) years of the reign of the Ten Brothers. Siggava died when 14 years of the reign of Chandragupta had elapsed. In other words, Siggava was the custodian for a total period of 30 (16 plus 14) years.

Chandragupta does not appear to have succeeded the Ten Brothers, who began their reign not at Pataliputra but elsewhere, because the *Dipavamsa* and the *Mahavamsa* tell us that Susunaga had a son called Kalashoka who held power at Pataliputra for a period of 28 years. It appears after his governorship for 10 years during Susunaga's reign, Kalasoka reigned for 18 years (28 minus 10) as a king at Pataliputra, and the Ten Brothers continued to rule from the same place as Susunaga after the possible division of the kingdom. In other words, it appears that Chandragupta succeeded Kalashoka at Pataliputra and the Ten Brothers (possibly the Nandas) at Rajagriha. The *Dipavamsa* also tells us that Siggava was 64 years old when Chandragupta had completed two years of

---

Chandragupta Maurya

The founder of the Maurya Empire, Chandragupta was the first to unite the lands and peoples of the Indian subcontinent. He first rose to fame by reconquering the Indian lands his contemporary Alexander the Great had taken over, and soon conquered the Nanda Empire and expanded to the east. The Maurya Empire ruled by his dynasty was the most powerful period of ancient India, and the greatest to rule the subcontinent until India became a British subject for a (relatively) brief time in the modern era. It was a time of religious awakening for the subcontinent, not only through the birth of Buddhism but through Chandragupta's own conversion to Jainism. In his last days, the emperor voluntarily resigned from the throne and finished out his life as a Jain ascetic, fasting in a cave.

---

his reign. Chandragupta's reign began in about 317 BCE. This means that in about 315 (317 minus 2) BCE, Siggava was 64 years old. But as Siggava died at the age of 76, that means he lived for another 12 years after 315 BCE. This would put the death of Siggava in about 303 BCE. This statement is also supported by another reference in the *Dipavamsa* where we are told that Siggava died 14 years after the beginning of the reign of Chandragupta, that is, about 303 BCE.

Conclusion

The upshot of the calculations made above is that the death of Siggava took place in about 303 BCE. Sonaka died 30 years before Siggava. Dasaka died 8 years before Sonaka. Upali died 26 years before Dasaka. The Buddha died 30 years before Upali. In other words, between about 303 BCE and the death of the Buddha, 94 years had elapsed. This would mean that the Buddha died in about 397 BCE.

It must finally be emphasized that our sources are not always exact in their calculation of time if we do not accept a slight deviation. The number of years for which a particular king reigned or an elder kept the *Vinaya* is given in rounded-off numbers in our records, with months and days being ignored. A deviation of a couple of years one way or another cannot be denied in a calculation involving about 100 years or so. Thus, 397 BCE may only be taken as a rough approximation to the year in which the Buddha expired. Some of the scholars who initially played an important role in popularizing the long chronology have now reverted to the short chronology, thus adding to its growing popularity. For instance, André Bareau, shortly before his death, in his "The Problem Posed by the Date of the Buddha's Parinirvana," revised his position and proposed that "in placing the Parinirvana of the Blessed One around 400, with a margin of twenty years added or deduced from this date, we would probably not be very far from the historical truth, which unfortunately remains inaccessible to us with more precision" (1953).

References and Further Reading

Bareau, A. "La date du nirvana." *Journal Asiatique* 241 (1953): 27–62.

Bareau, A. "The Problem Posed by the Date of the Buddha's Parinirvana." In *When Did the Buddha Live?* (pp. 211–19). Edited by H. Bechert. Delhi: Sri Satguru Publications, 1995.

Beal, S. *Si-yu-ki: Buddhist Records of the Western World*, Vol. II. London: Trubner, 1906.

Bechert, H., ed. *The Dating of the Historical Buddha/Die Datierung des historischen Buddha*, 2 vols. Göttingen, Germany: Abhandlungen der Akademie der Wissenschaften, 1991–92.

Bechert, H., ed. *When Did the Buddha Live?* Delhi: Sri Satguru Publications, 1995.

Bhattasali, N. K. "Mauryan Chronology and Connected Problems." *Journal of the Royal Asiatic Society*, Pt. II (1932): 283.

Bühler, G. "Three New Edicts of Ashoka." *Indian Antiquary* 6 (1877): 149–60.

Eggermont, P. H. L. *The Chronology of the Reign of Asoka Moriya*. Leiden, Netherlands: Brill, 1956.

Eggermont, P. H. L. "New Notes on Ashoka and His Successors II." *Persica* 4 (1969): 97.

Frauwallner, E. *The Earliest Vinaya and the Beginnings of Buddhist Literature*. Rome: Is. M.E.O., 1956.

Geiger, W., ed. *The Mahavamsa or the Great Chronicle of Ceylon*. Trans. W. Geiger and M. H. Bode. London: Pali Text Society, 1912.

Halbfass, W. "Early Indian References to the Greeks and the First Encounters between Buddhism and the West." In *When Did the Buddha Live?* (p. 205). Edited by H. Bechert. Delhi: Sri Satguru Publications, 1995.

Law B. C., ed. and trans. *The Chronicle of the Island of Ceylon or the Dapavamsa*. Colombo: Ceylon Historical Journal, 1958.

Lienhard, S. "A Brief Note on the Date of the Historical Buddha and Classical Poetry." In *The Dating of the Historical Buddha/Die Datierung des historischen Buddha* (Vol. 1, p. 196). Edited by H. Bechert. Göttingen, Germany: Abhandlungen der Akademie der Wissenschaften, 1991.

Max Müller, F. "The True Date of Buddha's Death." *The Academy* (March 1884): 153.

Oldenberg, H. "Die Datierung der neuen angeblichen Ashoka-Inschriften." *Zeitschrift der Deutschen Morgenländischen Gesellschaft* 35 (1881): 472–76.

Pachow, W. "A Study of the Dotted Record." *Journal of the American Oriental Society* 83, 3 (1965): 342–45.

Rhys Davids, T. W. "The New Ashoka Inscriptions." *The Academy* (July 1877): 37.

Rhys Davids, T. W., and J. E. Carpenter, eds. *The Dagha Nikaya* (The Dialogues of the Buddha), 3 vols. Translated by T. W. and C. A. F. Rhys Davids. London: Pali Text Society, 1899, 1910, and 1957.

Sarao, K. T. S. "Urban Centres and Urbanization as Reflected in the Pali Vinaya and Sutta Pitakas." Ph.D. thesis submitted to the University of Cambridge, 1989.

Schmithausen, L. "An Attempt to Estimate the Distance in Time between Ashoka and the Buddha in Terms of Doctrinal History." In *The Dating of the Historical Buddha/Die Datierung des historischen Buddha* (Vol. 2, p. 143). Edited by H. Bechert. Göttingen, Germany: Abhandlungen der Akademie der Wissenschaften, 1992.

Stein, O. "The Coronation of Candragupta Maurya." *Archiv Orientalni* 1 (1932): 368.

Takakusu, J. "Pali Elements in Chinese Buddhism: A Translation of Buddhaghosa's *Samantapasadika*, a Commentary on the *Vinaya*, Found in the Chinese *Tripitaka*." *Journal of the Royal Asiatic Society* (1896): 436.

Thomas, E. J. "Theravādin and Sarvāstivādin Dates of the Nirvāna." In *B. C. Law Volume* (Vol. 2, pp. 18–22). Delhi: Poona, 1946.

Winternitz, M. *A History of Indian Literature*, Vol. II. Calcutta: University of Calcutta, 1933.

Index

About the Editor

STEVEN L. DANVER is a full-time faculty member in the Center for Undergraduate Studies at Walden University. He is a historian of the American West, American Indian peoples, and the interaction of people with the environment. He earned his bachelor's in religious studies at the University of California, Santa Barbara; his master's in historical studies from Graduate Theological Union in Berkeley, California; and his doctorate in history at the University of Utah. His dissertation, *Liquid Assets: A History of Tribal Water Rights Strategies in the American Southwest*, to be published by the University of Oklahoma Press, examines the long history of one of the most important issues of modern relevance to American Indians in the West.

Among the many historical reference projects he has edited or co-edited are ABC-CLIO's *The Great Depression and New Deal: A Thematic Encyclopedia, Seas and Waterways of the World: An Encyclopedia of History, Uses, and Issues,* and a four-book set on *Popular Controversies in World History*. He is currently completing work on an encyclopedia on *Revolts, Protests, Demonstrations, and Rebellions in American History*. Since 2004 he has been managing editor of *Journal of the West*, a respected journal on the history of the North American West for nearly fifty years, and has always sought to publish articles that are both academically sound while at the same time interesting to the non-academic readership.